MW00574864

SELLING
SEXY

SELLING SEXY

VICTORIA'S SECRET AND THE UNRAVELING OF AN AMERICAN ICON

LAUREN SHERMAN AND
CHANTAL FERNANDEZ

Henry Holt and Company
New York

Henry Holt and Company
Publishers since 1866
120 Broadway
New York, New York 10271
www.henryholt.com

Henry Holt® and ⓗ® are registered trademarks of
Macmillan Publishing Group, LLC.

Library of Congress Cataloging-in-Publication Data

Names: Sherman, Lauren, author. | Fernandez, Chantal, author.
Title: Selling sexy : Victoria's Secret and the unraveling of an
    American icon / Lauren Sherman and Chantal Fernandez.
Description: First edition. | New York : Henry Holt and Company,
    [2024] | Includes bibliographical references and index.
Identifiers: LCCN 2024008744 | ISBN 9781250850966 (hardcover) |
    ISBN 9781250850959 (ebook)
Subjects: LCSH: Victoria's Secret (Firm) | Lingerie industry—United
    States. | Sex—United States.
Classification: LCC HD9948.3.U64 V5374 2024 | DDC 687/.22—
    dc23/eng/20240403
LC record available at https://lccn.loc.gov/2024008744

Our books may be purchased in bulk for promotional, educational,
or business use. Please contact your local bookseller or the Macmillan
Corporate and Premium Sales Department at (800) 221-7945, extension
5442, or by e-mail at MacmillanSpecialMarkets@macmillan.com.

First Edition 2024

Designed by Meryl Sussman Levavi

Printed in the United States of America

10 9 8 7 6 5 4 3 2 1

For Dan and Fritz —L.S.

For Daniel—C.F.

All good work requires self-revelation.
—Sidney Lumet, *Making Movies*

Contents

SELLING SEXY

Prologue: Dreams and Fantasies

In mid-October 2015, a twenty-year-old model named Gigi Hadid visited Victoria's Secret's Midtown Manhattan offices with high hopes. She wanted nothing more than to walk in the lingerie brand's annual televised fashion show, by then an American pop-culture institution. If she landed the gig, Hadid would prove her burgeoning modeling career was more than just a passing fad. She could become a super. For a young model seeking stardom, Victoria's Secret once meant everything.

Waiting for her inside a brightly lit white conference room was Edward Razek, the perma-tanned, silver-haired chief marketing officer, dressed sharply in a checkered suit. Then in his midsixties, Razek was preparing for the twentieth edition of the fashion show he had overseen since its inception. He liked to call it the "Super Bowl of Fashion," but a more accurate comparison would have been something like the Ziegfeld Follies meets Moulin Rouge—with a dash of the Grammys.

Hadid emerged from behind a screen, having changed into the requisite uniform: black high-cut briefs and a smooth push-up bra. Her long blond hair was parted down the middle and flowed in loose waves. She almost teetered on her high heels while demonstrating her notoriously brusque runway walk across the room. Victoria's Secret cameras were rolling, as they often were during these casting sessions, poised to capture the next TV-ready moment. Like this one. Razek sat behind a wide table at the far side of the room with three colleagues, watching Hadid carefully. She finished her walk with a pouty pose and a twirl. She stood politely in front of the table of judges.

"What are you doing on November ninth and tenth?" Razek asked, hiding a smile.

"I don't know?" Hadid nervously replied.

"Why don't you come join us?" he said.

Hadid shrieked. "Really?!" She almost collapsed to the floor, only to pull herself back up and run over to embrace Razek. Hadid began instantly crying in joy and relief.

Later that week, Victoria's Secret's social media accounts, and Hadid, posted a video of the moment. "One of the happiest moments of my life," she wrote. The clip—and Hadid's emotional reaction—went viral. A few weeks later, Hadid realized her wish inside Manhattan's Lexington Avenue Armory. During the runway show's grand finale, she waved and danced for the television cameras, dressed as a sexy firefighter (red sports bra, low-slung stiff yellow trousers), standing arm in arm with all the Angels under a shower of confetti.

Like many women born in the 1990s, Hadid grew up watching the television extravaganza every year and imagining herself walking down that stage. Through Victoria's Secret, she discovered supermodels named Gisele Bündchen and Tyra Banks strutting down illuminated runways in bedazzled bras and feathery wings. Where else did women seem so powerful and desirable?

Hadid's modeling dream was more than a youthful fantasy. Her wealthy mother, Yolanda Hadid, was a former model and now a reality television star. She had helped her daughter land a starring role in a children's campaign for the denim brand Guess. Shortly after Hadid finished high school in Malibu, in 2013, her career took off quickly. Her lean-but-athletic body, soft round face, and almond-shaped eyes made her unique. She was also charming and down-to-earth, drawing millions of followers on social media by posting candid behind-the-scenes clips and selfies. And yet, even after she had worked with Chanel, Tom Ford, and *Vogue*, her grandest ambition remained elusive. Victoria's Secret had rejected her from its show in 2013 and 2014. She wasn't "ready," they told her. She needed to work harder—which meant *working out* harder.

///

By the time Hadid earned Razek's blessing in 2015, Victoria's Secret had become the MGM Studios of American retail: a multibillion-dollar machine in the business of blockbuster entertainment, a leader born in the golden age of its industry.

Its studio head was the Columbus, Ohio, billionaire Leslie "Les" Herbert Wexner, who had made his fortune in the 1980s by conquering the American mall. Instead of movies, Victoria's Secret released elaborate commercials set in European castles and staged its annual televised fashion variety show. And instead of theaters, the brand counted more than a thousand manicured stores, the flashiest of which boasted glass staircases and leather-paneled walls. Instead of tickets, Victoria's Secret sold five-for-$25 panties and $45 push-up bras. And instead of leading ladies, it had its Angels, personifications of idealized European American beauty. Each one the girl next door with a sultry streak. Chaste but alluring. Never bitter, always approachable. Pure and potent fantasies.

The target audience was young adult women, but the brand had an outsize effect on American girls born in the late 1980s and early '90s. This was a generation that would never remember a time before Victoria's Secret dominated shopping malls and Super Bowl commercial breaks. Like their mothers before them, these girls grew up on the same inescapable idea hidden in plain sight across American culture. They were told that female sexuality involved little more than simply being seen as sexy. It was a performance. And what did sexy look like? Victoria's Secret was happy to show them.

All the while, the company scaled to annual sales of more than $7 billion while consistently generating double the operating profits of its competitors. The unstoppable performance of Victoria's Secret was a testament to the retailing genius of Wexner, a self-made multibillionaire and, until 2020, the longest-running CEO of a Fortune 500 company.[1] (He had a two-year head start on Warren Buffett.)

Visionary merchants like Wexner dominated American retail in the twentieth century. They had taste and instinct and watched their customers closely. They picked the *right* goods, the ones people didn't even know they wanted. They knew how to package their products with dreams of a better life.

Wexner was twenty-five years old in 1963, when he opened the first location of his first store, the Limited, in Columbus. In the decades that followed, he capitalized on a great American pastime: shopping for things we don't need, but desperately want, at a sensible price. The Limited became the fast-fashion prototype, lifting trends from the European runways and reproducing them cheap and fast for middle-class Americans. Wexner went on to launch and scale other retail megahits, like Abercrombie & Fitch, Express, and Bath & Body Works. He liked to boast that a $1,000 investment in his nascent corporation in 1969 would be worth $45 million almost fifty years later. By that time, the crown jewel of his empire was Victoria's Secret.

In some ways, Wexner was not a traditional merchant. His genius lay in patterning, as he called it. He saw trends, not just in hemlines and silhouettes, but in images and symbols. He noticed that stores decorated with clean, white panels and black trim communicated luxury; the way colorful cotton underwear arranged across a countertop recalled the impulsive joy of shopping at a candy store. And in the 1990s, Wexner saw an opening for Victoria's Secret to borrow the allure of the high-fashion world and distill it down to a commercial essence. The brand could take the glamour of that rarefied industry, its beautiful people and exclusive parties, and strip away all the thorny bits: the avant-garde clothing, the self-seriousness, the high prices, the closed-door runway shows. What remained became the Angels, built on an American obsession with the rich and famous, with clubs that would never accept us as their members. They satisfied our fascination with biological impossibilities, women frozen at age twenty-three, their Jell-O-mold cleavage always jiggling and eyes always shining.

At Victoria's Secret, each delicate purchase, tucked into the store's telltale striped bags, fueled that fantasy.

///

Speak to anyone who worked at Victoria's Secret since the 1980s, and the conversation invariably turns to a sinister figure who has now cast a dark shadow over the entire business: Jeffrey Epstein.

Jeffrey Epstein was Wexner's financial adviser and confidant for nearly twenty years, partially during the time Epstein sexually exploited and trafficked girls and young women. In 2019, a month after he was arrested on federal charges in New York, Epstein killed himself in his jail cell. Wexner has insisted that he had no knowledge of Epstein's crimes when they worked together, and that they parted ways in 2007.

Their confounding association has tarnished Wexner's legacy, and the legacy of the brands he built. Epstein profited off their relationship, and then used his wealth and influence to lure and entrap victims. These women's stories, the ones we know about, are the stuff of nightmares. And Wexner, wittingly or not, enabled this behavior by granting Epstein access to his fortune.

Epstein's crimes raise obvious questions about his role at Victoria's Secret. Based on the testimony of multiple women, Epstein found some of his victims by posing as a recruiter for the company and pretending to audition models.[2] But while Epstein helped Wexner manage high-level deals with outside partners, served as the lead adviser on several of his financial transactions, and managed much of Wexner's personal finances, he was not a presence in the lives of most Victoria's Secret executives— save for the occasional mysterious run-in.

It would be easy to reduce Victoria's Secret to its association with Epstein. Or to write it off as simply a frilly brand that capitalized on women's whims and last-minute Valentine's Day gifts. But Victoria's Secret is worthy of a deeper examination befitting its commercial scale and cultural influence. This was no ordinary retail business.

From the beginning, most of the decision makers at Victoria's Secret were women, and their mission was to make other women feel good. To embrace their sexuality, to lead more satisfying sex lives and have healthier relationships. To experience their gender as an asset, not a liability. To feel powerful.

For much of the 1990s, Victoria's Secret slyly presented itself as a posh British brand, following a directive straight from Wexner. The world Victoria's Secret created in the pages of its popular mail-order catalog was an American conceit of English manors and manners, an aesthetic fetishized by self-made people like Wexner. "Victoria" was always white and undoubtedly heterosexual, but she had layers. The models were often wrapped in billowing floral robes, holding teacups. It wasn't all garter belts and bustiers.

When Ed Razek gained more control over the brand's marketing strategy in the first decade of the 2000s, "Victoria" was smoothed down and simplified. She became universally taut, tanned, and silicone-augmented. Where the domestic comforts of elite society were once part of the aspirational vision the company sold, the focus gradually narrowed. Just youth. Just "sexy." The annual holiday catalog became the "Dreams and Fantasies" edition. Its models were no longer nestled under Christmas trees, but draped over gleaming Lamborghinis.

Victoria's Secret's stores became supersized. Its bras became smoother and fuller. Revenues soared. The brand's idealized women echoed across the era's blockbuster films, television shows, and music videos, tying women's success to little more than their ability to attract men.

"[Women] dress to please men," Wexner told *Fortune* magazine back in 1985.[3] "You're not selling utility. That's why uptight women stockbrokers will put on a G-string when they get home. Like [Revlon founder Charles] Revson said, we're selling hope in a bottle."

/ / /

One generation's hope is another's burden. Hadid was one of the last new supermodels to join the Victoria's Secret universe before the Angels era ended abruptly in 2021. In the years after her successful audition, as popular culture increasingly celebrated social and political activists, the brand came to be seen as an anti-feminist relic controlled by old company men in Ohio. Victoria's Secret closed dozens of stores as profit margins evaporated. By the time Razek and Wexner made their exits in 2019 and 2020, respectively, the Victoria's Secret story was long overdue for a reboot.

Wexner declined to participate in this book. We made a full effort to tell his side of the story, the good and the bad. The current leadership at Victoria's Secret also declined to participate and said in a statement that the company is focused on "expanding our definition of sexy."

It is remarkable that the brand's allure lasted as long as it did. Most fashion brands have a creative shelf life of ten to fifteen years before a stale smell wafts in, the hype fades, and shoppers move on to the next new thing. And yet, despite the rise of countless would-be competitors, the decline of the shopping mall, and the rise of e-commerce and social media, shopping at Victoria's Secret remained, for decades, a rite of passage for teenagers and an indulgence for their mothers. Until, suddenly, it wasn't.

By the time Wexner realized Victoria's Secret was sinking, he was a billionaire many times over, inoculated from contrarian thinkers. He was so accustomed to knowing better than his customers that he had stopped listening to them. Perhaps that's what happens when a business has no real competitors. The groundswells shifting our culture can seem insignificant from the top of an empire.

The mythology of Victoria's Secret grew so powerful, it blinded him, too.

CHAPTER 1

Right Place, Right Time

For Bay Area entrepreneur Roy Raymond,
a taboo sparks a billion-dollar idea.

The story of Victoria's Secret begins not with a bra, but with a vibrator.

One day in the early 1970s in Manhattan, a young, soft-spoken marketing executive named Roy Raymond was tasked with an unusual errand.[1] His wife, Gaye, asked him to buy her a vibrator on the way home from work. After clocking in a full day at his respectable office on Madison Avenue, Roy ventured into what was then one of New York City's seediest areas, Times Square. The neighborhood was a red-light district, full of peep shows, strip clubs, porn theaters, pay-by-the-hour hotels—and sex shops.

Roy wasn't bothered by the environment or the request. He and Gaye were open-minded about just about everything, and she was a physical therapist who used vibrators to soothe her patients' aching backs. But the trip got Roy thinking. As women in the second-wave feminist era began to embrace their sexuality, why should they be forced to visit seamy and possibly dangerous parts of town to try something new? And how would they know that these types of products existed, or that other "regular" people were using them?

Roy was on the lookout for great business ideas. Instead of resigning himself to an office job or working up the ranks of a traditional name-brand company, he was determined to one day veer off the traditional course. "Roy was not driven by money, and I don't think he was into power, per se," said Gaye. "He liked being creative." And that night in Times Square, he dreamed up his first truly great idea.

Roy and Gaye met while they were at college in the mid-1960s—he at Tufts, she at Boston University. They lived in the same apartment building in the Boston neighborhood of Allston. He had dark hair, a beard, and kind eyes and had grown up in Fairfield, Connecticut, the son of an engineer. Gaye was a peppy, honey blonde raised in Saint Louis and New Jersey after spending her early childhood in Peru when her father, a chemist who had worked on the Manhattan Project, landed a job at a copper company there.

When the two realized they were both headed to the Bay Area after graduation, Gaye offered to help Roy move. He was planning to enter the business program at Stanford, and she was heading back to her parents' place in Menlo Park. Not long after arriving in California, in something out of *When Harry Met Sally*, Roy and Gaye discovered they were in love.

As part of his studies at Stanford, Roy developed a business plan for a budding local outdoor climbing brand called the North Face. Roy's strategy was never used—it was more of an educational exercise, according to Hap Klopp, then its CEO. Roy wasn't an A student, but he was excited by his work for the North Face. The project inspired him to create a business of his own, something with a keen and clear focus.

After Roy earned his MBA in 1971, he and Gaye married and moved again, this time to New York City. Roy got a marketing job at Vicks, the maker of over-the-counter medications like VapoRub and NyQuil, and Gaye continued her career practicing and teaching physical therapy. Hence Roy's quest for the vibrator, as a muscle stimulant—the errand that changed his life.

/ / /

Entrepreneurs love to talk about "white space," a part of a market where a consumer is underserved.[2] Until it's tested in the real world, however, a white space is just a thesis. Did the world really need, for example, an upscale, mass-produced solution to coffee in the 1990s? (Starbucks proved that the answer was "yes.") Did soda drinkers need a clear alternative to Pepsi in 1992? (Crystal Pepsi's flop proved "no.")

Roy was obsessed with white spaces. Shortly after the Times Square visit, the couple moved back to San Francisco for a change of pace, and he kept thinking about new ways to sell sex toys. The timing was ripe for such a business: in the 1970s, the sexual revolution that began a decade earlier evolved to focus not only on relationships with romantic partners, but also with one's own body. In the "Me Decade," as the writer Tom

Wolfe later dubbed the seventies, Americans were consumed with understanding and bettering themselves, especially when it came to sexuality. Sex books like 1971's *The Sensuous Man* and 1972's *The Joy of Sex* became bestsellers, teaching readers how to get each other off and encouraging experimentation. Unconventional sexual behaviors were reframed as just a matter of taste. While these books focused on heterosexual couples, the mentality they embraced helped broaden the acceptance of gay and lesbian relationships—especially in San Francisco, where the first gay pride parade was held in 1972.

Still, sex was a taboo subject for many people, including Gaye's clients with physical limitations. While working at Stanford, she attended a conference at the University of California, San Francisco, where she noticed "there was a reticence among the disability community to use [sex toys] because they were so tackily presented," she said. "I must have come home and said something to Roy about it."

Roy thought of catalogs, which had become a popular way to reach American shoppers, especially in the suburbs and other less-developed parts of the country. Selling sex toys through a catalog would maintain customer privacy and be more inviting than a store located in the wrong part of town. Potential customers could be gay men, straight men, straight women, queer people. Anyone whose idea of good sex veered just a little bit away from what was then the norm. Roy's white space was wide open.

A few years after they returned to San Francisco in 1974, the Raymonds started their first business together, a mail-order catalog selling "sexual aids." They called it the Xandria Collection. (Roy came up with the name. "I would go to bed early, and he'd get all these ideas, and then we'd wake up and discuss them in the morning," said Gaye.) The catalogs were discreet, mailed out in plain white envelopes. Inside, there were no photos, just drawings of the devices illustrated by an artist from an advertising agency whom Roy had met while working at a wine company, his day job after the Raymonds moved back to the Bay Area. "Our products range from the simple to the delightfully complex," read an ad for Xandria in *Cosmopolitan*, promising prompt and no-questions-asked refunds for the unsatisfied. "They are designed for both the timid and the bold. For anyone who's ever wished there could be something more to their sex life."[3]

Gaye's experience lent the catalog an expert voice, emphasizing that the products could be used for physical therapy. In everything they did, the Raymonds wanted to be viewed as *respectable*. Their provocative ideas were always couched in somewhat proper and prudish language. Try something outlandish, but do it in a sophisticated way. Roy's goal was to defang taboo ideas, and Gaye went along for the ride.

From the beginning, Roy's intention was to offer mail-order purchases only. He befriended other entrepreneurs tackling the same market in the city, like Joani Blank, the owner of Good Vibrations, a sex toy shop for women that opened in 1977 in the Mission District. But he wanted to reach people who were not living in liberal enclaves like San Francisco. It was the right instinct. Xandria quickly found an audience, especially in the Bible Belt.

Xandria became so successful that Roy was inspired to take the same model—repositioning an ostensibly embarrassing product to make it accessible and shame-free—and apply it to a category with even greater commercial potential. His next target was women's lingerie, a sexy product with a decidedly unsexy business model.

III

The history of lingerie is a story of manipulation, control, ingenuity, and, above all, identity. Despite their hidden nature, undergarments have, for most of human history, made their presence known beneath layers of clothing. They've restricted and reshaped women's bodies according to the beauty ideals and trends of the time, communicating everything from fertility to wealth to morality through the contours of the silhouette.

The earliest known version of a corset that survives today traces back to 2000 BC in Minoan Crete. A figurine of a goddess from the period appears with her waist cinched tightly and breasts unabashedly bare.[4] Later, in ancient Egypt, Greece, and Rome, where slaves were often naked and wealthy women wore layers of draped robes, there was little distinction between under- and outerwear. Greek women sometimes wore bands of linen around their waists and hips to flatten their figures, as did women of ancient Rome.[5]

In the fourteenth century, royal and aristocratic women began wearing corset-like contraptions, made from layers of linen stiffened by paste, underneath their clothing. In the 1500s, the paste was replaced by removable strips of silver, ivory, or, more commonly, elastic whalebone, a discovery of cross-Atlantic explorers commonly used in laced corsets until baleen whales nearly went extinct at the end of 1800s.[6]

Corsets ushered in a new silhouette for women—torsos squeezed into conical tubes, the breasts forced upward. The tighter the better, internal organs be damned. In the mid-1500s, Catherine de' Medici, the wife of Henry II of France and an early fashion influencer, dictated that fashionable waists be no more than thirteen inches in diameter. The corsets required to achieve such a look made the act of bending over impossible and potentially life-threatening.[7] (Ambroise Paré, one of the fathers of surgery and Henry II's personal doctor, once dissected the cadaver of a woman to find that her ribs overlapped from prolonged corset use.[8]) The torso-as-rigid-tube look remained popular for centuries, with a few reprieves in style. Minuscule waists communicated women's most prized aspirations: beauty, moral virtue, sexual propriety, and wealth. Breasts also suffered as a result. Around 1795, corsets were so tight as to squeeze breasts "up to the chin, making a sort of fleshy shelf," according to the *Times* of London.[9] The style resulted in near-constant nip slips. An advertisement in the same period advised mothers to help their daughters into corsets by having them lie facedown and placing one foot on their daughter's back before pulling the laces, to achieve the tightest possible result. In a letter from 1828, a tradesman wrote that when his daughter attempted to bend down while wearing a corset, "her stays gave way with a tremendous explosion and down she fell upon the ground and I thought she had snapped in two."[10] Corsets, mass-produced starting in the 1700s, rarely lasted more than a year from all the wear and tear.

By the end of the 1800s, it was a "a girl's ambition to have, at marriage, a waist-measurement not exceeding the number of years of her age—and to marry before she was twenty-one," explained a pair of British costume historians in *The History of Underclothes*, published in 1951.[11] This was a dangerous goal no doubt encouraged by anxious mothers. In the late nineteenth century, corset makers in Europe introduced artificial breasts, inserts made from chamois leather, quilted satin, or India rubber and sometimes held in place inside a woman's corset by suction cups. The technology was far from foolproof. A German newspaper described an incident at a Vienna dinner party in 1885, in which a young woman wearing inflated padding in her corset was mobbed by prospective suitors until one pinned a flower to her dress, and in doing so deflated "the charms that had so enticed him."[12]

Finally, English and American reformers began at the end of the nineteenth century to bemoan the health risks of corsets, which, along with overlapped ribs, included broken ribs and pregnancy complications. Maternity-friendly corsets mercifully emerged at this time, and young girls were discouraged from wearing tight corsets during adolescence. Efforts to make women's foundations more comfortable sometimes had the opposite effect. Arriving in the early 1900s was the S-curve corset, which extended long over the hips and flattened in front, forcing women to push their breasts forward and arch their backs.[13] Once again, bending over was impossible, especially because corsets were by then attached to a complicated system of garters and suspenders.[14] The look was made famous by the illustrator Charles Dana Gibson, who depicted these voluptuous so-called Gibson Girls in the pages of *Life* magazine.[15]

The tyranny of the corset began to wane in the twentieth century. A French designer living in Argentina named Herminie Cadolle created a new "breast girdle" that supported busts by the shoulders, not the hips. She returned to Paris after the turn of the century and opened her boutique, Cadolle, which became the go-to "foundations" shop for the city's fashionable Maxim's set.[16] Meanwhile, French designer Paul Poiret introduced a high-waisted silhouette and built early versions of bras into his clothing, becoming an anti-corset evangelist.

The revolution in women's underwear catered to a new generation seeking freedom from restrictive underpinnings. Some scholars attribute the death of the corset to the rise of fast dances like the tango, turkey trot, and bunny hug, which required women to be able to twist and turn, and became popular in the United States and Europe in the 1910s.[17] Enter the girdle, which extended from the top of the waist to the thighs or even the knees. The girdle could be much more comfortable (and cheaper) than full-torso corsets when worn with early versions of the bra, which began as little more than two handkerchiefs sewn together. Proto-bras resembled camisoles with some light boning for structure and support, with some early cups made from drawstring pouches. Later came molded cups, typically made from diagonally cut pieces of fabric layered over cotton foam.

Early bras weren't just less restrictive than anything women had encountered before, they were also simpler to manufacture and less expensive than corsets. In 1911, Macy's in Manhattan announced the opening of its first brassiere department. "This season's close-fitting gowns make the Brassiere more indispensable than ever," read the store's ad, boasting prices starting at 98 cents a pair. So-called breast supporters, at first available only from mail-order catalogs like Sears and Montgomery Ward, became more popular and readily available in department stores in the years that followed.[18]

By the 1920s, when flappers and their androgynous silhouettes ruled in fashionable society, bras were a mainstream woman's staple, and women whose corset ridges were visible under their clothes found themselves woefully out of style. Corset makers shuttered or pivoted their operations to bras and girdles. Powerhouse manufacturers like Maidenform and Playtex emerged and thrived. Rayon, an artificial silk or satin, became readily available and, for the first time, extended the market for beautiful underthings far beyond only the well-to-do.[19]

At the same time, the contours of women's daily lives were drastically changing. Women's employment began to quickly grow in the 1920s, after decades when only single women from low socio-economic backgrounds worked in factories or domestic roles. But as education became more available, single and recently married women joined the workforce, especially as typists, stenographers, and secretaries. By 1940, 27 percent of women over the age of fourteen were working,[20] and these women needed underwear that allowed them to sit comfortably for hours in front of a typewriter or to lean over nursing patients and assembly lines.

But by the 1930s, distinct, perky breasts and tiny waists came back into style—and they never really fell out again. After the Second World War, Christian Dior solidified the return of the hourglass shape for women when he introduced his "New Look" collection in 1947, driving women to find ways to accentuate their busts and hips and narrow the appearance of their waists by comparison. It wasn't just Dior. The war had made icons out of busty stars like Carole Landis and Jane Russell. And the use of elasticized fibers in formerly restrictive underwear like roll-on girdles allowed women to comfortably emulate those icons.

One of the first underwire bras with cups, created and patented by Broadway costume designer Helene Pons in 1931, looked like a bulkier version of today's styles, with cups lined by U-shaped wires designed to lay flat against the body. Around the same time, the American bra maker Warner developed the Alphabet Bra line, the first with increasing cup sizes for better fit. After World War II, "falsies," akin to felt padding inserts, became commonplace.[21] American women were inundated with advertising for the latest styles and design advancements, including bras with fanciful names like "Young You" and "Jezebel." In the 1950s, the most coveted bras had pointy, conical cups that poked out from under blouses and sweaters. The first modern push-up bras emerged in this decade, using straps placed at the outside edges of underwire cups to shove breasts up and together.[22]

The trendsetters of the time were no longer royalty and aristocrats, but Hollywood stars like Lana Turner and Rita Hayworth who both appeared on the big screen in slip dresses that emphasized their curves. Turner's corset in *The Merry Widow* (released in 1952) inspired a line of popular underwire corselettes sold by Warner, which also promised waist-whittling and bust-pumping effects.[23] After World War II, molded bra cups, prized for their nipple-hiding effects, emerged and steadily grew in popularity over the postwar decades.

In 1946, a young man named Frederick Mellinger, recently discharged from the army, saw an opportunity to leverage Hollywood's growing influence on American style. A son of a tailor and born in the tenements of Manhattan's Lower East Side, Mellinger landed a job when he was just a teenager in the 1930s as an assistant lingerie buyer for a women's wear catalog, Aldens, in Manhattan. Aldens was a valuable learning experience, but the catalog was too conservative for his tastes.

While serving in the Signal Corps in Missouri during World War II, Mellinger polled his fellow servicemen: What kind of women did they fantasize about?[24] The men all had posters and photographs of cheese-cake pinups, soft-core images of shapely women who seemed chaste but posed seductively. During the war, the military all but sanctioned these images to raise troop morale. Among the most popular pinup girls was the actress and singer Betty Grable, who, glancing over her shoulder at the camera, looked wholesome and all-American with her round cheeks and blond curls. "[The soldiers] leaned toward boobs and shapely ankles," Mellinger said. "A high zoftig" was also desirable, he said, using a Yiddish term for voluptuous curves.[25]

After the war, Mellinger moved to Los Angeles and opened his own mail-order business, Frederick's of Hollywood, selling "famous Hollywood fashions" at budget-friendly prices. At first, most of his products were mostly trendy women's wear and accessories, but soon he found his niche by playing to his army buddies' tastes. The illustrated women in his catalog were pure pinup fantasies, preening and arching and twisting to show off every angle, their attire barely containing their physical forms. Most pages showed the kind of clothing favored by wiseguys' girls on the side—cleavage-baring jumpsuits, hip-hugging flares, and ribbed bodysuits. Mellinger also offered every conceivable "body enhancer"—items rarely found in respectable department stores. He sold nylon lace panties that were completely open in the back and called them "the Living End"; clip-on thongs to be worn under clothing, with cutouts at the hips; and "orgy butter," a lotion for setting a romantic mood. He also sold rubber nipple pads called "Tender Tips" to slip under semi-sheer shirts, butt and hip pads to layer under girdles, and leg pads that promised to look seamless under opaque tights. "Be a SKINNY SHANKS no more!" beckoned the catalog. Mellinger's bras had the power to add inches or curves—or both, earning him a reputation as the "Pygmalion of Pulchritude."[26] His sales tactics were as subtle as his Tender Tips. "It's not what you've got, it's the way that you shape it with Frederick's add-a-full cup size bras!"[27]

In his catalogs, Mellinger made lingerie shopping seem as thrilling as a night out on the town. "It's up UP and away for this big lift-off bra!" declared a 1971 brochure. Some of his wares were his own designs—and new innovations in the market. Other items were imported from Europe or copied from upscale New York designers. Frederick's was one of the first places where American women encountered black lingerie and push-up bras.

All the while, Mellinger remained Frederick's central character. "If your breasts sag a little . . . he lifts them up. . . . If nature didn't, Frederick's will!" read one catalog. Hollywood soon approved, often literally, with legendary stars, including actress Jayne Mansfield and pinup girl Bettie Page, appearing in ads and catalogs to endorse the Frederick's effect.

Mellinger's ideal woman remained in the bullet-bra 1940s even as fashion trends moved on to the mod-1960s and the bohemian 1970s, when soft, sheer bras became popular, and some women abandoned bras altogether. Mellinger succeeded by trading on a nostalgia for Rita Hayworth's heyday among heterosexual couples. His illustrated advertisements in *Esquire* and *Playboy* veered on pornographic, with models heaving up their bare breasts while clinging to his most revealing merchandise. "I hate to see a flat-fannied girl,"[28] Mellinger once said. In an interview, he described his secretary's breasts as "poached eggs,"[29] as he explained how her complaints to him led to developing bras with inflatable cups. (They came with tiny straws.)

"Our merchandise is selected to make her as 'sexy' as possible," Mellinger told a reporter in 1958, back when he had only three stores in Los Angeles, Long Beach, and San Diego. His most famous store, located within a striking, purple-awning art deco–style building on Hollywood Boulevard, opened in 1960. His target customers were women over thirty-five "who may feel their physical charm is fading" and who believed him when he said his dresses were worn by glamorous movie actresses.

"One of the best reasons a housewife might like to dress this way is to be sure the man would come home," Mellinger said on an Atlanta TV talk show in 1975. When a woman in the audience, a member of the National Organization for Women, said his clothing reduced women to sex objects, he was unbothered. "If a woman wants to look like a non-sex object, so be it," he responded.[30]

By then, Mellinger had become a minor celebrity, appearing on *The Tonight Show* and other national television programs with his signature mustache and Givenchy suit. He was often accompanied by models in hot pants and bikinis, there to discuss the merits of sexy lingerie. His catalogs boasted: "As seen on Johnny Carson!"[31]

Mellinger eventually catered to men, too. In the 1970s, he introduced a line of sheer robes and rip-off leather briefs with the tagline "Dress for Sex-cess." By 1980, Frederick's was titillating housewives and husbands of Omaha and Youngstown to great effect, bringing in $33 million in annual sales through the catalog and more than 120 stores across the country.[32] "We serve a purpose," Mellinger said once. "If a guy likes what he sees when he gets home, the family's gotta be a happy family and that's all we're interested in."[33]

///

In the 1970s, Frederick's of Hollywood was a minor sensation but still a niche business. When it came to buying underwear, most American women had few retail options. Major cities had independent boutiques that ranged from cheesy to utilitarian, but their products were typically expensive. Or at least pricier than those offered by local department stores like Macy's or Gimbels, where most women shopped for basic bras and underwear. The department stores' foundations sections were often poorly organized and devoid of salespeople. Lace and printed fabrics were scant, but boring bras with beige straps and gummy, high-waisted briefs were piled high. Still, the typical American woman was unwilling to turn to racier boutiques like Frederick's. The women's liberation movement freed some younger progressives from their bras and piqued their interest in sexual adventures—like the suburban swinging made famous by rumors of "key parties," where women went home with a neighborhood husband by choosing a car key at random from a fishbowl. But most Americans were still uncomfortable talking about sex openly, much less shopping for anything sex-related, and that included lingerie.

Roy Raymond, observing the dour shopping experiences and dreary lingerie selection at department stores, arrived at his next great idea. He and Gaye had visited lingerie shops in New York City that offered meticulous customer service. Why not do the same with more style? Roy became a student of retail, reading every article about the intimates market in *Women's Wear Daily*, the leading fashion trade paper, and *Vogue*. In Europe, high-end lingerie shops were more common. At Cadolle in Paris, descendants of the influential designer Herminie Cadolle had expanded the family business, offering made-to-measure bras and corsets for clients ranging from European royalty to Texan socialites. At Sabbia Rosa, another Paris boutique that also attracted the wealthy and famous from overseas, the colorful silk chemises were beautiful enough to wear out to dinner on their own. The tiny store was a pleasure to visit, trimmed in velvet and covered in mirrors.

Roy wanted to bring these experiences to the States where, after World War II, shopping became a driving force of economic growth. Department stores remained community mainstays, offering everything from the latest dress collections to the newest home appliances, all under one roof. But new, fast-growing "specialty" retailers, typically selling only one or a few brands of only one category, were becoming shopping's hottest new concept. Boosted by affordable retail rents and easy access to small-business loans, these postwar chains disrupted department stores by presenting themselves as experts in a specific field. Shoppers came for the individualized service and for the sense that they were getting the best of the best. In the San Francisco Bay Area alone, the North Face, Esprit, the Gap, Banana Republic, and Williams Sonoma all launched thriving businesses between the late 1950s and 1970s. "We were really changing the world of retail, and it felt like San Francisco was ground zero for all of that," said a retail publicist of that time. But specialty retail was also a national trend. In Philadelphia, Richard Hayne was outfitting East Coast college elites with his Urban Outfitters concept. And in Columbus, Les Wexner was building a midwestern empire with his cheap-chic clothing boutique, the Limited.

Roy was eager to join their ranks. In 1977, he borrowed money from his family and a bank and pooled some of the profits from Xandria. He and Gaye researched the lingerie market at local department stores, writing down the brand names of the best pieces and using the phone book to look up those brands' headquarters. The Raymonds did the same on a trip to New York, combing the racks of Bergdorf Goodman and Henri Bendel for upscale labels. On that visit, they placed their very first order of inventory from the best suppliers they could find, buying around $30,000 worth of lingerie—silk robes, tap pants, and lace brassieres—all in cash. Six months later, the Raymonds' first store opened in Palo Alto's Stanford Shopping Center, an outdoor mall in an upper-middle-class neighborhood that would later become one of the richest zip codes in the world. The name he and Gaye chose was "Victoria's Secret": evocative, mysterious and inviting, with a wink to the Victorian-inspired interior design style they loved.

Roy and Gaye spared no expense outfitting the retail space with antique Eastlake furniture and decor and custom woodwork. Roy fussed over every detail. The store was meant to look like a boudoir, an ornate private room of the late 1800s. The walls were painted dusty rose. The floors were festooned with Oriental rugs. Decorated bay windows looked out onto the street. Merchandise was pinned to soft fabric panels and hung on brass racks. The aim was to communicate a private, romantic sophistication and offset any embarrassment customers might feel in shopping for lingerie.

The mood was au courant. In the late seventies, fashion trends turned away from the sharp, bright silver lamé miniskirts and acid-green shift dresses of the 1960s. New materials (polyester) and silhouettes (bellbottoms) became popular, as did a refound appreciation for vintage fashion, particularly from the late 1800s and early 1900s to World War II. The color palette was autumnal—browns, rusts, and marigolds.

The sepia-toned aesthetic in fashion was reflected by Hollywood, including Peter Bogdanovich's 1973 movie *Paper Moon* (set in the 1930s and the Great Depression), and 1974's *Daisy Miller* (set in the 1870s), based on Henry James's 1878 novella. Louis Malle's 1978 film *Pretty Baby* best demonstrated the mood Roy was chasing for Victoria's Secret. The film follows a twelve-year-old sex worker, played by Brooke Shields, who lives in a brothel in New Orleans's red-light district during World War I. (The film, although controversial, was a critical success and turned Shields into a star.) The brothel is a Victorian-era lovers' dream, lushly rendered in ornate fabric wallpaper, dark carved wood furnishings, and tattered lace. The aesthetic was hatched from the brain of the movie's screenwriter, Polly Platt, an accomplished set designer who worked on many influential films of the period. Like much art of the time, shaded by Watergate, the Vietnam War, and the social traumas of the 1960s, *Pretty Baby* mixed nostalgia and disdain for the past. Aesthetically, the film reflected women's simultaneous liberation and fetishization.

Roy's vision for Victoria's Secret also drew on a nostalgia for a frilly, feminine romance that had fallen out of favor in the 1960s and early '70s, when lingerie trends veered soft, sheer, and minimalist. Austrian-born American designer Rudi Gernreich's hit "No Bra"[34] was emblematic of the moment: his sheer nylon mesh bra neither offered much support nor molded the breasts into any particular shape. Gernreich helped reintroduce lingerie as fashionable at a time when the hippies were growing up and entering the workforce. They had money to spend and, as it turned out, an appetite for delicate underthings.

Roy stocked his store with Victorian-inspired cotton and silk nightgowns and garter belts trimmed in ruffles and lace, along with silk teddies, and stockings in jewel tones and soft pastels. He carried designers like Janet Reger, whose upscale line was gaining a reputation and helping revive an interest in pretty nightgowns. Sharing the space were upscale American and European brands—including Hanky Panky, Flora Nikrooz, Christian Dior, and La Perla—which were similarly heavy on silk, satin, ruffles, and sheer fabrics. Few items other than underwear were priced under $60, and the occasional bra-and-panty set (a rare concept in the States at the time) could run upward of $2,000—the equivalent of more than $10,000 today. A pair of his-and-hers kimonos designed by Eleanor Coppola, the artist and wife of Francis Ford Coppola, was listed for $1,200.[35]

The high price was part of the appeal. Victoria's Secret catered to a sophisticated clientele. This was *not* Frederick's of Hollywood. "We are not selling items for women who stand in doorways with a come-and-get-me pose," Roy said in an interview in 1981.[36]

Half of Victoria's Secret's customers were women shopping for themselves; the other half were men shopping for the women in their lives. (Or sometimes for men or for themselves. This was San Francisco, after all.) And despite the recession of the early 1980s, the store thrived, as did the broader upscale lingerie sector. Magazines like *Forbes* characterized the trend as a reaction to the conservative, masculine clothing women wore to work. (How else could they assert their femininity!) *Cosmopolitan*'s editor in chief, Helen Gurley Brown, who first became famous for advising young women to enjoy sex outside marriage in her hit 1962 book *Sex and the Single Girl*, was more direct. "Lingerie is an accessory to sex," she said. "As women have become more assertive sexually, sex is very available. This is what you wear to take off to seduce and appeal to a man."[37] Others thought the sex angle was overblown and attributed the lingerie trend to women rediscovering the simple comforts of a beautiful nightgown or silky tap pants. Whatever the reasons, suppliers like Lily of France and Maidenform began to see their sales skyrocket at the end of the 1970s.

Victoria's Secret arrived at the perfect time. In 1981, its fourth year in business, it generated around $6 million in sales—a strong start for just four stores and a mail-order catalog. The Raymonds knew the catalog business well from their experience with Xandria. But the Victoria's Secret catalog became more than just a sales channel for at-home shoppers. It made this small Bay Area business nationally famous in a way the Raymonds never could have imagined.

ııı

By the time Victoria's Secret entered the market, catalogs were a $40-billion-a-year industry with a long, fruitful history. The first catalog as we know it today was mailed out in 1872 by Chicago's Montgomery Ward, a wholesale business catering to rural families and farmers. Chicago rival Sears, Roebuck and Company soon followed, and both "books," each offering thousands of items, made the formula famous, especially among rural Americans. By 1936, about 17 million Americans (of a total population of about 128 million) received catalogs from the two leading distributors. By then, many pages were printed in color and featured photographs. Shoppers could comb through hundreds, sometimes thousands, of products, from children's clothing to enameled stoves, in one sitting and fill out a simple form to place an order.

By the 1950s, well-to-do suburbanites, having fled major cities for white picket fences, marked the start of the holiday season when thick "wish books" from department stores arrived in their mailboxes. The upscale Dallas department store Neiman Marcus, known locally for bringing "good taste" to Texas, became famous nationally for its almost absurdly excessive Christmas edition catalog. Its gift ideas included a pair of live tigers, "giant or economy size," which the store promised to come outfitted in diamond and ruby bracelets—all for a cool $1 million.[38]

Catalogs were a godsend in the American suburbs before the giant malls arrived in great number in the 1980s. "Catalog buyers tend to be younger, more venturesome, and to express greater self-confidence," read a 1971 survey of shoppers.[39] In the industrious postwar culture, being able to afford the best products was an expression of pride and a mark of one's social status.

Given the competition in the catalog market, Roy knew that Victoria's Secret needed strong photography to stand out in American mailboxes. His first issues, published in 1978, prioritized a strong concept over aiding sales. They looked "trite, not very commercial—you couldn't see the product," said Ross Carron, an art director the Raymonds later hired. "They looked kind of homemade." The image on the covers resembled a worn oxblood leather photo album, with "Victoria's Secret" embossed in gold, somewhat cartoonish in its cursive letters. On the very first page, a small paragraph of italicized copy announced: "Welcome to my album of silk and satin delights. I know you will enjoy all the elegant and glamorous styles that are a part of my secret collection. It is a true pleasure to share with you the most enchanting designs in fine lingerie . . . Be sure to visit my new boutique when you are in Palo Alto." It was signed, "Victoria."

Tap pants (or side-cut shorts) were $16 (today, about $75), but an "antique-style" robe with a drawstring Empire waist and high-neck collar was $100 (about $470). In one early edition, the models recall actresses of the silent film era, lounging in front of trompe l'oeil wallpaper in an ornate home. In many of the images, a man in a three-piece suit played the role of photographer, posing next to a large-format view camera.

Soon Roy hired Carron, the art director, and Peter Ogilvie, a photographer, to take over. Ogilvie was a contributor to another publication that showed plenty of skin: *Wet: The Magazine of Gourmet Bathing*, a Venice, California–based art magazine. In its pages, slick models sprout from wading pools, nipples peeking out from between splashes of water. Like a lot of art from the 1970s, the magazine carried an air of humor and irreverence. (*Wet* published a cartoon by *The Simpsons'* creator Matt Groening called "Forbidden Soaps," where the protagonist explains, in excruciating detail, the pros and cons of a variety of bar soaps.) "*Wet* never took itself all that seriously," wrote its founder, the artist Leonard Koren, in 2012. "To paraphrase one of its contributors, *Wet* was a parody of all enthusiasms, or more accurately, a parody of all enthusiasms taken a bit too far."

Ogilvie was inspired by the work of Guy Bourdin and Helmut Newton, photographers known for their provocative, innovative images of nearly naked women. In 1976, a forty-page lingerie catalog Bourdin photographed for Bloomingdale's, entitled "Sighs and Whispers," had scandalized shoppers and become instantly influential in the fashion community for its surrealistic images. (In one scene, three models in silk robes stand transfixed around an illuminated conch shell, suggesting a séance.) While Bourdin's aesthetic was deemed too risqué for the Victoria's Secret catalog, his ambition inspired Ogilvie.

Victoria's Secret also took inspiration from photographers like Barry Lategan, whose black-and-white photos of the mod-era star Twiggy were soft and fuzzy, evoking pencil illustrations. "Prettier, sweeter," Ogilvie said. "Not so edgy." That soft focus was evident in a 1981 Victoria's Secret catalog cover featuring a hazy, closely cropped image of a curly blond model wearing a lace kimono jacket—no visible cleavage, her kohl-rimmed eyes almost wary. Inside, the models pose in groups of two and three dressed in camisole sets and shiny satin robes. They look pensive, slightly annoyed, and completely elegant. There are no arched backs or spread legs. Ogilvie, who had strong relationships with modeling agencies from his work in New York City and beyond, oversaw casting and location scouting, working side by side with Barbara Dunlap, the Raymonds' head of marketing.

Finding the right models was essential. The women needed to be thin, fair skinned, as blemish-free as possible—this was before easy retouching—and blessed with the right proportions. Busty but not too busty, with narrow, but not boyish, hips. Few models at the time had breast implants, which meant that bust sizes varied wildly. "Victoria's Secret wanted a 34B," Ogilvie said, but not all 34B busts fit the bras the same way or filled out the cups evenly. Sometimes models would call Ogilvie to let him know they had gotten breast implants, hoping it would land them more work. Sometimes it did.

The hair and makeup took on a heavy-handed style. Carol Perkins, a Ford model, compared her Victoria's Secret look to that of Miss Kitty, the saloon owner on the long-running TV series *Gunsmoke*. Hair was typically curled and pinned up high. Lips were painted hot pink.

Every single model in the early Victoria's Secret editions was fair skinned. While Black models were becoming more visible in high-fashion editorials in the 1970s (although not by much), most commercial catalogs stuck with a stereotypical blond or fair "all-American" look. Victoria's Secret was no different.

There could be no airbrushing. At the time, retouching a photograph to erase even a few pimples could cost $1,000 (around $4,000 today). Instead, Ogilvie and the photographers used more forgiving lighting that cast fewer shadows. "The more contrast you have, the bigger chance it's going to show a blemish," he said. But a lot could be covered with makeup. White powder was used to camouflage pubic hair, for example, because the powder reflected the white light of the flash—for the most part. But it did not always work, and pubic hair was often visible in the published catalog.

From the very beginning, even before anyone outside of San Francisco had heard of Victoria's Secret, modeling in its catalog was a sought-after job. Since the images required showing more skin than regular catalog work, the models were often paid double their typical day rate, around $1,500–$2,000 (now $6,000–$8,000). Some of the models were aspiring actors, like the Canadian Melody Anderson, best known for later starring in the space opera *Flash Gordon*. A young Geena Davis was another early Victoria's Secret model—but not for long. After she submitted some of her photographs from the lingerie catalog to director Sydney Pollack, he cast her in *Tootsie*, the 1982 comedy starring Dustin Hoffman[40] and Jessica Lange.

The catalog's creative team prided itself on finding the best shooting locations around San Francisco, like the city's ornate, vaulted Opera House. Perkins remembers that her first shoots were frequently set inside beautiful local private homes—a mansion on Nob Hill full of dark wood and soft lighting. Other shoots were set in similar locales in the outskirts of Paris, where Ogilvie later moved.

"When we did a shoot, there was a mood to it; it wasn't just lingerie," said Barba Kandarian, a graduate of Macy's legendary executive training program, who joined Victoria's Secret in the late 1970s as a buyer. "On every photoshoot, we pored over the pictures, selected the final shots as a group. It was a labor of love," she said.

The catalogs started to gain a following. In 1981, *GQ* recommended the catalog to readers for its "shamelessly sensual undergarments." Customers wrote letters, sometimes directly to "Victoria"—claiming, for instance, that a "picture of the black teddy on page fourteen saved our marriage," or that one particular red outfit had driven a woman's husband wild. Many of the catalog captions were written in the voice of "Victoria," who identified "my favorite teddy" or described private-label pieces as "my own designs" and others as "favorites of my boutique customers."

The most memorable letters came from prison inmates, Ogilvie said. "[They] would say, 'We don't care about *Penthouse* or *Playboy*; we just wait for the Victoria's Secret catalog.'" He added, "We used to say on the set, 'Let's do a photo for the prisoners.'"

///

In early television interviews promoting Victoria's Secret, Gaye Raymond often took center stage. She was the more gregarious of the two. Roy puzzled reporters who expected a swanky ladies' man, not a shy, soft-spoken fellow in wire-rimmed glasses and a conservative suit. Gaye was happy to step in and regale interviewers with tales of "Victoria." The made-up backstory: Victoria was a British woman the couple had once met during a journey on the Orient Express, the storied luxury train that ran across Europe and into Asia. (In reality, the Raymonds had never even traveled on the train.) The Orient Express was sophisticated, exotic, and out of reach for most Americans—yet it was entirely familiar, thanks to frequent mentions in literature, film, and television, from Bram Stoker's *Dracula* to Agatha Christie's Hercule Poirot novels.

In Gaye's telling, Victoria had been sitting behind the Raymonds at a table in the dining car when she leaned over to start up a conversation with the couple. It was a story straight out of a murder mystery. Victoria had an English rose complexion and brimmed with confidence. She wasn't just sexy and elegant. She was also an executive, oozing success. When it was time for the Raymonds to say their goodbyes, Roy leaned in and asked, "What's your secret?" And Victoria responded, "Fantastic lingerie."

It was a tall tale, a pure marketing gimmick that Gaye aptly sold to local television reporters as reality. On TV, Gaye would wear neat little suits with a silk tank top peeking out, a hint of what they were offering in their boutiques, and she was "positive, smiling, and encouraging," said Michele Rivers, manager of the first store and eventual head of retail.

As their business slowly grew, and the Raymonds opened four small stores in the Bay Area, the team drummed up business by hosting lunchtime fashion shows at nearby restaurants and Men's Only nights. Rivers recalls a Valentine's Day when she painted the windows of the San Francisco store magenta, leaving unpainted a keyhole-shaped section of glass, where passersby could "take a peek of what she really wants for Valentine's." Inside, models reclined in lingerie and silk robes. The *San Francisco Chronicle*'s Herb Caen, a popular local columnist, wrote about it. "There were lines out the door," Rivers said.

What sold best? "Tap pants," said Kandarian, the buyer, referring to silk shorts, sometimes trimmed in lace, that were often paired with a silk singlet and worn as pajamas or instead of underwear. Lace teddies were popular, too. First sold in the early 1900s under the name "camiknicker" or "envelope chemise," teddies combined a slip and underwear into a light-weight bodysuit. Women had worn them under the more body-conscious clothing that trended in the 1910s and '20s, but by the 1970s the teddy had been recast as loungewear. In 1981, actress Margot Kidder (Lois Lane to Christopher Reeves's Superman) came by the Victoria's Secret store in San Francisco and spent $2,000 on a stack of pieces, including a peach silk teddy.[41]

About four times a year, Kandarian traveled to the trade shows in New York City and to Europe to shop for Victoria's Secret's next assortment of lingerie. Often, Roy went with her. These shows were a long-standing industry ritual. Each season—a period of three to six months—retail representatives like Kandarian would place orders with manufacturers for the products they would sell in the months and years ahead. Typically, the buyers had a strict budget for each season, mostly dedicated to restocking the latest hit sweater or dress. Some of the budget was reserved for unexpectedly attractive styles, or for a new brand that was generating outsize attention, but such purchases were risky. Retailers could not predict the future. Most major retail successes are unexpected, meaning stores will often understock what turns out to be a popular product, frustrating consumers when it's not available, and then overbuy the style in the next season in the hope of meeting demand, only to be stuck with leftovers after the item's moment has passed.

When Kandarian first met Roy Raymond, his office was piled high with boxes of "mistakes," items he had come to regret ordering. Her first task was to get rid of them. Her second was to find better inventory. When it came to merchandising, Roy's primary strategy was that he wanted the very best for his store shelves, no matter the expense or risk. Kandarian consulted with him and Gaye closely and tracked sales at the stores, but she was largely free to buy what she liked each season. "We looked for elegance," she said. "Our goal was to elevate lingerie to something that was considered nice, sensual, and wasn't tacky."

Roy gave his employees an unusual amount of freedom, preferring not to meddle in the day-to-day decisions. While his soft-spoken nature made him difficult to read, the familial tone he set created a tight-knit work environment as the workforce reached thirty employees and kept growing. His employees often worked overtime, including Christmas and weekends, for the good of the business, but they also organized themed costume days for laughs. An advertisement in the *Chronicle* for a bookkeeping position at Victoria's Secret in the early 1980s called for the candidate to have, along with four years of experience and good communication skills, "honesty, a sense of personal caring and individual worth." In return, the candidate was promised a competitive salary, health insurance, an education allowance, and a "challenging and supportive work environment."

But growth came with heavy costs. Victoria's Secret was losing money, in large part because of Roy's lack of spending discipline. One employee estimated that Roy spent $1 million just furnishing each store. That's about $4.7 million per store in 2023 terms—an extraordinarily large budget even for a luxury goods store. Profits from Xandria, the sex toy catalog company, provided Victoria's Secret with some cash to keep expanding. (The Raymonds had hired someone to run Xandria while they focused on Victoria's Secret.) Still, ballooning overhead costs became an increasing problem—one that Roy insisted on handling himself. "I wanted to be a part of the meetings that involved finances, and he was never able to arrange it," said Gaye, who knew enough to realize Roy lacked a solid financial plan. "It could have been that he was embarrassed."

In so many ways, Victoria's Secret was a success. The Raymonds had managed to pinpoint a change in social mores that few saw coming. Second-wave feminism had ushered women into the workforce in larger numbers than ever before—50 percent of US women worked in 1980, compared to 34 percent in 1950.[42] As the bra-spurning days receded from memory, delicate satin lingerie no longer seemed like a relic of the past. Femininity came back into style. Beautiful loungewear and soft underwear could be a romantic indulgence and a personal tonic for independent, modern women on a quest to embrace their sexuality—what today we call self-care or self-empowerment. Roy and Gaye identified that impulse at the right time. But their cultural savviness couldn't make up for their lack of financial discipline.

Roy sought outside funding beyond the typical bank loans, but his options for early-stage investors were limited. In the 1970s, the now famous venture capital firms Sequoia Capital and Kleiner Perkins had set up on Sand Hill Road in Menlo Park, just down the road from the Stanford Shopping Center. But those firms were investing in technology, not bras. While Roy knew some venture capitalists, convincing them to take a chance on a lingerie shop—even one with a robust catalog business generating several million dollars a year—was next to impossible. And the business was too small to raise money in the public markets.

Victoria's Secret's debts were quickly rising. So when one interested buyer emerged—the assertive founder of runaway retail success the Limited—Roy could not stave off his proposal for long.

CHAPTER 2

The Rise of a Retail Savant

Les Wexner and the invention of fast fashion.

The origins of the modern American fashion business can be traced back to a dingy Midtown Manhattan joint called the York Hotel, where guests paid for rooms by the hour. One afternoon in 1971, Martin "Marty" Trust rented one of those rooms for what would end up being the most significant meeting of his career: an encounter with Les Wexner, the thirty-four-year-old owner of the rising women's retailer the Limited. Wexner was in town from Columbus, Ohio, with his chief merchant, Verna Gibson.[1]

Wexner, unassuming at five foot six, managed to tower over Trust, who was a whole four inches shorter. But Trust was brash and loudmouthed. "He could get twelve fucks into a six-word sentence" is how one former colleague put it. Trust overwhelmed the reserved Wexner. Not enough, however, to scare him away.

Trust owned Mast Industries, a firm he had recently launched to import apparel from Asia, mostly Hong Kong, into the United States. His career was something of an accident. The son of Russian and Polish immigrants who settled in Brooklyn, Trust graduated with a scholarship-funded business degree from the Massachusetts Institute of Technology in 1958. When a New Hampshire knitting firm hired him to install its computer system, he stayed on afterward to learn the manufacturing business. The company sent him to the United Kingdom to purchase machinery and to Hong Kong to learn from manufacturers who were ramping up their production capabilities in the hope of selling more products to foreigners like him.

Trust was struck by the quality of the clothing he found in the factories in Hong Kong, where labor costs were lower than in the United States, driving down the costs of manufacturing. In the 1950s, most American shoppers assumed garments made abroad, especially in Asia, were inferior to American-made ones. Americans bought far fewer items of clothing each year then than they do now, and they were better at clocking flimsy fabrics or shoddy stitching. These Hong Kong factories, though, were skilled, Trust realized. No American customer would know the difference.

After a decade with the knitting firm, Trust struck out on his own. He would find the best knitting factories in Asia and import sweaters for American retailers to sell. His business was slow getting off the ground, though. One client fired him because its other domestic manufacturers had complained about being undercut by foreign competitors. But Trust knew that his price would win out, so he kept touting Hong Kong.

Wexner had come to the York Hotel to see for himself if Trust's clothes looked as cheap as they cost to make. Trust laid out his latest imports on the hotel room's made-up bed. His Shetland wool sweaters in saturated colors and geometric Fair Isle patterns cost half of what Wexner was paying the Shetland Woollen Co. to make similar styles in Scotland. Back then, before cashmere was commonplace, Shetland sweaters were prized. Their wool was shorn from Scottish sheep and known for its texture and range of natural colors.

Trust's sweaters looked good—so good, in fact, that Gibson worried that she and her new boss were being conned. Wexner seemed unconcerned and promptly placed an order with Trust. "If the sweaters show up, great; if they don't, what difference does it make?" he said to Gibson afterward, noting that he had not yet cut Trust a check.

Weeks later, a batch of Trust's wool sweaters arrived in Columbus. Wexner weighed every single one on a postal scale, because he knew manufacturers often cut corners by thinning out their yarns. The sweaters made weight, and Wexner was delighted.

His business was about to change. Working with Trust would make the two men both very rich. It would also change the trajectory of American retail.

///

Like many Jewish Americans of Russian descent, Les Wexner grew up in the *schmatta* business—otherwise known as the rag trade, otherwise known as the business of making and supplying and selling clothes. The Industrial Revolution ushered in the rise of mass-produced, ready-to-wear clothing, and the American garment business had fed on inexpensive immigrant labor, as waves of poor people emigrated from Ireland, Sweden, Germany, and Italy. At the turn of the twentieth century, many garment workers were Jewish immigrants who came to the United States to escape religious persecution in eastern Europe and Russia. They gathered in the overcrowded tenements of New York City's Lower East Side, where they made most of the nation's garments in factories and sweatshops.

Garment manufacturing had relatively low barriers of entry. One man could set up his own small production outfit with a handful of employees, who often worked for less than a living wage, and subcontract production from larger firms looking to cut costs or quickly deliver orders—and, if he was lucky, step up into the middle class. Jewish Americans leveraged their community networks to find complementary suppliers or unofficial financing, and found success in what was, even then, a highly decentralized garment industry.

Many Jewish Americans also found work selling "dry goods" like clothing directly to customers across the country, carrying on a tradition with a long cultural history. In early modern Europe, Jews had often been excluded from owning land or practicing a profession, so many made a living lending money, peddling, and shopkeeping.[2] As the United States expanded west, Jewish immigrants traveled between frontier towns selling textiles and other nonperishable staples, and then parlayed those operations into dry goods stores and wholesale outlets in major cities across America. Many Jewish American families built thriving family-owned, multigenerational retail operations. (They had competition, of course. Prominent businesses such as Nordstrom in Seattle and Dillard's in Arkansas were run by gentiles. Even after the waves of immigration in the early 1890s, Jews represented only 4 percent of the total US population by 1930.)

One Jewish retail family set up shop in the heart of Columbus, where a German immigrant and rabbinical scholar named Simon Lazarus opened a menswear store in 1851. While there were many other such small stores in the city, Lazarus differentiated itself at the end of the Civil War by betting big on a recent invention: ready-to-wear suits. Before the war, most men's suits were made to measure. But ready-to-wear appealed to returning soldiers, who had just stepped out of some of the first American mass-produced garments—their military uniforms. As Lazarus expanded in the years that followed, the store became one of the first in the country to set standard prices for its garments, eliminating the hassle customers felt when haggling for their purchases.

The opening of a new, expanded Lazarus store in downtown Columbus in 1909 was a historic retail event. The six-floor mega-flagship, on the northwest corner of Town and High Streets, contained the city's first escalator and an aviary of singing canaries. (The escalator was ahead of its time. The store removed it after five years because it "scared the daylights out of people," said Simon Lazarus's great-grandson Charles.[3]) This flagship was the first Lazarus store to expand beyond menswear, eventually selling everything from children's clothing to fine china to records, and it became a civic hub for Columbus for decades. Generations of families visited "Mr. Tree," a talking Christmas fir, every holiday season and attended the store's annual Thanksgiving parade.

What distinguished Lazarus from most similar operations in cities across America was the tenacity of its leader. Fred Lazarus Jr., Simon's grandson, dropped out of college at Ohio State University to begin working full-time in the family business when he was still a teenager. Standing at barely five feet, with a permanent tremor in his hand from a childhood illness, Fred was more formidable than he looked. He was a retail innovator. Fred ushered in new practices and traditions in the 1920s and '30s that soon became industry standard. He organized clothing by size instead of price, an idea he brought back from a visit to Printemps, in Paris.[4] His was also the first major American retailer to offer sales on credit without a down payment.

Fred even changed how the stores were staffed, giving the top employee in each department of each individual store the responsibility to choose the products their department would sell. The simple idea was revolutionary: the buyer knew his or her local customers better than anyone else. (Department stores used this model until the 1980s, when data-driven strategies took over the retail industry.) In 1939, Fred also successfully lobbied President Franklin D. Roosevelt to move Thanksgiving earlier in November to lengthen the all-important holiday shopping season.[5] (The date, however, returned to its original schedule three years later.)

Fred was a rare breed: meticulous but always thinking about the bigger picture. In 1929, he proposed the formation of a national department store group, Federated Department Stores, to pool individual companies' resources and thus protect them from economic instability. The conglomerate began as a joint venture of Lazarus, Bloomingdale's in Manhattan, Abraham & Straus in Brooklyn, and Filene's in Boston. But Fred quickly became the dominant leader in the group, dictating its overall strategy. After World War II, when Fred was in his sixties and still as ambitious as ever, he led Federated on an acquisition spree, consolidating the most beloved family-owned department stores across the country into one even bigger group, which eventually became today's Macy's Inc.

The Lazarus stores made "the Lazari," as the family was nicknamed in Columbus, fabulously wealthy. For decades, they wielded widespread influence over the city's development (even after Federated's headquarters moved to Cincinnati). Family members were ubiquitous in the city's civic committees, and they sponsored everything from a children's hospital to the construction of Ohio State University's football stadium. In the 1920s, the Lazari were the first Jews to set up homes in Bexley, a Columbus suburb. In the decades that followed, the neighborhood became a hub for Jewish families. Bexley was also home to many of the city's most prominent people, including governors, presidents of Ohio State, and, briefly in the 1970s, Larry Flynt.

One of Fred's many employees was Les Wexner's mother, Bella Cabakoff, who landed her first job at Lazarus in Columbus when she was just sixteen years old, the same year she won a local Jewish beauty pageant. Bella had arrived in Columbus as a toddler from Williamsburg, Brooklyn, where she was born in 1908 to Russian immigrant parents. In Columbus, her parents sold fruit and vegetables at the market, and much of the family time was spent centered on her sister, Ida, who had a physical disability in her hips.[6] Bella was immensely proud of her job at the prestigious Lazarus, where she eventually rose to oversee the store's most important category, women's dresses. She claimed to be the youngest person ever hired to such a position at the store, where she worked for ten years until she married Les's father.

Harry Louis Wexner came to the retail business at an early age. He was born Hersch Wechnis in 1899 in Zhytomyr, Ukraine, then part of Russia, and came to the United States as a child in 1912. His family settled in Chicago, where his father worked for a tailor, and by his early twenties Harry was working as a salesman at one of the city's largest department stores, Mandel Bros. When he and Bella married in the mid-1930s, he was an executive at Miller-Wohl, a national retail chain selling cheap women's apparel.

Les was born in 1937, when the Wexners lived in Dayton, Ohio. As Harry worked his way up the ranks at Miller-Wohl, the family moved around the country frequently, making it difficult for Les to make long-lasting friends. From Dayton, they went to Kansas City, then Milwaukee, then Chicago. "It was painful," Les later said of the lack of stability during this time.[7] His parents turned to him for advice at an early age, he said, asking for his thoughts on Harry's career or where the family should live. "I remember being at the age of ten or eleven going to bed and crying, and saying they won't let me be a kid and I can't be an adult," he said.[8] Along the way, his sister Susan was born. Midway through Les's high school years, the family made its final move to Columbus.

Back in Ohio, Bella and Harry took a risk and decided to open their own store together. The store was Bella's idea—she was the tenacious one who loved fashion and had modest, classic, sophisticated tastes. The couple had been saving money to fund their business for years, but they were still short on cash. To save more, they moved to Columbus to live with family, including Bella's sister Ida, who helped look after the children while Harry and Bella worked late, and they even sold some of their household furniture.

Leslie's, named after the couple's beloved son, opened in downtown Columbus in March 1952. A short notice in the *Dispatch* marked the opening with a photograph of the inside of the small store, showing crowded racks lining the walls. An accompanying blurb highlighted the couple's "vast amount of apparel buying experiences."[9] The store carried smart women's wear—circle skirts and jackets reminiscent of Dior's New Look, as well as sportswear. Bella and Harry worked around the clock, struggling to make ends meet and borrowing money to keep it going. Les and Susan helped out after school. A second Leslie's would open four years later, in a new suburban shopping center west of the city.

In Columbus, the Wexner family settled just outside Bexley, home to so many of the Lazari. The public secondary school Bexley High was close enough for Les to attend, but non-Bexley residents had to pay tuition. Harry and Bella managed to cover the fees. Bexley was an upper-middle-class neighborhood, and Les felt an income disparity. He commuted to school by bus while many of his peers arrived by private car. And he always worked—mowing lawns, washing windows. "It was kind of tough when everyone's going away on their winter vacations and you're hoping it would snow, so you could make some extra money," he said.[10]

As a teenager, Les was an industrious "fat, little Jewish kid" who wore suspenders, according to an early Limited executive, Bob Morosky. A former classmate, Pete Halliday, described Les as "very reserved." His personality sometimes held him back. Wexner was a literal sideliner who managed the high school baseball team. "He was not athletic, but he was very supportive," Pete said. "He had a close circle." Bella was an exacting parent who held Les to high academic standards, but she also encouraged him to be ambitious.

Even from a young age, Les could be inscrutable. It was clear he was highly intelligent. He would be chatty and full of ideas one moment, closed off and cold the next. Some call him "shy"; others say "conflicted." Many people who have interacted with Wexner over the years have used the idiom "on the spectrum" to describe his personality, although he was never publicly known to have been diagnosed with any form of autism. Before the 1990s, few children were.

After graduating from Bexley, Les went to college across town at Ohio State University, earning a bachelor's degree in business in 1959. Afterward, he seemed at a loss. He signed up for basic training with the Air National Guard but soon dropped out. He went to law school at OSU for two years, before dropping out again. He pondered a career in real estate. He dreamed of being an architect.

Along the way, he worked with his parents from time to time. Leslie's remained steady but small. By their son's estimates, the business never generated more than $150,000 in sales annually, and Harry never took home more than $10,000 per year. Les wanted more from his life—he always had. His mother had pushed him to be assertive, and, finally, when he was still a young man in search of purpose, he took a risk. He dared to challenge his father's entire approach to the retail business.

/ / /

The trouble started in late 1961, when Les agreed to mind the store while his parents were on holiday after the Christmas season. Despite his best efforts to pursue a career outside of retail, he kept getting pulled back into the family business. He had begun accompanying his mother on buying trips to vendors in New York City and Europe, where they would buy designer dresses and sweaters to later sell in Columbus. But he didn't enjoy working with his father. Harry frequently described his son as clumsy and once even told him he'd never be a merchant.[11]

Meanwhile, many mom-and-pop shops like Leslie's were facing new competitors. Big-box discount retailers, like Walmart and Kmart, were about to expand nationally, taking advantage of the limited retail options in rural America and smaller cities. General stores felt the threat first, but so, too, did the apparel and smaller specialty stores. Many small shops did not survive through the 1960s.

Alone after Christmas, as 1962 approached, Les deduced that prices at his namesake store were too high. Most customers weren't even swayed to splurge on brands with national name recognition. So, he figured, why bother paying manufacturers in New York City a premium for those items? When his parents returned from their holiday, Les pitched them a strategy shift: instead of selling brand names, buy cheaper garments from lower-cost suppliers and slap a Leslie's label on them. These types of items are known in the fashion business as "white-label" garments.

The idea was a nonstarter for Harry and Bella. They were proud of the quality of the clothes they sold, and they believed their customers were, too. Leslie's reputation was paramount. They didn't want to go down-market. Les was frustrated, and he and his father continued to argue about the future of the business. Eventually, Harry told Les to find other work. "Son, our store can't support you and us," he said.[12]

Less than a year after his Christmas epiphany, Les decided to take his rejected suggestion, start his own business, and prove his parents wrong. He borrowed $5,000 from his aunt Ida and convinced his parents to guarantee a $5,000 inventory purchase order from suppliers in New York City. He didn't have enough capital to buy a wide range of products, so he focused on casual sportswear, the uniform for '60s young adults. No fancy coats or dresses. Les instead went for collared-shirt-and-skirt sets in geometric prints, peg-legged pants, and simple sweaters. The name he chose for his business reflected its narrow inventory: "The Limited."

Wexner was only twenty-five years old in August 1963 when the doors of the Limited opened in the Kingsdale Shopping Center, not far from Ohio State's campus. The Limited catered to young people, offering trendy, well-priced women's wear, like skirts and blouses. The price points were lower than what shoppers could find in Lazarus and in boutiques like Leslie's, but higher than the cheaply made stuff at Walmart.

The Limited sputtered at the start. The first day, Les sold $473 worth of clothing. The next day, just $128.[13] But Wexner was not going to give up. He was intense and competitive, but he wasn't a stickler or exacting. He took big bets on inventory he thought would be a hit, even if the wait could be nerve-racking. He also wasn't worried about losing money—he knew he had to spend money to make it.

"When he first started, he didn't have a balance sheet," said Pete Halliday, Wexner's classmate and former business associate, who helped him raise money for the Limited in the early years. To get more items on his shelves, Wexner bought some of his products on consignment—meaning that he didn't have to pay up front for them but was required to pay the manufacturer a large percentage of the final sale. The stress was overwhelming. He developed an ulcer. But in his first year in business, the Limited reached almost $165,000 in sales and managed to turn a tiny profit. It was enough to keep going and, a year later, open a second store in the north side of Columbus.

In 1965, women were flocking to the Limited for its flirty A-line skirts and ribbon-trimmed cardigans.[14] When he was on track to reach $400,000 in annual sales, Wexner received a call from Milton Petrie, the founder of several successful chains of discount women's wear stores.[15] Petrie wanted to invest in the Limited, telling Wexner he saw a path to $30 million in total sales and locations across the nation. Wexner was shocked. His goal was to reach $1 million in revenue, and he imagined opening only four stores in total. Wexner turned down Petrie's offer, but the phone call changed his perspective. He knew he had found something special with the Limited—a sweet middle spot between discount and department stores. So instead of cashing out, Les decided to expand. But he needed capital. He borrowed $2 million from a bank and in 1969, when the Limited counted six stores—four in Columbus, one each in

Dayton and Milwaukee—and $2 million in annual sales, Wexner began to sell shares in the business.[16] The Limited was still too small for a formal exchange, so instead he took an "over-the-counter" approach, selling to investors directly through a broker—in this case Wexner's high school friend Pete Halliday, whose investment banking firm Vercoe and Company raised the $345,000 Wexner needed to float the Limited at $7.25 a share.[17] (Members of the Lazarus family were rumored in town to be among the initial investors.) Between 1969 and 1971, Halliday and Wexner raised another $1.25 million. Wexner began opening stores in major cities across the country at a rapid clip. (Years later, a poster that dated back to the Limited's early years remained on display in the Columbus corporate offices. The poster read: "Ready, Fire, Aim.")[18]

In 1972, when the Limited had reached twenty-eight stores in ten cities, Wexner's accountant at Arthur Andersen, Bob Morosky, joined the business as chief financial officer. He became Wexner's most important business partner, followed by Bella and Harry—trusted advisers despite the sometimes tense history with their son. Their own business, Leslie's, had finally failed, bought out by the Limited. They joined their son's growing enterprise, swapping one family business for another. Bella served as the secretary and Harry as executive chairman until he died in 1975.

As Les Wexner expanded the Limited's distribution, he leaned on his growing partnership with Marty Trust, the Hong Kong manufacturing expert he met at the York Hotel in 1971. Wexner quickly realized Trust's factory connections could offer him a discount not just on production costs, but also on speed and flexibility. Wexner could bypass New York City's Seventh Avenue, where suppliers and design firms worked as middlemen between retailers and factories. These suppliers saved retailers from the headaches of dealing directly with factories, but they delivered collections at an established seasonal pace. Orders typically then took six months to land in their clients' shops, and if a style was a hit, the Seventh Avenue firms needed another six months to deliver a fresh batch.

Trust was a middleman, too, but he approached the business differently. He was eager to contract Asian manufacturers, for starters, and he was willing to fund their purchases of equipment or fabrics to jump-start or expand their businesses. In exchange, he became the most important client for many of these factories, with orders always at the top of their priority lists. Trust wasn't just interested in taking advantage of the low

labor wages in Hong Kong and Taiwan. After World War II, Asian manufacturers pioneered innovations to accelerate production schedules.
Their strategy relied on vertical integration: owning the entire process
of manufacturing, from sourcing raw materials (like cotton); to milling
fabric; to manufacturing items; to shipping, distributing, marketing, and
sales. While the Limited's competitors waited months for collections to
arrive in their stores, Trust could reorder garments for the Limited and
get them back in the United States in a matter of weeks. "My father's ability to take the manufacturing cycle from six months to thirty or forty-five
days was revolutionary," said Laura Trust, the daughter who later joined
the family business.

With access to Trust's manufacturing network, Mast, the Limited could
charge shoppers less than its competitors for the latest, trendy looks of
each season without sacrificing quality. And the Limited could generate
stronger profit margins, as much as 60 percent of its sticker prices. (At
the time, 40–45 percent margins were normal for a mass-market apparel
retailer. Today, those numbers typically hover around 20–30 percent or
even lower.) Few if any of its competitors were pursuing similar strategies.
At the end of the 1970s, more than 70 percent of apparel bought by Americans was made in America.[19]

The Limited's secret weapon, Mast, was not yet appreciated by the industry at large. But Wexner's rapid success was gaining national attention. He
expanded quickly throughout the 1970s—too quickly at times—but for the
most part, the Limited was growing exponentially and profitably. Its ninety-
eight stores across twenty-one states generated $70 million in sales in 1976,
up from $8.6 million four years earlier.[20]

When Wexner took on more debt to acquire Mast in 1978, for about $15
million in stock, many of his investors were confused. But Wexner knew
he had to cement his relationship with Trust to secure the Limited's future.
He was opening twenty to fifty new stores a year, and the rapid growth
strategy was working: the Limited's stock had split five times since 1969. As
soon as the Limited acquired Mast, it invested in three factories in China,
boosting its manufacturing capabilities.[21] And it opened a new $15 mil-
lion, 500,000-square-foot headquarters on the northeast side of Columbus,
a shiny black glass-covered office and distribution center. The Limited was
widely considered the fastest-growing retailer in the United States.

Even Sam Walton, the founder of Walmart and Sam's Club, took notice.

He called Wexner directly one day during the 1970s with an offer. "Sam Walton wants to buy me!" Wexner told Halliday. "I think I've got something." As he'd done when Milton Petrie came calling, Wexner turned Walton down and kept building.

III

What explained Wexner's retail success? Ask the many people who worked for him over the last sixty years, and the answers will vary. Some describe him as a terrific marketer; others stress his intense drive and willingness to take risks. But at his core, he was a merchant first.

The most talented merchants relied first on their own instincts. And none more so than Millard "Mickey" Drexler, a man with a unique talent for predicting the irrational whims of shoppers—and something of a foil to Wexner. While Wexner scaled the Limited in the 1970s, Drexler was rising through the retail ranks in New York City. In the 1980s and '90s, he earned his reputation as a major talent when he orchestrated a series of impressive retail turnarounds, overhauling Ann Taylor and then the Gap, which became synonymous with American style under his leadership. In the early 2000s, he did it again, transforming J.Crew into a multibillion-dollar brand.

Drexler's merchant instincts intertwined with his personal taste. His sense of style meshed with the designers redefining American fashion at the time. He favored the clean, preppy look that Ralph Lauren popularized beyond the country club crowd, and he took inspiration from the gray flannel and clean lines of Calvin Klein. He responded deeply to unfussy, elegant clothing. And he relied on his own preferences to predict what the rest of America wanted, too. Drexler once defined a merchant as "someone who figures out how to select, how to smell, how to identify, how to feel, how to time, how to buy, how to sell, and how to hopefully have two plus two equal six—there's a rhythm," he said. "You see goods as numbers. You see stores as numbers. And the numbers have to work out."[22]

Wexner, for his part, was not led by his own tastes. He couldn't look at two similar sweaters, for example, and predict which one would sell better simply by their color or cut. That's not to say he didn't have a personal style. He dressed in classic suits and slacks; suspenders became his signature. He also developed an interest in interior design and, when he started making real money in the late '70s, began to collect fine art and classic cars. "He had taste," said Morosky, his CFO. But when it came to choosing the clothing he sold in his stores, Wexner put his personal preferences aside.

Instead, Wexner became highly skilled at learning what to copy from others, and he trained his merchants to do the same. "Be a fast second," he told them. First and foremost, he was a keen observer of trends. By the 1980s, newly wealthy thanks to the success of the Limited, he traveled constantly for inspiration, crisscrossing Europe and Asia five times a year in his private Gulfstream jet. He and his team sometimes visited multiple cities in a day. Everywhere he went, he had a list of stores to visit. He could spend hours in a place like Selfridges in London, walking his merchants rack by rack, floor by floor. He had no qualms about copying competitors or high-fashion designer pieces. But he wasn't just copying blouses and skirts. Once in 1977, while on a trip to Paris with top merchant Verna Gibson, Wexner noticed a streetside flower seller commanding a larger crowd than his competitors. The seller had pinned flowers to the side of his booth rather than laying them across a table. When he returned to Columbus, Wexner directed his store designers to find a way to pin clothing flat against the walls, above his shoppers' heads. On another trip, he noticed that Europeans were wearing butter-yellow clothing. Butter yellow would soon be a trend within his stores. There were endless examples like these.

He would later dub this process "patterning," a term he borrowed from the consultants who started billing hours from his office in the 1990s. They were trained to evaluate companies by looking for similarities, or patterns, with other successful businesses or strategies. Venture capitalist investors also used the term "pattern matching" to describe a method of investing based on the idea that success is replicable. What Wexner's patterning strategy neglected was the value of taking a risk. Patterners follow a trend once they've seen it can work; they never create it.

In the early 1980s, Wexner did not need to take creative risks, thanks to Marty Trust. The Limited could be the first store to offer the season's trendiest items, and the cheapest versions of them. Take, for example, the colorful shaker-knit Forenza sweater that established the Limited as the most important American retailer of the 1980s.

Forenza was born unexpectedly. Early in the decade, Wexner saw brands across the market, from Giorgio Armani to Ann Taylor, embrace office attire and power suits. The Limited was missing it. Wexner asked the staff to develop a new collection that was "Armani-ish but affordable." A young marketer named Laura Berkman ignored the prompt and pitched a brand that reflected styles that were just then bubbling up in European youth culture. She took her cues from Marithé François Girbaud, from France, and the United Colors of Benetton, from Italy. Berkman named the collection "Forza" (literally, "force" or "power") for a dose of Italian sophistication.

Forza wasn't the work wear line Wexner had hoped to develop, but he recognized Berkman's reference points. The Limited's president Verna Gibson had already brought back a bulky knit sweater from a research trip in Florence that reflected the same ideas. Wexner tied it all together and greenlit a collection of V-neck shaker knits in bright Benetton-inspired colors.[23] The name "Forza," it turned out, was already taken, so Ed Razek, the Limited's marketing lead, tweaked it to "Forenza."

With Mast's help, the Limited tested a first batch of about five hundred Forenza sweaters in three stores in 1984. They sold quickly, and the Limited reordered for the entire store network in time for the holiday season. The sweaters became a full-blown phenomenon. The chain sold three million of them in the first year, at $30 each, even as the Limited's competitors rolled out copycat versions.[24] Ads for Forenza merchandise in local newspapers declared, "Finally in America," presenting the line as genuinely Italian. (The tags inside the sweaters read, "Made in Hong Kong.") Within two years of Forenza's launch, the knit was said to be the single most popular sweater in the country, and the Limited was considered the largest women's apparel retailer in the world.[25] The Limited's president, Wexner's longtime partner and top merchant Verna Gibson, commissioned a bronze-cast version of the Forenza sweater and hung it in her office.

Wexner wasn't one to relish in his victories. Even before Forenza hit stores, he had turned much of his attention to acquisitions. He needed more retail chains to plug into his sourcing model, impress his shareholders, and reach customers who might not fit the Limited's narrow clientele—primarily working women in their late twenties and early thirties. "The theory behind that was, McDonalds' biggest competitor is Wendy's," Morosky said. "Why didn't McDonalds develop Wendy's? We wanted to court the teenager, the young adult, the woman."[26]

In 1982, the Limited surprised Wall Street when, instead of cashing out by selling to a larger regional firm, it acquired Lane Bryant, the largest specialty plus-size women's wear retailer in the United States, for about $100 million in cash.[27] And Wexner was just getting started. In the following years, he targeted a range of retailers, including a small lingerie firm out of San Francisco that everyone advised him not to buy.

CHAPTER 3

One Man's Failure Is Another's Opportunity

**Roy Raymond and Les Wexner are both shy men with
colossal dreams. Only one will see them come true.**

In 1982, Victoria's Secret was on the brink of bankruptcy.[1] Roy Raymond,
a creative at heart, was ill-equipped to properly manage its finances and
too stubborn to relinquish control. His million-dollar-plus splurges on
antique furnishings for each new boutique and his unwillingness to set
firm budgets had caught up with him. He refused to close stores and
struggled to fire staff to stop the losses even as the business, and his personal life, suffered. As his debts grew, he continued to exclude his wife,
Gaye, from important financial meetings, leaving her unaware of the full
extent of the problem. Raymond needed a bailout. Fast.

Les Wexner offered an out. In the early 1980s, the Limited was a retail
powerhouse. Revenues grew from $295 million in 1981 to $720 million in
1983, while his store count and net income doubled. Wexner, the leader of
one of the fastest-growing American firms, was a billionaire—on paper,
at least. His employees cheered him on like a rock star at the Limited's
annual meetings. Once, he flew a sales associate into Columbus for what
she thought was a routine meeting, only to meet her at the airport with a
seventeen-piece brass band to celebrate her breaking a sales record.[2]

Though Wexner was becoming one of the wealthiest people in the
country, he was no less driven. He watched his competitors closely, frequently traveling across the United States and Europe to visit their newest
stores. He looked for new brands to acquire and new ideas to build out.
A youthful spin-off of the Limited, called Express, opened its first stand-
alone store in 1980 and was soon rolled out nationally.

In 1979, Wexner was in San Francisco overseeing a store opening when
he stepped into Victoria's Secret for the first time. He quickly recognized a

kinship with the brand's founders. Wexner, like the Raymonds, believed in the value of theatrical store design. He admired the look and feel of the Raymonds' stores. "I had never seen anything [like it]," he said later.[3] Wexner could have simply tried to copy the Victoria's Secret model. But he recognized the value of the business the Raymonds had already created beyond its four beautifully designed Bay Area stores. For starters, the business boasted a catalog mailing list of more than one million customer names and addresses. Such a large database, plus data on customers' shopping habits—from frequency of purchases to average order value to favorite items—was invaluable to someone like Wexner. If he was going to get into the lingerie business, he wanted to grow as quickly as possible. Victoria's Secret had small competitors across the country, and someone else could easily copy the model. But not at Wexner's pace: he had ample capital from the Limited to pour into opening new Victoria's Secret stores.

In later years, Wexner would take credit for the Victoria's Secret concept himself, often recounting how, one day on a long drive, he figured out how to disrupt the lingerie market. But when he walked into Victoria's Secret for the first time, he saw a golden market opportunity with national potential. For Wexner, the best ideas came out of common sense, and Victoria's Secret could provide a fast and relatively affordable way to break into a fast-growing category.

In the fall of 1981, Wexner brought a whole team out to San Francisco to tour the Victoria's Secret boutique on Sutter Street near Union Square. He also flew the Raymonds to Columbus to try to convince them that the Victoria's Secret brand would be safe under his watch. (And Roy was struck by Wexner's concern for safety, noting his intense personal security detail, guard dogs and all.)

Raymond and Wexner found common ground. Both were keen observers of customer behavior, and both were often described as shy but stubborn. Neither was particularly driven by money. Wexner, however, was far more ambitious than Raymond, who loved creating exquisite shopping experiences, but he had no concrete plan for how to expand Victoria's Secret to fifty stores, let alone a thousand.

Wexner saw infinite expansion on the horizon, and he knew how to move quickly. He was happy to throw money into building a business if he could figure out how to yield a juicy return. He was obsessed with sales figures. And he knew that the more volume he produced and sold, the bigger his profit margins would become.

Wexner had approached Raymond several times about acquiring the business before Raymond was finally ready to sell in the summer of 1982. "The attraction was that Victoria's Secret didn't really have any competition," said Bob Morosky, Wexner's operations man. "There was an opportunity to upgrade [Victoria's Secret's] image"—which the Limited team felt was antiquated—"get our arms around it."

Still, Wexner's senior executives didn't quite understand his interest in Victoria's Secret. When his inner circle—including Marty Trust and Verna Gibson—met to review Raymond's financials, they advised Wexner to pass on the deal. No one was in favor of buying the business. Wexner listened, told them he was going to get some air, and left the room. Half an hour later, he returned and apologized. He valued their perspective, he said, but he was going to buy Victoria's Secret.

By then, Raymond had little negotiating power. His debts were mounting. Wexner and Morosky would pay him only $1 million in the Limited stock, no cash. "Roy didn't have a lot of choices," said his lawyer Barry Reder, who worked on the deal.[4] "[Roy] had a big ego, a Stanford MBA, and thought he had the Midas touch," Morosky said. After a back-and-forth, Morosky cut to the chase. "Take it or leave it," he told him.

Raymond took the deal.

Wexner assured him that Victoria's Secret would remain based in San Francisco and that the employees would be protected. And Wexner promised to retain the brand ethos the Raymonds had created. Raymond had no illusions that he would join Wexner's trusted circle of executives, but he told Reder he thought he might learn something, calling it a "tuition-free supplement to business school."[5]

/ / /

Barba Kandarian, Victoria's Secret's first buyer, remembers the day everything changed. One morning in the fall of 1983, she showed up at the office on San Francisco's Bluxome Street to find several middle-aged men in jackets and ties roaming around. "Suits were not our thing," she said. "Roy wasn't in his office, which was unusual. It didn't pass the smell test."

A year had passed since Roy Raymond's sale of Victoria's Secret to Limited Brands, Wexner's growing corporation. Raymond had parroted Wexner's promises, telling the employees that business would go on as usual in San Francisco. And it had, for a while.

But there had already been one ominous sign of change: the introduction of what one executive remembered as a "$20 red lace teddy" produced by Mast Industries. It was flimsy, tacky, and scratchy. To Roy's employees, this "value" item felt woefully out of place with the rest of the Victoria's Secret designer label assortment.

Kandarian wasn't naive—she predicted that Roy would leave Victoria's Secret eventually. She knew he thrived on the chaos of building a new business. He embraced "start-up culture" before there was a term for it. He was eager to pursue other ideas. But Kandarian had hoped his strategy, and his team, could carry on without him.

That fateful fall morning, Kandarian and the other staff were called down to the lunchroom, where an executive from the Limited announced that Victoria's Secret was moving to Columbus. He told the assembled employees that the Limited would "entertain your request to stay with the company," Kandarian remembered. Ultimately, five people were offered the chance to stay with Victoria's Secret on the condition that they move to Columbus, too. Nobody went for it. Kandarian finished up the buying for spring and left the business six weeks later.

The overhaul shocked Victoria's Secret's original employees, who saw the Limited's takeover as the shameless corporate destruction of a one-of-a-kind company. But the new owners never hesitated. In San Francisco, Wexner and his executives saw a casual, unstructured organization that reeked of West Coast liberalism and leniency. "They weren't hippies, but it was hippy-dippy," said Laura Berkman, the marketing executive who started at the Limited in the early 1980s (and worked on Forenza) before being reassigned to work on Victoria's Secret full-time in 1985. "There was wine and beer in the fridge."

Wexner had initially intended to keep Victoria's Secret in San Francisco. But the three-hour time difference and frequent flights added up. "We concluded that we couldn't continue to develop the brand that way," Morosky said. And again, there was the clash of cultures. The square midwesterners balked at the habits of the laid-back Californians. "It was not managed well," Morosky said. "People were going to lunch and coming back half-stoned. Retailing doesn't work effectively on the West Coast."

Roy wasn't naive. He figured, despite Wexner's promises, he would be pushed out of the business eventually. So he was not shocked when, shortly before the suits showed up in San Francisco, one of the Limited's executives summoned him to New York City. "[They] fired him at the airport, and flew him right back," said Gaye Raymond, who was about to give birth to their second child.

Roy did not dwell on what had happened to Victoria's Secret. "There was no break to mourn, no coming down," Gaye said. He returned to the office where he had started the business and started over by launching an upscale children's department store and catalog. It was called My Child's Destiny, selling toys and clothing, as well as furniture, computers, and video games. But he still owned Xandria, the successful sex toy catalog. To prevent any reputational harm associating children's products with dildos, Roy sold Xandria to his accountant for less than a million dollars. (Xandria expanded successfully, went online in 1997, and changed ownership several times. It finally closed in 2016.)

The Raymonds made almost as much from the sale of Xandria as they did from handing off Victoria's Secret. To finance My Child's Destiny, Roy eventually sold all the Limited stock he had been granted in the acquisition. Gaye was kept too far away from the finances to know exactly how much the stock sales netted. But a senior Limited executive with knowledge of the acquisition said that Roy's $1 million in initial shares would have been worth $4 million by the time he was fired. If he had held the shares instead of selling them, the stock could have netted the Raymonds around $20 million by 2000, maybe more.

Roy's next business idea was, once again, driven by changes in social mores. In the 1980s, the once "hippy-dippy" baby boomers had grown up and were wearing Italian suits and French party dresses. The young urban professionals—or yuppies—had officially arrived. And when they had kids, they wanted to dress them up in posh clothes and fill their nurseries with chic European furniture. Or at least that was Roy's hunch.

Even if he was correct, his new venture stumbled right from the start. The store's focus on premium goods read as pretentious to parents in the Bay Area, where showy everyday materialism was more frowned upon than in many major US cities. The store sat a block away from Union Square, slightly out of the path of high foot traffic. Inside, shoppers were confused by the mix of reasonably priced brands, like Oshkosh overalls, next to Apple computers (which were still brand-new to the market) and expensive potty chairs imported from Europe. An early advertisement for My Child's Destiny depicted two blond children immaculately dressed as mini-adults—the boy in a suit and tie and the girl in a lace-collar dress. The image, also featured on the brand's catalog, made some parents feel inadequate.[6]

Roy quickly ran out of money—faster even than he had with Victoria's Secret. He didn't even try to find an outside investor like Wexner, to rescue him. He didn't want to be pushed out again. "I'll just do it by myself," he would say. The Raymonds drained most of their savings. "He just didn't want to wait," said Gaye. "He had skills, but money management was not one of them."

In 1986, Roy had no choice but to declare bankruptcy and close My Child's Destiny. To pay their debts, the Raymonds sold their Victorian-era home in San Francisco, their weekend house in Lake Tahoe, and their cars. Still, Roy was undeterred. He already had another business idea on his mind. And another and another.

///

Back in Columbus, Wexner moved quickly to reshape Victoria's Secret. The first store to open after the Limited acquired the business was significantly less Victorian than its predecessors.[7] The boutique arrived at the Los Angeles Beverly Center at the end of 1982. The brand's original cursive logo, with vines growing out of the V and S, remained. But the new store design was brighter and simpler. Less dark wood furniture, more light paneling. French antiques replaced Victorian ones. Fabric hung draped across the ceiling and Oriental carpets lined the floors. Roy Raymond was still involved then, but he was not in charge.

As Wexner began expanding Victoria's Secret nationwide, he pivoted the store's focus to the mass market. Most women in America were still accustomed to shopping for their bras at department stores, where "100,000 brassieres [hung] on trees like a forest," according to Howard Gross,[8] the merchant whom Wexner promoted to lead Victoria's Secret's stores after Raymond's exit. Wexner had appreciated the founder's original store concept—ornate, mysterious Victorian homes full of treasures. (One executive recalls Wexner removing the wooden awning of one of the Raymonds' original stores and shipping it back to Columbus to inspire his visual merchandising executives.) But many shoppers bypassed Victoria's Secret stores, assuming the lush, antique-filled boutiques were too expensive. After all, the brand had once prominently advertised a $2,000 mink-collar robe.[9]

Wexner's mandate for Gross was simple. First, open dozens and dozens of self-standing stores in shopping malls across the country as quickly as possible. Gross followed through, launching new locations at a prodigious rate that would have been impossible without the Limited's profits and network of real estate connections. Wexner also directed Gross to bring down prices by replacing the inventory with cheaper lingerie produced by Mast or major intimates manufacturers, like Vassarette and Lily of France.[10] Soon, the new stores overflowed with Victoria's Secret–branded teddies and nightgowns that were both less expensive for customers and more lucrative for the retailer.

The transformation culminated in 1987, when Victoria's Secret unveiled its first self-standing store in Manhattan. By then, five years after its acquisition, it counted 165 stores across the country's best malls—often alongside its corporate siblings the Limited, Express, and Lane Bryant—and was generating more than $100 million in sales and counting.

The Manhattan shop was polished and modern, spread across two stories and six thousand square feet of prime shopping real estate at Fifty-Seventh Street between Park and Madison. The floors were marble, the walls mirrored. The antiques, once Victoria's Secret's signature, were all but gone, the final remnant of Raymond's unscalable vision.

CHAPTER 4

The Making of the American Mall

Les Wexner hooks the shoppers of the 1980s.

Few people felt the magic of American malls, those controlled commercial utopias, more deeply than A. Alfred Taubman.[1] By the end of the 1970s, the Detroit-based real estate developer had amassed a glittering portfolio of the nation's most sophisticated shopping centers, including the Mall at Short Hills, in New Jersey, and the Beverly Center, in Los Angeles. Taubman designed his malls as perfect versions of the American downtown, planned in a way that real cities, with their congested traffic lanes and inelegant parking lots, could never rival.[2]

Taubman, a master of retail design manipulation, relied on a strict set of principles to draw people to spend. He designed his malls across two stories, instead of a single, sprawling floor. He set the length of his mall's corridors based on several studies, including one conducted by none other than Leonardo da Vinci, that argued that most people prefer to walk no more than the equivalent of three city blocks on discretionary outings. He placed high-traffic anchor department stores, like Neiman Marcus and Bloomingdale's, on outer ends of the malls, forcing shoppers to walk past smaller stores on their way from one major destination to the next. He used clear glass balcony handrails so strolling shoppers could spot storefronts above and below them. Taubman even built parking lots that deposited shoppers on the upper level of the mall because he found that "people, like water, flow downhill much easier than uphill."[3]

Instead of allowing tenants to choose any space they wanted, Taubman "merchandised" his real estate—with Brooks Brothers across from Johnston and Murphy, Brookstone next to the Sharper Image. He kept smelly restaurants and hair salons away from luxury stores. He lined his floors with terrazzo tiles because he determined they were more comfortable for women wearing thin-soled shoes. Artificial lighting was installed in the skylights to maintain the same brightness even as the sun set, so that shoppers would not notice the passage of time. "With essentially every object or vista I see, I think about how it could be better," he wrote in his memoir.[4]

In the early 1970s, Taubman turned his critical eye to one of his tenants, the Limited. This was before Les Wexner had transformed himself into the cultured global traveler. Then, he was still just trying to keep his new business afloat. Taubman found Wexner's stores messy and unimaginative with their burlap-lined walls and chaotic racks. No magic. Taubman summoned Wexner to Detroit and took him on a helicopter tour of his three shopping centers in the area's suburbs: the Fairlane Town Center, Lakeside Mall, and Twelve Oaks Mall. Each had a location of the Limited. Even though Wexner had opened his first store outside Ohio in a Taubman property in Milwaukee a few years earlier, the two men barely knew each other. That day in Detroit, Taubman told Wexner that his stores were a "blight on my shopping centers." Taubman had a leasing clause that allowed him to boot out tenants who did not maintain appealing store spaces. "You'd better fix them or I'm going to have them torn down," he said.[5]

Wexner immediately got to work redesigning his stores at great expense. He enlisted his own personal interior designer, Chicago's Richard Himmel. He was known and beloved (particularly among the Palm Beach set) for his lavish interiors, often centered around a curvy mid-century loveseat. Himmel turned the Limited's stores into clean-lined white-and-gold salons.

Taubman was impressed. Over the next decade, he and Wexner developed a close personal and professional partnership. Wexner came to see Taubman as a father figure, a mentor not only in business but in life. The Limited became one of the three largest tenants in Taubman's malls, with first access to prime real estate. The two men would later develop shopping centers together. In the process, Wexner became an evangelist of carefully crafted store design, believing that it was as important to seduce the customer through ambiance as it was through fetching product. This focus served him well for the next four decades, even after malls started to lose their luster.

///

"Meet you at the mall" could have served as a slogan for American life in the 1980s. For many Americans, society revolved around the vast shopping centers dotting suburbs across the country. With their temperature-controlled environments, always-on food courts, and skylit central domes, malls provided an epicenter of ease and leisure unlike any other American social structure of the time. They were the town squares of the suburbs.

Although Taubman liked to say that malls were as old as the bazaars of Istanbul, the American mall as we know it today was born in 1956 in Edina, Minnesota, a suburb of Minneapolis. A Viennese architect, Victor Gruen, dreamed up an entire shopping complex in one enclosed space. Most stores were accessible only from inside the mall's main corridors, not the street, allowing for innovative storefront designs without the worry of weatherproofing. Gruen's first mall, Southdale Center, cost $20 million to build and featured a central court with eucalyptus trees and caged canaries. The major funding came mainly from one of the biggest tenants, Dayton's, the Minneapolis-based family-run department store that would later create a booming retail chain, Target.

Southdale was an instant success. *Time* declared it a "pleasure-dome-with-parking."[6] A reported 75,000 people visited on the first Sunday after the mall opened, but just to see the building itself: the mall's stores were closed on Sundays. Southdale's overwhelming reception helped spur a mall-building spree across America that was already beginning, thanks to a recent addition to US tax law. In 1954, Congress introduced a new rule about depreciating assets that allowed investors to designate shopping centers as highly favorable tax shelters—regardless of how many shoppers they attracted.[7] Developers rushed to open malls as quickly as possible. In 1960, the nation had 4,500 malls, which generated 14 percent of total retail sales. By 1987, 30,000 malls accounted for more than half of all total retail sales and 13 percent of the US GDP.[8]

Shopping became a way of life. It was social; it was a hobby. As the country emerged from the recessions of the 1970s and early 1980s, Ronald Reagan ushered in a fiscal policy era of low taxes and lax corporate regulations. The number of Americans earning over $1 million annually would spike by more than 1,000 percent in the 1980s. The Levi's generation had become suit-wearing yuppies with money to spend. Conspicuous consumption was on trend.

Malls were epicenters for youth culture and gateways to adulthood, places where parents felt comfortable letting their kids roam free. For the children and teenagers of the 1980s, the mall was an entire world. Kids hung out there after school, eating at the food court, wandering the corridors, catching movies in the Cineplexes. The stores of this period became generational touchstones. There was Claire's, the jewelry boutique where girls flocked to get safe, reasonably priced ear piercings (with, of course, 14-karat gold Claire's studs); Spencer's, a novelty gag gift store that stocked edgier, PG-13 fare; and 5–7–9, a teen fashion emporium and a precursor to Forever 21. Food court chains like Orange Julius and Mrs. Fields were ubiquitous.

In a world of seemingly limitless choice, Wexner's single-category stores were primed to thrive. The mall had "unbundled" the shopping experience. Americans no longer had as much use for department stores like Chicago's Marshall Field's, which sold everything from Armani suits to cutlery. Inside the mall, there was a separate store for seemingly every need, and once the car was parked, popping in from one shop to the next was really no bother.

The best mall stores presented a distinct identity, from the sales associates they hired, to the items they sold, to their window designs. Devotees of the Limited considered themselves fashion-forward and trend-savvy. The Gap's shoppers preferred preppy, all-American classics. J.Crew fans shopped to embody the wealthy New England WASP culture depicted in that brand's catalogs. Ann Taylor sold suits to women who couldn't afford Giorgio Armani. Brooks Brothers sold suits to men who were too traditional for Giorgio Armani. In the past, the places Americans shopped primarily reflected how much money they had. But at the mall, there was something for every income bracket.

As specialty retailers' popularity surged in the 1980s, department stores tumbled. None fell further than the kings of the pre-mall era: Sears, J. C. Penney, and Montgomery Ward. These old giants became best known for their blowout sales, especially on holidays like Black Friday, the annual day-after-Thanksgiving discount extravaganza. Even the mall anchor stores, like Bloomingdale's and Dayton's, suffered. Many of them pivoted to specialty store–like strategies, cutting out certain categories, like kitchen appliances, to focus on clothing. Other department stores consolidated. Columbus's own Federated—the national conglomerate of department stores controlled by the family behind Lazarus—owned about a dozen department store chains in the 1980s. Starting in 1959 and continuing into the 2000s, Federated merged many of its chains to stave off losses. Eventually, local names like Gimbels, Kaufmann's, Marshall Field's, and Lazarus disappeared, all replaced by Macy's, one of the only survivors—and America's de facto mall anchor.

Though Wexner pioneered the specialty retail model, he still believed well-run department stores could succeed. Or at least he wanted to give it a try. During the 1980s, Wexner twice attempted, unsuccessfully, to force a takeover of Carter Hawley Hale, one of the nation's largest department store groups. Wexner said he was specifically interested in the group's higher-end stores—Neiman Marcus and Bergdorf Goodman. For his second bid, Wexner partnered with the second-richest man in Ohio, the prominent shopping mall developer Edward J. DeBartolo Sr. But Carter Hawley Hale's chairman, Philip Hawley, who made no secret of his disdain for Wexner, outmaneuvered them.

Around that time, Wexner considered buying Federated, too, according to Marvin Traub, the former chief executive of one of its chains, Bloomingdale's. He said Wexner envisioned setting up Limited shops inside each Federated-owned department store, but the takeover deal became too costly. "You'd probably have to spend $3 billion just to fix up Federated's stores," Wexner said later. "We can grow much faster staying in the specialty field."[9]

In the end, Wexner came out of the department store downturn empty-handed, with one exception. In 1985, he bought Henri Bendel, the innovative Manhattan department store known for selling what its exacting president Geraldine Stutz once described as "dog whistle" high fashion—clothing so special that only a very select group of sophisticated, wealthy women could recognize its appeal.[10] Wexner planned to expand the chain across the country while promising to leave the original Fifty-Seventh Street location untouched. But the culture clash between Wexner's teams, accustomed to ruthlessly integrating acquisitions into Limited, and Stutz's old-fashioned, family-like associates was immediately clear. Stutz had no choice but to leave, and Bendel's never regained its influence.

The Bendel's struggle demonstrated that Wexner lacked the sensitivity required to cater to the most affluent tastes. He wanted to expand the chain and use the name to sell cheaper stuff, as he had done with Victoria's Secret and another one of his acquisitions, the preppy stalwart Abercrombie & Fitch. But Bendel's didn't have broad appeal or, under the Limited's watch, a sharp enough point of view.

In some ways, the Limited had more in common with McDonald's than with Marshall Field's. Wexner's great talent was leveraging the cumulative power of his network of stores, testing and refining to find the right products at the right price, and replicating that process over and over—the clothing equivalent of cooking Big Macs. Only, in his business, the menu changed every month.

/ / /

"I'm not fascinated with fashion for fashion's sake," Wexner told the *New York Times* in 1986. "A lot of people in the fashion business shoot in the dark. You can't just decide that purple is going to be big in the fall. Then you're a kamikaze pilot."

In the 1980s, as the Limited's stores multiplied across the country, Wexner tweaked and expanded the innovative test-and-learn system that had so successfully launched Forenza. It was the same way he introduced Outback Red, one of the Limited's most successful and theatrically named sub-brands. The line was conceived in September 1985, at a merchant meeting at which Verna Gibson and her associates reviewed purchases from a recent research shopping trip. Wexner's merchants were encouraged to visit major cities both at home and abroad (chauffeured by the company's private jets) and buy anything that might be applicable to the Limited. The best purchases became "key items": in this case, a safari jacket from Banana Republic (the San Francisco–based clothing label acquired by Gap Inc. in 1983), a floral shirt from Laura Ashley, and a pair of tan cotton trousers found somewhere in Europe. Gibson thought these assembled pieces were compelling enough to kick-start a safari-inspired collection, riding Banana Republic's emerging popularity and incorporating the rugged charm of Ralph Lauren's more outdoorsy collections. With a few alterations, the merchants planned to copy the pieces they'd bought and apply their stylistic details to a wider range of skirts, shirts, and jackets. Wexner had zero qualms about copying other brands' designs. "You can't patent anything in the clothing business," he told the *Times*. "You've got to get your stuff to the consumer first if you want to be successful."[11]

Copycat behavior has always played a part in the fashion industry, especially in the United States. The manufacturers who dominated Seventh Avenue in Midtown starting in the 1930s—*garmentos*, many of them second- or third-generation Americans—built an infrastructure of factories to make cheap versions of high-fashion designs a year or two after they hit the runways in Europe. Their clients were American department stores, whose buyers would fly to Paris for made-to-measure couture garments from the top designers. Back home, factories would reproduce the clothes in simpler and cheaper versions. On the sales floor, the copies were advertised on the label as the real deal. It wasn't totally a lie; the quality was good, and the brands were approved. (At department stores, you can still find pieces whose labels read, "Halston for Neiman Marcus" or "Karl Lagerfeld for Bergdorf Goodman.") The *garmentos* also made original designs commissioned by Americans with growing name recognition like Claire McCardell, the mother of American sportswear, and Bonnie Cashin, who designed for Coach.

Europe's couturiers, aware that others were profiting from their design ideas, eventually decided to grab a piece of the mass-market business, too. After World War II, Italian designers began producing ready-made garments in standardized sizes, and "ready-to-wear" designer fashion was born. Yves Saint Laurent, the French Algerian couturier who made his name running the house of Christian Dior, was the first of his generation to launch the business model. In 1966, his new line Rive Gauche became an instant hit and validated the practice among fashion's top-tier houses, most of whom followed suit.

Ready-to-wear was a sensation. Suddenly, American shoppers of means could wear designer fashion without flying to Paris to order custom couture. New York City designers Bill Blass, Halston, and Oscar de la Renta built major ready-to-wear brands, as did Ralph Lauren and Calvin Klein. Wexner saw Americans' growing desire for the latest styles, so he positioned his stores to offer a cheaper, faster version of the silhouettes trending among not just upscale designers, but also smaller, hipper labels. Outback Red would become a prime example of this approach.

First, Wexner's merchants needed to test their bet on safari style. Another retailer might have placed a significant order for a collection on

Seventh Avenue, where importers and factories needed as many as ten months to find the right fabric and sew the pieces. The Limited bypassed those middlemen by turning to the company's powerful sourcing division, Mast. Since the Limited had acquired the division in 1978, its founder Marty Trust had expanded his network of factories to keep up with the chain's rapid growth, acting as a liaison to manufacturers in different countries. His system was designed to find the highest-possible-quality raw materials and production facilities for the lowest-possible prices—as quickly as possible.

Outback Red got the Mast treatment. Throughout China and Southeast Asia, Mast agents trawled for the perfect tan cotton fabric for the trousers, personally ensuring that it would arrive quickly in Hong Kong for dyeing before being sent to other factories across the city or in Mauritius or Sri Lanka, for the manufacturing of the final pieces. Smaller factories were on call to produce limited runs of apparel in a matter of weeks—or even days. Mast agents would ship samples on one of the company's three Boeing 747 jets headed from Hong Kong straight to Columbus each week. The Limited's competitors lacked the same network of overseas manufacturers on speed dial, and even if they tried to develop one, Mast's executives could, and would, box out rivals by clogging the schedules of the best and fastest factories.

By late November 1985, two months after the merchants first agreed to create the safari-themed collection, a sampling of Outback Red pieces were quietly introduced in five of the Limited's stores across the American South, where the weather still called for only light jackets and layers. Wexner and Gibson carefully tracked consumer interest in colors, styles, and prices. Pleated trousers were more popular than flat-front styles. Shirts were selling best at $20. Jackets could move at $50. In just a week, Wexner's merchants had enough data to tweak the line for maximum success.

Sometimes, when the Limited's merchants lacked time to produce their own samples to test, they cut corners. Instead of reproducing a garment from another brand, they would simply buy duplicates of the garment—say, a cropped sweater—and switch out the labels with their own.[12] Over the years, more than a few unsuspecting shoppers bought pieces at the Limited that would have cost three or four times the price elsewhere. This practice continued at Victoria's Secret. It took a while, but competitors like Calvin Klein occasionally caught on and sometimes even took legal action. Wexner either paid to quietly settle the disputes or made a deal to buy or distribute the objecting brand, as he did with Italian lingerie line Intimissimi and British perfumer Penhaligon's. The data gleaned from these furtive tests were well worth some legal headaches.

After concluding the testing period for Outback Red, the necessary tweaks were sent back to Hong Kong, where Mast's factories produced five hundred thousand units to the new specifications in the subsequent thirty days. A department store would need at least ninety days to replicate the same process for one of its in-house lines. At the end of January 1986, Outback Red's first full, finished collection was shipped to the East Coast of the United States, where a fleet of trucks owned by the Limited waited to bring its Gurkha shorts, khaki skirts, and bomber jackets to the distribution center outside Columbus. Each year in the Limited's warehouses, two hundred million garments were priced, sorted, and shipped out, a process that could take weeks for other retailers but that in Wexner's automated warehouse averaged only forty-eight hours. From Columbus, the Outback Red collections made their way to six hundred stores across the country, where the garments debuted in the first week of February, just in time for the start of the spring shopping season. In each store, the window decor followed a corporate dictate with no deviation: palm trees and bushes surrounding mannequins decked out in floral shirts and posed in tan wicker chairs.

Outback Red's timing was fortuitous. *Out of Africa*, starring Meryl Streep and Robert Redford, had premiered in December 1985 and would go on to win Best Picture at the 1986 Oscars. Fashion columnists across the country declared safari style the top trend of the spring season, giving Banana Republic credit for jump-starting the trend but pointing to the Limited as the easiest place to buy the look. Outback Red expanded with new collections into the following year, by which point "every teenage girl with any fashion credibility, like, at all, owns a 10-button Outback Red henley," according to *Ad Age*.[13] The brand became so famous that many shoppers assumed it was itself a designer line, like Ralph Lauren. "Department stores cringe when customers ask for Forenza or Outback Red," according to a newspaper report at the time, explaining the success of the Limited and its specialty retail peers including Benetton, the Gap, and Esprit.[14]

But the Limited was operating on a higher commercial level than its mall neighbors. Wexner was now responsible for selling more women's clothing than any other retailer in the world. He was heralded as a rag trade revolutionary, a master of the American mass market. But no number of plaudits or personal wealth would have allowed him to stop there. He was not capable of feeling satisfied in business. As Wexner once explained to a reporter, he was haunted by "terminal *shpilkes*," a Yiddish term for nervous energy. His wealth couldn't quiet it. His restlessness was a relentless wanting for more. How would he satisfy it?

CHAPTER 5

The Not-So-Ugly Stepsister

Les Wexner underestimates the Victoria's Secret mail-
order catalog—until it becomes the brand's secret weapon.

As a model, Carol Perkins had never worked with men in front of the camera until the Limited acquired Victoria's Secret.[1] Any remnants of the once soft-lens, Victorian-era-style catalog ended the day male models turned up on set. It was 1985, two years since Roy Raymond and his team exited the business. By then, Perkins had already appeared in four of the lingerie catalogs and knew what to expect when she showed up to work in San Francisco. But she was shocked by the post-acquisition changes, from the way she was dressed for the camera to the company on set, including the addition of male models. "They kept the name, but it was night and day," she said. "It was the polar opposite of the original founders' vision."

Perkins was one of many models who posed regularly for Victoria's Secret catalogs throughout the 1980s, when none of the models were house-hold names. Even so, the experience was often exciting, especially after the acquisition. The original team had occasionally ventured to Paris, but they usually kept the shoots local to San Francisco. Now, instead of reporting to set inside mansions on Nob Hill, Perkins found herself summoned to sprawling homes in Barbados, St. Barts, the Adirondack Mountains, and Shelter Island, off Long Island, for as many as ten days at a time. "When you are on location for a week and you're in faraway places, it's all an adventure," said Perkins, then in her mid- to late twenties.

There were other changes. Perkins noticed that the lingerie she modeled became appreciably less luxurious—no more handmade silks. Male models were now not only hired, but often centered, getting equal placement with the women on the catalog covers as passionate, dashing partners. Inside the pages, the men were adoring supporting characters, gazing at the women or nuzzling them as the women laid their heads in their laps. "They were good actors," Perkins said of the men. "It was a lot of fun." The stylist Ripley Albright, who was known for his work with Ralph Lauren, stepped in and brought a lived-in quality to the images, dropping the shoulder of a robe or mussing a model's bangs. Instead of pinned-up hair and bright-blue eyeshadow, the makeup was pared back, almost natural.

Perkins was a good fit for the new era; her almond-shaped eyes telegraphed elegance and refinement. She described the new approach as something like "anti-modeling," more akin to a fashion magazine. "They wanted you to be natural, to look off-camera." Even the VS logo was reinvented: the original flowery script was dropped for a bold sans serif across the top of the catalog—again, more like a fashion magazine. The new mantra was aspiration and wealth, but in line with the decade's taste for voluminous hair and chrome spiral staircases. "It was fresh, it was new, it was different. There was so much thought and character being put into the set design and the location and the models," Perkins said. "It did have an editorial feel."

The catalog also became notably racier. Nipples were clearly visible through sheer mesh bras. The men were often semi-nude, with bedsheets covering their crotches or their bare butts visible in the background of a shot. One of the male models, Bruce Hulse, a favorite of Calvin Klein at the time, later said he often had to take breaks on set when tents appeared in his silk boxers. "I'd be like: 'Stop the shoot! Got a woody!'" he said.[2] Sometimes the catalog required paper wrapping to meet US Postal Service standards.

The suggestive images created problems for Perkins. Talbots, a growing retailer known for preppy, ladylike daily attire, was another major client of hers—until customers noticed that she was also modeling for Victoria's Secret and complained. She paused her Talbots work; Victoria's Secret was the better gig. The brand needed models almost seven days a week, and what it lacked in prestige in the modeling world, it made up for in pay: upward of $2,000 a day, compared to less than $1,500 for apparel catalogs, due to the extra skin exposure.

Little did Perkins know that, back at Victoria's Secret's offices, the catalog was in a precarious situation. It was a small, loss-making division in Les Wexner's empire of stores, and he did not see much value in the mail-order business model. "Fix it or lose it," he told his executives, a team of young women in the catalog's offices in New York City, far from the glare of the Columbus headquarters. Despite Wexner's skepticism, the women persevered. And they managed to turn the catalog into not just a major profit driver, but a brand-building sensation with a national reputation and a roster of top models.

///

Nurse or teacher. Those were the two career options for college-educated women in Dayton, Ohio, in the 1960s, as Cynthia "Cindy" Fedus-Fields saw it. "I wasn't going to be a good schoolteacher," she said. When, in 1971, the Federated Department Stores retail group came recruiting at her college, Miami of Ohio, Fedus-Fields was relieved to discover an alternative. The conglomerate owned Ohio's most famous department store, Lazarus, where Bella Wexner had worked as a buyer decades earlier, and it was searching for new students for its reputable retail training program. Fedus-Fields enrolled at Rike's department store in Dayton.

Since the 1950s, almost every department store chain across the country had recruited entry-level employees on college campuses for their training programs. For a year to eighteen months, trainees cycled through different divisions to learn the foundations of retail: how to spot trends, commission products, work with designers and vendors, evaluate sales, and serve the customer. The most talented graduates could stay with the department store chain for the rest of their careers; they could become future chief merchants or chief executives, and they could move to other store groups across the country. Many of the most successful merchants of the postwar era trained through the program at Abraham & Straus, a beloved department store in Brooklyn. Its graduates included Allen Questrom, who became CEO of Neiman Marcus and Federated in the 1980s and '90s, and Michael Gould, chief executive of Bloomingdale's in the 1990s and 2000s.

By the '90s, when the department stores had consolidated into essentially one group after Federated merged with Macy's, few merchant training programs remained. The entire sector was shrinking, and merchandising now relied on data more than on individual instincts. But when Fedus-Fields entered Federated's program in the early 1970s, merchandising was still respected as an art form that required specialist training.

The best merchandisers—better known as "pickers"—were considered visionaries. When Fred Pressman, the president of Barneys and son of its founder, introduced Giorgio Armani's menswear to the US market in 1976, he established his family store as the first destination for the roomy, fluid power suits that dominated the 1980s. Merchandising wasn't just about choosing products; it was also about how they were packaged and displayed. In 1973, Marvin Traub, the CEO of Bloomingdale's, commissioned the renowned Italian designer Massimo Vignelli to create the iconic "Big Brown Bag," which became a coveted symbol of the store's cultural cachet.

Fedus-Fields quickly discovered she was a pretty good picker. After finishing the training program, she landed a job in Pittsburgh at Joseph Horne, another regional department store chain with a beloved local reputation. (In 1947, Andy Warhol worked a summer job there designing window displays.) Fedus-Fields followed her husband to New York City, where her marriage ended. "I was devastated, miserable, depressed, and down," she said. But she had training and experience. She was quickly recruited by a friend who had a line of sweaters she sold through department stores. The friend wanted to start a catalog business to sell directly to customers. Fedus-Fields agreed to help her.

In the early 1980s, catalogs selling only one type of item were considered "cutting edge," as Fedus-Fields put it, mirroring the rise of focused specialty retail stores in shopping malls. There were catalogs for brides, aviators, cyclists, and mothers-to-be. They featured dramatic color photography and witty copywriting. Banana Republic's catalog even included musings on style written by novelist Herbert Gold and *Doonesbury* cartoonist Garry Trudeau.

Though the catalog business model avoided the costs of leasing and operating a physical store, it still required a heavy investment of capital to get traction. There were photographers, set stylists, and models to hire, and the steep costs for four-color printing and distribution. And then one had to purchase lists of home addresses from other brands. Most catalog businesses at that time, if properly managed, took about three years to achieve profitability.

Fedus-Fields's fledgling sweater business struggled, closing its catalog less than two years after it launched. But she was eager to give it another try; she had fallen in love again, this time with catalogs. Still, she wanted her next company to have ample financial backing to survive "that magic three-year period." Everyone knew the Limited had money to spend. So in the spring of 1984 she applied to work at her top choice, Victoria's Secret. Hoping to land an offer, Fedus-Fields sent a telegram directly to Wexner. (She had read the best-selling career development guide of 1970, *What Color Is Your Parachute?*, and took its advice to appeal to people of authority when seeking a job.) "Know you are aggressive and growing, you need good people," she wrote. "Am one, experienced in retail and mail order." Within a week, she was summoned to Columbus. A job at the Victoria's Secret catalog was hers.

/ / /

When Fedus-Fields reported for work, the Victoria's Secret catalog was foundering, spending about $3 million a year to generate roughly the same amount in sales. She spent her first year learning the business and traveling weekly from New York City to Columbus, where operators took orders by phone and the warehouse shipped out the packages.

In 1985, Wexner tapped a trusted executive, David Kollat, then the Limited's corporate head of marketing, to take over and revamp the division. Kollat understood the catalog's marketing potential and was eager to find a way to increase profits. He fired everyone on the existing team except Fedus-Fields, who had emerged as the company's resident catalog expert. He then brought in Laura Berkman, the marketer from the Limited, and Sarah Gallagher, a lingerie buyer from the New York City department store Lord & Taylor. While Kollat would remain based in Columbus, the trio of women were allowed to live and work in New York, where they had easier access to a stream of photographers, models, and stylists. The catalog became the only division of the Limited, besides Mast Industries, that Wexner permitted to operate outside of Columbus. Victoria's Secret's stores, along with the other units, remained based in Ohio. (The brand's catalog and stores were run independently. They didn't even sell the same styles of lingerie.)

In an office on Broadway, near Bryant Park, removed from the cut-throat culture at headquarters, Berkman, Gallagher, and Fedus-Fields had the authority and independence to develop a successful catalog strategy. It was a rare opportunity. They became a powerful triumvirate, an early paragon of empowered women with significant autonomy, despite the gendered expectations of the men who managed them. "I remember

[Limited Brands execs] teasingly saying to me, 'We really hope you come back after your maternity leave because no one ever has,'" said Berkman.

Berkman gave the catalog a point of view, within Kollat's directive: move away from soft, Victorian lighting and the Vaselined lenses of the Raymond years and embrace a slick, soft-core boldness—the shift that had so shocked the model Carol Perkins. The result was more *Basic Instinct*, less *Pretty Baby*, with models perched on ornate balconies or lying across disheveled bedsheets, cuddling with male hunks.

Despite his lingering skepticism, Wexner occasionally showed an interest in the catalog's development. At one point, he sent Fedus-Fields to Chicago to meet *Playboy* founder Hugh Hefner's daughter Christie Hefner, who was running the media empire at the time. Wexner hoped Fedus-Fields would get inspiration from what he viewed as Hefner's modern approach to "girl-next-door sexy." The two women had little to discuss. "We sort of just stared at each other," Fedus-Fields said.

Wexner also offered one of his homes in Palm Beach, Florida, for a photoshoot. Perkins remembers a butler guiding her through the quiet property, which was tastefully designed and full of fine art. Milton Avery paintings hung in the guest bathroom. She and the other models shot outside the home, mostly by the pool.

But the catalog did not start to grow in revenue until Kollat, in a moment of desperation, requested that it offer the Limited's famous Forenza sweater, the ribbed V-neck cotton style that had become a suburban-mom phenomenon at the Limited's stores. "I don't care how you do it; I want that sweater in the catalog," Kollat told them. Berkman thought to style the models wearing the oversize sweaters strategically draped off a shoulder, with no pants, only briefs underneath. The tops were an instant hit—the catalog's first major win in years. Kollat was encouraged. He wanted more sportswear in its pages, and the New York triumvirate obliged. Soon, the catalog featured knit dresses and silk blouses alongside its satin bras and lace teddies. Catalog sales picked up pace.

Wexner, typically reluctant to give compliments, shot off a memo to Kollat praising the catalog's performance in the first half of 1986, when the division became profitable for the first time. "You proved the concept, your gross margin was superb, and you far and away led the pack," he wrote, comparing the catalog to the Limited's many other divisions. Wexner added that he could see some "capacity issues" on the horizon— meaning that the distribution center might not be big enough to handle such rapid growth. "However, you now have the nucleus for a major growth vehicle and a major profit contributor—I'm looking forward to another 200% [incentive compensation] season this Fall." (Incentive compensations were a central part of the Limited's corporate culture. Twice a year, employees were eligible for hefty bonuses based on their divisions' performance, not individual performance. If your subsection broke certain goals, you could almost double your salary. But the approach could create resentment. If you were with a weaker brand in the portfolio, you were unlikely to reach those goals, no matter how hard you worked.)

Kollat officially retired in 1987, after eleven years as a senior executive. As one of Wexner's most trusted advisers, he remained on the board of Limited Brands for another three decades.

In Kollat's absence, Fedus-Fields was promoted to president and CEO of the catalog. By then, the division was generating $50 million in annual retail volume and $7 million in profits. Wexner came to her with another ultimatum. Though the catalog's progress impressed him, he was no longer interested in running any division that generated less than $1 billion in revenue—or that lacked the potential to get there. He told Fedus-Fields that if the catalog did not generate $100 million by the end of 1990, he would shut it down. As a motivational tactic, the threat was effective.

But Fedus-Fields had a major problem. Her best growth strategy was to simply mail the catalog to more potential shoppers, but she thought "there weren't enough names in the universe" to generate the required sales by the deadline. So she pursued two new strategies. First, she focused on maximizing the economics of every single catalog page, developing a formula for evaluating sales. Kollat had relied largely on instinct when choosing the products to feature in the catalog. Now, Fedus-Fields developed a "formula" to reflect how merchandising was evolving in the late 1980s across the retail industry.

Merchants were increasingly using past sales performance to help determine future sales trends. If a white button-down shirt sold out in a week rather than a month, it was worth ordering double the next time. Some people called it data mining; others called it common sense. However, Fedus-Fields had more data at her disposal than the average department store. She knew not only what her customers had purchased but what they called her customer service team to inquire about.

She developed a formula of sorts to guide the merchandising strategy. The best pages in the catalog were reserved for items that belonged to categories and price points that sold well in the past. The formula might dictate, for example, that a catalog should have ten different sweaters and that half of them should be under $50. If turtlenecks were trending that season, maybe five of those sweaters would be turtlenecks. And then when Fedus-Fields and Berkman designed the catalog, a $45 turtleneck might get a full-page image in the center break of the book. "We lived and died by that formula," Fedus-Fields said.

Her other major new strategy was to again revamp the look of the catalog, which had become a "must-see for teenage boys," she said. Wexner came to her with a new directive. "Make it English, make it refined," he told her. Such a radical shift was highly risky. "Nobody in their right mind takes a brand from hardcore sexy to refined Ralph Lauren overnight," she said. Wexner was adamant. (He often had a keen sense about shifting styles. In the early 1990s, when grunge and gamines ruled fashion, Wexner would notice that people were suddenly ordering more martinis. He told his merchants that shirts and pencil skirts were about to come back into style. "No one drinks martinis in flannel," he said.)

Fedus-Fields trusted Wexner's intuition—and what choice did she have? "I was working for the greatest retail merchant in the history of the world. He said 'Change it,' so we did," she said. The shift started with the spring 1988 edition of the catalog, which featured a model alone on the cover, leaning over the back of a white wicker patio chair wearing a modest baby-blue silk charmeuse chemise with lace trim. A solid white border surrounded the image, a striking deviation from the typical full-bleed catalog cover style.

That was just the beginning. The sets moved indoors, where models posed in floral pajamas or paisley robes inside gilded homes full of antique molding and decorated with plush leather sofas, Battersea boxes, and paintings of horses. Hot pinks were replaced by subtle blush tones or burgundy. The male models disappeared. The logo on the cover was redone again, this time in patrician style, topped with a symbol of a crown. Soon, the word "London" was added under the logo, later replaced by the actual address of the company's corporate office at 10 Margaret Street—a dinky walk-up in Fitzrovia. Inside the catalog's pages, Columbus, Ohio, was now described as Victoria's Secret's "North American Office." The captions adopted British spelling, using "jewellery" and "splendour." Victoria's Secret robes now had names like "The Cambridge" and "The Chatsworth." Fedus-Fields started offering gift cards wrapped in boxes covered in what became one of the brand's signature prints, an embroidered floral jacquard inspired by nineteenth-century English tapestries. The model Jill Goodacre, with her long, shiny hair, became the catalog's premier cover star, holding a cup of tea while lounging in a thick floral robe or sitting beneath a Christmas tree in a bright red chemise, barely a hint of cleavage visible.

Compared to the Kollat era, when catalog models often seemed either pre- or post-coitus, with parted lips and messy hair, the models in this Anglophilia era were reserved—sometimes smoldering, yes, but always composed. The *New York Times* fashion writer Holly Brubach described them as a reincarnations of Édouard Manet's Olympia, "passive women, waiting for a man to come along and fulfill them—not just any man but the man of their dreams."[3] Brubach likened the models to the Victoria's Secret customer, lounging at home and leafing through the catalog, imagining a life worthy of the protagonist of a romance novel. Brubach theorized that shoppers were enticed by what was a taboo idea in the careerist 1980s: the unspoken pleasure of projecting oneself into the role of a sex object. "The fact remains that for many women, looking at pictures of other women is an incitement to fantasy," she wrote, "not because they want to know those women but because they want in some vague way to be those women, to evoke in men the feelings they imagine the women in the pictures do."

While the Victoria's Secret teams would be reluctant to admit it, the English look they established in the late 1980s and early '90s was closer to the Raymonds' original vision a decade earlier than to what Kollat had later mandated. Customers loved it. "Response rates," or rate of purchases per mailings sent, jumped quickly, validating Wexner's aesthetic directive. Fedus-Fields was pleased. Her target was in sight.

As sales grew, the New York triumvirate mailed out as many as fifteen editions of the catalog a year. Women, and men, were calling 1–800-Her-Gift and ordering sweaters and nightgowns and bras from the "fashion consultants" who kindly took their calls, twenty-four hours a day, 365 days a year.[4] Popular items were frequently sold out, and rarely shipped on time.

Product quality and consistency also suffered. And yet sales continued to rise. The catalog reached Wexner's $100 million revenue goal almost one year before his deadline. By the end of 1994, it was generating $570 million annually.

Meanwhile, Berkman used the catalog's expanding production budget to hire models with European runway experience. Stephanie Seymour, one of the original supermodels who dominated Paris and Milan in the 1980s, signed on and became a frequent cover star. The Victoria's Secret team wooed her not only with money, but also by promising to hire all her favorite collaborators, including photographer Patrick Demarchelier (who was beloved by models, fashion editors, and Princess Diana) and the talented hairstylist Max Pinnell.

Seymour appeared in Victoria's Secret's catalogs throughout the 1990s, as did another young Dutch model, Frederique van der Wal. Represented by the top agency Elite, van der Wal frequently appeared in American *Vogue* and in advertisements for Tunisian-born French designer Azzedine Alaïa. She warmed to the idea of posing for Victoria's Secret when she heard that as part of the redesign, the catalog had hired such top-tier photographers such as Demarchelier and Max Vadukul, who rarely otherwise shot catalogs. Van der Wal had boundaries: she would not shoot with male models, and she would not wear garter belts.

Van der Wal worked so frequently with Victoria's Secret, she felt she was part of the team. In 1993, she even asked New York financier Donald Trump, an acquaintance from the city's social circles, if the catalog could shoot at his Palm Beach country club, Mar-a-Lago. "I said, the only thing is, you have to sign a contract that you can't come [to watch the shoot]." Victoria's Secret was granted access for a day, without Trump lingering around. Van der Wal posed in front of a doorway adorned with the property's famous Spanish tiles. The image became the cover of the 1993 summer edition.[5]

Van der Wal appeared in the Victoria's Secret catalog for more than ten years. "We became a very tight group," she said, recalling that most of the people on set were women. She once jokingly complained about being tired of "standing in my underwear" and suggested that the crew on set with her strip down to their skivvies, too. They agreed. "Everybody knew a lot about each other, which is very rare in the fashion industry," she said.

Van der Wal remembers one day when Berkman pulled her aside on set and told her about a denim handbag she modeled in a previous catalog that had become a surprise hit—having sold more than seven million times and counting. Van der Wal had no idea how many coffee tables, nightstands, and office desks across the country were covered with her images—or how big Victoria's Secret would soon become.

CHAPTER 6

Man About Town

Les Wexner takes on Columbus.

In the summer of 1981, Les Wexner had a near-death experience—or the feeling of one. Hiking up Vail Mountain in Colorado on a warm August day, he became enveloped in a sudden storm.[1] "I was in no immediate danger," he admitted later. "But it was snowing and raining and thundering, and I was on top of this damn mountain by myself in shorts and a t-shirt and at first I said, 'What if I die?'"[2]

Wexner was stuck in what he later called an "adult adolescence."[3] He was unmarried, approaching forty-five, and a newly self-made billionaire. He lived in a starter mansion across the street from the Ohio governor and referred to his German shepherds Samantha and Max as "the Wexner kids."[4] He owned half a dozen other properties, including an apartment overlooking Central Park and an estate in Palm Beach near his mother's house. His propulsive, lifelong desire to better himself made him restless. Work was his life.

Wexner had always been shy, even closed off, and his new stratosphere of wealth had only further isolated him. He was outgrowing his high school and college friends, who did not understand his new expensive tastes. "I felt very insecure in relationships because I didn't think they would last," he said of himself at this time.[5] When, in 1982, *Forbes* ranked him among the richest people in the nation for the first time, he felt outed. "When you have a lot of money, you're looked at as a freak," he said. "I was closet rich until this thing was published. . . . I liked it better when I was just another guy from Columbus, Ohio."

The frightening hike led to an epiphany, in his telling: "I got to thinking, if I died, how would I think I had lived my life?"[6] He could afford to live quietly and fabulously rich. But Wexner thrived on building his business—the planning and the organizing and the *patterning*.

Wexner often told the hiking story in the years that followed. It was a useful anecdote to explain why, well into his forties, he had decided to become more than the king of the American mall. He could still buy and sell cars, like his beloved Mercedes 500 SEC, then his chief hobby. But he was hungry for new problems to solve. He would apply his entrepreneurial instincts to the only place he had ever truly felt at home. He would turn Columbus into a great American city.

/ //

In the 1980s, Columbus had a national reputation as a cow town, devoid of culture or wealth. The state's capital lacked the natural advantages of major rivers and lakes that in the 1800s had turned Dayton, Akron, and Cleveland into economic engines of the Rust Belt. Cleveland, where Standard Oil was founded, dominated Ohio with its coal, iron and steel manufacturing, and access to both Lake Erie and the Erie Canal. But ironically, it was the very lack of those natural advantages that worked in Columbus's favor in the twentieth century. When manufacturing declined and abandoned mills began to plague neighboring cities, Columbus saw its population pick up. Immigrants and southerners poured in, and postindustrial businesses, like insurance and scientific research, emerged. Ohio State University and the state legislature provided a solid foundation for jobs and activity. When many citizens of Columbus started leaving the city for the suburbs after World War II, civic leaders shrewdly annexed those suburban townships as they expanded, preserving vital tax revenue. Still, Columbus's growth was slow. Some in the city blamed the controlling influence of a handful of families who discreetly ran the town through its organizing committees and civic organizations.

By the time Wexner was preparing to wade into city issues, John W. Wolfe was the most powerful man in town. Known for his forceful—and vengeful—nature, Wolfe and his family owned the city's only daily newspaper, the *Dispatch*, and had their hands in everything from investment banking to real estate to television affiliate networks.

The first Wolfes came to Columbus in the late 1800s. The next generation, John W.'s grandfather and great-uncle, Robert and Harry Wolfe, built a successful business manufacturing and selling men's shoes. (They had rag trade roots, but the Wolfes were not Jewish.) With those profits, the brothers bought a local bank and organized what would soon become Columbus's most powerful banking group. The brothers also bought the city's two major newspapers and used them to support and control their favorite politicians.

The Wolfes' grip on Columbus remained so strong that, even in the 1960s and '70s, candidates from both parties still relied on John W.'s support.[7] Any project he opposed ended up stalled or canceled. City officials who defied him were pushed out of their jobs, driven by scathing editorials or suddenly publicized scandals. Wolfe was also involved in expanding the Columbus Zoo and the Port Columbus International Airport. And yet the Wolfe family name was rarely mentioned in connection with civic developments or politics.

Wolfe's vision of Columbus was one of maintenance. He wanted to ensure that the current way of life was preserved, not transformed. "Columbus is a good place to live, so why fix something if it's not broken," he once told a reporter.[8]

Wexner felt differently. As with the retail business, which he upended in the 1960s by creating proto–fast fashion, he thought Columbus could and should change. He believed he had solutions for how to make the city more efficient and appealing to the rest of the country. And he wasn't afraid to knock down the past to create a more perfect future.

Wexner was also a straight shooter, often to a point of insensitivity. When it came to city affairs, he did not want to wield influence through back rooms. In 1983, he told the *Dispatch* that Columbus had "the worst downtown in America"[9] because it was too spaced out and lacked sufficient cultural institutions. He felt that the historic downtown Cineplex, the Ohio Theatre, should be demolished, and personally pledged $5 million toward the construction of a new "world-class" multipurpose performing arts center, so the city could attract a full-time symphony. This plan enraged a local nonprofit group that had formed in the late 1960s to preserve the Ohio Theatre. Wexner eventually capitulated, giving up on the idea of a new theater and instead joining the ongoing plan to renovate the Ohio and upgrade its acoustics. (But he was irritated when, less than a decade later, Cincinnati built exactly the kind of advanced performing arts center he had wanted, and that Columbus still lacked.)

The performing arts center kerfuffle established Wexner as a renegade or a bully. He had expected his ambitions to jolt the city's power structure. He did not care about the reaction, but the failed effort stung. Still, as Wexner's wealth grew, more people paid attention. If his brash approach wasn't always effective, he didn't let up. When the city's mayor Buck Rinehart skipped a meeting Wexner attended in 1986 about a tax proposal for a new convention center he supported, Wexner railed at him as if he had been there. "Where in hell are you?" Wexner said, as captured by the reporters in the room. "Why in hell am I doing this in my spare time? You're working for me full time, I think, to lead this issue!"[10]

Wexner later suggested to Mayor Rinehart that he could buy a plot of land downtown and donate it to the city for redevelopment. Instead, the mayor purchased the land on behalf of the city, and Wexner was left bewildered. Why would the city not want his gift, even with strings attached? Mayor Rinehart later said that dealing with Wexner was like "talking to a tree,"[11] and he called his proposals "embarrassing." The mayor was one of Wolfe's favored politicians, which gave a deeper meaning to his public rebuke. "There was a strong perception that the civic scene had been split into two camps: Wexner on one side, and the Wolfes . . . on the other," wrote *Columbus Monthly*.[12] The Wolfes had clashed with other prominent people in the city, including the Lazarus family, but those conflicts were, of course, never mentioned in the *Dispatch*.

Wexner took aim at the city's wealthy set, who he felt were not doing their part to fund new city projects and charities. "The individual giving is just the worst," he said in 1984. To galvanize his peers, Wexner that year hosted his first glitzy fundraising gala, spending a rumored $300,000 to stage an eight-course dinner and dance party to raise money for the nonprofit United Way. Tickets cost $5,000 each, and guests included the chairmen of the city's most important companies like Nationwide Insurance, CompuServe, Ohio Bell, and Bank One, along with emissaries from leading families. The theme was "fire and ice," with mock flames and shiny blue mylar plastic decorating the Limited's headquarters, transformed for the night. More than one hundred employees of the Limited worked the event, including dozens who had trained as mimes to entertain guests as they arrived. A twenty-six-piece orchestra played on an art deco–themed bandstand, as crooner Andy Williams and a swing dance band flown in from New York City performed. Ohio senator and former astronaut John Glenn told a reporter he had never been to a better party in his life.

The gala raised $1.3 million, twice as much money as it had the year before. It was Wexner's debut as an Ohioan with deep pockets and glittering taste. Nouveau *mega*-riche. The next year, *Forbes* named him the wealthiest person in the state, a ranking that he retains today.

Wexner's flaunting peeved many in Columbus. There were those of the old guard who felt that Wexner had not paid his dues, that he was a tacky ingrate. He had not spent years on civic committees, showing and earning respect. "I've been working" was Wexner's response.

"The prevailing ethic in Columbus was you wanted to do it behind the scenes," he said in 1984 when asked about his local critics.[13] "I know what people say about me. They say I'm outspoken and 'This isn't how it's done. You don't give money publicly. How crass.' That's bullshit. Look at the Rockefeller Foundation, the Ford Foundation, Carnegie Hall. I mean, who are they kidding? You can't tell me that leadership being visible is not the standard of the world. Don't tell me that's not how it's done."

Undeterred by the criticism, Wexner threw himself into his new passion. He joined the board of his Orthodox synagogue in Bexley and the endowment committee at Ohio State University, where he personally funded a new contemporary art museum. He started two foundations under his name to finance and support the education of Jewish leaders. And he turned his attention to Columbus's stagnant downtown, hiring an architect to design a redevelopment plan. Wexner took that proposal public, publishing a six-point pitch to increase density and commercial activity. He distributed booklets with schematics and gave speeches at local clubs. In 1986, he hosted a rally, attended by three thousand employees of the Limited, for a special tax to support a new convention center. After his remarks, a plane flew overhead towing a banner that read, "We believe in the future of Columbus!"

More problematic than Wexner's perceived lack of humility was his neighbors' provincial mindset. Not everyone wanted Columbus to become a regional hot spot. Some in the city still embraced its humble reputation, even though, in 1980, it had roughly the same population as Boston or New Orleans. "Many of us don't really care and are, in fact, seriously hostile toward Columbus becoming what some term a 'big league city,'" read a fiery 1986 editorial in the *Dispatch* further articulating Wolfe's views.[14] "People around here have had just about enough of Wexner. . . . The era of Downtown Columbus is over. To try to alter that is to put up a hand against the sea."

While his critics griped, Wexner persuaded his friend A. Alfred Taubman to take over the development of a proposed downtown shopping center development that had been stuck in bureaucratic limbo for thirteen years. Taubman agreed, in part because Wexner committed to leasing one-fifth of the total space. Each one of his retail divisions would open there. Most intriguing was the promise of Wexner's most recent acquisition at the time, the Manhattan luxury department store Henri Bendel. Soon, Lazarus and Marshall Field's agreed to sign on as the shopping center's anchors—a major coup for Taubman and the city of Columbus.

When the $200 million, three-story mall called City Center opened in August 1989, Wexner sat front and center at the celebration between Taubman and John "Jack" Kessler, a Columbus real estate developer and one of Wexner's closest friends. Confetti rained down on their smiling faces as they watched a dance performance in the mall's central atrium.

City Center was more popular than civic leaders had ever imagined. An average of sixty-five thousand people showed up each day for the first six months.

Wexner was becoming influential if not quite celebrated. "Les has not learned how to be a team player and doesn't understand why he's not appreciated by the community," said one friend. "That's why we affectionately call him 'Les the mess.'" Wexner admitted he lacked patience. "I like to go ninety miles an hour while they prefer thirty-five miles an hour," he said of his fellow Columbus leaders and philanthropists.

Still, Wexner had an effect on the city. In the 1980s, Columbus drew new attention from major newspapers across the country, who declared it one of the fastest-growing and most hospitable cities in the country. By the end of the decade, Columbus would outgrow Cleveland and become the largest city in the state. Amid the grumbling about Wexner among civic leaders, a new concern emerged: if Columbus did not appreciate Wexner's efforts to remake the city as he wished, his neighbors ran the risk of pushing him out of town. Most of Ohio's wealthiest people lived in Cleveland or Cincinnati. Wexner was a rarity, a homegrown Columbus billionaire. When would someone like him come around again? And what was stopping him from leaving? "The biggest hostesses in New York are dying to get him on their guest lists," said an unnamed source in the *Dispatch*.[15] "The easiest thing in the world for him to do would be to go off to New York City and become a force there, and don't think he couldn't do it."

/ / /

Les Wexner first drew the attention of New York City's elite in 1984, when he surprised Wall Street by making a $1.1 billion tender offer for Carter Hawley Hale, the department store group more than three times the size of the Limited. After a monthslong battle, the bid failed, but interest in Wexner remained. Then, he pulled off something even more unexpected in the eyes of Manhattan's elite society. He bought a New York City landmark, the beloved upscale department store Henri Bendel. (As one story goes, Donald Trump came up to Wexner at a party, when they met for the first time, and asked, "How did you get so fucking rich?")

Even as he emerged in Columbus as an indefatigable force for change, Wexner remained an intriguing mystery in New York City. "He could have gone to any black-tie gala—but he didn't want to go," said Laura Berkman, the Limited executive who moved to New York in the mid-1980s to work on the Victoria's Secret catalog.

Wexner skipped the galas, but he maneuvered his way into high-society positions. He joined the board of the American Ballet Theatre, where he hobnobbed with Jacqueline Kennedy Onassis. When Al Taubman acquired a controlling stake in Sotheby's in 1983, Wexner joined the auction house's executive committee. Taubman also connected Wexner with the Whitney Museum, where he became a trustee and joined the painting and sculpture acquisition committee. He started buying Picassos.

The consensus was that Wexner would one day make a permanent transfer to New York, as many small-town entrepreneurs had done before him—including Andrew Carnegie and Andrew Mellon, Pittsburgh's robber barons, and John D. Rockefeller, who moved Standard Oil's headquarters from Cleveland to Manhattan.

In retrospect, Wexner approached his lofty Manhattan appointments transactionally, using them to deepen his understanding of the art world or to boost other projects. When he was on the board of the American Ballet Theatre in the early 1980s, for example, his major contribution was a proposed clothing collaboration with the Limited, inspired by actress Jennifer Beals's slashed-sweatshirt wardrobe in the 1983 film *Flashdance*. Nothing ever came of it.

And while Wexner struck up friendships with some of the most important philanthropists in the city—among them, Ann Getty, wife of oil heir Gordon; and Liz Rohatyn, wife of his close friend the financier Felix—he never stayed in town long enough to get fully ingrained. He wasn't comfortable in Manhattan. Instead, Wexner hosted two formal dinner parties a year, in Columbus for Halloween and Vail for Christmas, and otherwise tried to avoid large gatherings. He preferred instead to dine with Senator Glenn in Columbus or to visit Minnesota senator Rudy Boschwitz at the senator's home outside Minneapolis.

While Wexner resisted Manhattan, he couldn't resist feeding into his mystique—and relishing opportunities to remind everyone that he was wealthier than his midwestern background might suggest. In 1989, Wexner purchased Manhattan's largest private residence, a former schoolhouse on Seventy-First Street between Madison and Fifth Avenue, for a whopping $13.2 million. "He's an art collector and needs the room," a source told the *Daily News* during the extensive renovations.[16] While Wexner never intended to make it his primary home, he took great pains to decorate it, hiring hotshot interior designer John Stefanidis and architect Thierry Despont to transform it into the epitome of 1980s opulence by way of aristocratic Europe.

Wexner's frequent absences from New York City left an alluring impression, amplified by the fact that Wexner was approaching fifty and still unmarried. When *New York* magazine profiled him in 1985, it declared him the "bachelor billionaire," detailing his collection of Ralph Lauren and Gianfranco Ferré suits bought at Wilkes Bashford in San Francisco or Louis Boston. Wexner seemed in no rush to settle down. He addressed the assumption that he was gay, a speculation that would follow him throughout his life. "A lot of people think because I am not married I am asexual or homosexual, but I enjoy a relationship with a woman," he told *New York* magazine.[17] When Al Taubman frequently encouraged him to get married, he would respond, "Me and the pope." Wexner broke up with a casual girlfriend in the late 1980s, a woman who had converted to Judaism and adopted a Jewish-sounding last name, seemingly in the hopes of marrying him. (He offered her $10 million to sign a nondisclosure agreement when they parted, according to two sources, and she never spoke publicly of their relationship.)

Wexner's friends attributed some of his personal idiosyncrasies to his intense relationship with his headstrong mother, Bella, a widow since her husband Harry died of a heart attack in 1975 at age seventy-six. Even though Les had clashed with his father, Harry was the milder and kinder one in his marriage. Bob Morosky, the Limited's longtime finance executive, "especially liked the father," he said. "As a male in a female-dominated household, he became both shy and dominant at the same time," said Les's former Ohio State professor and close adviser Arthur Cullman.[18] Others described the mother-son bond more crudely: it was "kind of a sick relationship," said one former executive at the Limited.

Les's associates inside and outside the Limited characterized Bella as a stereotypical overbearing Jewish mother. She was demanding, maintaining high standards for herself and for her son. "If fear were a color, she'd be colorblind," Les said.[19] Into Les's adulthood, Bella remained uncommonly close to her son, occupying an office across the hall from him at the Limited's headquarters in her role as secretary and then board member. Her exacting nature caused some executives to turn and walk the other way when they spotted her in the office. During the board meeting when Les proposed the tender offer for Carter Hawley Hale, he asked Bella to formally put forward the motion to mark what he considered a historic moment. Some saw this as his asking for her permission. "Stories about his devotion to his mother sometimes get under Les's skin," *Women's Wear Daily* wrote in 1985, the same year another reporter saw Bella change her seat at the last minute at the Limited's annual meeting to be closer to her son. Still, Les often deferred to Bella, referring to her as "Mother" when in conversation with other people and often introducing her as "the big boss."

As the years passed, Les gradually distanced himself from his mother. Friends recall that by the end of the 1980s, Les went out of his way to avoid Bella—even planning vacations in Florida at friends' homes, rather than his own near hers in Palm Beach. Her visits to Columbus dwindled as she spent more time in Florida and in New York City, where her daughter, Susan, lived. But Bella remained on the board of the Limited until 1997.

"Bella was a difficult woman who wanted tremendous control," said one of Les's business associates, who believed Bella served as a block to his marriage prospects. "Nobody was ever going to be good enough." Not even his future wife, Abigail Koppel, whom Les met sometime around 1990 in New York City. His mother did not hide her disapproval of the relationship. Abigail was twenty-four years younger than Les, and "[Bella] didn't like the age difference," said Bob Morosky.

But on paper, Abigail was arguably perfect. She came from a good Jewish family. Her father had served in the Israeli military, helping to establish the State of Israel as a leader of the Haganah militia before moving to the United States in the 1950s to open an office for Israel's national airline, El Al. Abigail was beautiful, intelligent, and well educated, with degrees from Barnard College and New York University Law School. She was also well connected. In Manhattan in her early twenties, she joined Junior International, a social club for ambitious young Americans and well-bred Europeans. (At one of its parties, she was described as a "vampy PYT" in a black bustier dress.[20]) When Abigail and Les met, she was an associate in mergers and acquisitions at the prestigious New York law firm Davis Polk & Wardwell. She could hold her own with Les, as she did early in their relationship at the black-tie gala celebrating the reopening of Henri Bendel in Manhattan in 1991. Guests included Jacqueline Onassis, Anne Bass, Brooke Astor, and Paloma Picasso, all of whom Les greeted with Abigail by his side.

And perhaps most important, Abigail was willing to quit her job and move to Columbus to join Les's civic and philanthropic efforts. (As it turned out, the city girl loved horses, dogs, and all the trappings of country life.) Even before she and Les were married, she helped him plan a retreat for the Columbus Foundation, a group for civic-minded businessmen in which Les was actively involved. Abigail had a knack for diplomacy and, unlike her husband, was easy to befriend.

Abigail and Les were married in January 1993, in the library of his vast new home just outside Columbus, with only thirty assembled guests present. Abigail wore a striking minimalist Givenchy gown. In the absence of actual snowfall, the lawn was sprayed with artificial snow. After the ceremony and a fireworks show on the lawn, more than three hundred people arrived for the reception. They were led to dinner in a heated tent adorned with chandeliers and a white trellis fence covered in roses. There was live music throughout the night, by violinists and French horn players and a klezmer band playing Jewish folk music. Guests had multiple after-parties to choose from, including a silver ball–lit disco in the main house's orangery and a speakeasy-style jazz bar in the library.[21]

Bella, then in her mideighties, attended the ceremony but did not stay for the reception. Her relationship with her son had been irrevocably damaged. A year before the wedding, Les had replaced her on the board of the Wexner Foundation while she was dealing with an illness. When she recovered and sought to retake her position, the foundation went so far as to sue Bella. The suit was eventually settled, but the business was ugly. By then, the Limited had made Bella one of the wealthiest people in the country, with a personal fortune of more than $300 million. Bella settled on the Upper East Side of Manhattan, where her daughter, Susan, lived.[22] "When Les finally married Abigail, the mother came to the wedding, moved to New York, and never saw them again," is how a former Limited executive put it. (It wasn't quite as drastic, but it wasn't far from the truth.)

Less than two years after the wedding, Abigail gave birth to a son, Harry, Bella's first grandchild. In a bid to repair the family relationships, Abigail flew the child to New York to meet his grandmother. When Bella finally retired from the board of the Limited in 1997 after serving for thirty-four years, Abigail replaced her.

"I could see the day [Les] decided to be married, he changed; he was perfectly comfortable," Abigail told *Columbus Monthly* in 1994. "I think he wondered if he would ever have a family. I think he found some peace."[23]

For years to come, there would be speculation about the exact nature of Les and Abigail's relationship. Was it romantic? Was it a business arrangement? Whatever the case, it was a partnership, one that would last longer than any other in his life.

When Abigail entered the picture, Les also found peace with some of his adversaries in Columbus's power circles. As a sign of goodwill toward the Wolfe family, the Limited signed on as a sponsor for the 1992 flower show AmeriFlora, a project championed by the Wolfes. Les said he played "the good soldier," even though he thought the flower show was silly. In the end, AmeriFlora's attendance came under projections, and the event lost millions of dollars. Two years later, John W. Wolfe died, ending an era of outsize influence in Columbus. His successor in the family dynasty, his cousin John F. Wolfe, took a gentler approach to politics and worked to build a much closer relationship with Les. The two men worked so well together that *Columbus Monthly* dubbed them "the Wolfener."[24]

/ / /

If Wexner's first passion was shopkeeping, as he often described the heart of the retail business, his second was architecture. His expansion into civic projects revealed his itch to tear things down and build them back better.

First there was the Wexner Center for the Arts, the museum on the Ohio State campus he endowed in the early 1980s with a $25 million donation (now equivalent to $80 million in inflation-adjusted dollars). While few associated Wexner with the arts at that point, he thought the museum would have more public use than a business school.[25] And he was determined to commission an architecturally significant building for the occasion, establishing a contest for proposals. When the museum opened in 1989, its deconstructionist building, designed by renowned architect Peter Eisenman, was heralded by major arts critics as an ambitious success. (The performance artist Spalding Gray described it as a "spaceship that crash-landed on the prairie."[26])

In 1984, Wexner bought a $10 million historic mansion in Palm Beach and promptly demolished it. The locals were shocked, and his attempts to build a new mansion on the plot—in an ornate eighteenth-century French style—were stymied by the zoning board. He gave up and sold the entire uncompleted property four years later. He was already building a $26 million home in Aspen, atop the fancy-house-dotted Red Mountain, which he finished by 1988.

Meanwhile, Wexner was in the early stages of planning his own shopping center, near the Limited's headquarters: the Easton Town Center, a $300 million-plus, 1,100-acre development with mixed office and retail spaces that would eventually open in 1999.

As the Palm Beach construction languished, Wexner looked for another personal project closer to home. In 1986, he went for a drive through the outskirts of Columbus with his friend the developer Jack Kessler. They ventured northeast of the city, near the Limited's expanding headquarters, and came across acres of sleepy farmland called New Albany, population 450. The area had dense woods, open fields, soothing creeks—perfect for a "country" home just ten miles from downtown Columbus. "It had all the appeal of the country and all the desirable features of the suburbs," Wexner later said.

Wexner saw the area's potential not only for his personal residence, but for what he envisioned as a carefully planned luxury suburban enclave that could outshine Shaker Heights near Cleveland or Lake Forest outside Chicago. With Kessler, he began buying as many acres in New Albany as possible, about six thousand to start. By essentially buying up the town himself, Wexner could avoid many of the zoning issues and red tape that had stymied his projects in downtown Columbus and in Florida. He could shape New Albany into a suburban utopia, a picture-perfect American town centered around education, nature, and family.

Wexner and Kessler seemed to have an unlimited budget for their preparations, enlisting leaders in architecture and city planning, including the architects Robert A. M. Stern and Gerald McCue, to advise them. Wexner approached his New Albany research as intensely as he researched trends for the Limited. He traveled abroad with a team of advisers to survey towns in the English Cotswolds and in northern France. They settled on a Georgian architectural style, which Wexner felt was timeless and warm. All buildings in the area would be closely regulated to ensure compliance with the Georgian style and the maintenance of open space. (Wexner was in favor of neighborhood rules when he was the one setting them.) Major properties and roads would be lined with the same distinct white wooden fence. Wexner brought in his close friend Marshall Rose, the New York real estate developer (and future husband of actress Candice Bergen).

New Albany's existing residents, mostly farmers, were not prepared for the changes in store. "We get a call every three or four months from a representative," one told the *Columbus Monthly* in 1990.[27] "The phone conversation always ends with the same question: 'By the way, if you're interested in selling . . .' They pay premium prices and I guess everybody has their price." Wexner, through his New Albany Company, would continue to buy acres in the area for decades to come, spending hundreds of millions of dollars, by some estimations, and reaping untold millions more. He admitted it was a "significant investment" back in 1994, when he was just getting started buying land.

As word of Wexner's plans spread, New Albany was nicknamed "Wexley": the new Bexley, completely controlled by its mastermind. The development became the subject of fascination and debate. There were public hearings about school districts, potential annexation, and sewage contracts. In the end, New Albany kept its schools independent from the Columbus system, but the city agreed to take care of its water and sewage—a plum deal for Wexner's growing suburb.

In November 1989, Wexner broke ground on his own mega-mansion, a sixty-thousand-square-foot Georgian manor on 340 acres of land. (It was named the Abigail House after Wexner met his wife.) Designer John Stefanidis and architect Thierry Despont were once again brought on to design the main home, which boasted a combined interior space larger than a football field. In the dining room, a hydraulically operated plat-form lifted the vast dining room table from the basement kitchen below. Staff could fully set the table downstairs before sending it back upstairs for guests. The property also featured a sizable guesthouse down a small interior road that was later occupied by Wexner's business manager Jef-frey Epstein.

Wexner had more than dinner parties in mind for his new lavish estate. He added a "party barn" to the property for large events. In 2002, about a decade after they were married, Les and Abigail hosted the first annual benefit for the New Albany Community Foundation, funding the con-struction of a library, arts center, and theater in the neighborhood. In the years that followed, the benefit welcomed high-profile speakers such as Presidents Clinton and Bush, former British prime minister Tony Blair, and writer Walter Isaacson. The VIPs were often hosted at the main house, too. Casual visitors would be told that George H. W. Bush or Margaret Thatcher had been for dinner the night before. (Some prominent guests had professional motives: in the 1990s, Wexner emerged as one of the top Republican donors in Ohio.) Guests ogled Wexner's serious art collection: an Edgar Degas bronze statue of a young dancer in the middle of the library near the home's entrance, a music room with half a dozen paintings by Pablo Picasso from his blue period. (Wexner had a wider-ranging art col-lection back in the early 1980s, when his decorator Richard Himmel con-nected him with the Chicago gallerist Richard Gray. Gray recommended that Wexner sell everything he had, deeming it embarrassing for a man of his status, and focus only on collecting Picasso, Alberto Giacometti, and Jean Dubuffet. Wexner took his advice with gusto. In 1999, he spent $45 million at auction on Picasso's *Nude in a Black Armchair*.)

As New Albany Company began selling homes in 1992, at an average listed price of $500,000, Wexner sought to brand the neighborhood as a white-picket-fenced luxury enclave. He tapped Dick Tarlow, a New York advertising executive who helped in the 1990s repositioning of Victoria's Secret, to create a marketing campaign for the neighborhood. By the time *Town & Country* magazine sumptuously profiled New Albany in 2005, the area claimed four thousand residents, one thousand homes, and a golf course at the exclusive New Albany Country Club. The prime real estate, a gated community called New Albany Farms, was adjacent to Wexner's own property. Its residents included Express CEO Michael Weiss (a longtime Wexner deputy), race car driver Bobby Rahal, and White Castle CEO Bill Ingram, each with his own mansion and multi-acre property.

The investment in New Albany paid off for Wexner, personally and financially. By the mid-2000s, his wealth had reached an estimated $2.7 billion, nearly tripling over the course of the prior two decades. And in Columbus, his influence was now seen as equal to Wolfe's.

While Wexner had learned from his outspoken period in the 1980s that keeping his opinions to himself often served his civic agenda, he sometimes let his frustration get the better of him. In 2006, when Ohio's Republican governor Bob Taft appointed Wexner to Ohio State's board of trustees, Toledo's newspaper slammed the pick as a political favor for a prominent donor. Irritated, Wexner called the writer and listed the millions of dollars he had donated to OSU. He was tired of being underappreciated. "If that makes you a fat cat," Wexner told him, "then that makes me the fattest cat."[28]

///

Before dawn on the last Thursday in August 1993, Roy Raymond drove his car to the base of the Golden Gate Bridge, left it in a parking lot, and started walking.[29] Inside the car was a list of requests and an apology letter to his loved ones. Around 5:20 a.m., Roy climbed over a guardrail somewhere along the bridge and jumped. The Coast Guard found his body in the bay off Tiburon, in Marin County. He was forty-six years old. At a memorial service the following week, friends and family released red balloons into the sky above Ocean Beach.[30]

With the money he earned from the Victoria's Secret sale, "[Roy] could have clipped coupons for a living and lived happily ever after," his attorney, Barry Reder, told the *New York Times* afterward.[31] But Roy was not the type of entrepreneur to let money sit and compound. He interrupted casual conversations to jot down potential business ideas and stayed up all night brainstorming ways to invest any money he did have. That's how he conjured up Victoria's Secret, after all.

When his upscale children's department store My Child's Destiny shut down, Roy was personally liable for its debts. He had not incorporated the business. He and Gaye lost almost everything.

Their marriage ended four years later. While their financial trouble caused a strain, Gaye said it wasn't the reason they broke up. She felt the relationship had run its emotional course. Their divorce was mostly amicable, and they shared custody of their two children as Roy kept searching for his next great idea. Several more ventures also failed, including a children's bookstore called Quinby's, which he started with financial backing from Ron Miller, the former chief executive of Walt Disney, and Miller's wife, Diane Disney Miller. That partnership ended in less than two years over disagreements about Roy's extravagant spending.

The day before Roy's death, Gaye received a phone call from a friend of his. The friend told Gaye that Roy had threatened to kill himself. (Someone reported later that they saw Roy, two days before his death, walking on the Golden Gate Bridge.) Roy was once again in start-up mode, developing a retail concept with his girlfriend Peggy Knight. That relationship was faltering, however, and his insecurities had caught up with him. "He felt trapped, again, in a different sort of way," said Gaye. "I saw fear. He was scared of being alone."

The public narrative painted a less complicated picture. The founder of one of America's fastest-growing retail chains was tormented by the success of a company he had not been able to scale himself. Victoria's Secret had surpassed $1 billion in annual revenue at the time of his death. "In trying to recapture his initial glory, Mr. Raymond sacrificed his fortune, his home, his wife, and ultimately, his own life," the *Wall Street Journal* wrote. "In that sense, it was the ideas that killed him," added Reder.

Gaye has largely come to terms with the circumstances around Roy's death and with the fact that the business they built made someone else extremely rich. In many ways, she has moved on. She still lives in the Bay Area, still works as a physical therapist. But it is impossible for Gaye to leave Victoria's Secret entirely behind. Her role in its creation will be the first line in her obituary. She even became a customer, albeit a disappointed one. Gaye remembers taking her daughter to the Victoria's Secret in their local mall when she was about thirteen years old, in the mid-

1990s. "I'm looking for silk chemise," she told a sales associate. "We don't carry silk" was the response.

It was a reminder that Wexner and his executives "changed everything" about the business she and Roy created. Everything, she thought, except the name.

CHAPTER 7

Victoria Grows Up

Grace Nichols classes up the joint, and a flashy bra launch
sets the stage for the Angels era.

The first "Victoria," the one Roy and Gaye Raymond conjured up one evening at home in San Francisco, was a glamorous British woman the couple imagined meeting while traveling on the Orient Express.[1] She was a confident businesswoman, they decided, alone on the train—presumably with a man in her life but unburdened by him. She was fabulous and mysterious. The "secret" to her appeal, she told them, was great lingerie.

Over a decade later, the image of Victoria had evolved. *Vogue* described her as a mix of "the sexy and the sensible," appealing to both men and women by subverting Sigmund Freud's Madonna–whore dichotomy.[2] "The Victoria's Secret woman is not a fashion model, nor is she the girl next door," wrote the magazine's art and fashion writer Dodie Kazanjian. "If she's a wife, she's somebody else's wife. But she's more likely a wife-mistress, with her loose, slightly disheveled hair and one shoulder strap falling down."

Grace Nichols, the merchant who became the head of Victoria's Secret's stores in 1991, did not waste time psychologically evaluating "Victoria" or the stores' customers. When asked by a reporter if women were drawn to the lingerie chain because they were not able to wear ultra-feminine clothing to work, Nichols was quick to retort, "I could tell you any bullshit you want to hear." Then she added, "Women want to look pretty. [But to] expand, it is important that our brand does not objectify women."[3]

An extraordinarily talented merchant, Nichols had come to retail by accident. Around the same time that Cindy Fedus-Fields was mulling the prospect of becoming a nurse or a teacher, Nichols chose the latter. While studying for a master's in US history at UCLA, she worked summers back home in the Bay Area at the department store Emporium-Capwell. The chain was owned by Carter Hawley Hale, the group Les Wexner would later try, and so publicly fail, to buy. Nichols caught the retail bug and switched courses in 1972, signing up for Carter Hawley Hale's merchant training program. She rose through the ranks at two of the group's California department store chains before her friend Susan Falk—whom Wexner would hire in the 1990s to lead Henri Bendel—convinced Nichols that the golden age of department stores was over. The future was in specialty retail. Nichols was persuaded, and in 1986 she moved her husband and two teen daughters to Columbus and joined Wexner's growing empire. She quickly became Howard Gross's right hand in the Victoria's Secret stores business.

Nichols arrived at Victoria's Secret at an inflection point. Gross was opening stores across the country at a relentless pace, while at the same time replacing the Raymonds' designer lingerie with trendy, yet affordable, styles that would encourage a wide demographic of American women to stop buying their bras and pajamas at department stores. The strategy was working. By 1987, 80 percent of the products Victoria's Secret sold carried its brand name. More than that: the company was generating nearly $100 million in annual sales, up from little more than $5 million at the time of the acquisition.[4]

But in the years ahead, Victoria's Secret would need to be more considered in its strategy to reach the mass audience Wexner wanted. Once again, sexual mores were shifting. The conspicuous consumption that ruled the 1980s had started to wane, but the social conservatism of the decade remained. The nuclear heterosexual family was alive and well in America—at least the concept of it. In her seminal 1991 book *Backlash: The Undeclared War Against American Women*, Susan Faludi pointed to a series of forces across American culture that, knowingly or not, undermined women's rights advances from the 1960s and '70s.[5] Across American politics, media, and fashion, women were pushed "back into their 'acceptable' roles—whether as Daddy's girl or fluttery romantic, active nester or passive love object." The "cocooning" domestic lady of leisure was another popular trope, Faludi wrote.

Victoria's Secret's first major national advertising campaign launched in 1989 in the form of a ten-page insert in premium magazines like *Vogue* and *Vanity Fair*. The brand presented a decadent vision of the safety of traditional marriage. In its images, a striking blond couple wearing wedding rings strolls across their sprawling home, the landmark Sledmere House, a castle in Yorkshire, England. In one scene in a bathroom, the wife character prepares to enter a freestanding bathtub filled with bubbles, clutching a floral robe slipping off her shoulders. Her husband, wearing a suit and tie, is visible in the reflection of a large mirror set in a carved wooden frame, watching her intently. The tagline is direct: "What do women want? That's Victoria's Secret." The swanky New York City agency behind the ad, FCB/Leber Katz Partners, described the concept as "love in marriage."

The ad campaign was a ballast against the tawdry associations with selling lingerie. Victoria's Secret didn't want to be confused with Frederick's of Hollywood, the nipple tassell emporium of the 1970s. The chain's lascivious exuberance seemed tacky and outdated in the Reagan era. Frederick's profits started to fall at the start of the 1980s just as its aging leader, Frederick Mellinger, began showing signs of Alzheimer's disease and retired. Mellinger stepped down in 1984, and the chain shifted strategies to project a softer, more sophisticated message. But the changes at Frederick's could not come fast enough to convince the real estate developers who were rapidly building the biggest shopping malls across the country. They wanted to appeal to family values, too. And not only was Victoria's Secret more respectable, but it was also part of Wexner's powerful empire of stores. Frederick's was stuck in the dingier malls—and couldn't shake its racy reputation. In 2000, saddled with debts, the company filed for Chapter 11 bankruptcy protection. It wouldn't be the first time.

A gentler view of sex guided Victoria's Secret in the early 1990s. By the time Howard Gross exited in 1991—Wexner promoted him to lead the Limited's stores—the brand's offices had become filled almost exclusively with women, many of whom felt they were part of a powerful mission to help women embrace their sexuality. "It was very much about self-indulgence—not necessarily about being powerful, but being confident," said Joanna Felder, who led marketing in the early 1990s. The brand's copywriting encouraged shoppers to see lingerie as a "gift you give yourself." Anne "Linda" Enke, a director of product development during this period, said she joined the company "with this perspective that lingerie is good for women" because it could help them love their bodies—and cut back on the growing divorce rate in the United States. "A normal girl would buy something from Victoria's Secret, and she would feel glamorous, you know?" said Cate Lyon, a designer who created patterns and samples for the brand in the mid-1990s. "It was about being romantic, pretty. It was a feel-good look."

And not just pretty, but posh. To grasp the level of sophistication Victoria's Secret needed to exude, Wexner expected and encouraged his women executives to travel like well-heeled British ladies on the company's corporate jets—and abundant dime. The merchants and marketers went to Europe four times a year for research and comped shopping, checking out the windows of the Hermès boutiques in Paris and loading up on designer goods from Christian Lacroix and Guerlain. "One of the things that Les drilled into us was 'Don't invent things. Just be like the Japanese and copy. Copy the best,'" said one merchant.

Wexner would often invite his executive team to ride aboard his own private jet, a twelve-seater where business was conducted as if he were in the office complex back in Columbus. He would call each executive to sit next to him, one at a time, for meetings. This upscale lifestyle was expected to extend to Columbus, too. "We were encouraged to live the brand, to live a bit glamorously. Drive nice cars, wear smart outfits, be well groomed always," Felder said. Once, after an executive meeting with Wexner, he had a manicurist come to the office to polish everyone's nails, Enke remembers. "He had very definite ways that he wanted us to look." Wexner was known to prefer to hire blondes.

Grace Nichols was an exception, and not just because she had dark hair. She refused to play any kind of role to appease Wexner. "There wasn't anything delicate about her," said a former colleague. "Grace was not a Victoria girl by nature or looks," said another.

Of course, no one wondered if Howard Gross was enough of a "Victoria girl" when he was running things. But when Nichols was promoted to CEO in 1991, as she focused on increasing sales and profits, the press also judged her as an avatar of the Victoria's Secret customer. "Her legs aren't particularly long," Stephanie Strom wrote in the *New York Times* in 1993, describing Nichols as an example of the "older customer" Victoria's Secret needed to court to grow the business.[6] "Her thick, dark hair is cropped short instead of cascading down her back. Her lips are more likely to bow in a friendly grin than pucker in a sultry pout."

Back in Columbus, Nichols's team understood the pressures she faced.

"She had a hard road with Les, but stood up for her business decisions, and never got enough credit," said one of her executives. But she did get credit from her team. They often described her as "open"—encouraging of new ideas and willing to take suggestions—which was an unusual trait in the Limited's competitive environment. She also backed up her promises with action. "Grace was an amazing leader, a tough leader," said one former employee. "She was toughest on the people she cared about the most." (Nichols declined to be interviewed for this book.)

Wexner expected Nichols to double sales to $2 billion in less than a decade and to open at least two hundred new stores. To get there, she and Fedus-Fields, who operated independently, were aligned on a critical point: they were adamant that regardless of the type of product they sold or the images blanketing their stores and catalogs, Victoria's Secret did not sell sex. "We never use that word in our merchandising and marketing meetings," Nichols said in 1991.[7] Instead, she and Fedus-Fields spoke about sensuality and emotion. "We concentrate on the appeal of this merchandise to the woman, and how it will make her feel." Fedus-Fields summarized her vision of the brand with the initials "CC, SS, TT": "classic and classy," "simple and sensual," "tasteful and timeless." No fantasies, no illusions.

If Wexner had let her, Nichols would have sold bras in sizes larger than the standard 36DD, knowing that doing so would instantly expand the potential customer base. But Wexner was strongly opposed. He had a different view of Victoria's Secret. "We don't want to be for everybody," he would say. Victoria's Secret should be exclusive in its branding and products if not in its prices. His sizing strategy had some logic: in 1992, the average bra size in the United States was 34B, anyway, and Wexner wanted to focus on selling the sizes that were most popular and, therefore, the easiest to manufacture at scale. (However, the data on average sizes were faulty, gathered from small-scale surveys conducted by different retailers over multiple years and enshrined as conventional wisdom in the intimates industry. Today, while the data remain imperfect for the same reasons as before, the average size is thought to be around 34DD.)

Instead of amping up the cleavage or increasing the size range, Nichols used other strategies to grow the business. Under her purview, more than five hundred Victoria's Secret stores were redesigned under what was internally dubbed the "Queen of Hearts" design. It was an explosion of fuchsia: bright pink carpets and pink-striped wallpaper trimmed with gold crown molding in the shape of twisting vines. The stores looked like nothing else in the mall, nor like the boudoirs Roy and Gaye Raymond had designed.

Shoppers now took their purchases home in fuchsia boxes covered with the brand's new signature symbol—a tilted, jazzy heart with an overdrawn curl at the center, like a strand of hair escaped from Elvis's pompadour. The Victoria's Secret stores also started playing soft classical music at all times. The soundtrack became an unexpected business success when Victoria's Secret released its own album, *Classics by Request*, recorded by the London Symphony Orchestra. By 1994, Victoria's Secret had five platinum disc sets, each selling more than a million copies. (As with much of Victoria's Secret's strategy, the recordings were made with ruthless practicality, including only single movements, or excerpts from larger works, for maximum easy listening. Tchaikovsky's *Romeo and Juliet* fantasy overture, usually about twenty minutes, was cut down to a bite-size three.)

In her first years as CEO, Nichols also moved quickly to improve the quality of the products Victoria's Secret secured from its manufacturers. "Everything [at the stores] was 'buy one, get one free,'" remembers Enke of the state of the business when she joined in 1987. Victoria's Secret was known as a trendy and cheaper alternative to designer lingerie, but not for its quality. Enke was a fashion director Wexner hired to develop a home goods line for Victoria's Secret. Her duties expanded after he tasked her with manufacturing a perfume bottle that resembled one he had picked up from the French perfumer Marcel Franck on a trip to Marseille. Over the course of three trips to Taiwan, where Mast staffers connected her with local factories, Enke ordered a copy of the bottle and gave feedback on the samples, going so far as to visit the glass pits to direct the blowers to use more or less sand. Back in Columbus, she presented Wexner with his original bottle, which had cost him around $400, and the knockoff, which cost only $8 per bottle to produce. Enke asked him to identify the original French one. He guessed wrong and was overjoyed. Enke's bottle sold in Victoria's Secret stores for $40—an 80 percent profit margin.

Enke's role expanded to overseeing the production of more categories, including items like pajamas and robes. Soon, she was in Asia every month, visiting Mast offices in Taipei, Hong Kong, and Seoul, where she encouraged factories to invest in upgraded machines and finer raw materials while keeping costs low. Victoria's Secret's growing store network became powerful leverage. Enke could order one hundred thousand perfume bottles at a time, using the promise of such a giant order to negotiate a few cents less here and there. Once, in Seoul, under strict instructions from Nichols not to pay more than $2.05 per yard for a brushed jacquard fabric for robes, Enke managed to secure the price by ordering more total yards—eventually committing to what was then considered the largest fabric order ever commissioned in Korea.

At one point, Enke said Tom Hopkins, the Limited's vice president of personnel, passed her a message from Wexner. "We want you to take more risks," he told her. "At your margins, we can easily clean up your failures." The guidance was indicative of Wexner's strategy and of the power of his stores. He had the capital and the means to test, and to gamble on, products. And if an item was a dud, to mark it down and move on. The hits more than made up the difference.

III

Maybe it was Pamela Anderson, whose cleavage first filled the famous red *Baywatch* swimsuit in 1992; or Karl Lagerfeld, who sent Chanel models down the runway with extra padding underneath tweed bra tops the following year; or Madonna, who styled an entire tour around Jean Paul Gaultier's canonical brassiere in the early 1990s. Or perhaps it was the temporary ban of silicone breast implants over safety concerns. Whatever the reason, by the mid-1990s, push-up bras surged in popularity. New cleavage-enhancing "fashion technology" promised to offer what nature had not. And in the battle for padding supremacy, two sides emerged as the dominant players: Playtex's Wonderbra and Gossard's Super-Uplift. Victoria's Secret sold neither.

The war broke out in the United Kingdom, where both companies released expensive advertising campaigns in 1994. Wonderbra's starred the lingerie-clad model Eva Herzigová, photographed by Ellen von Unwerth, gazing down at her buoyant cleavage next to a simple slogan: "Hello Boys." The ad became a global sensation. City officials in Birmingham pulled the image from billboards, fearing it would cause traffic accidents. When the Wonderbra arrived in American department stores in the spring of 1994, the Herzigová campaign was already so famous that

Playtex sold it as a poster. The Wonderbra ad wasn't just clever, it was unusually ubiquitous.

By targeting men, Wonderbra ensured its message reached far beyond the pages of women's magazines and overshadowed every other push-up bra on the market—including Victoria's Secret's "Miracle Bra," a new product released in 1994 as the push-up trend was gaining popularity. Since the brand had advertised the Miracle Bra's arrival only in the catalog and in its stores, the Herzigová hoopla dominated the public conversation. While the Miracle Bra sold fine, it never rivaled the Wonderbra, even after Victoria's Secret released a television commercial and magazine campaign starring the model Heather Stewart.

"We got creamed in terms of awareness," said Nichols.[8] And no wonder. When Jill Beraud arrived at Victoria's Secret in 1995, she was surprised to find that the marketing department was little more than a "sign shop." Each Tuesday, the marketing team would meet with the merchants and "take orders" for the coming days and weeks' in-store banners. "All we spent money on was paper," said Beraud. While the catalog had its mailing list, the stores division lacked any data on its customers, including their ages and their purchase history. Beraud had come to Victoria's Secret from Procter & Gamble and from agencies that specialized in consumer packaged goods. The makers of grocery store staples used specialized strategies to target different types of customers, like creating sub-brands within a hit product line and using national television commercials. Nichols knew Victoria's Secret needed to adopt some of those highly orchestrated approaches.

Wexner was long resistant to paid advertising, preferring to use his store windows to announce new arrivals. But the Wonderbra experience confirmed that his old tactics could get Victoria's Secret only so far. To eclipse department stores and dominate the intimates market, he needed more than the hundreds of stores in malls across the country. Victoria's Secret needed its own traffic-stopping ads. And to get there, it needed stars.

///

As the Victoria's Secret catalog grew in scope and scale in the 1990s—two hundred million catalogs went out to ten million people annually—many of the models featured in its pages became minor celebrities. There was Elaine Irwin, then the wife of rock star John Mellencamp, and Jill

Goodacre, girlfriend (and future wife) of singer Harry Connick Jr. "People come up to me: 'Are you the Victoria's Secret model?'" Goodacre recalled. "In my head I say 'I'm not just their model.' If you see my book, it's a million other jobs."[9]

When Stephanie Seymour joined Victoria's Secret's cadre of models in 1992, several of her late-1980s supermodel peers, including Linda Evangelista and Karen Mulder, soon followed her. (Evangelista's tenure with Victoria's Secret was brief, and she modeled only the catalog's ready-to-wear, not its lingerie.)

Victoria's Secret couldn't match the clout that Seymour and Mulder gained when posing for luxury fashion brands like Chanel and Alaïa. But the catalog came along at just the right time. Modeling was a fickle, fast-moving business. Seymour was twenty-four but had been modeling since she was fifteen; she was no longer a new face in the industry. Fashion's most prestigious jobs had shifted to a younger generation. "The big European fashion companies are phasing out the faces of the Eighties," *Women's Wear Daily* wrote in 1993.[10] Kate Moss, Shalom Harlow, and Aya Thorgren were now landing big luxury campaigns over Christy Turlington, Linda Evangelista, and Naomi Campbell. "Linda is history," sneered one unnamed photographer in the same *Women's Wear Daily* piece, which described the Victoria's Secret catalog as "high in pay, but comparatively low in prestige."

Luckily for Victoria's Secret, models like Seymour and Mulder looked fantastic in lingerie because they had breasts, visible hips, and strong shoulders. They had posed for *Playboy* while modeling for Versace. Their bodies were a natural fit for the shoulder pads and hip-hugging pencil skirts of the late 1980s. When fashion trends turned severe and minimalist in the early 1990s, the faces on the runways changed, too. Designers preferred to showcase their clothes on leaner bodies. "Glamazons just didn't look good in Jil Sander suits," *Vanity Fair*'s Bob Colacello later wrote. Designers such as Helmut Lang and Calvin Klein—with their clean-lined and narrow suiting—cast ultra-skinny models with chests so flat they didn't even need bras.

Androgyny was in, as was a smoker's silhouette, later described as "heroin chic." Former *Interview* editor Ingrid Sischy coined that infamous phrase after twenty-year-old fashion photographer Davide Sorrenti died from what was assumed to be an overdose. (He was a heroin user but died from a hereditary blood disorder.) His images in the indie magazine *Detour*, styled by fashion director Long Nguyen, recalled the strung-out youths in the films of Larry Clark (*Kids*) and Danny Boyle (*Trainspotting*). Even President Bill Clinton felt compelled to condemn the images. After reading about Sorrenti's death, he said American fashion was "glorifying death."[11] Fashion's tastemakers did not care. Moss and her lean peers continued to score the top jobs. Aspiring models were advised to cut the carbs.

Except at Victoria's Secret. Wexner challenged Laura Berkman—the catalog's creative director, who oversaw the booking of the catalog models—to ramp up the star power. He wanted Americans to open the pages of a Victoria's Secret catalog and see the supermodels they recognized from *Vogue* and MTV. Above all, Wexner wanted the German sensation Claudia Schiffer. He promised Berkman every resource at his disposal, from money to private jets, to woo the model. "It was like getting the hottest music band to play at your prom," Berkman said. In the 1990s, Schiffer's career was ascendant. Frequently described at the time as a real-life Barbie, she was one of the highest-paid faces in fashion, earning upward of $8 million a year posing for Guess, Revlon, and Chanel, where she served as a muse to creative director Karl Lagerfeld. And at the time, she was dating the star magician David Copperfield.

When Victoria's Secret came calling, Schiffer wasn't desperate for money, but she was entering an entrepreneurial phase. Soon, she would appear in a commercial for Fanta soda and sign on as a partner with the Fashion Cafe, an ill-fated attempt to copy the Hard Rock Cafe business model. Schiffer was also a resident of the tax-haven Monaco and needed to work there a certain number of days per year to claim resident status. That provided an opening for Berkman, who proposed a catalog shoot at the Hôtel de Paris in Monte Carlo. Schiffer was not yet comfortable posing in her underwear, which was no problem for Berkman. In the spring 1994 catalog, Schiffer appeared on the cover of the Victoria's Secret's catalog for the first time, wearing the brand's popular jeans and a fitted, scoop-neck top.

Two years later, Berkman returned to Monte Carlo to work with Schiffer again, this time with another gimmick in mind. On the overnight flight to the shoot, she and Monica Mitro, a newly hired public relations manager, used a hot-glue gun to encrust a Miracle Bra with rhinestones.

It was a craft project made on the floor of a private jet. But when it was worn by Schiffer, who would believe the bra wasn't covered in diamonds?

Schiffer, finally comfortable enough to pose in lingerie, appeared in the "diamond rhinestone-bedazzled bra" on the cover of the 1996 Christmas catalog, which offered the sparkly bra she wore for $1 million, complete with a red velvet presentation box and a certificate of authenticity. It was Victoria's Secret's first "Fantasy Bra." "Please allow twelve weeks for delivery," the catalog advised. Not surprisingly, no one bought it.

///

Victoria's Secret was assembling its cast. But as the brand's leaders prepared to spend real money on print and television advertising, they needed a sharper identity—an update to the Raymonds' original "Victoria" story.

The task of filling in the details of her life fell to Joanna Felder who, with the Limited's head marketer Ed Razek, dreamed up backstories for sub-brands like Outback Red, the "uniform for explorers of Australian wildlife." She moved over to Victoria's Secret in 1991.

Wexner knew the power of a good brand story. When Express needed a refresh in the mid-1980s, a branding consultant named Marc Gobé invented a fictional character inspired by Princess Stéphanie of Monaco, who represented the ideal customer—rebellious, trendy, blue-blooded. The Express stores were even redesigned to (somewhat) resemble the palace where the princess lived at the time. Wexner found the exercise fruitful, and he wanted to use a similar process at Victoria's Secret.

"The goal was to get the merchant to think glamorously," Felder said of the strategy at Victoria's Secret. She wrote Victoria's life story in the form of a mini-memoir, an elaborate "brand book" complete with calligraphy and photographs Felder took of historic homes in London.[12] The character's full name was undeniably posh: Victoria Stewart-White. Her father was a wry but quiet English financier, her mother a fiery Frenchwoman with a "quick temper" who ran the family homes in London and Kent with "style and grace." As a young woman, Victoria accompanied her mother on shopping trips to Paris, Milan, and New York, while her father taught her "everything he knew about business." Victoria grew up to be a "true beauty" with a "sharp mind for figures" and a worldly education: "Men loved that I spoke my mind." When she was only twenty-four years old, tragedy struck. Victoria's mother was killed in a car accident. After months of mourning, Victoria took her inheritance and opened a lingerie shop on Sloane Street, in London, and an office at No. 10 Margaret Street, the latter dubbed "Victoria's laboratory for luxury." Victoria's best clients were her friends, and her friends were all models. They dropped by frequently to try on her latest designs. Soon, Victoria's shop "became the toast of London," visited by fashionable women on their every trip to the city. Her life was fabulous in every way.

Victoria was beautiful and successful—what else could she need? A husband, of course. Her father introduced her to a handsome, successful barrister named Thomas, and they fell in love and got married. (Fictional Victoria was still only twenty-nine years old at this point.) Their son, Alex, completed their family, which spent the weekdays in the city and weekends in the country. Their homes were decorated with a mix of English antiques and contemporary furniture. The store continued to be a "phenomenon." The couple traveled frequently, often driving down to Monaco to spend the weekend with Princess Caroline and her family. Or they'd go sailing on their fifty-two-foot schooner *My Victoria*, which Thomas had bought for her. Winters were spent in St. Barts, where Victoria often sunbathed topless (a crucial detail). Designer friends asked Victoria to preview their collections before the Paris fashion shows to "lend her eye" and to bring some lingerie for the models. "After the shows, there's an endless stream of receptions and dinners and parties and one must simply be there," Victoria wrote. Still, she found the time to work out with a personal trainer four days a week and to get regular facials and massages. "I think a body must feel good, as well as look good." Her other personal philosophies included: "The taste for luxury, once developed, can never be surrendered" and "There are many ways to look sexy and beautiful." What was *this* Victoria's secret? "To look at life glamorously."

With the "Victoria" brand book project, Razek began taking a firmer grip on Victoria's Secret after years of focusing on the apparel brands. He and Felder translated Victoria's new life story into a promotional video, narrated by an actress with an English accent, to show to new employees. "We started to get more interesting, and Ed started paying attention," Laura Berkman said.

Razek's attention was notable; he was one of Wexner's closest advisers. Like Wexner, he was an Ohioan, raised in Cleveland by a single father. A former champion army boxer and winner of the Mr. Ohio bodybuilding competition in 1946, the elder Razek later worked in a steel mill. He saved enough to send his son to military school in Indiana at the age of twelve.

Ed Razek graduated from Ohio State with a degree in English, already dreaming of making commercials. He joined Shelly Berman, one of Columbus's top advertising agencies, whose clients included Frigidaire, Bob Evans, and, fortuitously, the Limited—back when Wexner had only six stores. At the agency, Razek was known as a talented marketer and a sweet-talking, relatively harmless type who brought Daisy Duke–wearing girls around the office back when such boys-will-be-boys behavior was not so unusual. Wexner took a liking to Razek, who was ten years his junior, and in 1983 hired him as vice president of marketing for the Limited. Razek proved his dedication to Wexner at every turn.

As an adman, Razek prized clarity and concision. He reminded his colleagues that, in retail, the most important ideas were "Free" and "2 for 1." He often referred to what he considered the greatest newspaper headline of all time: "Kennedy Dead." The message passed the "blink test"—a customer understood it instantly—as Razek explained in a memo he distributed to his team titled "Top Twelve Sure Fire Rules for Marketing Success." He wrote that customers "don't talk 'merchant.'" They use, for example, the word "pants" instead of "bottoms." He advised his team to write and design with a single person in mind. He outlined his vision of the ideal specialty store: "When you walk past our stores or into them, do you know what you're trying to sell? Can you tell from the windows, the front door, the table?"

Razek was also a micromanager. He required copywriters to turn in their work triple-spaced, so he had plenty of room for revisions. "There are always creative types who believe if someone changes their copy layout or concept, it's not theirs anymore," Razek wrote in his memo. "I have news for you. It never was. The work belongs to the brand." Wexner, Razek wrote, was not a Medici; his employees were not artists. All that mattered were sales and profits. "If you're not building the brand, you're eroding it," he said.

A former colleague said Razek "thinks he's the greatest copywriter that ever lived." But Razek's ambitions extended far beyond copywriting.

///

On a hot night in early August 1995, Victoria's Secret staged its very first runway show. The timing was odd: fashion month in Europe did not start for weeks. Many fashion models were on vacation, taking advantage of the lull in the industry calendar. The producers worried that guests would not turn up in the ninety-five-degree heat.

But Wexner and Razek didn't care about the fashion calendar. Staging a series of runway shows for several of the Limited's brands, they hoped, would generate some excitement and boost sales. As the Limited and Express raced to respond to trends, shoppers were confusing the two brands with each other. Earlier in the summer, Lerner, the discount chain, had been the first of Wexner's divisions to stage a fashion show at the Bryant Park Grill in Manhattan. Express came next. Even Structure, the men's division at Express, later staged a men's underwear show.

Wexner had other motives for staging a new stunt. In two months, the Limited would spin out Victoria's Secret and Bath & Body Works, together, into an independent company and offer a 16 percent stake to the public. Wexner and his advisers had devised the strategy to raise money to placate Wall Street. His apparel brands were struggling, and analysts were growing frustrated. In the meantime, Victoria's Secret would host the men in suits for a titillating evening.

Razek, ever the marketer, told reporters that a lingerie fashion show had been attempted—a claim that went largely unquestioned. In fact, New York *garmentos* had staged negligee and lingerie shows for department store buyers as far back as 1926. Roy Raymond himself had hosted a series of small lingerie shows for Victoria's Secret in San Francisco restaurants in 1979. In New York City, designers like Bob Mackie would regularly hold lingerie runway shows. And, more recently, in 1994, the hosiery brand Wolford had staged a splashy show on the Spanish Steps in Rome, capped off with a live performance by Grace Jones.

Razek correctly assumed that his audience, American press and shoppers, would see a lingerie show as novel. The public fascination with all things fashion was just starting to grow. As soon as Wexner greenlit Victoria's Secret's first show, Razek got to work. He called Ed Filipowski, who was emerging as one of the most influential publicists in fashion. Filipowski was a partner at KCD, the public relations agency, and fresh off a major win: a few months earlier, he had managed to get his client Versace on a cover of *Time* when the magazine featured Schiffer in one of the designer's white suits.

KCD had a relationship with the Plaza Hotel and secured its largest ballroom—where, in 1966, Truman Capote had hosted his celebrated Black and White Ball—as an ornate setting befitting the catalog's reputation. Kevin Krier, a fashion show producer known for his sophisticated theatrics, staged the show. The respected casting director James Scully chose the models. Victoria Bartlett, a stylist who typically worked with Versace and Miu Miu, sorted through boxes of lingerie to choose the pieces for the runway. She wanted to avoid conjuring any images of Playboy Bunnies or pinups and instead channeled a bygone era of Italian screen stars—women like Sophia Loren and Gina Lollobrigida, who accessorized their tight-fitting bodices with prim handbags, pointy heels, and pearls. Bartlett chose simple lingerie like black-and-white cotton briefs and shiny champagne-colored bustiers paired with pencil-thin stilettos and soft cardigans tied around the waist or hung over the shoulders. Several models carried little top handle purses that they swung sassily as they strutted the runway.

Bartlett's Sophia Loren concept did not carry through the whole show, however. Razek found it overly complicated. "They wanted way more sexy, va-va-voom," Bartlett said. Some of the models walked out looking like off-brand Bond girls, in black knee-high boots, black gloves, and wraparound sunglasses.

To Razek's relief, the guests showed up. Nearly five hundred, mostly men, clamored to get in the door. "The audience was a bunch of cigar-smoking Wall Street guys who wanted a model as arm candy," said Scully. Gossip and culture columnist Michael Musto covered the event in his widely read column for the *Village Voice*. Record executive Russell Simmons and art dealer Tony Shafrazi were among the New York celebrities and tabloid lotharios in attendance. The Plaza crowds weren't the only ones watching. Footage from the runway was simulcast on a giant screen in Times Square.

Scully roped in a respectable group of models, including one of its catalog mainstays, Frederique van der Wal, and rising star Veronica Webb.

Catalog cover girl Stephanie Seymour was tasked with the unusual job of host, coming onstage before the show officially began to explain why a mall chain was putting on a runway show in the first place. "Because lingerie is fashion . . . lingerie is magic," she declared.[13]

Seymour, however, did not herself appear in lingerie. She closed the show covered from neck to ankle in an aqua cheongsam-style dress. While a few models walked the runway in only their bras and underwear, most were styled in silk slip skirts or shorts, or were wrapped in plush bathrobes they would teasingly pull down to their shoulders. It wasn't that nudity or revealing clothing on the runway was unusual or scandalous at the time. As Bartlett remembers, many models were hesitant to expose themselves for Victoria's Secret. On the runways of Alexander McQueen and Thierry Mugler, uncovered nipples and butt cheeks were justified as serving an artistic purpose. Here, there was no avoiding the men hooting and hollering from the front row—or the blatant commerciality of the entire enterprise.

Despite its awkwardness, Victoria's Secret's first runway show delivered enough excitement and press coverage to be considered a success worthy of a repeat. (And when Intimate Brands, Victoria's Secret's new parent company, went public in October, it opened at an impressive $17 a share, generating $680 million.)

Eight months after its first fashion show, Victoria's Secret returned to the Plaza with a sharper strategy. Razek tweaked the timing of the event to align with Valentine's Day. Major models Naomi Campbell, Karen Mulder, and Tyra Banks were convinced to join the lineup. Cardigans were banned, as was anything too loose or too long. The robes were shorter; several women wore garter belts. Everyone's skin glistened with baby oil. The model Veronica Webb, one of four Black models in the show, described the event as "WASP porn."[14] Seymour walked the runway in actual lingerie this time. ("The company is good to me," she told *Entertainment Tonight* backstage.[15])

Many of the runway looks were by Chantal Thomass, the Parisian lingerie designer whose sassy, namesake luxury brand had just filed for bankruptcy and fired her. Seymour wore a sheer, white cape with a matching bra-and-panty set to close out the 1996 show. The look nodded to the fashion tradition of closing runway shows with models dressed in bridal dresses, a practice that began with French couture designers in the 1940s.

Once again, the crowd at the New York runway event was mostly men, including the writer Christopher Buckley and the restaurateur John McDonald. *New York* magazine teased the crowd for "looking as if they had good, solid reasons to be there."[16] There was no "fashion" to speak of, even though the brand's publicists argued that Victoria's Secret's baby doll dresses represented a "return to femininity." The excitement was all about the models and the strange characters in the audience. One back-stage fixture was Monica Mitro, a Minneapolis-bred cellist who first came to the Limited around 1993 as a "fit model"—models who work exclusively behind the scenes, trying on clothing at studios and ateliers for designers as they tweaked styles. A year later, during the Miracle Bra debacle, Razek hired her as one of the first press managers at Victoria's Secret.

Around this time, before Mitro joined the company full-time, she and Razek dated. "We were told we needed to help Monica succeed," one executive said, referring to the understanding among the rest of the team that Razek and Mitro had a special connection. Mitro, to her credit, made herself indispensable, translating Razek's visions into reality and thinking of new gimmicks. "She came in and learned her trade," the executive said. (She embraced the role as Victoria's Secret grew, wearing flashy designer labels with Chanel boots and often toting a Birkin bag. The model Heidi Klum became one of her closest friends.)

The influential New York City publicist Desiree Gruber, then with the agency Rogers and Cowan, was also backstage, helping the models navigate the spotlight. Gruber encouraged models to ditch the scowls they typically wore on high-fashion runways. "In Europe, or New York, or wherever, it was much more like you're a stick figure wearing clothes," said model Catherine McCord. "This was much more about the personalities."

As a reward for orchestrating the hoopla, Wexner promoted Razek to lead a new, centralized advertising group, Limited Brand and Creative Services, which oversaw a ballooning advertising budget. In 1993, Victoria's Secret had spent $5 million on advertising. By 1996, that number reached $13 million. In 1998, it was $85 million.[17]

///

The first Victoria's Secret Angel wasn't a supermodel, but a bra—and a flimsy one at that. In the mid-1990s, Grace Nichols was shopping in

Europe when she came across a sheer set designed by John Kloss. When it had first hit the market in the 1970s, the lightweight and shimmery Kloss bra was a bestseller, known for its bright colors—and semi-scandalous nipple-revealing fabric. (Kloss, who had been discovered by Henri Bendel's president Geraldine Stutz in the 1960s, also had the honor of designing underwear for First Lady Mamie Eisenhower, working with her gown designer Arnold Scaasi.) Nichols brought the Kloss bra to Columbus and proposed turning it into a new product collection at Victoria's Secret, rendered in nine soft but vivid hues.

Wexner came up with the name. One executive remembers him calling from a museum in Europe with the simple directive to "do something with angels." Another remembered him doodling Cupid-like figures wielding bows and arrows during a meeting, prompting his suggestion to do something with wings. But what, exactly? A rising art director in Victoria's Secret's marketing department, Nancy Binger, researched inspirational images and found *the* picture. Herb Ritts had taken the photo in 1989 on the deck of his home in Hollywood for *Rolling Stone*. In the image, the five most important models of the early 1990s, the original "supermodels," were closely nestled together, naked: Stephanie Seymour, Cindy Crawford, Christy Turlington, Tatjana Patitz, and Naomi Campbell. Binger took the photo to Razek and said, "These are our angels." He loved it.

With the lessons of the Miracle Bra fiasco still fresh, Razek turned to a respected New York City adman, Dick Tarlow, to create a splashy commercial. Along with his wife, Sandy Carlson, Tarlow was responsible for some of the most important fashion and beauty advertising campaigns of the 1980s and '90s. Since 1979, Carlson had overseen the lavish print and broadcast advertising for her main client, Ralph Lauren. By the time Razek hired Tarlow, the husband and wife ran separate but deeply intertwined namesake agencies operating out of the same office and often sharing accounts. (The legend was that Ralph Lauren loved Carlson but hated Tarlow, so, to appease Lauren, the couple spun out Carlson's agency but continued to work closely together.)

Tarlow's side of the agency was owned by his biggest client, Revlon. It was an unusual arrangement for a client to acquire an advertising agency. But Tarlow had orchestrated Revlon's most memorable ads, campaigns starring supermodels such as Cindy Crawford and Claudia Schiffer. And he had a brutal honesty that charmed powerful men like Ronald O. Perelman, Revlon's owner. "You got Dick's opinion whether you wanted to hear it or not," said one of Tarlow's colleagues. The relationship between Tarlow and Perelman ended years later when, rumored among the employees, Tarlow refused to cast Perelman's wife at the time, actress Ellen Barkin, in a Revlon campaign. (Perelman, through a representative, said this did not happen.)

Tarlow's first commercials for Victoria's Secret in 1996 were a disaster. Thinking the brand should chase an edgier image, Tarlow hired basketball star Dennis Rodman to front a series of flirty spots with model Helena Christensen. In one ad, a shirtless, tattooed Rodman suggests he'd like Christensen to wear her new seamless bra "under" him. ("Victoria Stewart-White" would have been appalled.) Nichols hated both the commercial and the name of the line: "Perfect Silhouette." On top of everything, the bras were uncomfortable and barely sold. The whole thing was a wash. Nichols fired her head of marketing, and Tarlow forwent his fee as a form of apology.

One of Tarlow's art directors, a young woman named Carol Clarke, took charge of the Angels project. She suggested Herb Ritts, the photographer behind the inspiration image, direct the commercial, too. Clarke also brought in Tom Jones, the Welsh crooner known for "It's Not Unusual" and his cover of Prince's "Kiss." Jones was nearing sixty, but his reputation as a pop heartthrob prevailed. "No matter what I say or what I do, underwear is thrown at me and has been for a long time, so why not go with it?" Jones said in an interview later, explaining how he ended up in the commercial.[18] (His contract for the shoot stipulated that no one throw their underwear at him on camera. At that point, Jones had been dealing with flying panties for almost thirty years.)

Clarke also commissioned an essential part of the Angels' uniform: fluffy white feathered wings. They were small enough to remain at least partially visible on screen during close-ups, but large enough to seem otherworldly. Razek approved and chose the five models who would star in the campaign: Seymour, Christensen, Daniela Peštová, Karen Mulder, and Tyra Banks. (Banks was a favorite among the Victoria's Secret catalog team. Her images moved product.)

Perched atop clouds in bright blue skies, the models in the commercial giggled and cooed, "Not those kind of angels," as Jones interjected with some minor comic relief. Opaque pads added to the sheer bras ensured the network censors' approval. The women were directed to be "bitchy" with one another, nudging each other off the cloud. "If she's an angel, I'm a—" Mulder says. "Don't say it, Karen!" Banks responds.

The commercial was just one part of the launch strategy. A few weeks before it first aired in May 1997, Victoria's Secret hosted a party at Laura Belle, a trendy supper club in Midtown known for having a female attendant in the men's bathroom. The design of the space—giant chandeliers and Georgian-era antiques—was perfect for Victoria's Secret at the time. Wearing matching cropped corsets, the models took the stage one by one, each escorted by a young man in a bright white tuxedo. Tom Jones arrived last, with a microphone. "Ladies and gentlemen, Victoria's Secret's Angels," he declared, followed by lusty applause and a shower of gold confetti. A week later, MTV dedicated an entire episode of *House of Style* to Victoria's Secret, showing footage from the set of the Angels commercial, the early Victoria's Secret Fashion Shows, and some of the company's catalog shoots in New York and the Caribbean. ("I will not have my butt on the runway, ever," Banks says in an interview with the show's host, model Daisy Fuentes. "It's not that gorgeous." Fuentes demurs: "I don't know, I saw *Sports Illustrated*." Banks grabs her microphone and leans in close, responding, "Retouching, retouching!")

Jill Beraud made the most of the media attention in Victoria's Secret stores. Store associates filled the windows with images from the campaign. Television sets were rolled out from employee break rooms and loaded with tapes of the ad, playing on a loop. The Angels' "soundtrack"—featuring abstract New Age and electronic tracks with names like "Behind the Waterfall" and "Bliss Abyss"—played on store speakers and was available to purchase as a six-track CD. None of the choices were random: in the weeks before the launch, Beraud and her team had tested various strategies, putting different combinations of models in the store windows, alone and in groups, to see which versions drew in more shoppers. A few months later, a special edition of the catalog featured the Angels on the cover—another Beraud idea. The crossover was rare for Victoria's Secret. "It was the first time that we were firing on all cylinders and we leveraged all the assets of the company, meaning the catalog and the stores," she said.

The Angels bras were a sales sensation, despite a higher-than-normal price point of $24. At this time, most of Victoria's Secret bras were priced at $15 but sold for as little as $7 with discounts.

Razek saw greater potential for the Angels concept, and incorporated it into the next annual fashion show, in 1998. He summoned the models from the commercial to the runway in New York. Mulder opened the show wearing a pair of elbow-length feathered gloves that gave her birdlike wings, which she flapped as she moved down the runway in white high-cut panties and a push-up bra. That winter, model Laetitia Casta wore a similar pair of wings on the front of the holiday catalog, renamed the "Christmas Dreams and Fantasies" edition. Inside the issue, she and five other models appeared in feathered lingerie, draped across a white Lamborghini Diablo sportscar with swooping silver V and S letters across the side.

Cindy Fedus-Fields was dismayed to see the women as glorified car girls. She had loved the catalog covers with Jill Goodacre in a plush robe or silk pajamas, no cleavage to be seen. The vision of English manor refinement that had sent the catalog's sales numbers soaring only five years earlier was officially gone. With the Angels preening on the covers, the catalog's response rate started to decline. While it would have been easy to blame Razek alone, Fedus-Fields knew he was doing what Wexner wanted, with little regard for the version of "Victoria" she had so carefully crafted. Wexner knew Fedus-Fields wasn't on board with the new brand identity.

On a Tuesday in May 2000, Fedus-Fields flew to Columbus on a 7 a.m. flight from New York for a regularly scheduled quarterly meeting with Wexner. She knew rumors were spreading around the office that she might be fired, but she was confident in her performance. Despite a slight decline in the third quarter of 1999, the catalog generated a record $956 million in sales that year. The meeting didn't last long, she remembered. "It's time for us to part ways," Wexner said, giving no specific reason for firing her. He stood up to leave and reached out his hand to shake hers. "Let's part friends," he said. Fedus-Fields rejected the gesture. She felt betrayed.

After a debrief with the company's lawyer, security escorted her to a limousine waiting outside the building. Inside, she was annoyed to find a therapist who asked if she wanted to talk. "There's nothing to talk about," she said. The therapist accompanied her on the company's private jet back to New York, where Fedus-Fields's office was already being packed up. Her assistants had been fired, too. By the time she got home, it was late in the evening. On that extremely long day, she had worn a brand-new, beige Geoffrey Beene pantsuit. "It was beautiful," she said. "I got home, I took it off, and I put it in the garbage."

CHAPTER 8

Here Come the Consultants

The days of operating like a family business are over.

In the mid-1990s in America, no one knew anyone who didn't shop at the Gap. Its CEO, the obsessive merchant Mickey Drexler, had managed to conquer the hearts of shoppers at all ages and income levels.[1] Teens and moms alike discovered that khakis could be cool and agreed that white T-shirts were a birthright. The simplicity of the Gap's fits-everyone T-shirts and jeans offered Americans a shared cultural language. The brand's advertising featured archival photos of unlikely fashion stars like Ernest Hemingway and Amelia Earhart, both in Gap-style chinos, and Kim Basinger in a no-nonsense white button-down and pearls. Sharon Stone attended the Oscars in one of the Gap's turtlenecks paired with a ballgown skirt. Supermodels wore Gap jeans on the cover of an anniversary edition of *Vogue*. The brand was name-checked on *Seinfeld* and parodied on *Saturday Night Live*. The Gap declared 1998 the year of the khaki, and indeed it was.

Competing against the Gap was demoralizing. The brand had grown quickly in the '90s, opening new stores while the Limited shut down locations. Gap Inc.'s stock price and public reputation was always higher than Limited Brands', no matter how Les Wexner and his merchants tried to repair his apparel brands. As a former executive put it, Wexner could no longer merchandise his way out of problems. A decade earlier, his three largest brands—the Limited, Express, and Lerner—needed to deliver only one or two blockbuster items per season, and sell them at a slightly cheaper price than his competitors, to keep its edge on the market. But in the accelerating race to keep up with trends, Wexner's divisions had abandoned any sense of identity. The Limited was supposed to be a place for suburban moms to get smart pants and jackets, but now it sold halter tops and blue jeans. Express was aimed at younger, single cosmopolitan women, but it had a section of sensible office-ready separates. Specialty retail competitors, like Talbots, Banana Republic, and Ann Taylor, had sharper identities. The Gap, in particular, had a point of view as defined as many European designer labels. The Limited was just their copycat.

Wexner was acutely aware of the problem, not just because several lengthy newspaper and magazine articles speculated that he had lost his touch. (The *New York Times*, in one biting piece, suggested that "the merlin of the mall" had become distracted by concerns around his own legacy.[2] By contrast, Drexler was the "merchant prince" who couldn't miss.) At one point, the Limited's three largest women's apparel brands generated more than half the company's sales, but only 10 percent of the profits due to their rampant discounting. The decline prompted something of an existential crisis in Columbus.

Throughout his impressive career, Wexner had always relied on his own intelligence to evolve the business. He was constantly reading, studying, traveling, and "patterning." Shopping and copying from the best. But by the mid-1990s, he had little time for big-picture thinking. Two dozen executives reported directly to him.

Many entrepreneurs are micromanagers. Drexler was a self-professed one. Wexner, too, preferred to be deeply involved in his divisions. In the early years of the Limited, Wexner's direct mentorship and guidance of young executives, especially merchants and marketers, defined the company's corporate culture of nonstop work and hands-on research. His leadership style was not charismatic, and he could lose his temper: "Shit for brains" was a phrase he liked to hurl. But his staff admired his determination and decisiveness. The company's growing sales only further burnished his reputation. He had turned dozens of his employees into millionaires. "It's an enveloping world," said a buyer at a competitor in 1986. "If you sign up, you're owned. A lot of those people are like Moonies," referring to the cult-like church popular in the 1970s.[3]

Wexner's staff bonded through the intense ritual of his famous Monday night meetings, a practice that had started in the early days of the Limited and never stopped. Each week, executives within each brand convened to discuss and evaluate the prior week's sales. Wexner usually chose one brand's meeting to attend each week. If he arrived late to one, even by more than an hour, the meeting would restart from the beginning. The sessions often began at five or six in the evening and ran until close to midnight. The pressure was intense. Many executives would spend all Sunday preparing. Each week, the merchants examined the sales results, highlighted the problems and successes, and discussed what changes they could enact by the end of that very same week to increase sales during the upcoming weekend. Their focus was extremely short term. The merchants sometimes discussed future launches or seasons, but the priority was the upcoming week. There was no time for transformative thinking.

In the 1990s, the fashion industry was starting to rapidly consolidate into the conglomerates that dominate the industry today. At the high end, there are the European heavyweights LVMH (owner of, among other brands, Louis Vuitton, Dior, and Celine) and Kering (Gucci, Yves Saint Laurent, Balenciaga). At the lower end are companies like H&M (which today owns Arket and Cos) and the J.Crew Group (which includes Madewell). One major benefit of a conglomerate, or strategic group, is that brands can share resources as well as ideas. Wexner was early to the strategic group model, but in the mid-1990s, he realized that he was missing many of the centralized functions that are key to successful groups. He needed a better system for managing his many brands and sharing best practices and talent.

He tackled the problem like a diligent student, albeit one with elite connections and massive financial resources. He hired an executive coach. He sought out advice from Sam Walton, the founder of Walmart and Sam's Club; Jack Welch, the chairman of General Electric; and Wayne Calloway, chief executive of PepsiCo. In 1993, Wexner also hired a Harvard professor named Leonard Schlesinger to visit Columbus, observe the divisions, and diagnose their problems. Schlesinger, who studied successful businesses, recommended Wexner strengthen the brand identities of each of his businesses, lean on consultants for big-picture thinking, and hire experienced retail talents from competitors.[4]

In a matter of years, highly paid consultants with Harvard MBAs filled the halls of the Limited's headquarters in New Albany. Retail stars were poached from Ralph Lauren, the Gap, and J.Crew, lured with sky-high salaries and perks like easy access to company jets. "In Les's mind, the more voices, the better," said an executive who joined in the mid-1990s.

One person who eluded Wexner's advances was Mickey Drexler. The younger man never saw the appeal of working for the Limited, even when Wexner offered Drexler a $1 million signing bonus. Drexler preferred to work for Gap's owners, Don Fisher and his family, because they had no interest in running the company themselves. Drexler also felt that he and Wexner wouldn't work well together. Their approaches to retail were too different. Another factor was Ohio, where Drexler and his family had no desire to live. (Over the years, Wexner continued to monitor his younger rival closely. When Drexler launched Gap Body in 1998, the comfortable cotton intimates collection looked like the first genuine threat to Victoria's Secret to emerge in years. Wexner responded by pushing more cotton underwear and T-shirt bras.)

Other merchants and executives were happy to take Wexner's entice-ments. By the end of the 1990s, half of the Limited's retail divisions boasted new leaders.[5] Not everyone was the right fit. One executive remembered that new people would show up at meetings frequently without any intro-duction and often be replaced with just as little notice.

On Schlesinger's advice, Wexner set up central corporate divisions to handle the long-term, big-picture decisions his divisions' merchants were too busy to consider. For example, Ed Razek, after his 1997 promo-tion, led a central team focused on branding and advertising. Wexner created specialized teams in areas like store design and real estate to tackle projects across the company, regardless of division, and to share best practices.

One of the new divisions would have an outsize effect on the future of Wexner's retail empire. For the first time in his three-decade-long retail career, he started hiring proper fashion designers.

///

In the mid-1990s, if Wexner summoned a young retail executive to have lunch with him, no one in their right mind could turn him down. Wall Street was grumbling at him, but within the industry there was little debate that he was one of the best merchants of all time. Executives knew he was demanding, but working for him came with long-lasting rewards. "If you worked for the Limited in any capacity, you could write your own ticket," one of his merchants said.

Around 1993, Wexner called the head of design at Gap Inc.'s Banana Republic brand, Marie Holman-Rao, and asked her to lunch during one of his trips to Manhattan, thus beginning a yearly tradition of meetings. (They ate at his office. "That was one of his peccadillos," she said. Restaurants were too public and time-consuming.) Wexner was on the hunt for new executive talent, and in the years to come, he tried to hire Holman-Rao for different roles, including the CEO of Lerner. The attention was flattering, but Holman-Rao wasn't ready to leave her job yet. She was still ushering Banana Republic through the massive overhaul that had caught Wexner's attention in the first place. (He followed every other retailer "like a hawk," she said.)

When Holman-Rao first joined Banana Republic to oversee women's apparel, the safari trend that established the brand in the 1980s had waned. And yet, Banana Republic was still pushing the outdoorsy aesthetic. Its stores were decorated with actual jeeps and pictures of rhinos.

Mickey Drexler had never really cared about Banana Republic. The Fishers bought the brand right before they hired him in 1983, and he would have advised them against it. Drexler was more interested in wardrobe essentials—smart versions of the clothing everyone needed—than in novel concepts and trends. But, after he fixed the Gap and launched Old Navy, its cheap-chic counterpart, Drexler decided to give Banana Republic an "essentials" makeover, too. Before the Gap, he had successfully turned Ann Taylor into a popular destination for office attire. He thought Banana could fill the same role at Gap Inc. by selling the blazers and slacks people in the 1990s still wore to work. Holman-Rao, a die-hard Prada devotee, was the ideal person to bring the minimalist look of that Italian brand—and Jil Sander and Helmut Lang, too—to the suburbs. If Ann Taylor had been the 1980s alternative to Giorgio Armani for women, Banana Republic would be the place to buy a black Prada suit even if you didn't know what Prada was.

Holman-Rao, like so many others who climbed the retail ranks, wasn't a traditional fashion designer but a merchant with strong creative instincts, a quality possessed by many of Drexler's best executives. She was a graduate of Macy's merchant training program, eventually rising to president of Perry Ellis's influential menswear label. She stayed with the brand for two years after the designer's death from AIDS-related complications in 1986. (She later left when designer Marc Jacobs and his business partner Robert Duffy arrived.)

At Banana Republic, Holman-Rao took a page from the Perry Ellis playbook and headed to Première Vision, the fabric trade show outside Paris attended by all the top runway designers. There, she bought fine Italian wool crepe to turn into women's work suits. She priced them at a very low markup to not turn off Banana Republic shoppers before they had a chance to try them on. She kept repeating the process with different fabrics and styles: single-button suit jackets and straight-leg pants, everything cut narrower than the boxy, double-breasted 1980s styles. Customers looking for Banana Republic's chunky Irish knits and worn-in cargo pants may have been shocked by the changes, but the world had moved on. All those jeep owners were driving reliable Subarus now. Young professionals who couldn't afford designer clothing soon flocked to Banana Republic. Despite very little advertising, "we were selling cashmere sleeveless tops for $90 and they were flying out of the store," Holman-Rao said.

Wexner sought the same kind of transformation across all his businesses. In 1997, he presented Holman-Rao with an irresistible offer: build and lead a design studio to work with every division—an in-house design SWAT team, as he liked to call it. "You and I will decide which divisions to go into and what they need to have, and you and your group will provide that," he said. Holman-Rao would also be tasked with launching new brands.

When she arrived at Limited Brands, some of Wexner's divisions had already hired their first designers. The Limited had poached talent from Anne Klein, and Structure took the former head of men's design from Calvin Klein. Henri Bendel had picked up an entire team from Donna Karan, including Angela Ahrendts, to design its first in-house collection. (The Bendel collection folded two years later, as the department store continued to suffer. Ahrendts went on to become the CEO of Burberry and then the head of retail at Apple.)

By 1999, Holman-Rao had hired a team of twenty-four creative merchants and designers to support her central SWAT team and embed within each brand. She went to each division leader, explaining how the different pieces in the store should work together to tell a story. "Les not only wanted a coherent viewpoint, but also things that would really, really sell," she said.

Many of the merchants she encountered felt threatened. They did not see what value her team could bring to their brands. They complained that they were being turned into "corporate drones." Holman-Rao was startled by the pushback. "This was the first time I was not in a collaborative environment." But Wexner backed her and the move to embrace in-house design, so the merchants had to play along.

Holman-Rao's top priority was tackling the most challenged divisions, the Limited and Express, where the shop-and-copy strategy ruled. At an Express design meeting in 1997, as executives debated how to focus the brand's identity, Wexner—who had sent his wife, Abigail, to look for ideas in her own closet—said that he wanted to go in a "Ralph Lauren direction." Two weeks later, he changed his mind, directing merchants to pursue a "sexy look."[6] The team eventually landed on a younger version of Ann Taylor, like short skirts paired with blazers. At the Limited, the chosen design direction was a less expensive version of Banana Republic. Neither of those directions was compelling or differentiated, especially compared to Victoria's Secret. Its revenue was growing consistently, and the fashion show and commercials were generating attention. "The one thing that Les thought was that he had a lock on lingerie," Holman-Rao said.

But she disagreed. The executive saw an opportunity to expand beyond all the itchy lace, "the kind that you'd have on for five minutes before you took it off," she said. The Angels bra that launched with fanfare on television in 1997 was coarse and flimsy, and it was soon discontinued. "The women of the early aughts, coming of age, didn't want that kind of stuff," Holman-Rao said. They wanted beautiful but comfortable bras and underwear that could be worn daily. They wanted cotton and seamless styles. She also found the color palette antiquated. Instead of jewel tones and bright pinks, she wanted to see neutrals like black, white, beige, and soft pinks.

Consultants brought in from Boston Consulting Group (BCG) identified similar opportunities. A team based in Chicago began flying into Columbus regularly, shadowing different divisions and delivering endless PowerPoint presentations. The consultants surveyed one hundred single professional women in urban markets through at-home interviews. The subjects came from a very specific demographic: they were twenty-eight-year-old, unmarried college graduates with incomes between $50,000 and $125,000. They were ideal Victoria's Secret customers, young enough to have active social lives and earning enough to justify owning more than a couple of bras. The consultants looked at every item in the women's underwear drawers and asked which ones were their favorites and how much they had paid for them.

The research confirmed that women were wearing Victoria's Secret bras and underwear on special occasions, not day-to-day. "We came back and we said: sexy, glamorous, and comfortable," said Michael Silverstein, a BCG senior partner out of Chicago. "If we can put those three things together, you will win a big market."

When Holman-Rao proposed a new, nearly seamless lightweight Lycra-based line, a more comfortable, everyday version of the Angels line, Wexner and Grace Nichols gave the go-ahead. The new collection, Body by Victoria, promised "high-tech, soft microfiber that hugs and stretches in every direction you do." The bras, bralettes, camisoles, and briefs were available only in white, ivory, light pink, beige, navy, and brown. The black-and-white advertising campaign featured close-ups of models in ballet-like poses with the tagline "All you see is curves." Launched in the spring of 1999, the line generated a robust $209 million in sales its first year, despite the bra's higher-than-normal price, around $35.

Meanwhile, Victoria's Secret established its own in-house design team. In 1998, a designer named John Caleo was one of the first hires. He came from bra manufacturer Warnaco, where he had created some of the most successful bras in the intimates market. His designs included the Olga Secret Shaper—the first bra to be made with foam padding, creating lighter, smoother cups than those filled with traditional cotton fuzz.

Caleo and his initial team saw that Victoria's Secret lacked the infrastructure to support a high-functioning in-house design group. For starters, the team was missing several preproduction functions needed to turn sketches and samples into real products—like fabric specialists, print designers, and quality control systems. All that would come in time. Meanwhile, Victoria's Secret was cutting ties with manufacturers like Warnaco (the maker of the Miracle Bra) and Bestform (the maker of the Angels bra). In the years to come, its sister firm Mast Industries would increasingly connect Victoria's Secret directly with factories that could handle its growing demands for scale, quality, and speed.

/ / /

In early 1996, one of the only remaining bra factories in the United States closed its doors for good. Located in a tiny Alabama town called Monroeville, one hundred miles from the closest city, the plant employed 660 people making bras bound for sale at stores including Walmart and Victoria's Secret. Vanity Fair, one of the largest intimate apparel makers in the country, opened its first plant in Monroeville in 1937, lured to the South (like many other apparel manufacturers) by the promise of cheap labor and the lack of unions.

Then came NAFTA in 1992. The trilateral trade agreement between the United States, Canada, and Mexico minimized taxes and tariffs paid on goods imported into the US, incentivizing manufacturers to move their factories to Mexico, where labor was cheaper. Even before NAFTA, many apparel makers were opening factories in countries like Costa Rica, where laborers earned little more than a dollar an hour.[7]

By contracting out manufacturing, bra makers like Warnaco and Maidenform had less control over the process but more control over their spending. The flexibility allowed them to pivot quickly, moving production wherever trade rules and labor costs afforded them the best price for value. It was the very same strategy Wexner's partner Marty Trust pioneered two decades earlier with Mast Industries, and it had since become industry standard.

Vanity Fair was a holdout, paying $6.33 an hour in Alabama and at its plants in Tennessee and Florida. For a while, its investments in technology (such as automated bra strap–making machines) allowed the firm to keep producing at home. But American factories never caught up to their foreign competitors in efficiency or price. Chinese manufacturers had become so sophisticated that most consumers no longer thought twice about the countries listed on their labels.

When Limited Brands bought Victoria's Secret, in 1982, Mast began sourcing and producing pajamas and robes for the company, but not bras. Few apparel categories are more complex or more labor-intensive to produce than bras, which require thirty to forty pieces, including underwires and strap-adjusting sliders. Each piece is sourced from a different specialist with its own order minimums and timetables. Each piece must be available in a factory for assembly at the same time and in the same color. The assembly process is complicated, too. Bras are three-dimensional; special machinery molds the foam cups into their concave shape. Assembly cannot be totally automated as it can be for T-shirts or knit sweaters. In the 1990s, just four companies (Vanity Fair, Warnaco, Maidenform, and Sara Lee Intimates) manufactured 75 percent of all US bras through owned or contracted factories around the world.[8] And Victoria's Secret bought most of its bras from them, too.

Victoria's Secret would need to create an independent system. Marty Trust wanted to efficiently manufacture and restock the brand's lingerie without relying on the big bra makers. He had factory partnerships everywhere from Korea to Hong Kong, but he was bumping up against limits on the number of items he could import from each country. In 1974, the United States signed the Multifiber Arrangement, a multilateral protectionist measure intended to limit the volume of garments and textiles flowing from "developing countries" like China and Bangladesh to the United States and Western Europe, where local manufacturers could already see their gloomy fate. Every year, for example, only a certain number of cotton trousers could be imported from Hong Kong to the US. In the exporting countries, individual factories battled for the right to fulfill different quotas, which were reassessed every few years to account for countries where manufacturing was surging. (Japan and Hong Kong were the first regions to be heavily limited, creating more opportunities for Taiwan and South Korea, until tougher quotas in those countries pushed manufacturers to consider Southeast Asia, and so on.[9])

Trust thought of Sri Lanka. He'd first visited the island country during a tour of India in 1984 and remembered that it had a small garment district and few quotas. Sri Lanka was an odd choice for investment, as there was an ongoing civil war between the Sinhalese Buddhist majority and the Hindu Tamil minority. But the island's existing garment industry and high literacy rate were attractive. Trust had recognized a strong entrepreneurial spirit in many of the people he met there. And, of course, the cost of labor was dependably low.

Foreigners were not permitted to establish businesses in the country on their own, so Trust needed strong local partners. He met a charismatic

man named Mahesh Amalean who had just started a small apparel manufacturing business in the Sri Lankan capital Colombo with his brothers.
Trust's early partners also included Ashroff Omar and Ajit Dias, the latter
of whom has since left the business. Amalean and Trust each agreed to
invest $45,000 to build a new manufacturing division that would supply
the Limited with a simple category of items that Amalean had experience
making: women's dresses. However, by the time the factory was ready to
begin production, the trade rules had changed, and women's dresses in
Sri Lanka became subject to the quotas. Amalean needed to pivot.

Flipping through a Victoria's Secret catalog on Trust's desk during
a meeting in Colombo, Amalean suggested that his plant manufacture
women's underwear instead. In Sri Lanka, there was no quota for intimate
apparel. The problem was, Amalean knew nothing about making underwear, so Trust invited him to visit one of his plants in China to observe
the process. He also flew Amalean to Ohio to pitch Howard Gross, who
agreed to order a trial run of three thousand panties. Amalean's new plant
exceeded expectations on quality, and Gross committed to using 60 percent of the factory capacity for the next three years.

What Trust really needed, however, was bras. Around around 1990, he
asked Amalean to start manufacturing them, too. Amalean was initially
resistant. He knew how complicated bras were; he had tried and failed to
manufacture them before. Trust would not take no for an answer. He
told Amalean that his resistance left his factories vulnerable to competitors. "You can't cherry-pick the things you like to work on and then leave
the rest to others," Trust said.[10]

Trust suggested bringing in another joint venture partner with the
experience Amalean lacked. The German bra maker Triumph International, the market leader in Europe, was also looking to diversify its factory base, then concentrated mainly in Hong Kong. Triumph's executives
visited Amalean's plants in Sri Lanka and were impressed with his operation, called MAS Holdings. In 1990, Triumph, Mast, and MAS signed on
as equal partners in a new bra-making venture. Triumph would contrib-
ute its systems and process, Mast committed as a major buyer, and MAS
would handle the operations on the ground. A new plant, called Bodyline, located one hour outside Colombo, opened in 1992.

A decade later, more than four thousand workers—the vast majority
women—commuted daily by bus to Bodyline, where they made bras not

just for Victoria's Secret and Triumph, but also for the Gap and Britain's Marks & Spencer. By then, MAS Holdings had grown into a cluster of fifteen companies generating $250 million a year, with factories in the Maldives, Madagascar, Mauritius, and India. MAS had also established its own elastics and fabrics plants in Sri Lanka, to avoid costly imports of raw materials from China. By 2004, Sri Lanka was the largest exporter of intimate apparel in the world. MAS was its largest player and Victoria's Secret's single biggest supplier—the engine behind its unprecedented scale.

Marty Trust resigned from Mast in 2001, the year he turned sixty-seven. His global sourcing machine no longer required its founder's oversight. But Trust had left his mark on Wexner. Wexner could never have scaled the Limited without him and saw him as a true equal. He trusted him implicitly, and with good reason. Trust was no yes-man. Soon, Wexner would have a hard time finding anyone who dared tell him no.

CHAPTER 9

Making (Something Like) Movies

Victoria's Secret chases a high-fashion image as the
brand's top adman, Ed Razek, spins a cinematic fantasy.

In the 1990s, men were from Mars and women were from Venus, or so the decade's best-selling relationship guide would have it.[1] In the spring of 1998, the Victoria's Secret Angels were recast as intergalactic explorers. In the new television commercial, a silver saucer zipped across a purple galaxy of comets and planets before landing in a desert on the fiery, masculine red planet. Four leggy models emerged and gazed toward the sky. "First there was the miracle, then came Angels. Now Victoria's Secret introduces Angels 2000," a sultry female British voice announced. The models on-screen removed their sparkly jackets to reveal matching lingerie—including "the sexiest bra in the galaxy"—and seductively leaned against rock formations.

The production values were more *Spaceballs* than *Star Wars*. A single Union Jack flag, planted in the sand by one of the models, was all that remained of the genteel English heritage that had once been central to the Victoria's Secret story. The television spot was clearly meant to be light-hearted. Stephanie Seymour and Karen Mulder did not belong in outer space; they were high-fashion girls, through and through, and could barely get through their dialogue without laughing. ("The bra of the future . . . is here today!") In the final seconds of the spot, an alien popped out from behind a rock, flinging a bra up into the air à la *2001: A Space Odyssey*.

More than seventy-six million people saw this hokey commercial, an Ed Razek production, when it debuted during the two-part series finale of *Seinfeld*. The advertising trades, and even some of the executives at Victoria's Secret, scoffed at the ad. Les Wexner himself was displeased. A few months earlier, he had parted ways with adman Dick Tarlow because he felt Victoria's Secret needed the full-time attention of a dedicated in-house team of marketers, led by Razek. (Razek was happy to see Tarlow go. "I don't think he liked the competition," said one of Razek's colleagues at the time.) But Wexner thought "Angels 2000" was embarrassing, neither aspirational nor elevated.

"I can't argue with the success of these things, but I don't think you're building toward anything," Wexner told Razek, according to another executive. Where would the models go from Mars? Ten thousand leagues under the sea? What did all this have to do with fashion? Or supermodels? Or Victoria Stewart-White swanning around in her English manor? "It was a conversation that was overdue and had never happened because sales were good," the executive said, pointing back to the kitschy commercials that had preceded "Angels 2000" and featured models palling around with Santa Claus. ("I traded my elves in for Angels!")

Wexner's concerns were valid. By the second half of the 1990s, he was hyper-focused on the potential cinematic impact of his brands, particularly Victoria's Secret. Hollywood director Sidney Lumet's 1995 book *Making Movies*, part memoir, part filmmaking guide, had gripped him. He gave all his top executives a copy. (Wexner, who was obsessed with biographies of leaders like Winston Churchill and Napoleon, had a list of mandatory books for his executives, which also included his "bible," the influential *Profit from the Core* by Chris Zook and James Allen.) "In the movies you have an enormous group of creative people," Wexner said a few years later, adding that he had visited director Steven Spielberg on set to watch him work. "How do they bring all that creative talent together and not explode? Basically it is really a lesson in simple points of coaching and alignment. There is a lot of communication."[2]

While Razek greenlit his intergalactic take on Victoria's Secret, a different vision was quietly emerging from Grace Nichols's store division. The merchants and designers had developed a new collection of cotton bras and underwear, but Wexner was apprehensive about advertising it. Cotton wasn't sexy, he thought. "I don't want to be like Hanes," he said. "We are not an everyday brand." But Wexner's merchants knew women wanted more from Victoria's Secret than lace panties and push-up Miracle Bras. Cotton pieces were comfortable and less expensive.

Jill Beraud, then Nichols's head of marketing, knew she could change

Wexner's mind if she backed up her instincts with data. Instead of pitching him a commercial for the cotton collection, which he would surely reject, she suggested what was then called a "point-of-sale video," a clip that would play on the television sets in Victoria's Secret stores.

The concept was soft and sophisticated, set in the ornate Oheka Castle in Huntington, Long Island, once one of the largest private homes in the country. In the spot, three young, fresh-faced models wore the brand's latest collection of simple cotton bras and underwear while walking in and around the grand mansion. The portrait photographer Max Vadukul, known for his campaigns for Yohji Yamamoto and editorials for Italian *Vogue*, photographed the models for the catalog, and Jeff Madoff, the in-house videographer, shot the clip. Recalling the catalog's refined '90s era, the cameras focused on the models' faces, their taut bodies, the wind flowing through their hair. But this new approach was modern, stark and sophisticated in black-and-white. There was no lace to be seen. The models were younger, poutier. A delicate opera aria provided the soundtrack—Razek's suggestion.

Razek had approved the concept from a series of ideas proposed by Nancy Binger, the creative director in the stores division. For Binger, the campaign was about the comfort and freedom of being home alone in cotton lingerie. "I saw our business as a cosmetic company," said Binger. "We were in the business of making people feel confident." Razek saw the ad completely differently. He was overheard wondering to a colleague on set, "Who is the guy who has all these women that he can keep as concubines in this giant house?"

Months later, when the cotton collection arrived in Victoria's Secret stores, Beraud made the launch feel like an Angels-level event. The windows were decorated with Vadukul's images. A TV set running a loop of the video was wheeled out to sit just inside the entry of each store—what Beraud called "the third window"—and the company's opera music soundtrack was piped through the store's speakers. The strategy worked. The cotton collection sold massively; it would become a $500 million line of business in its first year. Wexner recognized that the video was compelling enough to use as a television commercial. When it aired in the spring of 1999, images from the shoot were also used as ads in *Vogue*, with the tagline "This, too, is Victoria's Secret."

The cotton commercial starred two models who would become central to the Angels narrative in the years to come: Heidi Klum and Adriana Lima. (The third model in the spot, the French Laetitia Casta, stopped posing for Victoria's Secret in 2000 and later said she felt objectified by the work.[3])

Lima was shy, only fifteen and far from home in the city of Salvador in Brazil, where she won a modeling contest and a ticket to New York City. In 1999, when she walked in Victoria's Secret's runway show for the first time, she was one of a few women given a thong bodysuit without a mini-skirt or dress to hide behind. (Lima's agent had told Victoria's Secret that Lima was already sixteen, according to a former employee. Lying about age was common in the youth-obsessed modeling world. The brand's team discovered the truth only later, when they surprised the model with a birthday cake on set, and she told them she was actually *turning* six-teen.) Lima would go on to become the longest-serving Victoria's Secret Angel and one of its most famous spokeswomen, able to flip seamlessly between cutesy and sultry.

But it was Lima's older and more assured costar Klum who would become the de facto face of Victoria's Secret in the early aughts. Klum fit the brand's image perfectly: her long legs, ample (but not too ample) bust, and wide smile offered a sophisticated version of the classic all-American (albeit German-born) beauty ideal. And she was a natural charmer on camera—relaxed, beaming, and delighted to toe the party line.

Klum was virtually unknown when she first walked the runway for Victoria's Secret, in 1997. As a teen, she had won a modeling contest in Germany and found herself catapulted from her small hometown outside Cologne to Paris and Milan. But she didn't have the look of high-fashion modeling's waifish, grungy phase. Designers and casting directors told her she was too short and too wide. "I was told over and over again that my looks were too normal, too girl-next-door, too American Pie," she said later.[4] She was also told to lose weight. Klum moved to New York in 1994 to try to break in with commercial clients, like mainstream catalogs and department stores.

Klum soon became a self-described catalog queen, modeling for Newport News and JCPenney. Eventually, Klum pushed her agency, Elite, to get her an audition with Victoria's Secret. The timing was right: the catalog's creative directors needed someone to fill in for Elle Macpherson, who was on maternity leave. Victoria's Secret quickly picked Klum for a catalog shoot in Mustique and then booked her for the annual fashion show in 1997, her first turn on any runway. In 1998, Klum landed the coveted cover of the *Sports Illustrated: Swimsuit Edition*, her biggest career break yet. As she promoted that cover on radio, talk shows, and late-night television, Klum proved to be a natural, always charming interviewers with her clipped German accent and love of yodeling.

Klum was a rising star, no question, but she existed largely outside of the insular high-fashion world, even as designers and luxury brands began to embrace the power of film and television. In the mid-1990s, MTV's *House of Style* was one of the network's most popular programs. Hosted by Cindy Crawford for its first six years, the show presented fashion personalities like designer Todd Oldham as pseudo–rock gods. VH1 and E! rolled out their own fashion programming, broadcasting runway shows from New York and Paris with backstage interviews with designers and celebrities. The 1995 documentary *Unzipped* followed charismatic designer Isaac Mizrahi, and *Catwalk*, released that same year, documented the drama and glitz of top model Christy Turlington's jet-set career. Calvin Klein and Ralph Lauren, among other designers, regularly appeared in their own labels' advertising campaigns. Gianni Versace was already famous for his supermodel posse when his 1997 murder became an international story. At the same time, a new class of under-forty designers, including John Galliano, Alexander McQueen, and Tom Ford, was using theatrical runway productions and celebrity endorsements to court mainstream fame.

VH1 boosted mainstream awareness of fashion when, in 1995, it televised its first annual Fashion and Music Awards. The variety show brought together musicians, actors, models, and designers to hand out awards for "most stylish music video" and "model of the year," among other categories, in between musical performances and mini–runway shows. The VH1 awards struggled to find the right tone during its seven years on air, and the fashion elite made for a touchy crowd. Nevertheless, the television exposure had an impact. "Housewives in Cleveland know who Tom Ford is ('that cute balding guy on the VH1 Fashion Awards who works for Gucci')," *New York* magazine reported in 1996.[5]

Still, fashion models in the late 1990s struggled to replicate the success of the original supermodels like Christy Turlington and Cindy Crawford, who became household names almost a decade earlier. The waif era had failed to produce any mainstream celebrities since Kate Moss broke through in 1992. Amber Valletta and Shalom Harlow had thriving runway careers, but few people outside fashion knew their names. Revlon, guided by Tarlow, had once exclusively hired the biggest supermodels to star in its ad campaigns. In 1996, the beauty giant chose Halle Berry as its first Hollywood actress campaign star. Competitors followed suit.

"Nobody cares about models anymore," said Linda Wells, the editor of Condé Nast's beauty magazine *Allure*, in an editorial meeting in late 1998.[6] When *Vogue* chose actress Renée Zellweger to front its influential September edition that same year, the message was clear: readers preferred Hollywood to high fashion. The magazine even described actresses as presenting "smarter" than models.[7]

Wexner and Razek didn't care about Revlon and *Vogue*'s new Hollywood obsession, and they used the industry shift to their advantage. They wanted shoppers to see Victoria's Secret as high fashion, and they needed to maintain its growing supermodel reputation by finding a Stephanie Seymour or Claudia Schiffer for a new generation. And in 1998 the perfect woman emerged. Her name was Gisele Bündchen, and she was a bona fide fashion sensation. Eastern European models had ruled the runways of the early 1990s after the fall of the Berlin Wall. But as trends turned sexier and sweatier at the end of the decade, designers preferred tanned Brazilians, especially those from the south of the country, where waves of German immigration since the 1800s had yielded unusually tall women.

Bündchen first caught the industry's attention in 1997, when she walked down Alexander McQueen's runway topless except for a slash of white paint across her chest. She was model-thin, of course, but she was no waif. She had breasts. Fashion editors and photographers, always looking for the next trend, quickly identified her as a signal that the heroin chic, grunge era was ending. Bündchen had a sexy body, but her face was unusual, somewhat androgynous, and sufficiently avant-garde to excite the same fashion community that had rejected traditionally beautiful women like Klum. Bündchen looked strong and healthy. She could credibly tell reporters that her childhood dream had been to play professional volleyball. "Say goodbye to bulimia, black lip balm and the girls from intensive care; hello, flesh and libido," *Newsweek*[8] declared, breathlessly describing the impact of Bündchen's runway rise. *Vogue* proclaimed that the "bodacious body" was back, thanks to her.[9]

Laura Berkman, the Victoria's Secret catalog's creative director, realized Bündchen was perfect for the brand. Razek and Monica Mitro, his leading publicist, agreed. They invited Bündchen to walk in the February 1999 runway show. She was just eighteen years old.

From Bündchen's point of view, the Victoria's Secret job registered as little more than just one of countless runway shows she walked that year, albeit one that paid well and required more television interviews. "I normally don't do lingerie but I think it's okay with [my parents], since I'm not wearing anything small or too sexy," she told the Style Channel.[10] Bündchen knew Victoria's Secret's runway show stylist Brana Wolf, who had styled her for a Steven Meisel editorial in Italian *Vogue* the year before. Wolf butted heads with Razek and Mitro. Her approach to fashion was subtle, minimalist, and sophisticated. Wolf was not interested in creating the kind of kinky costumes the brand preferred. Her taste in models was similarly esoteric: she preferred unusual faces like Carmen Kass over all-American types like Tyra Banks. But Bündchen was the rare model who pleased both Wolf and Razek—she was a star from everyone's point of view.

"Gisele is probably, if not the hottest model in the world at the moment, certainly one of the hottest models in the world," Razek said proudly in 1999.[11] "Gisele wouldn't have done the show, say, four years ago."[12] No matter that "four years ago," Bündchen was fourteen years old and had only just started modeling in São Paulo. Razek spun the story to highlight his brand's growing status in fashion. And he positioned Bündchen as the central character. She had plenty of personality, even if she would never convincingly cross over into acting. She also represented exactly what Victoria's Secret wanted to be: tasteful and high fashion, but with sex appeal.

Bündchen's agent, Anne Nelson, knew that fashion's most influential editors, photographers, and designers likely had no idea she was working with the lingerie brand. The fashion community was based mostly in Paris and Milan, and no one outside the US market paid much attention to Victoria's Secret. But American fashion gatekeepers did bristle at the brand's casting success. *Vogue*'s editor in chief, Anna Wintour, and its creative director, Grace Coddington, in particular, "hated that the major girls worked for Victoria's Secret," said one of the many people who worked on *Vogue* and Victoria's Secret sets at the time. "They thought it was degrading for the girls to run around in their underwear."

But Victoria's Secret money was nearly impossible to turn down. In fashion in the 1990s (and still today), even the most innovative designers and most influential magazines often could not afford to pay models, stylists, and photographers much, if any, money. Models are still sometimes paid only in clothes. And the high-paying luxury jobs, reserved mainly for once-a-season print campaigns, were few and far between. Almost everyone in fashion relied on big commercial clients like Revlon and Calvin Klein to earn a living. Victoria's Secret followed those brands' example, offering not just good salaries but also ample production budgets to hire the best creatives in the industry. Victoria's Secret could afford, for example, to hire Herb Ritts to direct a television commercial or Naomi Campbell for a runway show. "It was very lush budgets, and there was never any sort of restriction on anything," said someone who worked on the runway shows during this time.

Bündchen approached modeling like a serious job, not as a ticket to fame. She told *Rolling Stone* that being a supermodel diva was "so over, it's ten years ago."[13] She was determined to earn as much as possible in her notoriously short-lived profession, for herself and for her family. Her childhood in the small southern Brazilian town of Horizontina was rustic and simple. Her father was a teacher, her mother a bank clerk. She grew up sharing one bedroom with five sisters. As her profile rose, Bündchen and her agent strategically balanced safe, commercial jobs, like ads for Ralph Lauren or appearances in *Vogue*, with edgy and often nonpaying gigs, like editorials in the industry magazine *Big* or runway appearances for little-known designers like Hussein Chalayan.[14] And throughout it all, Bündchen built a reputation as a ruthlessly professional modeling machine: on time, sober, never complaining, and drama-free. She reportedly earned $5 million in 1999, when she appeared on the cover of American *Vogue* a whopping three times; starred in campaigns for Valentino and Dior; and earned the Model of the Year award from VH1 and *Vogue*. As if that wasn't enough, the following year she started dating *Titanic* heartthrob Leonardo DiCaprio.

Razek and Berkman moved quickly to tap Bündchen as an Angel, a term that Razek would soon reserve only for contract models. By paying her top dollar, the company could signal to the fashion industry that it was no longer a tacky mall brand, that it no longer needed to rely on models considered past their initial peak. "In that way, VS bought its way into the high-fashion industry," said a modeling agent. Razek described the strategy with Bündchen as "dipping her in gold," according to a colleague.

In 2000, Bündchen signed a five-year contract with the company, earning her about $5 million a year, according to sources with knowledge of her deal. Bündchen's days were extremely valuable at that time; she was commanding as much as $100,000 for a single-day shoot. Years later, Bündchen admitted that signing on to model lingerie was a "tough choice," but one that gave her "financial freedom."[15] And she was able to insist that the brand never send her down the runway without something covering her butt.

///

In the late 1990s, a mania infected Wall Street. Virtually any stock in a company with a tangential connection to the internet, no matter how obscure, skyrocketed in price. "If one or two of them work, it'll make up for the five that likely will blow up," one money manager told the *Washington Post* in 1998, describing the dot-com boom that had not yet gone bust. "They definitely are 'the field of dreams.'"[16]

Wexner wanted to ride the wave. The stock price for Intimate Brands (IBI), the public parent of Victoria's Secret and Bath & Body Works, was stagnant for much of 1998, despite the bull market. The catalog had reported some bum quarters, which its executives publicly blamed on too many catalogs and some merchandising mistakes. But IBI's share price started to pick up at the end of the year, following a few key announcements. Wexner had managed to poach Robin Burns, a talented beauty executive at Estée Lauder, to expand Victoria's Secret's beauty division. The category already generated $475 million in sales a year, but Wexner knew it had the potential to be much bigger. In December 1998, Victoria's Secret also launched its first website. It was little more than a lo-fi digital version of the catalog, but shoppers could register their email addresses and request subscriptions. A Columbus-based agency, Resource Marketing, which worked primarily with Apple on projects for the Midwest, had designed and launched the site.

The website desperately needed traffic. Few people knew it even existed. Before the 1998 holidays, with the fashion show coming up in

February, Wexner and Razek asked the website team if they could air live video from the show online. At the time, streaming video was rare. Most users relied on sluggish dial-up connections and were still learning how to use basic functions like search engines.

But there *were* a few companies that professed to see the future. One was the Dallas-based start-up Broadcast.com, cofounded under another name in 1995 by the serial entrepreneur (and future Dallas Mavericks owner and *Shark Tank* star) Mark Cuban. The site streamed live and recorded audio and video from concerts, sporting events, press conferences, and even President Clinton's grand jury testimony, taped and released in 1998. For most Americans who lacked broadband internet connections at home, Broadcast .com's video streams often resembled stop-motion films. They were grainy and rarely occupied more computer screen space than the size of a business card. The technology for multi-thread streaming, which allowed multiple users to watch the same stream at the same time, was primitive. "It was like a seven-lane highway when it needed to be a *seventy*-lane highway," said Ken Weil, the head of the Victoria's Secret website at the time. Still, Wexner and Razek decided to try live streaming the Victoria's Secret Fashion Show on the brand's website, powered by Broadcast.com.

Less than a month before the show, Nancy Kramer, the founder of Resource Marketing who worked closely with Razek, suggested advertising the webcast during the most important television event of the year: the Super Bowl between the Denver Broncos and the Atlanta Falcons. Kramer's team pitched Razek several ideas, including one ad featuring a montage of footage from past fashion shows. He and Wexner loved it. Victoria's Secret paid $1.5 million ($2.8 million today) for a thirty-second ad.[17] More than eighty-four million viewers tuned in to the game. The ad's copy was simple, just as Razek always wanted: "The Broncos won't be there, the Falcons won't be there. You won't care. Victoria's Secret Fashion Show, live in 72 hours only on the world wide web exclusively at www .victoriassecret.com."

Kramer's team also placed ads for the internet show in the *New York Times* and *Women's Wear Daily*, targeting financial analysts. "High Tech, High Fashion, Hi Wall Street," read the copy accompanying a full-page image of a glowing, busty Tyra Banks in a bra and briefs, a floor-length floral robe billowing around her. "This Wednesday, tickers will be racing after the markets close," the ad continued. "It's proof positive that you can turn more than profits on the internet." (The *Wall Street Journal* rejected the original ad with Banks for being too risqué, but agreed to instead run one with an image of Karen Mulder in a camisole and tap pants.)

The day of the show, Stephanie Seymour rang the closing bell at the New York Stock Exchange before crossing the street to the show at Cipriani, where Wall Street analysts mingled with the likes of Donald Trump, actor Wesley Snipes, and *Vogue* editor Polly Mellen. The lingerie show, advertised that day on the banner on Yahoo.com's home page, started forty minutes late, adding to the anticipation online. As Klum and Bündchen hit the runway in their silvery thongs and gauzy capes, the web stream overloaded, leaving many users with blank screens. While Broadcast.com had prepared to host as many as five hundred thousand simultaneous views, few people were able to watch the stream. Those who did were rewarded with little more than dark, jagged pixels resembling women walking up and down a runway. Back in the Victoria's Secret offices in Columbus, Beraud remembers, the mood was funereal. People were crying. Their expensive stunt had completely failed.

But in New York City, Razek proved his talents as a spin doctor. "Of course we melted the computers—we knew we would," he told one reporter,[18] boasting that as many as two million people had logged on to the brand's website to try to watch the show. He later described the traffic spike on Victoria's Secret's website after the Super Bowl commercial break as "the biggest collective behavioral shift in the history of mass communications." In the days that followed the show's "airing," every major paper ran a piece about the internet milestone, declaring the snafu a pop cultural event and blaming the crash on subpar technology, not Victoria's Secret. *Adweek* named the webcast the marketing event of 1999. IBI's stock price shot up 11 percent the day after the show, reaching its highest point in a year.

"This is very much a perception-and-momentum business, and all of a sudden they're the talk of the industry," Mark Cuban told the magazine *Adweek*, doing some spinning of his own. Two months later, he sold Broadcast.com to Yahoo for $5.7 billion in stock. Cuban shrewdly hedged his Yahoo shares, buying a form of Wall Street insurance to protect against stock price declines. As Cuban anticipated, Yahoo's share price plummeted a year later when the dot-com bubble burst and his billions were protected.

/ / /

The 1999 webcast elevated the Victoria's Secret Fashion Show to a global front-page story. But a blurry stream wouldn't seem charming a second time around. The 2000 fashion show needed to outshine the earlier runways in every respect.

Razek turned to an energetic Frenchman named Alexandre de Betak—once dubbed "the enfant sublime of the catwalk" by *New York* magazine.[19] At thirty-one years old, de Betak was already respected for staging the most ambitious runway shows in fashion. He'd created a forest with falling snow for the American designer John Bartlett, and a motion-activated runway floor that controlled the soundtrack for Donna Karan. Models loved de Betak. Designers, famously a volatile and insecure set, trusted him to turn their fifteen-minute shows into unforgettable spectacles. De Betak was an uncommon specialist in fashion. Unlike his competitors in runway production, who oversaw public relations and myriad other image-related strategies, de Betak was focused only on the runway.

Razek needed to ramp up the spectacle for Victoria's Secret. But how? Immediately, he and de Betak explored staging the show abroad. London, Victoria's Secret's faux hometown, was the obvious choice—until Razek received an unexpected call and a compelling offer from Hollywood's most influential power player, producer Harvey Weinstein.

Weinstein and his brother Bob were the founders of Miramax, the most important independent film studio of the 1990s. They were known for producing and distributing stylish, highly anticipated, award-winning films—from Gus Van Sant's *Good Will Hunting* to Quentin Tarantino's *Pulp Fiction*. Weinstein wielded his growing power and influence each summer during the Cannes Film Festival. The movie industry's most prestigious event was just as famous for its films as for the surrounding hoopla—ten days of nonstop glitzy galas, yacht parties, and black-tie events filled with top actors, Russian oligarchs, and media barons. The festival's unofficial, but closely followed, dress code said it all: women were required to wear high heels on the red carpet, no exceptions.

In the 1990s, Miramax dominated the festival, premiering and ruthlessly acquiring coveted films, and hosting exclusive parties. Weinstein was known as a notorious bully even then, but he had not yet been unmasked as a criminal abuser of women. (As the world learned later, Cannes was the site of at least three of his alleged sexual assaults.)

Weinstein's favorite party was the annual amfAR Gala, benefiting

Elizabeth Taylor's American Foundation for AIDS Research. Under his influence, the party had become the most exclusive event of the film festival, assembling the most stars per square foot in the French Riviera.

Weinstein wanted Victoria's Secret models at the 2000 amfAR dinner. Why not stage a fashion show there? From Razek's perspective, the association with the legendary festival and its hottest-ticket event, with Elizabeth Taylor and Elton John due to cohost, was unbeatable. De Betak agreed. "I understood the challenge," he said, describing the earlier Victoria's Secret shows as "borderline misogynistic." Razek and Mitro "were really open to anything," de Betak said. "It was a huge challenge to make something interesting out of a commercial product, which objectively, fashionably speaking, had no place on the runway."

De Betak hired the in-demand stylist Charlotte Stockdale, whose own background could have inspired the fictional Victoria. Half French and half British, Stockdale was the daughter of a baronet and had grown up in an eighteenth-century home in the English countryside. She'd attended boarding school with the actress Sienna Miller and dabbled in modeling before starting her styling career assisting Katie Grand on early issues of the London indie magazine *Dazed & Confused*. Stockdale's styling exuded a confident eccentricity that would later earn her long partnerships with Karl Lagerfeld and Dolce & Gabbana. De Betak also brought in John Pfeiffer, formerly of the communications agency KCD, who was establishing himself as a casting director, another newly emerging specialization in fashion.

De Betak was adamant that the Victoria's Secret Fashion Show should extend further than the runway. After all, the excitement of the Cannes Film Festival spilled over to the Promenade de la Croisette, the central boardwalk filled with street performers and people watchers, and to the Hotel du Cap-Eden-Roc, the uber-luxury hotel where actors like Mark Wahlberg and Sharon Stone holed up with their entourages for the week. To garner any attention amid the chaos, Victoria's Secret needed to lavishly announce its arrival.

De Betak thought of the Concorde—the supersonic passenger aircraft that crossed the Atlantic in less than five hours—which he considered the "sexiest plane in the world." With tickets at nearly $10,000 a pop, flying on the Concorde was a status symbol for the global elite—people like Ronald Perelman and Michael Jackson, whose time was infinitely more valuable than money. De Betak had a vision of a Concorde emblazoned with the Victoria's Secret logo flying low over the film festival, so everyone would look up and know the Angels were in town. He went to Air France, the only company flying Concordes in the South of France, and asked to charter a direct flight from New York to Nice.

Air France said no, according to de Betak. The airline no longer offered direct Concorde flights from New York to Nice, only to Paris. De Betak was adamant that the models ride the supersonic plane all the way over the Atlantic to their destination—otherwise, what was the point? Undeterred, de Betak asked Air France to allow him to join a Concorde training flight from New York to Paris, where he spoke directly with some pilots. The problem was excess weight, they told him, and de Betak offered to cut the passenger list down to just forty from one hundred and send the luggage on a separate plane. Could Air France do it then? The answer was yes.

Next step, branding. The Victoria's Secret logo was emblazoned on both sides of the plane, just behind the cockpit. Inside the cabin, special pink menus were made up for the guests, who included not just the models but also a handful of reporters brought along to document the fantasy experience. "It has to be said that there are worse ways to spend an afternoon than traveling at Mach 2.02 with some of the most beautiful women in the world," wrote Simon Mills, milking his assignment for London's *Sunday Times*, even though most of the models spent the flight sleeping. Mills spent a paragraph describing the models' "bottoms," which he saw as "dinky little orbs of steely flesh and bone when their owners are standing still, a brace of cantaloupes getting jiggy in a denim tote bag when they are on the move."[20]

De Betak, fastidious and obsessive, stage-managed the Concorde's touchdown in Nice. He chose the exact time of the landing so that the sunset would light the models as they descended the staircase from the plane to the tarmac. Photojournalists were on hand to capture the moment. "I wanted it to be the perfect picture," he said. The models wore matching baby pink leather jackets with angel wings embroidered on the back, with the Victoria's Secret and Air France logos gleaming on the aircraft behind them.

The Concorde negotiation was just one of many logistic complications Victoria's Secret encountered in France. The company was not accustomed to working at such a grandiose scale, much less in a foreign country. The teams scrambled to obtain special permits to bring real animal feathers and fur for the costumes into the country. Several of the American models lacked work visas. By the time the team flew to the South of France, the seamstresses had finished only half the show's looks. They worked all night before the show in a "war room" at the Hôtel Martinez.

In the days leading up to the show, the backstage at the Palm Beach Casino was chaotic and cliquey, said Libby Callaway, one of the reporters covering the event for the *New York Post*. "It was like high school back there," she said. The eastern European models all hung together, as did the Brazilians. Eva Herzigová and Daniela Peštová were feuding and had to be kept apart. Few of the models spoke English, and many were teenagers (one, an American named Danita Angell, was fourteen). The American and British models were more relaxed, cracking open beers and tanning between rehearsals. The most famous models had their own area, cordoned off by a curtain, and for good reason: amfAR and Miramax executives, especially Weinstein, were frequently roaming around.

The model casting was also in flux until the day of the show. Claudia Schiffer was expected to join, according to employees who helped produce the event. But Schiffer wanted a higher rate and would participate only if she opened the show, typically considered the most prestigious slot. This jostling was common in the fashion business. Often, models waited until the day of the production to push Razek for a bigger paycheck, especially if they caught wind of the rates of their peers. This year in Cannes was special. The opening slot was better spent on Bündchen, whose schedule was so packed that she arrived in Cannes just a few hours before showtime. Razek had just invested a ton of money in her, and he needed to make a clear statement that she was now the face of the brand. Instead of finding a way to placate Schiffer, he allowed the producers to call her bluff. The model eventually agreed to walk the show anyway, employees remembered, but it was too late to include her in the runway lineup.

Bündchen opened the twenty-two-minute show in a light teal sequined open cape-top worn over tiny matching briefs. A giant screen framed the top of the runway and set the mood for the elements-themed show: first water, when models wore shimmery blue lingerie; then heaven, when out came the white wings; and next hell, marked by red lingerie with bondage-style details. Then, the stage went dark, and the screen filled with lightning and an explosion of gold. Out of this big bang, the models reappeared for a final turn down the runway decked in gold bustiers, G-strings, and micro-miniskirts. The model lineup featured original supers—including Stephanie Seymour, in her last appearance for Victoria's Secret—and new stars like Lima, Klum, and another rising runway favorite, sixteen-year-old Czech model Karolína Kurková. The least-known models were the most exposed on the runway. Overall, the lingerie at Cannes was skimpier and more transparent than the brand had ever shown before.

The audience included Monaco's Prince Albert and actors Gregory Peck and Joaquin Phoenix, the star from *Gladiator*. (He left for the bar mid-show.) Afterward, Weinstein roped Klum into donating a massage during the gala's live auction. He asked actors James Caan and Kenneth Branagh to lie across a grand piano onstage so Klum could demonstrate her skills to the audience. "I remember looking back, and Joan Rivers was disgusted," said Callaway. (Caan won the bid for $31,000.)

Online, the Victoria's Secret Cannes webcast did not crash. In the year since the first live-streamed show, the brand's tech team had worked with Broadcast.com to upgrade the site, hosting it on powerful servers and learning from other large-scale video streams how to handle the traffic. An overflow of people still logged on to watch the show, but instead of crashing the entire video, some users were redirected to a "waiting room" page, where they could wait to watch the show after its initial stream. Razek later boasted that two million people tuned in for the video stream,[21] which went live in the afternoon in New York City and during lunchtime in Los Angeles. The show's success cemented his reputation: a few months later, *Brandweek* named Razek marketer of the year. "There isn't a photographer, art director or model today we couldn't work with," he told the outlet. "That wouldn't have been the case five years ago."[22] Victoria's Secret was untouchable, and Razek was just getting started.

CHAPTER 10

What Is Sexy?

With Victoria's Secret's "fashion credibility" intact, the
Angels invade television.

Nearly nude supermodels made Victoria's Secret famous for bejeweled push-up bras and sparkling gold corsets. But the brand's actual customers had different priorities.[1] The comfort-oriented Body by Victoria line was an instant hit, generating more than $200 million in sales in 1999 and over $520 million two years later. "That's bigger than many bra brands," Grace Nichols, the chief executive of the stores division, told analysts.[2]

Twenty years after opening its first store, Victoria's Secret was a roaring success. The brand was no longer just the plucky disruptor with a catalog. It was the most dynamic player in a rapidly growing retail category. US sales of intimate apparel grew from $10.3 billion in 1996 to close to $12 billion in 1999. Every American retailer wanted a piece of it. And the competition was finally taking proper notice of Victoria's Secret. In the mid-1990s, most major American bra makers, including Warnaco and Maidenform, counted Victoria's Secret as a client at one point or another. But as Mast Industries developed its own network of bra manufacturers, Victoria's Secret shifted from client to outright competitor. Take Warnaco, the maker of Victoria's Secret's Miracle Bra. Its demanding chief executive Linda Wachner cut ties with Victoria's Secret in 1998 because she suspected the brand was copying her firm's designs and producing them with cheaper manufacturers.[3] Warnaco responded by releasing and marketing its own version of the Miracle Bra. The style, called Nothing But Curves, was a strong seller at department stores but not successful enough to keep Warnaco from filing for bankruptcy protection just one year later.

Scrambling to avoid a similar fate, American bra manufacturers poured more money into advertising than ever before. In 2001, Playtex, one of the country's oldest bra makers, tried to shake off its prim reputation with a $20 million campaign to rebrand its most successful style, the "18 Hour" bra. The ads featured a glamorous woman wearing red lipstick and a black bra with the tagline "A Woman Has Many Sides, We Support Everyone." Meanwhile, Victoria's Secret's mall peers tried to grab a piece of the intimates market, too. Gap Inc. expanded GapBody, its unfussy cotton intimates sub-brand launched in 1998, and J.Crew quietly began selling simple bras and panties.

To differentiate itself from the pragmatic department store bra lines and the clean and classic mall brands, Victoria's Secret's advertising rarely mentioned the functionality of its bras. Whenever the brand's executives suggested highlighting fit or comfort, Les Wexner would repeat an old maxim: "We sell hope, not help." Ed Razek agreed with Wexner. "I don't get into product attributes," he said. "We're telling a story."

In the nineties, Calvin Klein reigned as American fashion's most provocative marketer. His black-and-white advertising campaigns brought a rare sophistication to mass-market goods, namely men's boxers printed with the Calvin Klein logo along the waistbands. Brooding models leaned against blank studio backdrops, leaving all the focus on their bodies—whether skinny or chiseled. Klein's advertising featured minimal slogans or taglines. The images invited viewers to fill in the blanks. A series of 1992 ads costarring Kate Moss and Mark Wahlberg, then known as Marky Mark, exemplified the brand's stark and seductive style. Klein's ambiguity often provoked controversy in the press: some observers interpreted what they saw as glamorizing drug use or sexualizing children. In any case, the ads always got people talking.

As Victoria's Secret distanced itself from the campy tone of its original Angels commercials, the brand created its own version of Calvin Klein's sensual, evocative sophistication. French portrait photographer Dominique Issermann shot a series of print and TV ads presenting Victoria's Secret with a new creative direction. Nearly all the ads featured models in a studio setting, their bare bodies shot in intimate close-ups, under high-contrast lighting, and in black-and-white. Issermann's work was dramatic, mysterious, and elegant. No naughty Santa, no Angels wings.

Issermann had started her career collaborating with avant-garde filmmakers, including Jean-Luc Godard, and photographing actors on Federico Fellini's sets in the late 1960s. In the 1970s, French designer Sonia Rykiel, known for outfitting a new generation of stylish, self-possessed French-women, asked Issermann to shoot her advertising campaigns. Their part-nership continued for a decade and led to more fashion campaigns for Issermann. She often worked with the cinematographer Darius Khondji, known for films directed by David Fincher and Bernardo Bertolucci. (She was also a longtime romantic partner of the meditative singer-songwriter Leonard Cohen.)

Issermann directed a memorable fall 1999 commercial for a new line of Victoria's Secret bras, dubbed "Desire." In the spot, lingering close-ups of six models' faces were interspersed with quick shots of cleavage, as a narrator asked, "What is desire?" Each woman responded with a different conceptual answer while giving her best bedroom eyes. "Desire can never be satisfied, but it keeps me going," offered Eva Herzigová. Razek wrote the copy for the ad, which drew mixed reactions. *Adweek*'s columnist Bar-bara Lippert lambasted Victoria's Secret's efforts to be "arty, intellectual" as "boob noir" in 1999,[4] and later described the ads as *Playboy* for the late 1990s." (*Saturday Night Live* spoofed the ad in a sketch featuring a model's breasts that "spoke," when pressed together, in a French-accented falsetto. A voice-over called it "the new voice of sexy."[5])

Issermann's striking style was most evocative without dialogue. In another of her Victoria's Secret commercials, from 2000, Gisele Bünd-chen shimmies and throws up her hands while sitting on a rotating chair in a black-box studio set to a soundtrack of Daft Punk's "One More Time." The future hit song was not yet formally released, so many Americans heard it for the first time in the ad. Bündchen appears free and confident, wearing a simple Body by Victoria black bra and briefs. Several Body by Victoria commercials during these years communicated a similar feeling of confidence and intimacy. "We want your personality to come through, we want this to be about you and you connecting with the women on the other side of the camera lens," Nancy Binger, head of marketing for the stores division, told the models during these shoots. The Body by Vic-toria campaigns translated into striking print campaigns, which were installed in stores, decorating alcoves in thick black frames, and in 2000 began appearing more frequently in *Vogue*, *Harper's Bazaar*, and other women's fashion magazines.

By the early 2000s, Beraud had created a robust in-house market-ing division, launching new bra styles with multipronged Angels-style strategies. Her team amassed and analyzed data from Victoria's Secret "Angels" credit cards, customer loyalty programs, and surveys. In the first years of that decade, one survey showed that nearly 90 percent of the brand's customers "loved or liked" the Angels. Heidi Klum and Tyra Banks were, by far, the most popular. (Wexner had periods in his career when he forbade focus groups. He felt customers didn't know what they wanted, and that surveys represented customer preferences in the past, not the future. But during the first decade of the 2000s, Wexner allowed his executives to survey customers and present their findings in monthly brand meetings. Still, he preferred his merchants to spend time in stores, watching and talking to shoppers themselves.)

Beraud also introduced one of Victoria's Secret's most powerful ongoing marketing strategies: the free-panty mailer. In the 1990s, half the shoppers who bought bras at Victoria's Secret never bought underwear. Beraud suggested mailing customers a card offering them a free pair from the stores, with no other purchase required. "Sampling was kind of very common in beauty and food but completely unheard of in the fashion business," she said. Beraud's initial tests were promising. Half of the customers who visited a store with the mailer ended up buying something else. "Treat yourself to a free Body by Victoria Panty," read one of the postcards mailed in May 2001, featuring an image of Bündchen in a black bikini briefs kneeling in a gray studio, her crossed arms covering her bare chest. More than four million shoppers received that version of the mailer, which generated $6 million in incremental sales.

Victoria's Secret adopted a coordinated marketing strategy that changed every one to four weeks. Beraud and her team synchronized everything from the messages on easels set up in stores announcing the latest launches and promotions, to the national television commercials, to the flyers mailed to customers at home. Each medium aligned with a broader strategy, planned as much as a year in advance. When a new delivery of Body by Victoria bras arrived in stores in March 2001, for example, the windows featured campaign images and slogans that had already been tested in select stores in February. (Not surprisingly, the winning posters were ones announcing Body by Victoria as "The Most Comfortable Bra We've Ever Made.") The everyday line became a massive hit for the company. In 2001, Body by Victoria brought in more than $500 million of Victoria Secret's $3.3 billion annual sales, and it was growing 20 percent year over year.

And yet Wexner saw a problem. Wexner did not consider Body by Victoria sufficiently sexy, and he worried that its success would overwhelm the brand's reputation. In one of his regular meetings with Victoria's Secret's top executives in 2000, Wexner proposed launching a new push-up bra line called "Sexy." Several executives, including beauty division CEO Robin Burns and head creative Marie Holman-Rao, opposed the idea. What would it mean for all the other existing lines? That they were *unsexy*? Wexner compromised, agreeing to a slight tweak to the name: "Very Sexy."

/ / /

When Victoria's Secret's Miracle push-up bra debuted in the early 1990s, on the heels of its highly publicized competitor Wonderbra, few American women were wearing heavily padded bras. But by the end of the decade, push-ups were ubiquitous. In 2000, sales of bust-enhancers with names like X-Bra (from the VF Corporation in the US) and Ultimo (from the British firm MJM International) accounted for about 10 percent of the total US bra sales. At Victoria's Secret, push-ups generated 20 percent of Victoria's Secret's annual sales.[6] But the Miracle Bra, its most famous style, was quickly becoming obsolete. Competitors were experimenting with different ways to make push-up bras more comfortable and effective. Victoria's Secret needed its own new "high-tech" bra to draw women into its stores.

Designer John Caleo, head of the newly created in-house design team, went to work developing a push-up bra for the new millennium. He experimented with different types of padding. Foam worked well enough and it was lightweight, but it would eventually collapse inside the bra. He designed a style with inflatable padding, which Victoria's Secret called the "air bra," and even an adjustable version called the "click bra." But the results were too flimsy and, when worn, the bras didn't look like they held natural breast tissue. Silicone gel inserts, not unlike what women were having surgically implanted in their breasts, turned out to be the most realistic material. For months, Caleo tested his first gel pad bras on company employees before introducing them in small runs in stores.

In the fall of 2001, after two years of development, the new "Very Sexy" bra arrived in Victoria's Secret stores nationwide. Marketed as an evolution of the Miracle Bra, it was the company's most technologically complex design to date. Such a milestone product needed a shiny, new advertising strategy. While the moody and mysterious Body by Victoria campaigns stood out among the glossy ads in *Vogue*, Wexner and Razek wanted to set an edgier tone, especially with Victoria's Secret's television commercials.

High fashion was in a horny phase of its own. Designer Tom Ford signaled the beginning of the end of '90s minimalism when he debuted his first collection for the Italian luxury house Gucci in 1995. His models, with tousled hair and smudged eyeshadow, wore dangerously low-rise trousers with tight satin shirts unbuttoned down to their cleavage-free sternums. They wore literal, Gucci-logo G-strings. "It's a long time since we've had sex in clothes—real, beautiful, attractive sex that's about touching," the designer told *Vogue* after his debut. His ads were full of sexual inferences, with models semi-undressed and caressing each other. Ford's most controversial ad from this time was for Saint Laurent's perfume Opium. (In 1999, he also became the head designer at that luxury brand.) In the Opium campaign, model Sophie Dahl appeared completely nude and reclining on a fur rug, legs spread, cupping one breast, her mouth open in apparent ecstasy. Three years later, Ford provoked again with a Gucci ad featuring the model Carmen Kass pulling her underwear down, revealing a *G* shaved into her pubic hair.

Ford kindled fashion's growing fascination with sex and nudity. But Victoria's Secret's ubiquitous stores and commercials would bring that sensibility to far more people than Gucci's $300 logo G-strings ever could.[7]

To capture the MTV generation, Razek hired two new men who would shape Victoria's Secret's next phase of visual identity. First was the gregarious Australian photographer Russell James, whom Stephanie Seymour had introduced to Victoria's Secret in 1999 after the two met on the set of an Italian *Vogue* shoot. James would be the main photographer for Victoria's Secret for almost two decades. Razek also enlisted America's most masculine director, Michael Bay, whose saturated and stylized action films relied heavily on technical effects and lit women's bodies like shiny automobiles. Before Bay directed blockbusters like *Armageddon* and *Bad Boys*, he had been a prolific director of commercials, including the original "Got Milk" spot, and music videos for the likes of Meat Loaf and Lionel Richie.

As it turned out, milk appeared again in Bay's first commercial for Victoria's Secret. He filmed the ad at the same mansion on Long Island, Oheka Castle, where the first black-and-white cotton commercial was set two years earlier. In Bay's spot, Gisele Bündchen rolled around on a bed in bright blue lingerie, and Heidi Klum showered with a male model. In one cut, Adriana Lima drank from a glass bottle of milk, which dripped from the corner of her mouth and spilled down the front of her chest. The British narrators and the opera arias of previous commercials were replaced by the thrumming bass of the English trip-hop group Massive Attack. Bay's commercial featured no narration at all, let alone any conceptual discussion about desire. Instead, the campaign's tagline filled the screen in giant trembling typeface, one word at a time: "WHAT IS SEXY?" The message was simple, urgent, and effective. "Very Sexy" brought in $51 million in sales in the last months of 2001. Within a year, the push-up was not only the highest-selling bra at Victoria's Secret. It also spawned a best-selling fragrance and an entire collection of bra variants: new cuts of bust boosters as well as camisoles and bikini tops.

Bay's oiled-up, striptease version of Victoria's Secret was emblematic of early 2000s American culture when, as journalist Ariel Levy wrote, "Both men and women alike seem to have developed a taste for kitschy, slutty stereotypes of female sexuality resurrected from an era not quite gone by."[8] In her 2005 book *Female Chauvinist Pigs: Women and the Rise of Raunch Culture*, Levy identified young women's Y2K-era exhibitionist turn as a reaction against the austerity of their mothers' generation. The attitude also reflected an "if you can't beat them, join them" mentality, she argued, a way to cope with the sexism that continued to pervade culture.

Fashion trends reflected the attitude of the moment. Young people embraced crop tops and bandage dresses. Thong underwear, which Britney Spears and Paris Hilton wore peeking out of low-waisted jeans, became a new staple of lingerie drawers. In 2000, 40 percent of Victoria's Secret's underwear sales were thongs, up from just 10 percent five years earlier.[9] More women opted for breast implants, with rates increasing by nearly 600 percent in the decade ending in 2002, when American surgeons completed 226,000 augmentation surgeries.

The erotic obsession went beyond fashion trends and body modifica-
tions. Certain cultural taboos were also dissolving quickly. Porn, more
accessible than ever thanks to the internet, was an obvious culprit. The
adult entertainment industry's unabashed tackiness became a shorthand
for modern liberation. The female body, long a symbol of sex, rarely represented anything else. The message to women was clear. "What it means
to be sexy is to not feel pleasure, but to represent someone else's pleasure,"
said Jill Filipovic, a writer on women's rights, pointing to a telling admis-
sion by Hilton in 2003: "My boyfriends always tell me I'm not sexual.
Sexy, but not sexual."[10] The participants in the popular VHS series *Girls
Gone Wild*, who jumped at the chance to flash their breasts for cameras,
may have internalized the same confounding ideas.

The sexual charge was also apparent on network and basic cable television, a medium bound by its own historically conservative conventions.
In the 1999–2000 television season, nearly three-quarters of prime-time
TV shows depicted sexual activity, according to a report from the Kai-
ser Family Foundation.[11] *Adweek* explained the rise of sex, violence, and
"potty talk" on television as a bid for younger viewers. "Who is eager for
this edginess? Teens and young adults, mostly men 18–34, who advertisers want but can rarely find in large numbers. The demo is elusive and
media-jaded, and will come to the TV only if content boundaries are
explored."[12] The key phrase was "mostly men." Despite women's career
progress in the 1990s—entering the workforce in larger numbers, delaying marriage and motherhood, gaining representation through state and
federal elections—women were still considered a niche audience in the
early 2000s.

Razek seized the moment with an ambitious proposal: Victoria's Secret
could take its runway show to network prime-time television. He would
create a supercharged variety-show-meets-infomercial on a scale unlike
anything America had seen before.

/ / /

The Victoria's Secret Fashion Show almost made its television debut one
year earlier, in 2000. The setting was appealing: the glitzy amfAR Gala
at Cannes. The previous years' webcasts proved that there was a wide
audience for the show, and broadcast television promised a much wider
reach than primitive web technology ever could. ABC was interested, but

amfAR insisted the runway show include a message about the importance of practicing safe sex. Wexner was dead set against the idea, according to a creative executive at the time. The fantasy of Victoria's Secret did not include talk of AIDS. (Similarly, employees said Wexner turned down proposals over the years to link Victoria's Secret products with breast cancer research fundraising. Not sexy.)

In early 2001, Razek went back to ABC to pitch a prime-time version of the runway show filmed stateside, without amfAR's involvement. ABC agreed to an unusual arrangement for what was essentially a one-hour commercial airing at the start of the all-important holiday season. Victoria's Secret would cover all the costs of the show and buy half the advertising slots. ABC's teams would film the show and package it for airing two days after it was staged.

The timing became unexpectedly complicated after the terrorist attacks of 9/11. The fashion industry had avoided hosting any large-scale events in the weeks following the attacks, which had occurred halfway through New York Fashion Week. A few weeks later, when major designers Ralph Lauren and Donna Karan finally presented their collections to the press and buyers, they opted for small, no-fuss productions in their corporate offices. No brand wanted to be the first to host a celebratory fashion show after a national tragedy.

And yet, less than two months after 9/11, Victoria's Secret was set to stage the most glamorous, blowout runway show it could possibly muster—in New York City. The show would coincide with the holiday shopping season and ABC's sweeps season, when viewership had the biggest impact on advertising rates. ABC was desperate for a ratings boost as advertisers prepared to pull their budgets in anticipation of a gloomy holiday shopping season. The country was still in a state of shock, especially in New York City, and the invasion of Afghanistan dominated the national conversation.

Razek and Mitro massaged the show's narrative, framing their decision to stage the event as a modest act of patriotism. Razek told reporters and Victoria's Secret staff that the brand had considered canceling the show, but that New York City mayor Rudy Giuliani, now a national hero, had personally requested that they keep going (a great anecdote, regardless of whether it was true).

Razek and ABC's producers tried to give the runway show emotional gravitas. Its location, Bryant Park, home to New York's most exclusive Fashion Week shows since 1993, provided some fashion industry credibility, which helped. Razek rejected a proposed design of the stage because it was too "Fifties kitsch," requesting a backdrop reminiscent of "the cathedral of Notre Dame." Mitro was at his side to explain what this request could possibly mean. "What Ed's saying is that we've never had this much space before and what can we do with it?"[13]

The run-up to the show itself was a media event. Victoria's Secret's models appeared on five top ABC shows during the week of the taping. Model Rhea Durham, for example, guest-starred on *Spin City* as herself. In the episode, she invites Richard Kind's character to the lingerie show before confessing her love for him.

Finally, showtime. Andrea Bocelli opened the program with a plaintive performance of "Sancta Maria" on a stage adorned with two hundred lit candles. (He had previously collaborated with Victoria's Secret on a best-selling soft pop album.) Karolína Kurková emerged first to walk down the runway in a white retro bikini with fur-lined red Santa stockings, followed by Gisele Bündchen in a white bandeau and miniskirt. In the closing segment, each model strapped on the requisite feathered wings as a Black gospel choir belted *Hair*'s "Let the Sunshine In," a song Razek personally chose, while winged acrobats floated above the stage. "Before September 11th, it was corny to do a message of hope," Razek said. "Now it seems like the right idea."[14] Models got on message, too. "This is about being a woman and being powerful and using your assets," model Rie Rasmussen said backstage. "It's liberating, and I'm proud to be a part of the Free World."[15]

The telecast wasn't all sanctimonious. The puckish British actor Rupert Everett, on hosting duty, guided television viewers through the evening with some light ogling and lewd jokes. He was well known for his role as Julia Roberts's gay confidant in 1997's *My Best Friend's Wedding*, giving him something of a free pass to wink knowingly at the audience. "Security is tight, and so are the girls," he said, leading the cameras through the backstage tent. The actual runway clips in the hour-long special lasted only about fifteen minutes, so Everett had plenty of time between commercials to set the scene. At one point, he rubbed Klum's legs, careful to show the cameras only her outer thighs, not her inner thighs, following an odd ABC censorship rule at the time. Before a commercial break, he

*Welcome to my album of silk and satin delights.
I know you will enjoy all the elegant and glamourous
styles that are part of my secret collection.
It is a true pleasure to share with you
the most enchanting designs in fine lingerie.
You may find my selections both romantic
and inspirational. They will almost certainly allow
you to be exquisitely expressive. Be sure to visit
my new boutique when you are in Palo Alto.*

Victoria

The very first Victoria's Secret catalog arrived in 1977. At first, founders Roy and Gaye Raymond prioritized a distinctive visual concept over pushing sales. The Raymonds created the character of Victoria, a fabulous and mysterious British woman. The "secret" to her appeal was great lingerie.

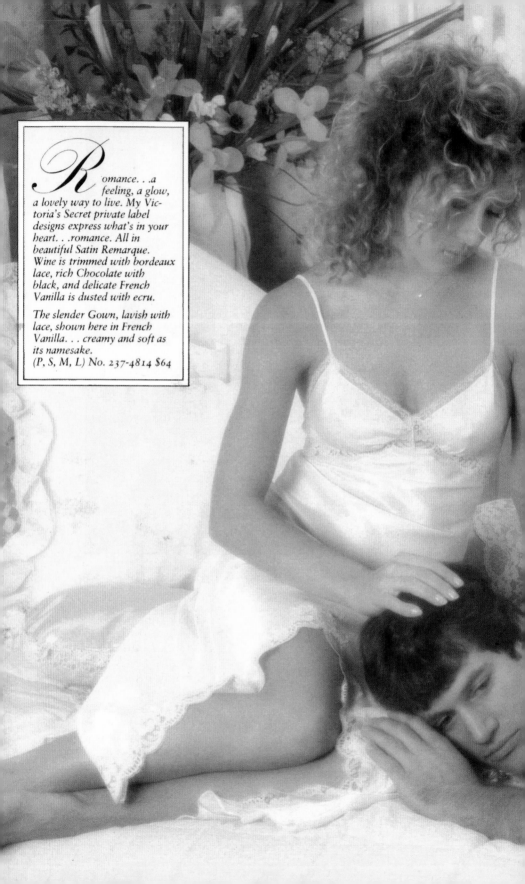

In early catalogs (1981, left; 1977, above), the photography was soft and sweet, while the images were vaguely provocative. Pubic hair was often visible (retouching was prohibitively expensive), and sheer bras and garter belts were de rigeur.

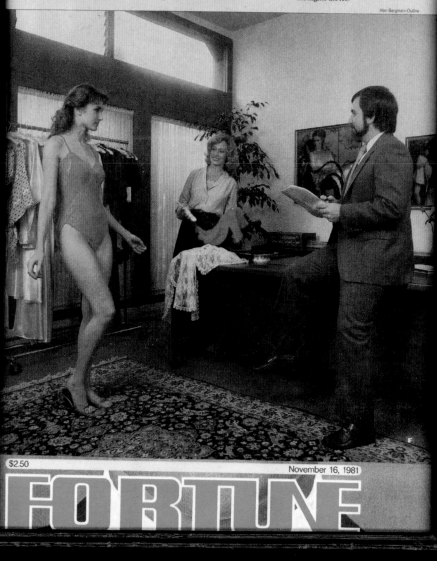

Victoria's Secret

Stanford MBA Roy Raymond, 34, got "tired of being treated with smirks" when buying lingerie for his wife, Gaye, also 34. So in 1977 he left his marketing job with a winery to start Victoria's Secret. Raymond claims that with four California stores and 50,000 mail-order customers, he will double sales to $6 million this year. That com-pares with some $40 million for Frederick's of Hollywood, the pioneer in the sexy-underwear trade. Victoria's glossy catalogue uncovers everything from an $8 G-string to a $340 silk robe. Most sales are to women, but Raymond reports that "couples shop the catalogue together; we get that from their letters."

Owners Gaye and Roy Raymond admire a $36 teddy. Lingerie models earn as much as $1,200 a day for catalogue photography: the skimpier the garment, the higher the fee.

Alan Bergman–Outline

$2.50

November 16, 1981

FORTUNE

Courtesy of Gaye Raymond

In the early years of Victoria's Secret, Gaye and Roy Raymond's
business was often compared to Frederick's of Hollywood—
but with more sophisticated lingerie and customers.

Leslie Wexner, seen above in 1985, went against the advice of many of his executives when he acquired Victoria's Secret as part of an acquisition spree in the early 1980s. By the end of the decade, his clothing empire operated more than 3,300 stores across his many divisions, including Abercrombie & Fitch and Express.

Wexner hugged his mother, Bella, as two thousand employee shareholders cheered at the news of a two-for-one stock split in 1990. Well into his adulthood, Les and Bella remained uncommonly close. Her office was just across the hall from his at the headquarters in Columbus. "If fear were a color, she'd be colorblind," Les once said.

At the annual
investor meeting in
New Albany in 2014.

Wexner's sixty-thousand-
square-foot mansion,
photographed in 1999, is
set within 340 acres of land
northeast of Columbus,
just minutes from the
Limited's headquarters.
The Georgian-style home
was designed by architect
Thierry Despont.

Ed Razek, the brand's top marketing guru, chatted with models during a break backstage before the 2014 Victoria's Secret Fashion Show in London.

Gisele Bündchen at a meet-and-greet in a Victoria's Secret store in Miami Beach in 2004. The Angels were contractually obligated to promote the brand through interviews and appearances. "Les wants them in the stores" was a common refrain.

Naomi Campbell wore angel wings on the runway during the 2003 Victoria's Secret Fashion Show. At the show's peak, more than ten million people tuned in for the annual televised event. But ratings steadily declined after 2013, drawing just three million viewers at its final airing in 2018.

© Eileen Blass, USA TODAY

tried on a pair of Angel wings. Interspersed with Everett's hamming were wholesome prerecorded interviews with the models. They recounted their big breaks and their dreams to, for example, one day walk on the moon. Razek and Mitro appeared, too, hitting the key points they had been peddling for years: every model in the world wanted to be in the show, but only the most beautiful women—supermodels!—had made the cut.

When the first televised Victoria's Secret Fashion Show aired, on Thursday, November 15, 2001, at 9 p.m. eastern, 12.4 million viewers tuned in. In network television terms, this was a mediocre result. (For the time, at least. By comparison, fewer people in 2023 watched *Yellowstone*, the year's most popular television series.) Twice that number of people watched the mega-hit *CSI: Crime Scene Investigation* on ABC's rival channel CBS. But for Victoria's Secret, the audience was immense. *Time* named the show one of the top-ten best advertising stunts of the year. "As a play for viewers, it was pretty transparent. (So was the clothing.) As advertising, it was a coup."[16] The production's price tag totaled $6 million—chump change for Victoria's Secret.

Nichols respected the show's publicity value, according to colleagues, but hated the concept. Like many other executives within Victoria's Secret, she found the event tacky. She also didn't care for Michael Bay's testosterone-filled commercials, which soon became an annual tradition. But Nichols knew how to pick her battles. "Part of her success was recognizing the bond between Les and Ed," said a colleague.

The debut fashion show managed to generate backlash from both conservative and feminist groups. On the day the show aired, representatives from the National Organization for Women protested the brand in Manhattan. One activist admitted to a reporter that, despite her moral qualms with the brand, she owned a drawerful of Victoria's Secret lingerie.[17] Where else could she get a decent bra at a decent price? (After investigating numerous complaints about the telecast, the Federal Communications Commission determined that ABC had not violated any decency rules.)

Razek welcomed the ultimately empty controversy. It only fueled perceptions of Victoria's Secret as a provocative brand. Publicly, he played it cool. "The misperception is that we try to appeal to men," he told *Vogue*. "It just simply isn't true. Men come along for free. The brand is designed for, positioned to, and talks to women. Period. The end."[18]

/ / /

In the fall of 2002, Victoria's Secret opened its largest store in Manhattan's Herald Square, brazenly situated across the street from Macy's flagship, then the largest department store in the world (until 2009, when it was surpassed by the Shinsegae in Busan, South Korea).

The 25,000-foot store marked a new chapter in Victoria's Secret's approach to retail design, aligning with its slick TV identity.[19] Gone were the fuchsia wallpaper and carpeting, the gold trim and ornate chandeliers. Instead, the updated store took inspiration from the leather-loving architect Peter Marino's designs for Chanel stores. White walls were rimmed in black and silver, with more breathing room on counters and in display windows. Upholstered leather covered some walls, television screens looping footage from runway shows covered others. The floors were marble and terrazzo. Framed studio portraits of the Angels, photographed in black-and-white by Russell James and Dominique Issermann, dotted the walls. Specially designed mannequins wore makeup and had real human hair. Any semblance to the Victorian bordello look that had defined Victoria's Secret in the 1980s and '90s was gone. In the years that followed, the top-performing locations in Victoria's Secret's network of over a thousand US stores would be renovated and expanded to match the New York City design. The Herald Square store sold close to $20 million of product in its first year. The average Victoria's Secret store at the time drew in $2.5 million.

The Herald Square store opened the first week of November. The timing was strategic: the holiday shopping season approached, with the second Victoria's Secret Fashion Show due to air right before Thanksgiving. CBS, eager to reverse its network's reputation for aging viewers, outbid ABC for its production in 2002. Phil Collins and Destiny's Child were set to perform.

Alexandre de Betak, the show's returning creative producer, and Charlotte Stockdale, the stylist, had rethought the approach to the "fashion" in the show. De Betak was accustomed to working with high-fashion designers who provided the stylists and producers with the raison d'être for each show he produced. Victoria's Secret's shows had no such creative heart; they lacked a thematic through line. De Betak suggested that the team conjure up several distinct themes that could justify the different costumes and set backgrounds. They created mood boards—fancy collages of trends and themes he thought could feature in the next show.

"The idea was to bring fashion and to bring storytelling to the show," he said. "To give it substance that it didn't really have otherwise." The 2002 show opened with a staging that looked like a chapel dome, with the models entering the stage dressed as if they had just stepped out of a Pre-Raphaelite painting. The next vignette was animal-themed, with models wearing leopard print with their wings. That was followed by a quasi-Latin interlude: models walked down the runway in red-and-black lace as a Spanish guitar played.

Tyra Banks, always game for a bit, briefly performed some flamenco-esque dancing before heading down the runway, only to break a long-standing runway show convention. Instead of ignoring everyone but the photographers and keeping a straight face, as models usually did, Banks played to the audience. She clapped to the beat, gesturing and pointing to the stands with a big smile. This crowd wasn't just full of stoic fashion editors, after all. The celebrities and suits wanted some acknowledgment. They cheered as the show reached its finale, a loosely themed carnival. Bauhaus neon lights in the shape of a woman's body (modeled after Gisele Bündchen's) illuminated the stage.

At least that's how eleven million viewers saw it go down from home. (The ratings were, once again, great for Victoria's Secret but just fine for CBS, which competed against the finale of The Bachelor on ABC.) But audiences were spared the evening's most unexpected moment. Unbeknownst to the producers, some attendees were animal rights activists, including one named Kayla Rae Worden. Wearing a bland gray pantsuit, her hair in a sophisticated blond updo, Worden had walked confidently into the venue, the historic 69th Regiment Armory, on Lexington Avenue in the Twenties, hours before showtime. She told the staff checking names at the door that she was a makeup artist, and no one questioned her. (The same trick had worked for her a few months earlier, at a Versace couture show in Paris.) Now, backstage at the Armory, she quickly located her target, Gisele Bündchen. When Bündchen emerged on the runway during the "flamenco" segment, Worden and three other protesters quickly jumped onstage, unfurling signs that read, "GISELE: FUR SCUM" and speeding toward the end of the runway, where the cameras were clustered. Somehow, Bündchen never hesitated or broke her stride, hitting her mark at the end of the runway and coolly turning back, as if security guards were not violently yanking protesters offstage all around her. "I landed right beside Madonna," said Worden, who was arrested that evening, but detained for only a few hours. The police officers even took her out for a drink after booking her downtown.

The show restarted, allowing the cameras to capture enough footage to remove any evidence of the disturbance from the televised version that aired a week later. The only casualty of the kerfuffle was a guitarist stuck in the rafters, meant to be dropped in slowly on a wire but held up by a computer malfunction caused by the abrupt pause.

Once again, controversy proved to be excellent publicity for Victoria's Secret. The unscripted chaos—fashionistas clashing with lettuce lovers—made global headlines: "Fur Flies at Victoria's Secret Taping." "Blonde Activist Eclipses Madonna." The stunt proved formative for Bündchen, who later wrote PETA a letter of apology and supported its cause.

Victoria's Secret learned a lesson, too. Moving forward, it would stage and film the runway show twice in one day, to get two takes—and double the guest list. The production also became more tightly controlled by Victoria's Secret and CBS. In 2004, CBS decided not to stage the show in the aftermath of the Super Bowl, when Janet Jackson's partially visible breast at the end of the halftime show became a national controversy. The FCC fined CBS $550,000 for what it deemed an indecent incident and increased its scrutiny of television content. Even daytime soap operas shifted their storylines in the year that followed. Razek and de Betak disagreed with the decision to pause the show, as it was carefully edited beforehand anyway, but Wexner supported CBS's decision. Razek and Mitro organized television coverage for a replacement event, a tour they called "Angels Across America." The brand's five contract models—Heidi Klum, Alessandra Ambrosio, Gisele Bündchen, Adriana Lima, and Tyra Banks—hosted events in New York, Las Vegas, and Los Angeles..

But there were few real concerns about indecency. The Victoria's Secret show on television was not live. Any nip slip or stumble could be edited out. The camera cut away before any butt cheek came fully into view. The show wasn't supposed to be provocative. It was family-friendly programming, designed to entertain and sell at the same time.

Brands have sponsored television shows since before most Americans owned a set, but rarely was a brand the producer and subject of the show itself. Victoria's Secret was not just any brand. In 2004, it surpassed

$4 billion in annual sales, generating nearly as much revenue as all Wexner's other brands combined. Nearly 80 percent of its lingerie sold at full price. "No other specialty retailer has passed this level," Nichols told her merchants and marketers. "There are no paved roads here to follow. There is no road map."

CHAPTER 11

On Wednesdays We Wear Pink

A breakout sister brand challenges the Angels playbook.

A statue of a pink polka-dot dog as tall as a double-decker bus blocked a lane on a corner of Thirty-Fourth Street and Sixth Avenue in Manhattan.[1] It was a bright Thursday in the city in the summer of 2004.[2] A white stretch Hummer, also covered in pastel-pink polka dots, pulled up behind the pup. A chauffeur opened the passenger door, and out popped Alessandra Ambrosio, the twenty-three-year-old Brazilian model and Victoria's Secret Angel, in a pleated miniskirt and tank top, her perfectly highlighted hair shining in the midday sun. On the sidewalk outside the Victoria's Secret megastore in Herald Square, a small crowd had assembled. Held back by barricades, the people cheered as Ambrosio threw them pink plastic frisbees. She had a crew of non-Angel models with her: two wore brightly colored "boy brief"–style underwear (essentially tiny shorts), sitting low and wide across their hips, with ribbed tank tops, while another model wore cropped pink sweatpants rolled down at the waistband to reveal the top of a fuchsia thong.

Ambrosio had a long day of interviews and photocalls ahead. Victoria's Secret's latest product launch wasn't just a push-up bra, but a whole new "lifestyle" brand—this time for young women. It was called Pink.

Inside the megastore, the second floor had been transformed into a brightly lit polka-dot playland: the Pink-dedicated salon. Its central feature was a wide table covered with striped cotton underwear arranged in shallow piles, looking like bins of sweets in a candy shop. Dog figurines filled the space. Display cases in the walls featured the brand's key items, like a cotton wire bra and the boy-short underwear the visiting models wore. Covering the walls were tank tops, T-shirts, polo tops, and sweatpants in girlish colors—lime green, sky blue, and lemony yellow.

The event followed a familiar Victoria's Secret marketing strategy: summon an Angel or two to a well-appointed store for a photo op and a couple of quick, anodyne interviews. The photos of the models were usually enough to guarantee coverage in local newspapers and weekly tabloids. And this time, Ambrosio didn't even have to do all the talking herself. Victoria's Secret had a new group of spokeswomen, so to speak, including one named Amy Porter, a rising junior at Ohio State University. That day, Porter wore two layered tank tops, each with a different version of the Pink logo across the bust, and loose pajama pants printed all over with the silhouette of the mascot dog. Porter described the collection to reporters as Ambrosio posed for photographs behind her: "It's comfortable, you can go to sleep in it and get up for that 7 a.m. class and just go, throw on a sweatshirt and go."[3]

Porter was one of twenty college girls from across the country who had successfully auditioned to serve as something like Avon ladies for Victoria's Secret's new brand. One of Porter's sorority sisters had encouraged her to apply, and after several rounds of taped interviews to see how she would respond to media questions, she passed. The New York City trip was a highlight of the "job." Most of Porter's other duties involved hosting events on campus back in Columbus, where she handed out gift certificates and coupons for the brand. Her apartment was filled with boxes of promotional products, including toy dogs and pink strawberry Vitamin Water. "The whole thing was to get awareness out about the brand," said Porter, who still works in fashion and marketing. "The experience was somewhat life-changing for me at the time," she added, remembering her training about community-based marketing.

Back then, she thought of Victoria's Secret as "froufrou" and "constrictive." But Pink was different. It was comfy, cute, and cool. It was also an instant hit. And no one at Victoria's Secret was prepared for just how successful Pink would soon become.

///

In the early 2000s, American culture turned its attention to a mysterious phenomenon: the new millennium's teenage girls. Few demographics were the subject of more think pieces, marketing decks, and screenplays during this time, and for good reason. The children of baby boomers, rapidly outnumbering their elders, were eager to grow up. The kids' toy industry was in crisis due to what child psychologists called "age compression": tweens couldn't wait to act and dress like teens. By the mid-1990s, young American girls in were also physically developing faster, growing breasts more than a year earlier than previously recorded, at around age ten on average.[4] Once they hit their teenage years, they were more likely than their predecessors to be sexually active at younger ages. Boomers looked disdainfully at Paris Hilton, the ditsy, wealthy Los Angeles teen who had parlayed a leaked sex tape into a starring role on a hokey reality television series and a career as professional It girl and tabloid magazine star. (Later, this career track would be renamed "influencer.") But for many teens of the time, Hilton encapsulated an intoxicatingly irreverent glamour they wanted to channel.

As the children of the boomers transitioned toward adulthood, they became voracious shoppers. American teenagers spent $155 billion in 2000, according to one study, mostly on discretionary categories like fashion that helped shape their identities. After school, teens roamed malls in packs, picking up colorful plastic jewelry at the cheap-and-cheerful piercing stores, like Claire's, and scoop-neck tops at Wet Seal or American Eagle. They took their cues from TV's *Dawson's Creek*, from MTV's music video stars, and from half a dozen new teen magazines, like *Elle Girl* and *CosmoGirl*, which recommended the latest hair straighteners and tube tops.

The urge to shop was more than a fun hobby for teens, girls especially. Trends were social currency. Take, for example, a Missouri high school junior named Jessica Travis. In 2002, she told the *New York Times* that she made her friends "dress up" on Mondays for school—meaning show up in skirts instead of jeans. "You want to remind people how cute you are in case they forgot over the weekend," she reasoned.[5] When one of her friends dared break the rules, Travis banned her from sitting with the rest of the clique at lunch. She saw nothing wrong with this policy: to make her high school's "A-list," you had to play by the rules.

"Girls treated their own lives like the soaps, hoarding drama, constantly rehashing trivia," offered the same *Times* piece,[6] describing the "seething underside of American girlhood." Adults were waking up to a dark reality: girls frequently bullied their classmates in subtle and psychologically destructive ways. The problem was so prolific that Rosalind Wiseman, a teacher and the author of the 2002 book *Queen Bees and Wannabes: Helping Your Daughter Survive Cliques, Gossip, Boyfriends, and Other Realities of Adolescence*, developed a thriving consulting career, traveling the country to lead seminars for frightened teachers and parents. Her book was the source material for the hit satirical 2004 comedy *Mean Girls*, in which the popular bully Regina George mandates that her clique always wear pink on Wednesdays.

In girl world, only a select few could be "cool" and "popular" at any given time. But it was difficult to resist the urge to try. The mall stores that understood this concept—and exploited the inevitable insecurities it created—thrived in the early 2000s. None more so than Abercrombie & Fitch, whose popular magazine-like catalogs and campaigns, with their semi-naked teenage models in provocative poses, filled its stores with hordes of young shoppers.

Les Wexner had bought the heritage brand in 1988, when it was a sleepy sporting goods chain best known for outfitting hunters like Theodore Roosevelt and Ernest Hemingway. In 1992, Wexner appointed a quirky, aggressive young merchant, Mike Jeffries, to recast Abercrombie as a trendy teen retailer. Jeffries refashioned the brand as a dark and fragrant, strictly preppy, sex-addled teenage dream by partnering with Bruce Weber, the go-to photographer for Calvin Klein and Ralph Lauren. Weber's sexualized (and often homoerotic) images scandalized conservative groups and titillated teens. At Abercrombie's dark and clubby stores, salespeople were hired primarily for their physical beauty. The brand grew faster than even Wexner had anticipated, passing half a billion dollars in annual sales in 1997, the year before Wexner spun out the brand as an independent public company.

Wexner wanted to find other ways to target teens. He was already familiar with this demographic, having previously repositioned the boring childrenswear companion to the Limited, called Limited Too, as a premium, ultra-girly mall staple targeting pre-teens. The store became a generational status symbol in the 1990s, selling leopard print bomber jackets and rhinestone-covered T-shirts. Its clothing sizes ran small, punishing young girls whose bodies were growing faster than those of their peers and thus adding to the brand's alluring sense of exclusivity. Wexner also spun out that business as a public company, in 1999, when Limited Too's net sales were growing more than 20 percent each year.

Wexner wanted to bring the new teens—the generation already known as "millennials"—into the world of Victoria's Secret. It was a tricky proposition. While young girls fancied themselves older than they were, they weren't ready to jump into Body by Victoria bras. The Victoria's Secret stores posed their mannequins across elevated displays like Playboy centerfolds. The bras were silky or lacy. It was all too much for most young women. (Plus, odds were high that their mothers shopped there. How lame!) Teens felt more comfortable browsing Gap Body, which marketed itself as more wholesome than sophisticated. Gap's cotton tank tops, with built-in bras, were also comfortable and affordable.

Wexner turned to his in-house design SWAT team, as he called the Limited Brands central design group. In September 2000, during one of his monthly meetings with the group's head Marie Holman-Rao, the talk turned to teens. He asked her to propose a concept for a younger, sister brand to Victoria's Secret, something fresh and playful that would speak to college-aged girls. They agreed that translating Victoria's Secret's high-octane sex appeal to teens would be a challenge. Wexner also wanted to keep the main brand's focus on single professional women in their late twenties. But a new, casual sub-brand could be rolled out to draw in younger women until they were ready to graduate to the main brand. "Above all, he wanted a feeder system," Holman-Rao said. And if the new line also appealed to younger teens or older women, all the better.

Holman-Rao and her team coined the assignment Project Pink. They began with the kind of comprehensive market research Wexner had come to expect from his executives. What did young women want? And how could that apply to bras and pajamas? Two brands that encapsulated the youthful zeitgeist of the early 2000s fed directly into the idea for Pink: Abercrombie & Fitch and Juicy Couture. Both presented a vision for casual clothing that was daring and titillating, yet traditional at its core. Abercrombie upgraded staples like jeans and button-downs by making them look vintage and cutting silhouettes close to the body.

Juicy Couture succeeded by hitting on a deeper trend. Launched in 1994 by two Hollywood-adjacent friends, Gela Nash and Pamela Skaist, the line began as a collection of playful and girly fitted shirts in bright colors and emblazoned with the brand's Old English–inspired logo.

Barneys and Fred Segal sold the line to women looking for flirty, casual tops to wear with their designer jeans and luxury handbags. In 2001, Juicy Couture introduced what would quickly become its trademark item: a bright, textured two-piece tracksuit in candy-colored pinks and teals. The trick of the look, rendered in humble terry cloth and cheap velour, was that it was *tight*. The hoodies were closely fitted, emphasizing busts when partially zipped up, and the pants were low-rise, emblazoned with a cheeky "Juicy" label across the butt. The Juicy look set off a pervasive trend in unapologetically youthful clothing—cozy but sexy, comfortable but glamorous, casual but trendy, girly but sporty. The aesthetic appealed not just to teenagers but also to younger moms. And Juicy's success marked a new chapter in the casualization of American wardrobes: the rise of higher-end athletic apparel meant to be worn not while exercising but when out on the town. Later, the category would be dubbed athleisure.

As Pink was incubating, some of Victoria's Secret's competitors, including La Perla and Natori, rolled out playful collections of camisoles and boy-cut briefs in bright colors and prints, and pajama shirts featuring sassy messages like "Meow" and "Boys Lie." In department stores, "young contemporary" became a new category in intimate apparel.

Holman-Rao saw an opportunity to build a new sub-brand from a collection of cotton underwear in girly prints and patterns like pink stripes and polka dots. "There was just so much whitespace opportunity there for what was essentially cotton underwear, which Victoria's Secret had never [focused on]," she said. Her team tested an initial collection of the cotton underwear in a handful of Victoria's Secret stores across the country in October 2001. The line sold quickly despite the post-9/11 slowdown hitting malls at the time, exceeding even Wexner's high expectations. "When he saw [the results] with his own eyes, he was like, 'Oh my goodness, this is amazing,'" Holman-Rao said. Mothers were buying Pink, too. "Older women didn't think of themselves as older anymore," she said. Wexner had insisted bras should be central to the product mix. "You cannot be in the lingerie business without a bra," he told Holman-Rao.

Her team kept testing, and at the end of 2002, Wexner greenlit Pink for nationwide expansion. To get there, Pink would need a store design strategy. Liz Elert, a visual merchandiser on the central store design team, came up with the idea for a mascot: a dog of nonspecific breed covered in polka dots. She proposed using the dog to decorate the store windows instead of Victoria's Secret's usual photographs of models and provocatively posed mannequins. Razek was opposed. The idea undermined the supermodel strategy. Wexner, however, loved the dog. The mascot communicated something unexpected and friendly. (It also called to mind Abercrombie's moose mascot.) Wexner saw the pup's literal commercial potential, too. "I think we could sell those," he said at a run-through of a potential store layout. "They would be perfect GWPs," he said, meaning "gifts with purchase." Victoria's Secret was *always* on the lookout for GWPs.

The Pink dog became the brand's logo, and polka dots its signature print. Despite Wexner's insistence on marketing bras as the main product, customers preferred the hip-hugging cotton underwear, sold in bulk deals, like five for $20. As Pink went nationwide, it overtook dedicated rooms inside existing Victoria's Secret stores. The line soon expanded to include all the dorm life staples—sweatshirts, boxer shorts, knit socks with pom-poms. The brand's T-shirts were emblazoned with playful messages like "I Like Boys" or, playing into the collegiate theme, "Phi Beta Pink."

But it was Pink's brightly colored sweatpants that became the brand's signature item. The designer behind the style was Kim Schraub, a new hire brought in from Abercrombie at the end of 2003. She was critical to the brand's success over the next decade. (Schraub left Pink in 2013 to work for Kanye West's apparel line, Yeezy, before moving to Kim Kardashian's intimates and loungewear brand Skims, where she became the head designer.) When she joined Pink, Schraub noticed an emerging trend of chunky sweatpants with large, graphic logos from smaller Los Angeles brands like FreeCity and C&C California. Celebrities like Paris Hilton and Jennifer Lopez alternated these sweatpants with their Juicy Couture velour tracksuits. Schraub's version for Pink featured "PINK" emblazoned in big, block letters across the seat or down the upper leg of the pants. The ankle hems were elastic, allowing the pant legs to be scrunched up and styled as capris. The sweatpants sold out quickly, especially after Pink's merchants sent a pair to Jessica Simpson, who wore them during an episode of her reality show, *Newlyweds*, in early 2004.

In 2008, Juicy Couture would sue Victoria's Secret for trademark infringement on the sweatpants. The two brands settled out of court. But by then, the velour trend had faded, Juicy Couture was in decline, and Pink was exploding—on the verge of becoming a $1 billion brand.

Pink's success came down to more than just a pair of trendy sweat-pants. The brand had captured a series of emerging trends and presented them in a bright, shiny, easy-to-shop package for average American teens, most of whom didn't live anywhere near a Barneys—and couldn't afford its $200 Juicy Couture tracksuit pants if they did. (Even the teens with Barneys budgets loved Pink.) But most important, Pink was more approachable than Victoria's Secret. Its models were not perfectly toned runway stars with chiseled abs and arched backs. Gisele Bündchen was nowhere to be seen in its advertising. Shopping at Pink didn't require a sex life or even passing through puberty, as all the bras were lined with at least a little push-up padding.

The fantasy at Pink was a feeling of girl-world acceptance: entering a slumber party at a sorority house where the perfectly thin "sisters" in matching T-shirts spoon at containers of Ben and Jerry's and invite you to gossip. No boys allowed. Even young women whose busts had outgrown Pink still came to its stores to stock their underwear drawer with striped thongs and hip-hugging briefs. Where else could they buy cute under-wear, anyway?

Growing up two hours outside of St. Louis in the first decade of the 2000s, Casey Lewis exclusively wore Pink underwear. Victoria's Secret was one of the few standout stores in her small regional mall. Pink's appeal was its approachability. "It was never overtly sexual," said Lewis, now a writer about youth culture and trends. Pink's logo was a status symbol, too. "I remember so vividly the waistbands that said 'Pink,' they didn't say 'Victoria's Secret.'"

Pink's cutesiness also tapped into an impossible dichotomy for teen girls in the early 2000s. Young women were often sexualized in the media, but just as often shamed for being sexually curious. Britney Spears, first famous as a sexy schoolgirl in the ". . . Baby One More Time" music video, caused global headlines in 2003 when she confessed to having had sex with her first public boyfriend, Justin Timberlake, after having previously promised she was waiting for marriage. Sexual stigmas pushed the next generation of Disney stars, like Miley Cyrus and the Jonas Brothers, to wear purity rings during their teen stardom years. Their fans internalized the same dynamics, but felt largely insulated from them at Pink, with its polka dots and puppies.

Though Pink was more approachable than Victoria's Secret, it wasn't more progressive. Most of Pink's bras weren't available in anything larger than a size 36C. Its main models were mostly thin, white, blond (or blond-ish), and conventionally beautiful. And the brand's kitschy T-shirts and underwear often featured phrases that suggested traditional female roles, like "I Like Boys" or "I'm with the Band." In later years, Pink negotiated licensing deals with major universities and NFL teams to use their logos on T-shirts and sweatpants, positioning itself as the go-to brand for young female football fans. "[It was] extremely heteronormative, for sure. But what brand wasn't then?" said Lewis. Still, Pink proved there was an appetite for even a slightly different view of femininity than what Victoria's Secret offered. Boosted by its proximity to Victoria's Secret in malls and its catalogs, Pink rarely advertised. But its success showed that an intimates brand could scale by appealing to young women, and just young women—not their boyfriends.

// //

Despite Pink's unstoppable growth and profit margins (as high as 70 percent in some categories), the brand struggled to mature out of its pseudo-start-up phase. Even by the mid-2010s, it remained a scrappy operation, and within Limited Brands, it was always considered a second-class business next to Victoria's Secret.

In the first decade of the 2000s, Victoria's Secret was essentially three independent and fiercely competitive companies: Grace Nichols's Columbus-based stores division; the New York City–based catalog division, run by Cindy Fedus-Fields's successor Sharen Jester Turney; and the New York City–based beauty division, led by Robin Burns. Pink would have fit naturally within the stores division, but Nichols and her merchants did not want it. They had little time to deal with an entire new category, for one, but they also knew that giving Pink room to grow would mean sacrificing square footage already reserved for other, more established collections under the Victoria's Secret label. A key factor in a particular bra line's sales performance was simply how much physical space it had on the floors of the more than one thousand Victoria's Secret stores. And no one wanted to sacrifice any of their category's space for Pink.

Pink clearly merited its own dedicated division of merchants, designers, and marketers. Holman-Rao's team launched it but would need to hand it off to permanent leadership. Rao hoped to be the one to lead

Pink, and she shared her wishes with Len Schlesinger, then Wexner's chief operating officer. It would not be so, and she was confused when, without warning, Schlesinger hired an outsider as Pink's first CEO in 2005. That executive lasted less than a year before being terminated.

Fed up, Holman-Rao surprised Wexner by resigning in 2006. She never told him that Schlesinger had passed her over, which had forced her decision. The central design team she led, so integral to Pink's development, carried on a few years before Wexner disbanded it and reassigned its team into the divisions.

Eventually, Pink found its permanent leadership in Denise Landman, a former hosiery merchant. Unlike many of the top executives who arrived after the influx of consultants at the Limited in the late 1990s, she lacked the pedigree of an Ivy League MBA. But Wexner greatly respected her and formally appointed Landman as Pink's chief executive.

Pink retained a plucky start-up attitude as it grew. Helpfully, Razek barely involved himself in Pink's marketing. He had bigger priorities, so Pink could ignore many of the Victoria's Secret brand codes. Its college ambassadors served as local influencers in a pre-Instagram era. Its press events did not always revolve around the models, either. Instead, Pink hosted outdoor parties in New York City and Miami with age-appropriate musical performers like Ashlee Simpson. Guests were given coupons to draw them into stores.

Pink's distinct aesthetic took inspiration from the fashion photography style dominating the mid-2000s, thanks to photographer Terry Richardson: studio-style snapshots with bold lighting and an undone quality that communicated authentic glamour. Richardson, however, leaned into hypersexuality in his images, often encouraging models to remove their clothes and allegedly sometimes assaulting them. Pink never worked with Terry Richardson and its images were never as sexualized as his. But the team took the flash-camera snapshot aesthetic he popularized, stripped it of its lewd associations, and adopted it as Pink's house style.

Wexner hoped Pink's success would encourage executives across his other brands to take more risks. Instead, as many Pink employees saw it, Victoria's Secret simply copied many of their tactics. In 2006, for example, when Pink sold colorful printed pajama bottoms in green polka dots and embroidered logo dogs, the main line offered in its catalog its own brightly colored pajama sets covered in cats and horses. While Pink offered its own sweats version of the Juicy Couture tracksuit, complete with Old English–typeface logos across the chest and butt, Victoria's Secret sold velour tracksuits in midnight blue and magnolia pink: the same idea, just a tad more sophisticated.

The overlap became a point of friction among executives, complicated by the fact that Wexner was unwavering in his insistence that Victoria's Secret was the priority over Pink. "Pink was successful and creative, and Victoria's Secret wanted that," said a Pink executive at the time. "They copied everything we did."

***

In 2006, as Pink cemented itself as one of the decade's fastest-growing retail brands, a new teen-friendly underwear brand emerged, hoping to pick up some of Pink's market share. American Eagle, another shopping mall staple and teen retailer, debuted its Aerie line in 2006.

Pink's new competition had close ties to Columbus. American Eagle had been founded and headquartered in Pittsburgh, but it was owned by a branch of one of Columbus's most revered and influential families, the Schottensteins. The family grew from three Orthodox Jewish brothers who had immigrated to the city in the late 1800s and early 1900s from Lithuania. In 1917, one of their sons, Ephraim Schottenstein, opened a department store that his four sons would later turn into a local discount store empire. Ephraim's grandson Jay Schottenstein took over the family's retail business when his father died in 1992 and has run the portfolio ever since. Its holdings include American Eagle, acquired in 1980; footwear retailer DSW; and Value City, an outlet store for clothing and furniture, along with a significant portfolio of retail real estate and shopping centers. (In the early 2000s, Jay Schottenstein was one of the wealthiest people in Ohio—thought to be second only to Wexner. But Schottenstein was old money, living in Bexley; and Wexner was new money, living in New Albany.)

When Aerie launched, American Eagle counted 850 stores in US malls and its teen-friendly jeans and T-shirts generated over $2 billion in annual sales. American Eagle was Abercrombie-light, offering simpler, more affordable products in the same styles, but without the trendy edge and provocative marketing. Like Pink, Aerie offered a sweet and playful collection of sweatpants, as well as bras and leggings.[7] But Aerie was comparatively understated to the point of blandness. Instead of the bright soft pink associated with its rival, Aerie's main color was a dusty cornflower blue. Its campaigns featured conventional teen girls, without much makeup, relaxing on softly lit window seats wearing striped "boy brief" underwear and hoodies and giggling with friends. Their bras were sometimes visible through a shirt or camisole. But no cleavage. The tagline was "Sweetly sexy, flirty and fun."[8] In one holiday commercial, a model posed on a bed in a padded bra, with the words "Made with love for the girl next door."

By 2014, Aerie's sales were lagging. American Eagle had expanded the line too quickly, installing Aerie-branded corners in many American Eagle stores. Aerie's future was in question. That's when Jennifer Foyle, the chief marketing officer, proposed an advertising campaign of "unretouched" images featuring models who were not slimmed or perfected by the magic of Photoshop. The marketing stunt was a success, even a minor revelation, creating a media conversation about body image issues among young women and the lack of "real" images in advertising. Sales picked up. Aerie had stumbled upon a gradual, cultural shift: the growing distaste for performed perfection. The sentiment was building among shoppers, but not yet pervasive. Very soon, it would be.

CHAPTER 12

Scaling Sexy

The Great Recession whacks retail, but Victoria's Secret
emerges as a bona fide blockbuster.

By 2008, the Victoria's Secret Fashion Show was a marquee television event, drawing millions of viewers each year with its long-established premise: beautiful women in lace, leather, and feathers; lots of skin; pop star performances; and a confetti cannon finish.[1] The $15 million production resembled a multi-camera sitcom, presenting a carefully crafted supercut of the live event taped in Miami Beach three weeks earlier. The intro felt like a sitcom, too. "How lucky can one guy be . . ." The music surged as Heidi Klum emerged from a convertible, grabbed a martini glass, and winked at the camera. Cut to Alessandra Ambrosio strutting past a crowd of eager paparazzi. Cut to Doutzen Kroes flipping her hair back inside a shiny chrome elevator. Their names flashed on the screen with a gold sparkle, Dean Martin's voice ringing clearly in the background, reminding the viewers of simpler times.

Adriana Lima, the last model to be introduced, walked down a red carpet as she slowly removed her earrings, necklace, and, finally, her dress. We didn't see her body at first, just the garment pooled around her ankles. The program cut to the runway stage and the thousand-odd guests. Lima emerged onstage in a soft gray bra-and-panty set with a gauzy lavender cape, blowing a kiss to Usher as he sang "What's Your Name." The models began their parade with hair bouncing and skin glowing. The night before, a spray gun–wielding expert had given everyone artificial tans, painting their abs sharper and their cleavage deeper. The show's theme was glitz and ritz, inspired by the location: the Fontainebleau hotel, newly reopening after a two-year, $1 billion renovation. The television special wrapped up with red fireworks as Klum again winked to the crowd with a massive sequined red bow strapped to her back. Men in suits and A-list actors filled the stands, along with fashion editors from all the major titles. Carine Roitfeld, the editor in chief of *Vogue Paris*, made a point to never miss the Victoria's Secret Fashion Show.

"It felt like good, clean fun," said Mickey Boardman, the editorial director of one of fashion's most influential fashion magazines, *Paper*. "As insidery as fashion is, it felt nice for fashion to be celebrated and recognized in a mainstream way—even though it wasn't fashion."

When the show aired on the evening of the first Wednesday in December, 8.7 million viewers tuned in to watch the eighth annual tradition, now a reliable mix of musical performances, behind-the-scenes clips, and flirty runway poses. More people that night watched *Law & Order* and the annual rerun of *Rudolph the Red-Nosed Reindeer*. But still an impressive turnout for what was essentially an hour-long ad.

"Now the new sexy is glamour," Sharen Jester Turney said in an interview after the taping.[2] She was two years into her tenure as the first person to hold the CEO role across all Victoria's Secret divisions—the stores, catalog, website, and even beauty. She had recently become the third-highest-paid female executive in the country. (In 2008, the annual report showed she earned $20.3 million.) Turney was facing a job-defining test: the United States was officially in a recession, seeing its sharpest downturn since the 1940s.[3] Shoppers were spending less money on Christmas gifts during the most critical period of the year for retailers. The national consumer mood was gloomy and apprehensive. Not that there was any evidence of that at the fashion show, of course. The show was an homage to the lifestyles of the rich and famous of the 1960s, long before Lehman Brothers went bust. Victoria's Secret persisted with shimmer and shine. "What are we supposed to do—wear cotton?" Lima asked a reporter backstage.[4]

Back in the real world, the mood was darkening. An average of seven hundred thousand Americans were losing their jobs each month. The finance, construction, and manufacturing sectors announced some of the deepest employment cuts, as did advertising-supported businesses like magazine publishing and entertainment. Nothing kills the joy of retail therapy like the fear of not being able to make ends meet.

The Great Recession brought an abrupt, painful end to a golden age of American retail, built on networks of shopping malls and biannual sales. The immediate impact was painful. Stores had little choice but to essentially

give their goods away by slashing prices—a strategy with escalating consequences. In retail, the smallest slowdown in sales can be crippling. Products
start to pile up. The instant that a new batch of spring dresses, for example, arrives in a store, an invisible countdown clock starts ticking. That
clock reflects changing weather, evolving trends, and, most important, the
impending arrival of a new batch of sweaters that will push the dresses to
the back of the store, where they are less likely to be seen and bought. To
keep the cycle moving on time, retailers often begin reducing the prices
of those dresses before they land on end-of-season clear-out racks at even
lower prices. (Les Wexner was a proponent of not delaying discounts,
advising his merchants to accept failures and get the offending product
out of the stores as quickly as possible.) While discounts typically boost
short-term sales and can appease a public company's shareholders, they
can, if offered too frequently, transform a store known for quality into
one defined by its bargains. To protect against that perception, and to
help off-load the growing glut of unsold products, retailers often funnel
goods to off-price retailers, like T.J.Maxx and Burlington. (Many brands
also burn their unsold goods, though the practice has become controversial. A former merchant remembers that recession-era Victoria's Secret
sent bras to foreign countries to be destroyed.) A new category of online
retailer emerged during the 2008 recession: the flash sales site. Dot-coms
like Gilt Groupe and Rue La La capitalized on the downturn by selling
high-fashion brands' leftover inventory for pennies on the dollar.

The deepest pain in retail fell on the many small boutiques and designers dotting the malls and shopping districts across the country, businesses
that had operated for decades out of one or a few storefronts or by selling
their small collections through department stores. In Chicago, for example, over two dozen boutiques closed along Armitage Avenue, a popular shopping area, and designer Maria Pinto, known for dressing First
Lady Michelle Obama and Oprah Winfrey, shut down her business after
twenty years. Similar stories were common across the country. Even after
the economy recovered, the business of selling clothes would never be
the same. Foot traffic in American malls had begun a precipitous decline,
triggering a wave of bankruptcies, store closures, and the rise of nearly
abandoned "ghost malls."

Wexner later likened the recession to riding inside a free-falling elevator with its cable cut, plunging to unknown depths. But he and Turney

navigated the downturn more deftly than many of their peers. Victoria's Secret cut prices, but typically only on specific categories or collections, so as to limit the perception that the brand was in trouble. Turney also temporarily stopped selling many of the brand's less-successful styles and smaller product lines (including a new activewear brand, VSX) that distracted from the best-selling collections and had smaller profit margins. Instead of languishing in Victoria's Secret stores, those lines and other excess items were funneled to charities and discount retailers in foreign countries, sometimes with the brand's labels removed to disguise the practice.

Meanwhile, Wexner had the foresight to see beyond the crisis. He insisted that none of his executives cancel product orders with their factories or stiff their stores' landlords on rent—common tactics for retailers in jeopardy. "He basically said, all of our competitors are going to cancel orders left, right, and backwards," said a finance executive at the time. "We are going to reestablish our partnership in a very important way." In 2009, Victoria's Secret's annual revenue shrank for the first time in eight years, and sales at stores open more than one year fell by 6 percent. Operating income fell, too, by about 5 percent. But the brand's reputation remained largely intact. Consider that two years later, Kanye West and Jay-Z performed their hit song "N**gas in Paris" live on television for the very first time during the brand's fashion show. Over ten million people tuned in for the rap duo's appearance, and the program had its best ratings in a decade.

When Americans started shopping with gusto again, their perception of a good deal was forever warped. Shoppers expected the same level of nonstop discounts from 2008 and 2009, especially when buying clothing and shoes. But less so at Victoria's Secret. As soon as consumer spending started to recover at the end of 2009, the brand's stores were quickly filled with new merchandise, including the launch of what was soon to become its most famous bra style: the "Miraculous," later renamed the "Bombshell."

The rocky economy had not deflated Americans' obsession with pert, augmented breasts, and Victoria's Secret's latest launch was built with enough padding to make bust sizes appear two cups larger, roughly four inches wider around the bust. The slogan "Hello Bombshell" recalled the "Hello Boys" Wonderbra billboards of the 1990s. The new bra became a quick bestseller, despite the nearly $50 price tag. (At the time, most Victoria's Secret bras were in the $30 range.) The brand was perfectly positioned as an easy indulgence in post-recession America, reaching record revenues of nearly $6 billion in 2010. A Victoria's Secret bra or body spray fell into the category of a $5 daily vanilla latte at Starbucks or a $40 weekly blow-dry at Drybar. And three-quarters of Victoria's Secret sales were in-store, not online. Digital purchases still represented less than 10 percent of total retail sales, with the mail-order catalog making up another chunk, but the online category was growing quickly.

Wexner had seen some of the changes of the post–Great Recession market coming. He was confident in his view that Victoria's Secret, with its theatrical store designs and strong profit margins, would be immune to the aftershocks of the recession—and strong enough to survive the challenges his first success story, the Limited, could not.

/ / /

"We are an enterprise of shopkeepers," Wexner wrote in Limited Brand's annual report in 2006, when Victoria's Secret crossed $5 billion in revenue for the first time. For Wexner, the shop was a physical space, not a cyberspace. The store was where he felt he understood his customers: what moved them, what excited them, what kept them coming back. "If specialty retail was about technology and systems, it would be easy," he continued, before invoking one of his retail heroes. "Walt Disney constantly walked his theme parks and would stop to talk to any child about their experience," he wrote.

Wexner had walked through his own Disneyland and drawn his own conclusions. The business of selling mid-market sweaters and jeans was doomed. He had already sold off many of the smaller women's apparel stores he had bought in the early 1980s: Lerner went in 1989 and Lane Bryant in 2001. The Limited and Express, his final two remaining apparel chains, were beyond rescue. The Limited had a particularly steep decline, dropping from a peak of $1 billion in annual revenue in the early 1990s to just $493 million in 2006. Try as they might, his merchants had not been able to repeat the success of Forenza or even Outback Red.

The problem was deeper than a muddled brand identity, the issue that had preoccupied Wexner in the 1990s. The foreign production method that differentiated his business when he first scaled the Limited in the 1970s was now industry standard. Walmart, Target, and every other major mass-market retailer was producing apparel overseas and pumping stores full of decent cotton separates. Europe had spawned new fast-fashion giants, Spain's Zara and Sweden's H&M, that were not just cheap, but trendy. Zara could beat Mast at the runway copycat game because it used just-in-time manufacturing methods in its wholly owned factories in Spain. There, the brand produced clothing components before their final designs were even decided: the pieces were cut and dyed right before production. The Gap's sister brand Old Navy had found fast success by undercutting the Gap's prices on casual clothing. Old Navy's giant, warehouse-style stores, typically located in self-standing retail space along popular suburban streets, never inside a mall, shrewdly appealed to shoppers who already felt the mall experience was old-fashioned.

The Limited and Express languished by comparison. Their clothes were more expensive than Walmart's, less trendy than Zara's, and less convenient to shop than Old Navy's. Wexner's apparel chains had become low-margin commodity businesses, driven by discounting first, quality and style last.

Wexner had also lost confidence in his merchants' abilities to shift the stores' public perceptions. In one meeting with the Express team, Wexner complimented a merchant's jeans, an ultra-skinny style that was gaining popularity at the time. She told him she found them at Barneys New York, then arguably the most important multibrand luxury retailer in the country, and known for its designer denim. Wexner asked why Express wasn't selling jeans just like hers. "Oh no, our customer wouldn't understand," the merchant responded. An executive who witnessed the exchange said Wexner was livid. "If he could have taken her up the elevator to the roof, he would have thrown her off," the executive said. "Les couldn't stand when people didn't give the customer credit."

But he also couldn't stand losing money. In 2007, after much speculation from Wall Street investors eager for Wexner to cut his losses, Limited Brands announced that it was finally parting ways with both its once-mighty apparel brands. The private equity firm Golden Gate Capital picked up Express for $602 million.[5] The Limited went to another private equity firm, Sun Capital Partners, in two transactions: after the first, in 2007, Wexner's corporation registered an after-tax loss of $42 million from the deal. When it sold off the rest of the stake three years later, Wexner's firm only got $32 million in return.[6] But after nearly two decades of trying to fix his apparel brands, Wexner was out of the clothing business. (For the most part, at least. Victoria's Secret still had a line of jeans and dresses available through its catalog.)

Publicly, Wexner told analysts he was "happy and delighted" to have the two businesses off his plate.[7] His empire now largely consisted of Victoria's Secret and Bath & Body Works, both of which had merged back into the Limited corporation in 2002. Years after the sales of the Limited and Express, he acknowledged feeling some sadness in letting his first business go. He admitted he'd held on to the brands too long. The Limited provided the corporate name of his retail portfolio. It inspired the name of his super yacht, *Limitless*. The brand had served as a daily reminder of how he defied his father's expectations and revolutionized an industry. The Limited was Wexner's signature accomplishment, embodying his core strategy: target a specific category, gain the consumer's trust, and then milk it for all it was worth. In the end, though, the Limited's point of view was not specific enough to survive. If the Limited was past its prime, perhaps so, too, was Wexner.

"You can't put in all those hours, all that sweat and all that anxiety, and not have feelings about it," he said years later about letting go of Express and the Limited.[8] "The other part of it is, I began thinking this when the business was 10 or 15 years old. Someone said, 'Your legacy will be The Limited,' and I thought, If I'm defined by a brand, what a sad commentary about life. There's more to life than that. What really matters is what you think about yourself in the here and now. Are you proud of what you're doing? You should be proud when you think about what you've done for your community."

Wexner was referring to his philanthropic efforts and his civic projects in Columbus. But he was not ready to dedicate himself full-time to that role. Instead of retiring or stepping back, he raised his ambitions. The Limited brand, in its best years, had barely exceeded $1 billion in annual revenue. Victoria's Secret had long passed that milestone, ending 2007 with $5.6 billion in revenue, and he was determined to get it to $10 billion over the next five years. But for Victoria's Secret to scale through its next multibillion-dollar growth spurt, it needed a new strategy. And it needed new leadership.

///

Turney first came to the Limited at the end of 2000, just as Victoria's Secret was preparing to open its thousandth store. Her remit then was the website and catalog business, which still operated independently from the stores. (By the mid-2000s, however, both channels finally sold mostly the same lingerie.) In Columbus, Turney quickly distinguished herself among Wexner's top lieutenants. She was shrewd and tough, despite the cutesy demeanor her voluminous blond bob and southern accent suggested. "As a business woman, she was spot-on," said a colleague, remembering that Turney could glance at a page of sales figures and "find the wrong number immediately." Another executive described her as refreshingly straight-forward. "With Sharen, you knew where you stood with two words—her tone and demeanor was very clear."

Turney grew up hauling hay and driving tractors on her family's land in Oklahoma, where her father raised cattle and farmed peanuts. She was an outstanding student and thought about becoming a teacher after graduating from the University of Oklahoma. But a career day fair put her on a different track. Intrigued by retail, she joined the management program at the Houston department store Foley's, then owned by Macy's. She stayed there eight years, rising from trainee to become the buyer of junior sportswear. In 1989, she joined the Dallas high society's favorite department store Neiman Marcus, where she moved quickly through various ascending roles before ultimately becoming the head of the store's catalog business, known for its flamboyant Christmas book. She launched Neiman's e-commerce business, and she was the first woman in the department store's history to be named CEO of a division. Then Wexner called.

At the Limited, Turney fostered a beneficial dynamic with her new boss. Wexner considered himself a teacher with more than four decades of retail knowledge to impart. When he spoke at length, Turney listened. "[She is] one of my best students, maybe the best one," Wexner said in 2006 after promoting her to a newly formed position at the head of Victoria's Secret's three divisions.[9]

Turney's appointment came at a crucial time. Victoria's Secret's most important leader to date, Grace Nichols, had just retired. Wexner was planning to sell his apparel brands. He was nearly seventy years old. Questions were emerging about his next act. The king of the mall brand was entering the digital era. Were his best years behind him?

Wexner's answer, of course, was: absolutely not. In 2006, he blocked a shareholder proposal to require the company's board of directors (several of whom were closely tied to him, including his wife, Abigail) to stand for election every year. The board would remain immune to serious scrutiny for another decade.

Around this time, Wexner also parted ways with his most obvious successor, the former Harvard professor Len Schlesinger. In his nearly fifteen years with Wexner, Schlesinger made sweeping changes to the corporation, pushing forward necessary infrastructure investments (like the digital systems the merchants used to place product orders across brands), helping Wexner hire retail executives from rivals, and standardizing the corporate culture.

But Schlesinger had become a polarizing figure. Some top executives felt his projects were distracting at best and damaging at worst. In 2006, Schlesinger oversaw the acquisition of La Senza, a Canadian lingerie chain, which represented the Limited's first step toward international expansion. But La Senza languished as an irrelevant sideshow to Victoria's Secret. When L Brands (as Wexner renamed Limited Brands in 2013) sold La Senza in 2018, the division was operating at a loss. During the final years of his employment, many executives across the Limited blamed clashes with Schlesinger for a wave of exits, from Marie Holman-Rao to Grace Nichols to Neil Fiske, the former Boston Consulting Group partner whom Wexner had hired to lead Bath & Body Works.

Right before Schlesinger's exit, Wexner had put him in charge of all beauty and personal care categories across the portfolio, on top of his role as vice chairman and chief operating officer. The promotion signaled Wexner's faith in Schlesinger, even though he had little operational experience outside of his work with the Limited. But a year later, in 2007, their partnership came to an end. The rumor among the other executives was that Schlesinger had gone around his boss to propose to some board members that Wexner be forced to retire and that he take over. "It was like Brutus and Caesar," one executive recalled. Except this Caesar survived. The board alerted Wexner, so the story went. (When asked about this incident, Schlesinger, who did not participate in this book, said, "That is completely untrue and not even within the realm of possibility.") In the summer of 2007, Schlesinger abruptly resigned with no explanation and a hefty severance deal, including $2.6 million to buy his

New Albany home, located directly across the road from Wexner's own vast estate.

By then, Turney was already in her new position, where her mandate was clear: double the Victoria's Secret revenue and maintain the premium perception that allowed the brand to charge twice as much for a bra as Walmart or Target could.

/ / /

As Turney focused on the Victoria's Secret business in the United States, Wexner had international expansion on his mind. Although the brand had a global reputation, thanks to its supermodels and fashion shows, Wexner had always been averse to opening its stores abroad. For decades, he even considered Hawaii too far. Wexner knew how to take trends and ideas from European boutiques and digest them for Americans. But Wall Street analysts pressured Wexner to expand. Where would the next billions come from if not overseas? "Something really funky happens in international specialty retailing," Wexner cautioned analysts in 2011,[10] without naming examples of American brands, including Gap and Abercrombie & Fitch, that had struggled abroad. He pushed back on questions about when Victoria's Secret could open in France: "I don't think there are three people in the company that speak French."[11]

Finally, in 2008, Wexner relented. He hired Martin Waters, an understated Englishman from the British drugstore chain Boots, to oversee all international business, reporting directly to Wexner, not Turney. Waters devised a low-risk strategy for expanding Victoria's Secret's appeal abroad. He opened a series of small stores, primarily in airports, carrying beauty products, the brand's simplest inventory. Foreign partners, eager to seize a piece of a famous American brand, built the stores, agreeing to put up all the cash and run all major decisions by Waters's team. These little airport stores turned out to be profit machines. Buoyed by their success, Wexner started opening proper lingerie stores abroad, too, slowly but surely. He personally oversaw the design of Victoria's Secret's first mega-flagship store in London. When that location finally opened in 2012 in the city's prized shopping district, on Bond Street, a few blocks from Louis Vuitton and Cartier—women queued down the block.

Meanwhile, Turney focused on extracting more business from the US market. Earlier in its history, Victoria's Secret had grown by opening new stores and raising prices. In Turney's era, Wexner had another idea: make the existing stores bigger and fill them with more stuff. The Limited's weight as one of the largest tenants in American malls gave it a strategic advantage when leasing bigger retail spaces. In 2004, at the CoolSprings Galleria outside Nashville, Victoria's Secret swapped spaces with Bath & Body Works and connected to an adjacent opening. The new store doubled in size to about nine thousand square feet. The brand repeated these tactics across the country.

There was no shortage of product lines to fill Victoria's Secret's larger, renovated stores. The assortment included bra collections like Body by Victoria and Very Sexy. There was also the brand's wide-ranging selection of fragrances, lotions, and makeup and outside brands like Intimissimi, an Italian lingerie label that Victoria's Secret had been producing and selling in the United States through a licensing agreement for a few years. Swimwear, once available only in the catalog, started appearing in stores every spring. In some stores, Victoria's Secret also carried upscale lines designed by French lingerie designer Chantal Thomass and other designer-licensed labels, like Betsey Johnson and Dolce & Gabbana. The retailer began to resemble a miniature department store, like it had in the 1980s, when the shops carried mostly outside brands like Bob Mackie and Hanky Panky. And then there was Pink, which took over more retail space as it grew throughout Turney's tenure. Her team eventually found that a side-by-side model was the best strategy, giving Pink its own entrance in the mall but connecting it inside the store to the main brand. That way, mothers and daughters, or sisters of different ages, could shop together.

Turney's strategy for Victoria's Secret went beyond square footage and product diversification. She understood that success in retail required being a few steps ahead of the customer—repairing weaknesses before they became apparent. So she set out to revamp the brand's product design and marketing, which she thought could be much more sophisticated.

Turney was responding to wider changes in the fashion market. In the late 2000s, European luxury brands like Chanel, Louis Vuitton, and Gucci grew rapidly across the globe. At the same time, American accessories brands like Coach, Michael Kors, and Kate Spade became popular domestically by offering European-style handbags at better prices—a few hundred dollars rather than a few thousand. These brands marketed themselves as pseudo-luxury houses by hiring notable designers, investing in quality-focused production, and pumping out *Vogue*-worthy advertisements. Their success proved American bargain hunters would splurge if given a compelling reason to do so.

In 2007, Turney hired British designer Janie Schaffer to upgrade the entire Victoria's Secret assortment. Schaffer was a known quantity in the intimates industry. After she and her future husband Stephen launched a successful Victoria's Secret–esque retail brand called Knickerbox in 1986, the British tabloids dubbed her a "knicker queen."[12] The couple had met while working as frustrated buyers at the British department store Marks & Spencer, which dominated the UK's intimate apparel market. Knickerbox's bright, lacy pieces were quick hits, but the couple struggled to manage the growing retail chain. The business went into administration (the British term for bankruptcy protection) shortly after they sold it in 1996, when it had more than 150 stores. Janie Schaffer took a career break to raise their daughters. She had returned to work, designing a smaller lingerie line, when Victoria's Secret came calling.

Schaffer had a British design sensibility for making avant-garde ideas commercially appealing. She brought a high-fashion approach to the Victoria's Secret design process, setting a conceptual "direction" (for instance, the beach style of Saint-Tropez) for each of the year's six seasons, to align the designers and merchants behind one big aesthetic idea. One of her first projects was to launch a "designer" collection made through a traditional process—starting with sketches, reviewing fabrics, and working with pattern makers to develop a design. Victoria's Secret had rarely operated that way in the recent past. Much of the designers' time had been spent updating existing styles, like a version of the Body by Victoria bra with adjustable straps, or another iteration of a turquoise-blue "sexy maid" apron that merchants needed specifically for the Miami market. (The piece was a hot seller there because it matched the team colors of the Miami Dolphins.)

Schaffer's designer collections used higher-end fabrics, like Swiss lace and hand embroidery, and the fabric upgrades extended in some form or another across most of the store. Turney loved her work. "[Turney] wanted everything to look better," said a designer at the time. But Turney and Schaffer's vision of "better" didn't always match the expectations of the women shopping at Victoria's Secret. When designers proposed a line of underwear made in real silk, the merchants pushed back. "She doesn't like silk" was the response (referring to shoppers in the third person singular had become common in the retail business).

The merchants were partially right. While Schaffer and her design
team's influence helped fuel Victoria's Secret's growth, especially after the
2009 crisis, many of the brand's best-selling pieces reflected the cleavage-
heavy, Michael Bay–styled vision of the brand more than a delicate, La
Perla–inspired one. And no wonder: Victoria's Secret's commercials and
runway shows had defined a new generation's sense of beauty, or at least
sexiness. The typical twenty-three-year-old American woman in 2010
had been aware of the Angels since she was a teenager. The catalogs and
commercials with Angels biting their lips, draped across beds, were ubiquitous. "Bombshell" became a key word for Victoria's Secret, whether it
referred to a push-up bra, a new fragrance, or the Angels' signature voluminous blowout hairstyle.

But Turney knew that if invoked too frequently, the hypersexualized
vision of Victoria's Secret would eventually bore shoppers. She turned her
attention to Victoria's Secret's brand identity. "We have moved off of our
brand heritage," Turney told analysts in early 2008,[13] describing the brand's
identity as "too sexy" and off-putting to customers who were older than
twenty-six. (She may have been thinking of a commercial that Victoria's
Secret had released the prior fall, featuring Heidi Klum joking around
in a black bra, exclaiming, "I have great knockers," while pretending her
breasts were machine guns.[14]) Turney wanted to pivot to a "feminine" and
"sophisticated" identity that could connect with more women. "Some of
those 400 million catalogs the company mails out each year must have
finally landed in the hands of some women," added the *New York Times*.[15]

Turney's instincts were right. A spray-tanned raunch had dominated
the aughts. But that pop-culture era defined by tabloid magazines, paparazzi,
cable television, and shopping malls—all channels that Victoria's Secret
dominated—was drawing to a close. The next era, the social media era,
had not yet fully begun. Only 20 percent of Americans had smartphones
in 2008. What was left in the interim was a sort of *Us Weekly* hangover.
Aughts celebrities like Britney Spears, Lindsay Lohan, and Paris Hilton crashed under the pressure of their fading youth. Kim Kardashian
competed on *Dancing with the Stars*, seemingly hitting the limits of her
fame. Neither Beyoncé nor Rihanna had yet to appear on the cover of
Vogue. The cast of every hit TV show posed for the requisite sexualized

photoshoot for *Rolling Stone* or *GQ*. "Feminism" was still a loaded term, rejected as a label by Lady Gaga and Katy Perry. Instead, it was a time of "good girls" (Taylor Swift), "good girls gone bad" (Rihanna and *Gossip Girl*'s Leighton Meester), "the sexiest bad girl" (Megan Fox), "very bad girls" (Rosario Dawson and Rose McGowan), *Bad Girls Club* (the reality show), and soon just *Girls* (the HBO series lambasting a generation raised watching *Sex and the City* reruns in Pink sweatpants).

Victoria's Secret had already developed a rubric to discern between, to put it as crudely as the headlines of the time, good girls and bad girls. "Every year, we would ask ourselves, 'What is sexy now?'" said Turney. In the early 2000s, the brand had created what was known internally as the "wheel of sexy," a corporatization of the feminine mystique. It was a matrix chart, with twenty quadrants, roughly defined by the words at the end of the two main axes: *naughty* versus *nice*, and *extroverted* versus *introverted*. The wheel was meant to remind executives that the shopper "experiences many different facets of sexy" and that Victoria's Secret had to appeal to the entire wheel. The brand could not present only as "for him" or for "divas"; it also needed to be "for me" and for "ingenues." The brand's marketing needed to cover the entire wheel, but from Turney's perspective it reflected only the overtly sexy spokes.

Turney hired a chief marketing officer, a new position in a newly unified Victoria's Secret. Ed Razek still held the equivalent of that title on a corporate level, across all the businesses within the Limited. He reported to Wexner, not the brand's chief executives. Turney now had her own person in the mix. She brought in someone Wexner and Razek both trusted and respected: Jill Beraud, the executive who had set up Victoria's Secret's first proper marketing division in the 1990s before moving to the central corporate division—or "the center," as everyone called it—to work with Razek across Wexner's other brands. Turney asked Beraud to oversee marketing for both the catalogs and stores, and to encourage the divisions to collaborate.

Beraud agreed with Turney that Victoria's Secret needed a new angle. "We felt like the Angels were over-sexualized, too mass-appealing to men and almost caricatures of ourselves," Beraud said. The provocative campaigns made sense in the early 2000s, when fashion imagery was highly erotic. "The world evolved and we needed to evolve with it."

In 2008, Turney and Beraud organized a series of big-picture meetings to discuss Victoria's Secret brand positioning and strategy. Beraud gave a presentation called "A Brand Is a Story Well Told." (The title was one of many "Les-isms.") In it, she reviewed the story of Victoria Stewart-White, the stylish British woman with a perfect personal and professional life, who still played a central role in the brand strategy more than a decade after her reinvention in the 1990s. Beraud defined what "Victoria's Secret is"—*sexy, sophisticated, forever young, ultra-feminine*, and *luxurious*—illustrated by black-and-white photographs of women in petticoats and old-fashioned corsets, Claudia Schiffer in a bustier pouting at the camera, and Scarlett Johansson smirking in a tank top. There was a slide dedicated to "what we're not"—an homage to Razek's tastes. (Neither Wexner nor Razek attended the presentation.) There were no words, just recent Victoria's Secret images: Adriana Lima in a leopard print bra-and-panty set, one hand pulling her waistband down and the other mussing up her hair, her lips parted. Other pictures showed Lima arching her back, lying on a bed wearing a pink Santa hat, and Miranda Kerr, in girly polka-dot pajamas and a bow in her hair, coquettishly biting a finger. Those images represented only a small slice of the wheel of sexy.

During these meetings, Beraud and her colleagues discussed the past, present, and future of "Victoria." Who should she be in the 2010s? The story of Victoria Stewart-White remained in play. But before Turney took over, Razek had introduced a different "Victoria" as the symbol of the customer in the new millennium. She was a twenty-six-year-old woman living in Chicago who had graduated from Northwestern University and was working at an ad agency in the city. She wore a size 6 in clothing and a 34C in bras. She was unmarried. "She is a sensual young woman with good taste and a European sense of appropriateness," an internal presentation from this time described her. "She wears beautiful lingerie as much for herself as for the man in her life. . . . She pampers herself, investing in her appearance and indulging her senses."

Faced with a new decade, Turney considered this "Victoria" to be outdated. Instead, she wanted to focus on the brand's supermodels. Customers loved the Angels, but Turney wanted to see them channel more romance and glamour, rather than just pure heart-pumping provocation. Razek often wanted the opposite. She respected his talent, but they had different visions for the brand. "Ed is a contrarian," said Turney. It took "a lot of work" to change his mind, but she knew it was possible and, over the course of her tenure as CEO, she felt that she was often successful in evolving Victoria's Secret's brand identity in the right direction.

The 2008 Christmas commercial was one prominent example. The setting was a baroque French château outside of Paris, the Vaux-le-Vicomte. The director was not Michael Bay but Michael Bernard, who worked frequently with Victoria's Secret, though usually not on the high-budget holiday campaign. (On the commercial alone, the brand usually spent around $5 million.) In the ad, the models—including Adriana Lima, Heidi Klum, and a new Angel, Marisa Miller—traipsed around the empty château and passed each other a ribboned Victoria's Secret gift box. The soundtrack was classical piano and strings, no throbbing bass. The women all wore red bras and long, puffy red tulle skirts. The final shot of the ad showed Lima outside the château, walking along its main drive, lined with illuminated fir trees, as she glanced over her shoulder to the camera with the gift in hand. The spot featured no bedsheets, no pouting, and no smoldering eye contact with the audience.

But Razek still ultimately controlled the brand's most visible marketing—and he reported to Wexner, not to Turney. After Beraud left Victoria's Secret at the end of 2008, for a bigger job as chief marketing officer of Pepsi, her successors had less influence over creative strategy. Razek and Wexner shared a deep trust built up over twenty-plus years of close collaboration. Their offices in Columbus were around the corner from each other. A running joke between the rest of the executives was that Wexner would always back Razek up with "Right again, Eddie." Meanwhile, Razek shrewdly gave Wexner credit for his best ideas. While Wexner was quick to turn on an executive who was underperforming—or, more likely, standing in his way—Razek always seemed protected from this treatment.

Razek's conception of "sexy" was the brand's North Star, "wheel of sexy" be damned. In his eyes, the brand represented a fantasy for the shoppers who wanted to look like Gisele Bündchen and who wore Victoria's Secret to attract men. "He was a rooster on his perch," said one executive. "He did not budge on this stuff." Wexner shared Razek's perspective. He often pointed to James Bond as an example of the importance of consistency, arguing that Bond would never abandon his "shaken, not stirred" martinis just because modern audiences preferred beer.

When Wexner turned seventy, in 2007, Razek gifted him a framed cover of a silly Photoshopped version of a *Rolling Stone* cover featuring Wexner with the headline "He's Bringing Sexy Back!"—a nod to the Justin Timberlake hit song. Wexner hung it in the conference room next to his office.[16]

The year after Turney's château commercial, Razek hired Michael Bay again to direct the holiday ad. This time, the models didn't pass around a gift—they *were* the gift. The tagline was "A Thousand Fantasies." The women showed off the brand's lingerie atop motorcycles and pool tables, in front of airplanes, tied flat against a wall, and in ballrooms wearing *Eyes Wide Shut*–style masks. They strutted in front of fiery explosions in the desert and low-flying helicopters on airfields. They looked breathlessly into the camera.

To his credit, Razek did expand Victoria's Secret's conception of sexy in the 2010s, in line with a larger cultural trend: an all-encompassing pursuit of health and fitness. Dieting for the sake of only losing weight was antiquated, conjuring images of repressed housewives sipping cabbage soup. Health, however, still correlated with low body fat. Thinness was an indicator that women had the time and money to spend on organic food, boutique fitness classes, or infrared sauna sessions. "Long and lean" muscles became a status symbol. Diet gurus who warned against eating gluten and sugar found eager audiences. Celebrities, who typically concealed the effort they put into their appearance, now went public with their support of the nutritionists, personal chefs, and trainers who kept them in shape for their nonstop public lives. The actress Gwyneth Paltrow launched *Goop*, as a newsletter, in 2008 to document the best juice cleanses to "detoxify" the digestive system and her favorite "natural" beauty products.

The health-is-wealth lifestyle justified a new uniform of form-fitting casual apparel—Spandex leggings, moisture-wicking tank tops, and water-resistant windbreakers. Lululemon, a fast-growing activewear brand out of Vancouver, helped transform yoga apparel into an everyday American uniform. In the mid-2000s, Lululemon was still small and just getting started expanding in the United States, but it quickly attracted a loyal American customer base. Its stretchy separates, known for their quality and their flattering, shaping effect on women's butts, were a hit with yuppies and college girls alike. Women increasingly wore leggings to restaurants and coffee shops. Sales of denim jeans began to decline in 2012, for the first time in decades.[17]

Wexner and Turney saw the commercial opportunity. Victoria's Secret had previously launched a Nike-inspired athletic apparel line, called VSX, in 2008. The line even opened a dedicated pilot store in Easton Town Center, the manicured outdoor mall near New Albany that Wexner had used as a retail testing ground since 1999. But the first iteration of VSX folded as part of recession cuts. By 2011, Turney was ready to try again. (As part of the preparations, one of the brand's merchants tested consumer interest by buying several pairs of Lululemon leggings, switching out the tags, and selling them in the Victoria's Secret store in Easton.) Victoria's Secret reentered the market, focusing on sports bras, a notoriously difficult product category. Most sports bras on the market were smashers—designed to compress breasts and reduce their movement during exercise. These bras were often uncomfortable and ugly, barely better than post-surgical garments. Victoria's Secret made a traditional compression sports bra, but also a version with underwires and cups, offering more support for women with larger busts.

Turney told reporters at the time that the underwire sports bras solved what she dubbed the "uni-boob problem" caused by compression bras.[18] The marketing for Victoria's Secret's new line, however, did not explain that the "uni-boob problem" could be more than an aesthetic issue. Instead, Razek's launch strategy focused on the novelty of padded sports bras: call it the "Bombshell" effect. One of the Victoria's Secret sports bras that came with two cup sizes' worth of extra padding—"for lift and cleavage" in the gym—was named the "Showtime." The Angels were deployed across the country to hype the launch, hosting lunches with fitness instructors in Los Angeles and Chicago and appearing on morning television shows in their new workout uniforms, discussing their exercise regimens. "Get a runway body!" read a banner in the Chicago store in 2011.[19] The sexy sports strategy irked many Victoria's Secret employees, who felt the messaging made it seem like the bras couldn't be worn during serious workouts.

VSX's sales started off slow. Even as Victoria's Secret stores expanded in the 2010s, they often lacked the square footage to showcase the line. But at a company so aggressively focused on bras and underwear, it wasn't cause for much concern. Victoria's Secret was a retail goliath during Turney's tenure. Between 2010 and 2015, its US revenue grew by $1.8 billion, fueled by sales of Bombshell bras, hip-hugging underwear, Pink sweatpants, and floral fragrances. The L Brands stock price peaked at $78 a share in December 2015, as Victoria's Secret surpassed $8 billion in annual sales. The brand counted over 1,100 Victoria's Secret and Pink stores in the United States, Canada, and the United Kingdom. Meanwhile, many of its mall peers, including Abercrombie & Fitch and Aéropostale, announced store closures by the dozens. It was during this period that Victoria's Secret "earned its perception stripes as something beyond a mall-based apparel retailer," said Simeon Siegel, a retail analyst at BMO Capital Markets.

While design, marketing, and store expansion factored into the growth spurt, operational strategies that had nothing to do with romance or sex also played essential roles. At a company as large as Victoria's Secret, retail fundamentals—hiring and training sales associates, restocking drawers, managing the number of cashiers—were difficult to optimize but hugely beneficial when well managed. Turney prioritized these strategies and invested in the brand's supply chain in Sri Lanka, creating smoother systems to restock best-selling items, like bikini briefs, in as little as fifteen days.

And then there was Pink. In the early 2010s, the sister brand for the college set grew twice as fast as the main line. Pink's logo T-shirts and sweatpants were more popular than its bras and underwear. By 2015, Pink had grown to nearly equal Victoria's Secret in revenue, despite its much smaller physical retail footprint. (Pink was available in only half of Victoria's Secret's 1,000 stores and in 128 self-standing stores.) The faster growth didn't worry Wexner so long as Victoria's Secret remained the market leader in its most important category, bras. He understood the cyclical nature of retail brands, and Pink was clearly on the upswing.

But as the 2010s continued, a troubling trend emerged. For the first time in more than a decade, industry-wide sales of underwire bras in the United States declined. Slowly but surely, women were growing tired of wearing bras that dug into their sides, left them with back pain, or rode up their chests. What was wrong with a more natural look anyway? Bras designed only to lift and mold breasts were uncomfortable, and women no longer accepted the pain.

/ / /

"Do you need a bra fitting today?"
Nichole Naprstek knew little about breast shapes when she landed a

part-time job as a sales associate at Victoria's Secret in 2006. She earned $6.24 an hour working at the store inside the Dover Mall in Delaware, down the road from the air force base where she also worked, as a technician. The retail gig was a fun way to earn some extra money and "offset all the testosterone that I was surrounded by at my full-time job," as she wrote on her Blogspot at the time. She had a talent for helping customers, once selling thirteen bras to one woman in a single afternoon. The employee perks were nice, too: 40 percent off merchandise year-round, 65 percent off during the holiday season. And each month, the company designated one item "gratis" for employees.

Over the course of nearly a decade working at Victoria's Secret, Naprstek witnessed waves of changes in protocol. She learned how to measure customers with a tape measure to determine their bra size. Although the measuring guidelines changed several times over her tenure, she always used the original fit method she had learned on the job: measuring shoppers around the rib cage, where the bra's band sits; above the bust, underneath the armpits; and at the fullest part of the bust.

Ultimately, the shopper decided which bra size was right for her, based on whatever ideas she had about how it should or should not fit. The right fit was difficult to judge because most bras are rather uncomfortable by design. The wires, band, and straps must be tight enough to hold unwieldy breast tissue and mold it into different shapes or positions. Women have been lifting and pushing and squeezing together their breasts for centuries, even before the advent of the modern sizing system in the 1930s. But that system often fails, even today, to account for the different density and shapes of breasts.

Victoria's Secret carried limited sizes, of course, so Naprstek was directed to recommend "sister sizes," meaning a bra with the same cup volume but a different band size, to give shoppers options. By that policy, for example, a 32C and a 34B could be interchangeable. Naprstek frequently watched customers buy bras that didn't fit perfectly, simply because it carried the Victoria's Secret logo. "It was still a status symbol," she said. Naprstek never questioned the fitting system. She was raised on it, as most American women were.

That was until the summer of 2015, when Naprstek realized everything she thought she knew about bra fitting was wrong. She had stumbled across a discussion page on Reddit called "A Bra That Fits," which offered advice and an online calculator to determine bra sizes based on six measurements taken while standing, leaning over, and lying down. She tried the method on herself. The improvement in comfort when she tried on her new "right" size—a 36H instead of a 36DDD—shocked her. Naprstek, like many other women who had never questioned their bra size, had not realized how uncomfortable she had been before. Or that the "armpit fat" that poked out from her cups before was simply a sign the cups were too small.

Victoria's Secret did not carry Naprstek's new size. At work, she now felt ethically compromised while helping customers find their sizes. "[The brand] offered thirty different band and cup combos, but what they needed was four hundred band and cup combos," she said. Naprstek was no longer an outstanding bra saleswoman. Before her Reddit experience, she sold $4,000 worth of bras in a month. The next month, her sales plummeted to around $1,000. Her manager asked what was going on, and Naprstek told her the truth: she was referring customers online or to a small nearby boutique that offered sizes Victoria's Secret did not (namely, cup sizes larger than a DDD). Disillusioned, she left Victoria's Secret four months later, moving to another sales job.

Naprstek wasn't alone in her frustration. A generation of women who were too young to remember the Wonderbra were fed up. "A bra fitting is the worst shopping experience you can have," said Michelle Lam,[20] one of the half dozen entrepreneurs in the early 2010s who leveraged the internet and venture capital money to try to tackle the bra business. Lam's company, True & Co., launched in 2012. The website asked shoppers to fill out an extensive questionnaire with questions like "What is your shape?" with answer options including "wide and low" and "slightly flatter at the top." The site's branding was simple and clean. Lam's angle was strategic: she would convince shoppers that they could find their true size without trying on bras in a store. In its first two years, True & Co. sold around five hundred thousand bras. This was paltry compared to Victoria's Secret, but impressive for a new brand without any paid advertising or established legitimacy in the market. (Lam had an advantage: she had worked with Victoria's Secret as a consultant for BCG in the early 2000s.) Another new lingerie start-up that emerged around the same time, called ThirdLove, gained traction by asking shoppers to submit a photograph of their torso (in a fitted top) so the brand could scan the image and recommend a bra size. Yet another emerging label, Negative Underwear, focused not just on fit, but on feeling. Its bras were available only in simple colors, like black and gray. The founders hoped to attract women who did not care for padding or lace. "So much of lingerie is sold in a way that's all about the voyeur," said one of cofounders, Lauren Schwab, in 2014. "We've marketed it as—for you."[21]

While digital, direct-to-consumer start-up brands garnered press coverage and investment dollars, the idea that any could truly disrupt Victoria's Secret's market dominance seemed impossible. "We are nothing compared to Victoria's Secret," said Romain Liot, cofounder of the trendy and racy online shop Adore Me. "Every day they sell as much as we sell in one year."[22] Victoria's Secret and Pink sold more than 40 percent of intimate apparel in the United States in 2015. The next-largest brands, Frederick's of Hollywood and Aerie, accounted for only low-single-digit slices of the overall market pie. "In the lingerie sector, there's a lot of brand loyalty," said retail analyst Danielle McCoy, echoing the conventional wisdom back in 2014.[23] "Once women find a brand and size and style they like, it's extremely hard to try to get them to try on different ones."

But analysts underestimated that while American women may not have been trying new types of *underwire* bras, they were open to softer, stretchier bras. Women were embracing a new trend that aligned with the rise of athleisure, prioritizing comfort over cleavage and frills. Enter the bralette, a soft top that stripped away wires, metal clasps, and bulky padding. No molded cups or light-but-not-too-light foam padding required. As easy to manufacture as a T-shirt and, very soon, nearly as ubiquitous. An underwear revolution was underway, and Victoria's Secret would soon look clueless.

CHAPTER 13

The Last Great Contract in Modeling

The Angels, under pressure to meet exacting standards,
start to lose their allure.

She was neither the first Angel nor the last. But when Heidi Klum finally said *auf wiedersehen* to Victoria's Secret in 2010, she left a void that no other leggy blonde could fill.[1] As she took one last turn down a shimmering, V-shaped runway, Klum was Victoria's Secret's most famous model and, at thirty-seven years old, its oldest. That she lasted so long was a testament to her charms and resilience. She was unflappable on television—always on message, always in on the joke.

Her final runway appearance came just six weeks after she gave birth to her fourth child—any evidence of which Victoria's Secret obscured with a corset and a flouncy tulle skirt. Klum wore them with aplomb.

She had pulled off a remarkable feat, parlaying her Victoria's Secret fame into a television hosting career that did not involve wearing lingerie. As the host of *Project Runway*, a reality TV fashion design competition that debuted on Bravo in 2004, she cut contestants with a withering but empathetic gaze that made for delightful viewing. Klum had her longtime publicist Desiree Gruber to thank for landing her the gig. Gruber managed models like Klum—she had been calling the *New York Post* about Klum since before anyone knew her name—and her Hollywood-tied PR agency, Full Picture, oversaw much of the press coverage for the Victoria's Secret fashion show. One of Monica Mitro's closest friends, she had helped launch *Project Runway* and served as its executive producer. (Today, Full Picture is best known for representing the Kardashian family.)

Klum was the last in a wave of high-profile models who left Victoria's Secret in the first decade of the 2000s. Tyra Banks, another telegenic charmer, had left Victoria's Secret five years earlier to focus on reality and daytime television. Gisele Bündchen, the most important model for the brand throughout her contract, would soon follow. After reportedly requesting a contract valued at $10 million annually and being turned down, she walked away in 2007. Bündchen's representatives denied this story at the time. Years later, the model said she had tired of the brand's demands on her time and felt increasingly uneasy modeling lingerie. "Give me a tail, a cape, wing—please anything to cover me up a little!" she wrote in her memoir, explaining that she let her contract expire because she wanted to stop "living my life on the company's terms."[2]

This was not an overstatement. According to multiple sources, Angel contracts varied by model and tenure, but in the early aughts, many Angels had a starting annual salary of around $1.3 million for a minimum of forty-eight days' work. If the women worked more than forty-eight days, Victoria's Secret paid them on a per diem basis. Not a bad deal. And some models worked more, as many as 150 days, racking up major paydays. (Since Victoria's Secret regularly photographed models during weeklong trips to exotic beaches, logging extra days was easy.) Around 2015, the Angel contracts changed: most new models started with a minimum of $350,000 annually for twenty days' work. But they, too, could cross the million-dollar mark if they worked more. A specific number of contract days were reserved for photoshoots and for PR, of which there was no shortage. The company crammed the Angels' press days with interviews and meet-and-greets. They appeared on morning television and late-night shows. Camera crews often accompanied Angels on set, filming segments that ended up on E! or MTV or YouTube. (Some PR was less public. The models were often roped into mingling, on behalf of the brand, with the likes of commercial real estate bigwigs at industry conferences.) But nothing was more important to Les Wexner than in-store appearances. "Les wants them in the stores" was a common refrain. And so, they went, posing for photos with fans in Atlanta or ribbon-cutting a new renovation in Las Vegas.

Everywhere they went, the Angels were trained to be charming and kind, especially with reporters. "No matter how rude or intrusive they are, never lose your cool and always be nice," read a document of tips for the models, distributed backstage at one of the fashion shows in the 2010s. "Play nicely, as this will disarm most reporters and get them on your side. Remember everything is positive, and this is a great show."

The Angels were also required to live in New York City. (IMG agents for Lily Aldridge, who lived in Nashville with her husband, Kings of Leon front man Caleb Followill, negotiated a rare exception.) And a contract clause stipulated that an Angel's deal could be nullified if the model gained a certain amount of weight or became pregnant.

The Angels' appearances were also highly controlled. When the Angels appeared publicly anywhere, Monica Mitro dictated everything from their outfits to their hairstyles. This generated heavy drama. Many of the models hated being dressed and styled all the same. Each wanted to stand out in group pictures. "They had meltdowns over hair and makeup," said one employee. Mitro held firm, leading to early morning fights before morning television appearances or in-store signings. "It was a control thing," said the employee. Sometimes the models called their agents to intervene. Those closer with Razek called him directly to complain, which irked Mitro even more. (Karlie Kloss sparked a mini-crisis when she cut her hair into a bob days before the 2012 fashion show. Stylists gave her flowing hair extensions for the show. Images featuring her new short hairstyle were cut from the swimsuit catalog that winter.)

Victoria's Secret also prohibited its contract models from working for competing intimate apparel brands and sometimes even for mass-market beauty brands. Models with shrewd agents were able to negotiate a "poison pill"–style contract clause to preserve the possibility of lucrative fragrance campaigns for other brands. If another beauty player approached a model to advertise a perfume, Victoria's Secret had the right of first refusal.

Being an Angel was a lucrative but all-consuming job. Especially for Bündchen. By the time she parted ways with Victoria's Secret, the company was generating 80 percent of her income. But she had new priorities. Less than a year before her final contract expired, Ed Razek introduced her to the New England Patriots quarterback Tom Brady, setting them up on a date at the low-key West Village bar Turks & Frogs. Razek had been trying to link one of his models with Brady for some time, first playing matchmaker for him with another Brazilian model, Cintia Dicker. (It was a mutually beneficial association: Razek wanted his Angels to date famous people, and he was happy to build a relationship with notable bachelors like Brady.) Unfortunately for Razek, Bündchen's ambitions grew larger than her wings. Soon after she left Victoria's Secret, she and Brady got married and started a family.

Even after she left, Bündchen's patina remained. As high fashion's brightest star, she had validated Razek's vision of Angels as true super-models. Rising models were happy just to be mentioned in the same sentence as Bündchen. The strategy saved Razek money on model salaries moving forward. "It never got back to the Gisele days in terms of [total compensation]," one agent said.

And once Klum and Banks left, Victoria's Secret never quite recaptured Gisele's level of celebrity, either. (Adriana Lima and Alessandra Ambrosio, the two long-tenured Brazilian models, got more airtime after those exits, but neither emerged as mainstream celebrities until Instagram took off.)

One Angel who *nearly* fit the Gisele mold was Miranda Kerr, whose round face and dimples gave her a doll-like quality. The Australian began working with Victoria's Secret as the face of Pink in 2006 and signed with the main brand shortly before Bündchen's exit. Kerr became famous, in part, for dating actor Orlando Bloom during his run in the *Pirates of the Caribbean* film franchise. But unlike Bündchen, Kerr had never worked with high-fashion designers or brands. That changed in 2009, when Balenciaga creative director Nicolas Ghesquière cast her in the brand's runway show. In the following years, Kerr and other Angels long ignored by high fashion—Adriana Lima, Alessandra Ambrosio, and Doutzen Kroes, among others—showed up in designer runway shows and advertising campaigns for the likes of Louis Vuitton and Prada.

The European designers wanted the Angels for their comparatively voluptuous shapes. Most runway models were underweight teenagers then. The fashion industry considered Victoria's Secret models "healthy" and "curvy"—code for models who wore a size 6 or 4 instead of a 2 or 0. (In the 1990s, at least two of Victoria's Secret's main models wore size 12, and most had real or augmented breasts, something rarely seen on high-fashion runways.) When Marc Jacobs cast Lima in his 2009 Louis Vuitton show, *Vogue* described her and her peers as "sumptuous and voluptuous," deeming the casting trend "a big, fat hit."[3]

While the Angels-to-Paris crossover moment lasted only a few seasons, it broke down the rest of the industry barriers that Bündchen had chipped away at for herself years earlier. Victoria's Secret had emerged as the rare fashion brand offering both runway and swimsuit models the chance to build a lasting public profile—the holy grail in an industry that often treats its stars like clothing trends.

///

The business of modeling can be dehumanizing and dangerous. In reporting this book, we spoke with models who worked for Victoria's Secret in different eras over the last four decades. They often spoke of the industry's predatory nature. The job requires a degree of compliancy that is often exploited by people in positions of power. Photographers who pressure models to take off their clothes. Stylists who play on their insecurities to bolster themselves. Executives who expect a flirtatious rapport. Billionaires who pay models to show up to parties. Agents who tell them to ignore their instincts.

The writer Michael Gross once observed that models typically fall into two separate groups. At the top of the pyramid is a tiny, exclusive group of high-earning models, who enjoy power, wealth, and influence. They are recognized as future stars early enough in their careers to be shielded from the industry's most disturbing realities. "You never mess with quality merchandise," Gross writes.[4] All the other models occupy the bottom of the pyramid. They are a large group of working but nameless models, as young as fourteen, typically alone in a big city, often in a foreign country, hoping for their big break. These models are deeply vulnerable to predators.

We know now that not even the most powerful models are safe from abuse. In 2023, original supermodel Linda Evangelista said that at the height of her success, her ex-husband, the powerful modeling agent Gérald Marie, physically abused her.[5] (Marie, who has been accused of rape by multiple models, denies all the allegations against him.[6]) In the early 1990s, women like Evangelista commanded huge per diems and became famous personalities, independent of their clients. But in the decades that followed, brands and logos emerged as the real stars, and few models found fame and fortune in fashion. More models could occupy a third middle zone, working steadily for a decent living while remaining voiceless figures. And as the #MeToo movement revealed, many of those models regularly faced abuse, too. In 2018, more than fifty models spoke to the *Boston Globe*. Sixty percent said they had experienced a range of sexual misconduct, from inappropriate touching to assault, as they navigated their careers.[7]

Models have pitifully few legal protections. In the United States, they are considered independent contractors, lacking many workplace protections and benefits. They are often not told what their gigs will pay, or how much money they owe their agencies (for room, board, and travel costs, often arranged without their consent or approval). Sometimes models are not paid at all, compensated instead with free clothing.

In this unstable business, many models eagerly competed to work for Victoria's Secret during its heyday. Money wasn't the only factor. Victoria's Secret was one of the only jobs where a model's name might appear next to their image, especially before social media. The brand wanted its Angels to be celebrities and treated them as such. High fashion work, by contrast, was "all about mind games," one agent said, describing models' "tangible feeling of being disposable." Women who made the cut as Angels had a chance to build their personas, become television stars. The ultimate currency. "It was the last great contract in the modeling business," said James Scully, the former casting director.

For many women, Victoria's Secret was their first introduction to the idea of a supermodel. A generation of girls who bought their first bras at Pink were mesmerized by the Angels. One of those girls was Chanel Iman, who began her high-fashion career at age fifteen in 2006. When she turned eighteen, Iman's agents advised her to wait a few years before auditioning for Victoria's Secret. "People said, 'If Gucci sees you in the wrong campaign, your career is over,'" she said. "If [photographer] Steven Meisel sees you, he's never going to book you again!"[8] But Iman didn't want to wait, and Victoria's Secret was happy to have her. During her fitting for her runway costume, she cried with happiness as stylist Todd Thomas slipped her into a pair of wings.

Another of Iman's peers, the St. Louis native Karlie Kloss, followed a similar trajectory. By the time she was eighteen, Kloss was already a runway veteran who had worked with Prada, Dior, and Chanel on runway shows and ad campaigns. Beloved by designers and photographers for her energy and poise, Kloss had no shortage of career opportunities. Like Iman, Kloss was just a pre-teen when Pink opened stores across the country. For this generation, Victoria's Secret was a bigger deal than Louis Vuitton. "Growing up in St. Louis and an American girl, this is it," she said at her costume fitting in 2011, where she also shed joyful tears.[9]

Both she and Iman would soon be Angels, too. Razek was delighted to sign both Kloss and Iman as Angels. He wanted the Victoria's Secret shopper to recognize them in ads for luxury brands and in the pages of *Vogue*. It gave the brand an air of luxury, if only by association.

But Kloss and Iman didn't look like the other Angels, the women whom *Vogue* had called "voluptuous." Weeks after her Victoria's Secret show debut, Kloss appeared on the cover of *Vogue Italia*, photographed nearly nude inside the issue by the influential Steven Meisel. The magazine had to remove from its website one of the images of her, with one bony hip exposed in a sharp protrusion, after the picture began appearing on "pro-anorexia" blogs. The cover had declared Kloss "The (New) Body." And indeed, a new body type was coming to Victoria's Secret: in a few years, Kloss and Iman's ultra-lean shapes wouldn't be outliers, but new standards.

///

On a Wednesday afternoon in late October 2010, Adriana Lima stopped traffic in Soho, New York, when she pulled up to the Victoria's Secret store in the back of a white, vintage Rolls-Royce driven by a young handsome man in a tuxedo.[10] Lima channeled a 1950s movie star, surrounded by eager photographers zooming in on the diamond-covered, push-up Fantasy Bra she wore with her silk ball gown skirt and gloves. The bedazzled bra, a clever media stunt conjured up by Monica Mitro in the 1990s, never failed to generate press coverage. "It's such a great honor, it's my second time," Lima told a CBS reporter inside the store.

After more than a decade with the brand, Lima entered the 2010s as the top Angel on Razek's roster, often opening the fashion show or taking a starring role in the holiday commercials. She had grown up, now a mother of two in her early thirties, older than most of her fellow Angels. The age difference was particularly apparent at the annual fashion shows, where most of the models were under twenty-five and many were just eighteen or nineteen.

Lima responded by devoting herself to fitness, working overtime to get "in shape" for the yearly Victoria's Secret runway. Every Angel felt the pressure. The camera angles were flattering, but models couldn't count on airbrushing to hide their insecurities as they could in photoshoots. Angel Erin Heatherton said she took a dangerous off-market weight loss medication when word got back to her that the brand thought she had gained weight. An employee in the marketing division at this time said such requests were often simply implied—the brand's people were "masters of the unspoken word"—and not just about weight. Many models, eager to maintain their careers with the brand, returned from hiatus with augmented breasts, their surgery scars still tender and bandaged.

As Lima's longtime trainer Michael Olajide Jr. once put it, gaining weight "can be a death sentence" for a model.[11] When Karolína Kurková, then an Angel, developed hyperthyroidism and quickly gained thirty pounds in 2008, Victoria's Secret wrapped her in a wide leather corset belt during the runway show, reduced her television time, and cut her from the final edit of the holiday commercial. Fox News wrote an article addressing her "weight problem."[12] Kurková returned to the runway two years later, after having a baby, looking leaner and more toned than she ever had before. "It was terrible; she was counting grapes," said one fashion show staffer.

In the 1980s and '90s, high-fashion models did not exercise regularly, if at all. When those women weren't on the runway, they were on set or flying to their next job. There wasn't time or need for the gym. Their major food groups were cigarettes and wine. Exercise was for bulking up, not slimming down. Kurková's was a cautionary tale: anyone who didn't keep up with the new body type risked being body-shamed by the press and public.

Even Bündchen, whose toned curves always stood out, did not begin a regular exercise routine until after she left Victoria's Secret in 2007. At the peak of her career, she didn't have much time to go to the gym. "I was working until, last night, two o'clock in the morning. I was shooting," she said backstage before the show in 2003. "I arrived here this morning, and my preparation then is to sit at [makeup artist] Charlie's table and trust her to make me look pretty."[13]

That was before Victoria's Secret embraced the great American fitness craze. In 2011, Lima laid out her annual fashion show prep process for the London *Telegraph*.[14] In the months leading up to the taping, she exercised twice a day with her trainer, but was careful not to develop bulky muscles. She meticulously tracked her body fat percentage, downed protein shakes and energy-boosting supplements. In the final weeks before showtime, she entirely cut out solid food. In the final hours, she didn't even drink water.

Her comments spread widely across the internet. Articles revealing "what it takes to be a Victoria's Secret Angel" were great for clicks: readers were eager for any indication that models had body image issues, too. Lima later backtracked, saying that she'd been misunderstood. "Those teenagers out there, don't go starving yourself or only drinking liquids," she said. "I just have an athlete's mind, and I appreciate doing this thing."[15]

Razek revered Lima's fanaticism. His models needed more than just beauty and charm. He wanted his Angels to prove their dedication. "There are rare athletes and rare models who have very long careers because they do the work, prepare and don't take it for granted," Razek said.[16] He boasted that he told an unnamed model she had been cut from the brand because "I see a picture of you on Instagram from a club, night after night, and every night [while] you were doing that Adriana Lima was jumping rope for three hours."

A new standard emerged, one that neither Klum nor Banks could have fit: Victoria's Secret models were expected to fit a size 2 in clothing and a size 36B bra. Most had between 10 and 18 percent body fat. Increasingly, the models relied on their runway costumes to give them the illusion of curves they did not actually have. Padding was used strategically, not just in bras, but also in bums and hips.

Meanwhile, Razek rejected models who would have fit perfectly as Angels a decade earlier. Popularity was no guarantee. Take Kate Upton, the voluptuous, smiley blonde from Michigan—one of the first models to use social media to fast-track her career. In 2011, months before a silly video of her dancing in the stands at a Los Angeles Clippers game went viral on Twitter, the model was called to a photoshoot for the Victoria's Secret catalog, a common entry point to working for the brand.

Upton, like Klum, was effortlessly charismatic and confident—and exceptionally busty. Reportedly a size 8, she was too big for "straight-size" modeling. The shoot seemed to go well: producers told Upton they wanted her to have dinner with Razek, who was not on set that day, and refrain from shooting with other brands in the meantime. Victoria's Secret wanted to lay claim to her future success. But Upton had just posed for the upcoming *Sports Illustrated* swimsuit issue and had been sworn to secrecy about it. When the issue came out a few weeks later, Victoria's Secret abruptly dropped Upton, despite her soaring fame. *Vogue* soon declared her "America's favorite bombshell," borrowing a bit of Victoria's Secret jargon.

Upton's rejection reflected rivalry between *Sports Illustrated* and Victoria's Secret, whose Angels were sometimes barred from appearing in the magazine. But the more prevalent view inside Victoria's Secret was that Upton had been deemed "too *Maxim*" for the brand, a reference to the raunchy "lad mag" popular in the United States in the early 2000s. (The same had been said of other models who looked more like vintage pinups than ballerinas. Russian model Irina Shayk, for example, had unsuccessfully auditioned for the Victoria's Secret runway show eight times, despite having a close mutual friend with Monica Mitro, because she, too, was "too *Maxim*." Victoria's Secret finally cast her in 2016, after she started dating actor Bradley Cooper.)

Victoria's Secret runway show stylist Sophia Neophitou was harsher in her assessment of Upton. She told the *New York Times* in 2012 that Upton was "like a footballer's wife, with the too-blond hair and that kind of face that anyone with enough money can go out and buy." Neophitou called Upton a "Page 3 girl," referring to British tabloid the *Sun*'s daily photo spread of a topless woman.[17] The ire revealed a prejudice within Victoria's Secret. The brand wanted stars on its own terms, who would never outshine the Angel fantasy. Upton, propelled by the influential modeling agency IMG, became the first supermodel of the social media era.

Regardless, Upton did not have the exceptionally lean, toned body Victoria's Secret now sought. The brand kept building on the athletic angle in its marketing. Video after video showed perfectly sculpted models in sweaty workouts, clad in VSX-logoed attire. Women's magazines fueled the interest in their workout regimens—perfect clickbait for their digital media sites battling for traffic.

During the 2015 runway show, a lengthy pretaped segment featured the models prepping for the event by boxing and running. "It feels like we are training for the Olympics," model Elsa Hosk told the cameras. "There's nowhere to hide on that runway," Candice Swanepoel added.

Swanepoel, a white South African model, became one of Victoria's Secret's most popular Angels, encapsulating the post-Bündchen look. "She was a physical specimen who should not exist," said one casting director at the time. Swanepoel was extremely thin, with just enough fat in the "right" places. (Not unlike the side of creamed spinach Swanepoel once ordered as her entree at a dinner hosted by Victoria's Secret for models and the press in the mid-2010s.) Swanepoel came across as reserved during interviews, but she was a dedicated Angel, rarely associating herself with other brands. Victoria's Secret rewarded her with more catalog covers than any other model in the 2010s.

For many Angels, the pressure to be thin was contagious, fueled by comparisons and competition among the women. Even the contract models had hierarchies. Favored Angels got to wear the Fantasy Bra at the fashion show, for example, or open one of the themed segments of the fashion show or cover the swimsuit catalog.

The body pressures were nothing out of the ordinary for celebrity women. A 2014 video produced by *Cosmopolitan* magazine, featuring one of Victoria's Secret's newest models, Romee Strijd, follows along as she trained with Mary Helen Bowers, a former ballerina. (Bowers had whipped Natalie Portman into lean, prima ballerina shape for the 2010 film *Black Swan*.) In the video, the blond Strijd, a Dutch nineteen-year-old with a shy, albeit friendly, demeanor, plowed through a class of demi-pliés and bridges. She told the *Cosmo* editor that she exercised twice a day and avoided processed foods. She looked tired. "I'm sure there are some girls who have good genes and it's easier for them to stay skinny," she said. Years later, Strijd revealed that, during the peak of her modeling career, she didn't get her period for seven years, in part because her weight was too low. "My body was under constant stress," she wrote.[18]

///

"Ed's about to do his speech, I'm getting my shoes on as we speak," said Karlie Kloss, filming herself backstage at the 2014 Victoria's Secret Fashion Show in London, as a dresser laced up her knee-high gold gladiator sandals. "I'm nervous, I don't feel ready, but too late, gotta go!"[19] These clips didn't air on CBS but on Klossy, Kloss's YouTube channel, the first of many diary-style videos she published documenting her life as a twenty-two-year-old top model, mixing behind-the-scenes glimpses with straight-to-camera thoughts on self-confidence and her cures for jet lag. Kloss, who was active on Instagram and Twitter, too, was more focused on social media than many of her peers. Victoria's Secret was a boon to her audience numbers: when she posted backstage pictures while the 2013 fashion show aired on television, she gained sixty thousand Instagram followers in a few hours.[20] "It's shocking, the power of having a presence on these platforms," she said later.[21]

The Angels were uniquely positioned to succeed in the social media era. Between 2010 and 2015, the majority of cell phone–carrying Americans upgraded to smartphones and started spending unimaginable amounts of time on Facebook, Instagram, and Twitter. Stars, more than publications or brands or organizations, amassed the largest audiences online. Among fashion celebrities, like models and designers, Angels had more followers than most. The women documented trips to the Caribbean to shoot the latest swimwear campaigns and cold nights in Paris filming a holiday commercial. They posted silly or candid images of themselves and their celebrity friends, late-night workout sessions and yoga poses, and bouquets of roses from rock star boyfriends. Their images projected a carefully performed authenticity, a glimpse behind the television cameras. In the first years of Instagram, it was still novel to observe the "real" lives of celebrities. Seen through their iPhone pictures, models seemed like regular-ish people, sisters and girlfriends who liked baking and snapping selfies with their friends. And their fans could tune in every day for the latest updates.

Online, women's magazines and fashion sites fed into the Angels' fame. "We called it traffic Christmas," said former Fashionista.com editor Alyssa Vingan of the televised fashion show. Victoria's Secret frequently invited Vingan and other editors to "no-holds-barred, no-expense-spared press events," like workouts and dinners, with the Angels. "They seemed so happy to be there, very chipper, very charming," said Vingan. "The readers ate it up."

Victoria's Secret shrewdly embraced the Angels' digital stardom, posting their images regularly on the company's Facebook page, which ranked among the top-ten most-followed brands in the country. A video of the Angels lip-syncing Katy Perry's hit song "Firework," filmed quickly backstage before the runway show in 2010, drew millions of views on YouTube. The lip-syncing videos became a yearly tradition. In many ways, the brand began to operate like a women's magazine, too, publishing interviews with the models on its blog and posting behind-the-scenes featurettes from its swim campaign shoots on YouTube.

By 2014, social media played a central role in the fashion show's press strategy. Staff and models were sent memos with guidelines on what—and what not—to post online, including the hashtags they were required to use. Backstage, a giant screen tracked the hashtag's engagement and listed the latest selfies and tweets from the models. Traditional press remained important, coming along for the journey that year from New York City to London via a pink-hued, branded private jet, but their stories mattered less when the models were posting their own pictures from customs lines and late-night workouts. Between 2014 and 2015, Victoria's Secret more than doubled its Instagram follower count. During the week it published its swimwear campaign in 2015, the account gained one hundred thousand new followers each day.

Across all these posts and clips and tweets, one through line remained, the same idea Razek had first articulated two decades earlier: the Angels were the most beautiful women in the world. Why would that message need changing? Instagram and YouTube were media channels just like television, he thought.

But the Victoria's Secret audience would soon start to use the internet to talk back. In 2014, the brand advertised its latest Body by Victoria collection online with a campaign showing ten of its uniformly thin models, digitally retouched as always, below a new tagline: "The Perfect Body." The ad caused a Twitter furor after three British students petitioned for its removal, claiming the campaign was harmful and body-shaming. The controversy spawned a round of headlines, a rare example of negative press for Victoria's Secret. A decade earlier, Victoria's Secret CEO Grace Nichols had banned the use of the word *perfect* in marketing for this very reason. Razek agreed to change the wording of the ad to read, "A Body for Every Body," but there was no other acknowledgment of the kerfuffle. And no lesson learned.

///

Ed Razek was at the center of the Angels machine, a singular force in the modeling industry with a widespread reputation as an exceptional marketer. In 2004, he had convinced Bob Dylan, of all people, to not only license a song for a Victoria's Secret commercial but also appear in it himself. Over the course of his long career, Dylan had rarely "sold out," so Victoria's Secret earned itself an additional wave of unpaid advertising when every newspaper and magazine covered the unlikely pairing. His role in the ad, tastefully shot by Dominique Issermann, was cheesy but affecting. In it, Dylan smolders into the camera before tossing his black cowboy hat to Adriana Lima. On set in Venice, the shoot was so quick and seamless that Dylan lingered.

"Is there anything else you want me to do?" he asked a producer. The folk legend was paid "a good chunk of change" for his appearance, according to a former executive, and Razek sweetened the deal by offering to sell an EP of Dylan's song "Love Sick" in Victoria's Secret stores at Christmas.

As the man behind the Angels, Razek embraced a glamorous, celebrity-adjacent lifestyle, shuttling between the offices in Columbus and New York City to the European châteaus and Caribbean beaches of the Angels photoshoots. Razek bought a ranch in Aspen on the billionaire haven Red Mountain, a property Wexner had built and sold to him, and kept sprawling apartments in Manhattan and Miami. He loved to drop his A-list friends' names. Director Michael Bay and photographer Russell James became close, as did Robert Evans, the famed Hollywood producer of *The Godfather* and *Chinatown*.

By contrast, Wexner almost never appeared socially in Hollywood or New York City, and he rarely interacted with the models. He was engrossed in fatherhood, philanthropy, and his life in Columbus. He had barely wanted to attend the first Victoria's Secret Fashion Shows back in the 1990s, and it wasn't unusual for him to skip the shows entirely as the years went on. He never visited the sets of Victoria's Secret photoshoots.

For Razek, though, the fashion show was the highlight of his year. Friends and acquaintances jostled to get tickets. He appeared on camera every year, explaining the myth he had created. "When you're talking about major fashion events, there is our show. And then there's what?" he asked CBS cameras, defensively. "He wanted to be John Casablancas," a colleague said, naming the influential founder of Elite Models, the agency best known for launching supermodels in the late 1980s. Razek personally oversaw the selection of the musical guests, his own favorites being Justin Timberlake and the Weeknd.

Razek relished the opportunity to address the models in the minutes before the tapings, to inspire them to be their most beautiful selves on the runway. (It was a habit he adopted from Alex de Betak, the runway producer, who parted ways with Victoria's Secret in 2006.) "I want to be clear about this," Razek said backstage in 2015, microphone in hand, standing on an elevated platform surrounded by the models. "'I have made your dreams come true'—that is not true. You have made my dreams come true."[22] The women cheered, dressed and ready for showtime in cleavage-popping bustiers and lingerie, their hair teased and bouncing. In these speeches, Razek often became emotional as he described how hard the models had worked to be there.

On social media, Razek seemed to always be with models—on shoots in tropical locations, out to dinner in New York City, at launch parties and store openings. In 2013, five of the Angels showed up in Columbus for a charity dinner in his honor at the Smith & Wollensky steakhouse near the Victoria's Secret offices. That night, Wexner surprised his longtime friend by announcing the formation of a fund in Razek's name at the Ohio State University Wexner Medical Center, where Razek had been treated for a bout of cancer some years earlier. Wexner donated $100,000 to the fund and asked Razek's closest friends to also make contributions. (Tom Brady donated $50,000.)

Razek's relationship status was mysterious. He had an adult son, Scott, from a previous relationship. (Scott worked at Victoria's Secret for some years and left after a female colleague allegedly accused him of acting inappropriately with her. When these claims were published in the *New York Times* in 2020, Scott did not comment.)[23] Some colleagues knew Ed Razek had a longtime relationship with a woman in Columbus—they lived together and might have been married—but she rarely accompanied him publicly. Others knew about a lengthy relationship with a married coworker.

But mostly, Razek surrounded himself with the young women who fronted the brand, projecting an image as Victoria's Secret's very own Hugh Hefner. In 2016, Razek even introduced a *Playboy*-style tradition for the Angels. A few weeks before the taping of the fashion show, during costume fittings, he presented each Angel with custom identical gold-and-diamond rings in the shape of wings.[24] (Hefner had a tradition of bestowing each Playmate with a diamond-encrusted Playboy Bunny head pendant necklace.) The gifting became Razek's annual ritual, each year in different forms: a bracelet, a necklace, a belt buckle.

(A digression for Taylor Swift fans. While the yearly gift was reserved for the contract models, Razek commissioned an extra ring for the singer in 2016 because he was "obsessed with her," a colleague remembers. Around this time, Swift had cemented herself as a pop superstar and a close friend of many Angels, including Lily Aldridge and Karlie Kloss. Swift performed during the 2013 and 2014 fashion shows and licensed one of her songs for the 2015 holiday commercial. The day Razek gave out the rings, he knew Aldridge was having dinner with Swift that night, and he asked that she pass it along. Swift wore it publicly many times. But Razek's view of Swift soured a year later when, after agreeing to perform during the 2017 show in Shanghai, she pulled out just a few months before. "You never heard about Taylor from Ed again," a colleague said.)

Behind the scenes, agents and employees warned one another about Razek. He relished his power and "needed to feel like the star of the show," said one agent, who advised his models to maintain clear boundaries with Razek. "If you're going to dinner with Ed or traveling with him on the jet over the weekends, you are not going to have a career in VS," the agent told them. The agent suggested that models, instead, get close with the women who had some control behind the scenes, like Niki Baratta and Michelle Priano, who led the photoshoots for the catalog and could sometimes influence show casting and Angel contract decisions.

But following such advice could be complicated. "He had boundary issues," said one colleague, putting it mildly. At fittings for the fashion show, for example, Razek would often hang around, watching from a leather couch in the office. One colleague remembered a fitting with Swedish model Elsa Hosk, at which Razek adjusted Hosk's underwear, running his finger inside its elastic edge. "That's where it should be," he said, referring to the garment. Later, when the employee mentioned this behavior to Mitro, she said Mitro advised her to "write it down." Another time, Razek was riding in a car with one of the Angels and a female colleague, on their way to the Plaza Hotel for a video shoot, when he said, "I know what this is, ladies. You guys just want to fuck me at the Plaza in your PJs." The women giggled and brushed it off. Just another uncomfortable joke from Ed. (Razek declined to be interviewed for this book. When asked about this interaction and others described in these pages, he responded: "Fake news.")

Canadian model Andi Muise was one casualty of Razek's power games. In September 2005, she was an eighteen-year-old with blunt bangs and an exotic look. Five weeks before the fashion show, she started working with Victoria's Secret as a fit model, trying on looks in the New York City offices as the stylists and designers prepared the collection. The opportunity arose after Muise met and befriended the show's stylist Charlotte Stockdale, who styled for brands like Armani and Dolce & Gabbana and magazines like British *Vogue*. The fit model gig was fun, easy, and exciting.

Muise spent lunch breaks helping the seamstresses carefully cover bras with Swarovski crystals. During this time, she met Razek, who popped in and out of the office. He was nice and charming. "I wanted to impress him, because that's the main guy," Muise said.

One day, after hours of fittings, Muise received a call from her agent, who told her that Victoria's Secret wanted her in the runway show. Muise was elated: her career was about to take off. The day of the show, she felt a pure adrenaline rush. Backstage, dozens of photographers milled about, documenting the hair and makeup process. She mingled with supermodels Naomi Campbell and Tyra Banks, who never came to office fittings. "There's people running around everywhere," Muise said. "It was all happening so quickly." Her debut on the runway arrived during a (loosely) themed Russian segment. She wore a black bra-and-panty set with black thigh-high stockings and a silky white cape. Muise's first-time nerves were invisible to the cameras.

The show immediately boosted Muise's career. Dolce & Gabbana chose her for its runway show; Armani cast her in a campaign. Her relationship with Victoria's Secret was never guaranteed, but in 2006 and 2007, the brand brought her back as both a fit model and a runway model. She felt she was returning home to her fashion family. "There were more jokes and conversations," she recalled. Razek was friendly, and the two would text sometimes, as Muise did with Stockdale and the others.

After her second appearance in the fashion show, Razek asked her out to dinner, just the two of them. He told her he wanted to discuss her role in the show. She agreed to dinner, hoping it would benefit their working relationship and increase her chances of landing a coveted Angels contract. But she was nervous, too. She'd heard gossip, speculation that some of the Angels had slept with Razek to advance their careers. On the night of the dinner, Razek's driver arrived in front of her apartment downtown and Muise climbed into the backseat next to Razek. On the way to STK Steakhouse, she said Razek leaned over to try to kiss her. She turned away and pretended nothing had happened. The rest of the evening was unremarkable, but Muise remembers feeling shocked and uncertain what to do. After that night, Razek started sending her flirty emails. He knew she had flown down to the Dominican Republic for a photoshoot at Oscar de la Renta's home, and he advised her to speak to a real estate agent about buying property there. He said they could buy a place together. "I need someplace sexy to take you!" Muise remembered he wrote. Muise responded professionally and tried to ignore it.

A few weeks later, Razek again invited Muise to dinner, this time at his Manhattan apartment. She did not want to go but felt she could not say no. "This is the career and life-changing thing, and he's the decision-maker," she said. On the day of the dinner, she texted him to back out. She was scared. "I felt in my gut that something was wrong."

The canceled dinner marked the end of their relationship—personally and professionally. When her agent told her she would not be part of the 2008 show, Muise called Razek in tears, hoping he would reconsider. Razek did not budge. He gave her no reason. "It's not just my decision," he told her. "It's everybody else's, and I was really fighting for you." She chose to believe him. It was easier that way, even though, without the Victoria's Secret association, her career stalled. Muise never spoke to Razek again, except once, briefly, at a party years later. By that point, she was married with kids and had finally accepted that turning him down had tanked her career.

Years later, when Muise spoke publicly about her experience with Razek for the first time in the *New York Times*, he denied he ever acted inappropriately with any models. "I've been fortunate to work with countless, world-class models and gifted professionals and take great pride in the mutual respect we have for each other," he said.[25]

CHAPTER 14

The Epstein Factor

How did a convicted sex trafficker become a main character
in the life of Les Wexner?

In the fall of 1992, Cindy Fedus-Fields found herself at a dinner party in Columbus, seated next to an intriguing man she had never seen before.[1] The occasion was a birthday party for Les Wexner's mother, Bella Wexner. The setting was the cafeteria at the Limited Brands' headquarters. Sitting next to Fedus-Fields was a young Jeffrey Epstein, a financial adviser to Wexner who had quickly joined his inner circle.

Fedus-Fields had attended the dinner party somewhat reluctantly. She was the CEO of Victoria's Secret's catalog division, a job that left her with little free time or appetite for company social events. When she wasn't dashing off to catch the next flight home to New York City, she was working late during her frequent trips to the Columbus office. The catalog team operated largely independently in Manhattan, giving her cover for missing most events back at the headquarters.

When Al Dietzel, then the Limited's head of communications, called up Fedus-Fields and invited her to Bella Wexner's eighty-fourth birthday celebration, he urged her to show up this time. "Cindy, you don't come," he said, "and it's noticed." Dietzel's wife could not attend, so he offered to accompany Fedus-Fields, who was divorced. In the early 1990s, it was still unusual for a single woman to show up to a party alone, so she agreed to Dietzel's offer.

The Limited's cafeteria was spiffier than it might sound. Les Wexner often used the space for special events, sprucing it up with linen tablecloths, satin decor, and dimmed lighting. Fedus-Fields was seated at Table 2, just feet away from the Wexner family table, where Les, Bella, his sister Susan, and his future wife, Abigail Koppel, held court. Fedus-Fields was joined by Dietzel, members of the Wolfe family who owned the *Columbus Dispatch*, and, directly to her left, the "to-die-for, handsome guy"—Epstein, who came alone. She was surprised by his prominent seating place. "So, you're the stockbroker?" she asked. Epstein bristled at the suggestion: "No, I manage the money." Rather an oversimplification, as it turned out.

As the dinner ended and guests were getting up to leave, Epstein leaned over to Fedus-Fields and invited her to an after-party at Wexner's mansion in New Albany, the manicured neighborhood he was building on the edge of town. She had visited the house many times before, but only for executive meetings, company picnics, and civic events. This would be different. She felt uncomfortable showing up at a private party late at night, especially because Wexner had not invited her himself. "I was hired help," she said, noting that Wexner did not typically socialize with his employees, especially not the women. And she barely knew Epstein. She declined his invitation—"I said, 'Thank you, no, I'm calling it a night,'" and went back to the hotel.

A few days later, when Fedus-Fields was at her office in Columbus, Epstein called her direct line. "You know, I'm frequently in Columbus, and I could use some companionship," he told her. Fedus-Fields was unsettled. What an awkward, uncomfortable come-on, she thought. She didn't know how to respond and did her best to deflect. "I'm sitting one hundred feet from five hundred women who are answering telephones for the catalog," she told him. "Come over and take a peek," she told him. The awkward tactic worked—she thought.

Epstein tried again later in the year, right before the holidays. He called Fedus-Fields at her New York office at the Grace Building, the sloping travertine skyscraper across the street from Bryant Park. Epstein invited her to attend Wexner's annual holiday party in Aspen. "I'm going to go out in a private jet," Epstein bragged. "Would you like to come with me?" Fedus-Fields declined again, but she was puzzled by Epstein's interest in her. Hardly a wallflower—pretty, smart, with a reedy energy—she was confident and enjoyed dating. But she was also acutely aware of her place in both the corporate pecking order and society at large. Several years older than Epstein, she wasn't wealthy, and they didn't run in the same social circles. What was his motivation?

Fedus-Fields forgot about it—at least for a few months, until Laura Berkman, the catalog's creative director, walked into her office in the spring of 1993. Fedus-Fields remembers Berkman behaving frantically. "It had come to her attention that there was a person portraying himself as a recruiter of Victoria's Secret catalog models, and she asked me what she should do," Fedus-Fields said. Did Berkman have a name? Yes: Jeffrey Epstein.

Fedus-Fields recalls telling Berkman that Epstein "manages the money" and how she came to meet him. Fedus-Fields advised her to call Wexner and tell him what had happened.

Berkman remembers the incident slightly differently. She recalls Epstein rang her line directly, telling her that he wanted to introduce her to some beautiful young women who would be "good for your business." Because Berkman had been the main contact for supermodels such as Claudia Schiffer and Stephanie Seymour, she often received these sorts of "tips" from outsiders and uncouth company executives trying to make an impression. (Once, a few years later, producer Harvey Weinstein, at the height of his Miramax power, showed up at Victoria's Secret's New York offices with a so-called model. Berkman politely asked him to leave.) That day in 1993, Berkman told Epstein—of whom she was vaguely aware, although she had never met him—what she told anyone who offered to introduce her to a "great" girl: Victoria's Secret worked only with models who were represented by legitimate talent agencies. "It was just another day, another call, but it raised an alarm," Berkman said. She went to Fedus-Fields's office to relay the incident. And both women remember what happened next. Berkman called Wexner, and he told her he'd take care of it.

///

Les Wexner met Jeffrey Epstein in the mid-1980s. Back then, Wexner was a newly minted billionaire, still living in Columbus but spending more of his time in New York City. He'd recently bought the tony Upper East Side department store Henri Bendel and was making inroads with the city's high-society crowd. But he was far from a social butterfly. If he appeared in the pages of the fashion industry trade publication *Women's Wear Daily*, it was because of a development in his business. He rarely graced the pages of the paper's "Eye" section, which documented the city's latest fetes. Wexner needed an entrée into society, someone to connect him with the right people and protect him from the wrong ones.

Epstein seemed like the right man for the job. He had a growing reputation for shrewd money management. He was cute and charismatic and attended all the right parties. Wexner's introduction to Epstein came through Robert Meister, a respected insurance executive at the brokerage firm Alexander & Alexander. Meister dealt with high-profile, high-net-worth clients, exactly the kind of people Epstein was eager to meet.

Epstein's background was unconventional for a money manager. He was born to working-class parents in Coney Island. He didn't have a college degree, which was unusual but not unheard in finance at the time. His résumé amounted to little more than a less-than-two-year stint as a physics and math teacher at the prestigious Dalton School on Manhattan's Upper East Side and a few years working as a stockbroker at Bear Stearns. He landed that job in 1976 when the parent of one of his students recommended him to the investment bank's CEO Alan Greenberg.[2] Epstein proved himself to be a good salesman and was promoted to limited partner, one level below full partner. He was known for his expertise in tax avoidance, catnip for wealthy clients. Epstein left the bank in 1981, for reasons that have remained murky. Some sources said he was pushed out for alleged infractions, but Epstein said he left of his own accord.[3]

Epstein then struck out on his own as a financial adviser offering tax advice, estate planning, and accounting services for wealthy individuals. In the late 1980s, he linked up with Steven Jude Hoffenberg, a swindler who later pleaded guilty to conspiracy and fraud charges related to a Ponzi scheme he ran during his years working with Epstein. Epstein was never charged. Hoffenberg later described Epstein as "the best hustler on two feet" and claimed that it was Epstein who had been the architect of their fraudulent schemes.[4]

None of this was publicly known when Epstein met Wexner. Epstein told Wexner he had been very successful making money for other unnamed, prominent people. And even though Epstein had likely been pushed out of Bear Stearns, Greenberg and his deputy Jimmy Cayne still vouched for him. Wexner believed he could trust Epstein. And he needed someone a bit unconventional. He needed a hatchet man.

While Wexner could be ruthless in his business, he disliked confrontation. Over the years, he attached himself to deputies who were willing to do his dirty work—to say the things to his employees or partners or lawyers that he would rather not say himself. This cadre included good-looking, confident, and well-educated men like Ed Razek and Len Schlesinger, the Harvard Business School wonk who would lead Limited Brands through its consulting crusade of the 1990s and early 2000s. And men like Jamie McFate, a jack-of-all-trades chief of staff whom Wexner first hired as the fashion director of Structure in 1993, then recruited to travel the world on his behalf, researching market trends. And the attorney Bruce Soll, Wexner's longtime adviser, with whom he is still close today. For many years, there was no one closer to Wexner than Soll. Except for Epstein.

Early in his working relationship with Wexner, Epstein proved himself a tough operator. One of Epstein's friends recalled him saying that Wexner originally hired him when he suspected someone at the Limited was stealing company funds, according to a report by *Mother Jones*.[5] Wexner asked Epstein to come to Ohio and take a careful look at the accounts and find the culprit—an ideal task for Epstein, who knew how to think like a swindler.

As Epstein established his relationship with Wexner, he told a friend that Wexner was "completely socially inept," adding, "This guy has no life, and I'm going to give him a life."[6] The friend sat in on a meeting between Epstein and Wexner in Paris and found Wexner to be as awkward as Epstein had promised. Soon, Wexner began socializing less with his high school friends and early-stage business associates, and he broke up with his longtime girlfriend. He began spending more time with his new confidant, whose influence extended far beyond Limited Brands.

Wexner also cut ties with Bob Morosky, his financial adviser and his most important operational partner in the first decade of Limited Brands. The send-off was particularly cold. Wexner simply changed the locks on Morosky's office door over one weekend in 1987, according to one executive, and Morosky was never seen in the headquarters again. His exit was so shocking that the *Columbus Monthly* dedicated a cover feature to the breakup of retail's most powerful duo. But no one at the famously tight-lipped company would explain what caused the split. Morosky had at one point questioned Epstein's influence, but Wexner, in response, had insisted that Epstein could "introduce [Wexner] to important people." Decades later, Morosky didn't hold back his judgment in the *Wall Street Journal*. "Les is an insecure guy with a big ego . . . he had a lot of money but craved respect," he said. "[He and Epstein] played off each other's needs."[7] (In an interview for this book, Morosky said he had been misquoted.)

In 1991, Wexner made an unusual decision with lasting implications: he granted Epstein power of attorney, with the legal authority to act on Wexner's behalf—to cut deals and manage relationships, but also to invest, and spend, his money. Power of attorney is usually granted to close, trusted family members, friends, and in some cases lawyers. For Wexner, who at the time was in his early fifties and by all indications in sound health, Epstein was an odd choice. The two hadn't known each other for long, and Epstein was not connected to any of Wexner's other advisers. Though Epstein's résumé was thin, Wexner trusted him with not only investments but also personal projects. Epstein hired and fired personal employees, including nannies for the Wexner children who arrived years later. Epstein joined planning meetings about the New Albany community and helped Wexner commission a new, larger iteration of his yacht *Limitless*, overseeing its construction with ship captain Craig Tafoya in Germany in the mid-1990s. "I saw him as the money guy," said Craig's wife Mary Tafoya, who worked as a stewardess on the *Limitless*. (Craig died in 2021.) Tafoya saw Epstein aboard the yacht only twice: he was prone to extreme seasickness.

Shy and at times reclusive, Wexner was an unusual fit with the charming, handsome partier Epstein. But it was clear to those around Wexner that Epstein had a hold on him. "It just makes no sense why [Wexner] did any of that, to allow Epstein to manage all his money. It was baffling," said one of the company's former top executives, who echoed a near-universal sentiment among many people we spoke with. "Everyone thought Les was such a retail genius, then he did this. It was so bizarre."

It wasn't like Wexner to trust someone so easily, quickly, and with such conviction. His mother, Bella Wexner, was among those with suspicions about Epstein's motives. So was Alfred Taubman, the Detroit real estate developer and Wexner's close friend. He asked Wexner directly why he gave Epstein such expansive powers to operate on his behalf. Taubman later recounted the exchange to the journalist Edward Jay Epstein (no relation).[8] "If you knew how much money he has made me, you wouldn't ask," Wexner responded. Another wealthy man, a financier, who knew Epstein since the 1990s, explained his methodology to the same journalist years later. Jeffrey Epstein offered to run a "reverse Ponzi scheme" for the financier, essentially proposing to hide some of his vast wealth from the government. It was a service Epstein said he offered clients looking to avoid taxes or reduce their alimony payments. Clients who gave Epstein power of attorney to execute the scheme gave themselves a measure of protection, offering a way to claim plausible deniability should the IRS ever sniff out the illegal activity.

Thirty years later, Wexner said he did nothing unusual in signing over his rights to Epstein. "He was given power of attorney as is common in that context, and he had wide latitude to act on my behalf with respect to my personal finances while I focused on building my company and undertaking philanthropic efforts," Wexner wrote in a 2019 public letter to the Wexner Foundation, his family's philanthropic organization.[9]

Epstein settled into a consigliere-type role with Wexner. Epstein's rising influence in Wexner's life coincided with his marriage to Abigail in 1993 and the widening gulf in his relationship with his mother, Bella. Shortly before the wedding, Wexner replaced his mother, then in her mideighties, as one of the trustees of their family charitable organization, the Wexner Foundation, while she recovered from an illness. Epstein took her spot. When Bella tried to return to her trustee role a few years later, Wexner and Epstein blocked her. "If my client needs protecting—sometimes even from his own family—then it's often better that people hate me, not the client," Epstein later told *Vanity Fair*.[10]

None of the executives we spoke to in reporting this book told us they remember seeing Epstein join any Victoria's Secret meetings. Some, including Anne Enke, a former fashion director at Victoria's Secret, saw him traveling with Wexner on the corporate jet. During her flight with Epstein, he and Wexner discussed plans for the interior design of the yacht. "It was clear to me that he had Les's attention," she said.

But most executives said they were unaware of his involvement in the Limited Brands' day-to-day operations. Key people involved with the catalog and models said they had never heard of him before his arrest in 2019. He did show up for the fashion show in the early years, often sitting next to Wexner or his wife, Abigail, and often with his girlfriend, a striking woman named Ghislaine Maxwell. Naomi Campbell remembered "he was always front and center."[11]

Epstein did interact with executives on Limited Brands' corporate finance and investor relations teams. (One of those executives recalled

Epstein as nasty and dismissive in his dealing with executives, especially with women. "He was a very active force," said the executive.) In particular, Epstein was said to be deeply involved in a series of complicated financial maneuvers in the second half of the 1990s. As his women's apparel brands struggled, Wexner opted to spin out several divisions from Limited Brands. One was Abercrombie & Fitch, which became its own entity in 1996. The other was a combination of Victoria's Secret and Bath & Body Works, which became Intimate Brands, Inc., in 1998. Epstein drove the strategy behind both deals, according to former Limited Brands executives. The spinouts were billed as a boon for Wall Street, freeing the new divisions—and their stock prices—from the struggles of the Limited and Express. Limited Brands retained a majority stake in Intimate Brands until reabsorbing the business in 2002.

Wexner had other plans for Abercrombie. In 1997, he summoned every Limited Brands C-suite executive to his home in Columbus to announce that the Limited Brands would divest fully from the new entity. The decision bewildered many of his executives. The provocative teen brand was an impressive, highly profitable retail success story thanks to Mike Jeffries, its dogmatic chief executive. Its revenue had nearly tripled between 1994 and 1996 to $335 million.[12] But in 1998, two years after Abercrombie went public, Limited Brands sold its majority stake in the brand on the public market. The sale was meant to be tax-free to shareholders, allowing them to swap Abercrombie & Fitch stock for Limited stock, and vice versa.

Some executives speculated that Epstein had manipulated the stock sale to Wexner's benefit and to the detriment of others. Rita Trevino Flynn, the head of communications at Limited Brands in the 1990s, was one of those executives, according to a colleague. She resigned shortly after the transaction. (Flynn declined to comment about the deal for this book.) Other senior executives close to the deal denied any wrongdoing and said that divesting from Abercrombie was a practical decision with upside for shareholders. The transaction raised no red flags for outsiders or the business press at the time.

Executives also knew Wexner was eager to cut ties with Jeffries. It was not unusual for Wexner to argue with his most successful executives, especially Express CEO Michael Weiss. But the relationship with Jeffries was different. Jeffries was reluctant to listen to Wexner and often veered from his playbook: he hired designers years before Wexner mandated the same strategy at his other divisions.[13] Jeffries turned Abercrombie's catalogs into highly produced quarterly magazines, reflecting his provocative personality and connection with the art and fashion worlds. (Bruce Weber and his Montauk crew, including influential marketer Sam Shahid, were Jeffries's close friends, and Weber's photographs became synonymous with Abercrombie & Fitch.) Other executives thought Wexner was jealous of Jeffries's booming success, which came right as the Limited and Express were on the decline.

Meanwhile, Epstein's life only grew more extravagant, thanks to Wexner. Sometime in the early-to-mid-1990s, Wexner privately transferred to Epstein his lavish Upper East Side mega-mansion on Seventy-First Street, once the largest private home in Manhattan, for an unknown sum. Wexner had bought the property in 1989 for $13.2 million and spent tens of millions more redecorating its twenty-one thousand square feet in an opulent French Renaissance–inspired style.[14] The former schoolhouse dominated the block, presenting more like a museum or embassy than a home. The heavy oak front doors were fifteen feet tall. Wexner added a seventh floor, elevator, and heating panels underneath the front sidewalk, so snow would never collect there. "Les never spent more than two months here," Epstein told a reporter in 1998.[15] Wexner's representatives later said Epstein purchased the property for $20 million, while other reports maintain the price was much lower, tantamount to a gift.

Epstein had coveted the mansion for years. He quickly remodeled it in a garish style, with leather-paneled walls and leopard-print chairs. He replaced Wexner's Picassos with what guests frequently described as striking and disturbing art pieces and curios: rows of individually framed prosthetic eyeballs; a human-size chessboard modeled after his employees, in their underwear; a photorealistic painted portrait of Epstein in a prison yard; a life-size female doll hanging from a chandelier; and, most memorably to guests, a large painting of President Bill Clinton wearing Monica Lewinsky's famous blue dress.[16]

The mansion became the locus of Epstein's power. It was there where he entertained all manner of prestigious people who would one day express regret about their associations with him—scientists, artists, businessmen, and intellectuals, including linguist Noam Chomsky, former Treasury secretary Larry Summers, and Bard College president Leon Botstein.

And the mansion was where Epstein lured and trapped the vulnerable young women he sexually abused in systematic fashion for years to come.

/ / /

In 1991, a friend of Epstein's introduced him to a charming and beautiful British socialite named Ghislaine Maxwell. The two soon became inseparable. They were romantically involved for a decade, on and off, but their unique partnership lasted much longer.

Maxwell was born into money, but not gentry, in the United Kingdom. Her father, Ian Robert Maxwell, was a Czechoslovakian refugee who served as a minister of the parliament in Great Britain in the 1960s while amassing a publishing empire. He became a well-connected political power broker, locked in a fierce rivalry with Rupert Murdoch. At one point, Maxwell owned the country's largest commercial printer, the Mirror Group Newspapers (publisher of the *Daily Mirror*), and Macmillan, among other communications firms. In 1991, Maxwell disappeared from his yacht, the *Lady Ghislaine*, off the coast of the Canary Islands. His body was found in the sea the next day. Weeks later, his company collapsed and filed for bankruptcy protection. Maxwell, much to the British public's shock, was deep in debt and had been pilfering money from his companies' pension funds.[17] His business dealings were murky, and rumors spread wildly that his mysterious death was neither an accident nor suicide. (Conspiracy theorists still insist that Mossad, the Israeli intelligence agency, killed Maxwell after Israel refused to loan him money to cover his debts and Maxwell responded with threats.[18])

When her father died, Ghislaine Maxwell was newly arrived in New York City and had recently met Epstein. He had money to spare, largely thanks to his employer Wexner.[19] Maxwell was broke, forced to downgrade from a Columbus Circle high-rise to a Midtown studio apartment. Epstein later set her up in a nicer place, according to friends, and she became his personal and professional partner. She managed his properties and was an intriguing social asset by his side as he forged relationships with powerful people like Prince Andrew and President Bill Clinton.

Epstein and Maxwell met Clinton as early as 1993, his first year in office, when they attended a fundraiser at the White House. In the years that followed, Epstein was a frequent visitor at the White House, but it remains unclear what he was doing there and whether it had anything to do with Wexner. In the 1990s, Wexner actively lobbied against barriers on imported apparel and had cultivated his own relationship with Clinton.[20] The president invited Wexner to a small group lunch with other CEOs at the White House at the beginning of his administration.[21]

While Epstein and Maxwell were hobnobbing with princes and presidents, they were secretly and systematically abusing young women and girls. (Clinton maintains he knew nothing about Epstein's crimes.[22]) The couple drew young women into their world with promises of money and career support, as federal prosecutors later showed. They forced their victims to participate in sexual acts both in the United States and abroad. Around 2000, Epstein bought a Boeing 727 from Limited Brands. The plane, later dubbed the "Lolita Express" by Epstein and his friends, allowed him to travel freely between his homes in Manhattan, New Mexico, and Palm Beach, and his private island in the US Virgin Islands. Maxwell served as recruiter and trainer, introducing herself to young women, gaining their trust, and instructing them how to perform sexual acts on Epstein.[23] Maxwell, who was convicted in 2021 for her role in helping Epstein abuse underage women, pleaded not guilty and maintains her innocence as she serves a twenty-year sentence.

As Victoria's Secret became a powerful platform for models in the late 1990s, Epstein used his knowledge of the business to lure aspiring models into compromising situations. In May 1997, Epstein met a model named Alicia Arden in Los Angeles through a mutual friend who told Arden that Epstein could get her work as a model for Victoria's Secret. She called Epstein at his office in New York, and he asked her to mail him some pictures of herself modeling lingerie, which she did. He rang her back, and suggested they meet at the upscale Shutters on the Beach hotel in Santa Monica. When Arden arrived for the meeting, Epstein told her to undress and started to pull her clothing off, groping her, and said, "Let me manhandle you for a second." Horrified and in tears, she ran out and later reported the incident to the police.[24]

An Italian model, Elisabetta Tai, said she had a similar experience in Epstein's Manhattan home in 2004. She showed up expecting to meet the head of Victoria's Secret. When Epstein took off his clothes and instructed her to give him a massage, she fled, too.[25]

Victoria's Secret model Frederique van der Wal recalled about five separate occasions when models told her they were planning to meet with

Epstein. She cautioned them. "I would go, why? The guy has nothing to do with Victoria's Secret," she said. "Absolutely not."

Epstein allegedly met some of his model victims through the influential French modeling agent Jean-Luc Brunel, who became the head of Karin Models in Paris in 1978. In the decade that followed, Brunel was a fixture of Parisian nightlife, usually surrounded by young models, successful businessmen, and copious amounts of drugs. Teenage models just starting their careers in Paris often stayed at his apartment in the city.

Brunel was a predator, too. In a *60 Minutes* exposé that aired in 1988, several models accused Brunel of pressuring them to have sex with them and of drugging and raping them.[26] But Brunel was not charged with any crimes, and the next year, he and his brother quietly became partners in a new modeling agency in New York City, Next Models, run by the respected agent Faith Kates. Employees at the agency said they remembered seeing Epstein around from time to time or calling Kates at her office.[27] (In 2019, Kates, through a lawyer, denied having any significant relationship with Epstein.) Epstein dated several models represented by Next, including Alina Puşcău, who appeared in a couple of Victoria's Secret catalogs in 2003.[28] In 2005, Epstein even gave Brunel a million-dollar line of credit to open a new model agency in Miami, MC2 Model Management. Epstein told one of his victims, Virginia Roberts Giuffre, that Brunel brought in underage women from eastern Europe and elsewhere. Epstein told her he had sex with more than a thousand of them.[29]

In 2019, Wexner denied knowing that Epstein used his connections to Victoria's Secret to entrap women. He also denied any knowledge of Epstein's abuse of minors and young women. But some of Epstein's victims, including Giuffre, have alleged differently.

In 2000, Giuffre was seventeen years old and working as a locker room attendant at Mar-a-Lago, Donald Trump's resort in Palm Beach, when Maxwell spotted her and offered to train her as a massage therapist. Giuffre agreed. The first time she visited Epstein at his home nearby, he and Maxwell sexually abused her. They paid Giuffre several hundred dollars, much more than she made at Mar-a-Lago.

Giuffre was particularly vulnerable. She had been sexually abused by a family friend growing up and had run away from home, moving in and out of foster care. She needed money. She spent the next three years traveling with the couple, who directed her to have sex with Epstein and Epstein's friends, and taught her how to recruit other vulnerable girls into their masseuse ring. When Epstein traveled to Africa with Bill Clinton in September 2002, he sent Giuffre to Thailand to vet a young girl for him. Giuffre took the opportunity to flee, and started her life over in Australia. In 2009, Giuffre sued Epstein for sexually trafficking her as a minor; Epstein settled for $500,000. Two years later, Giuffre went public with her story in the *Mail on Sunday*, which published a picture of her arm-in-arm with Prince Andrew.

In 2016, when Giuffre was deposed as part of another Epstein-related lawsuit, she said she had sex with Wexner more than three times, following Epstein and Maxwell's directions. She also said that, on one occasion, she had sex with both Wexner and Jeffrey Epstein's assistant Sarah Kellen at Epstein's home in New Mexico. Giuffre also named other prominent participants, including two she sued herself: Prince Andrew (for sexual abuse) and Epstein's lawyer Alan Dershowitz (for defamation, after he denied ever having sex with her). In 2022, Giuffre dropped her suit against Dershowitz and said she may have made a mistake in identifying him. "I was very young at the time, it was a very stressful and traumatic environment, and Mr. Dershowitz has from the beginning consistently denied these allegations," she said.[30]

In 2020, Wexner lawyers disputed Giuffre's story, saying he never met her. "Mr. Wexner was unaware of, and was never a participant in, any of the abhorrent behavior engaged in by Epstein against Epstein's victims," said representatives.[31]

Another one of Epstein's earliest known victims, a painter named Maria Farmer, holds Wexner partially responsible for her abuse on his property.[32] Farmer, who has since shared her story with multiple publications, met Epstein in 1995 when she was twenty-five years old. They were introduced by the dean of her school, the New York Academy of Art, at a gallery show for her graduation. Epstein had been on the board of the school and soon hired Farmer to buy art for him and work on the renovation of his home, she said. The next summer, Farmer was commissioned to create some large-scale paintings for the film *As Good as It Gets*, and Epstein offered her his home in New Albany—on Wexner's gated estate, in view of his mansion there—as something of an artist's retreat. To leave the property, Farmer said she needed to call Abigail Wexner to get per-

mission from the on-site security teams. When Epstein and Maxwell visited the house toward the end of the summer, Farmer said they forcibly
groped her. According to Farmer, she fled and hid in a room in the house
and started calling friends and family for help. Farmer alleged that Wexner's security team would not allow her to leave the property for twelve
hours, and only let her go when her father arrived by car from Kentucky
to get her out of town. Farmer said Maxwell later called and threatened
her multiple times.[33]

Farmer soon discovered the couple had pulled her sixteen-year-old
sister Annie into their orbit, too. On a visit to Epstein's Zorro Ranch in
New Mexico, Maxwell groped Annie while Epstein watched, the younger
Farmer said. Maria Farmer tried to sound an alarm about Epstein, reporting her experience to the New York City Police Department and the FBI,
but nothing came of it. In 2003, she and her sister spoke to *Vanity Fair*
about their experience with Epstein, but the magazine decided not to
publish their accounts.[34]

All the while, Epstein cultivated a reputation as a dashing "international moneyman of mystery," as *New York* magazine called him in 2002.
In the piece, Donald Trump praised Epstein for his vibrant social life. "It
is even said that he likes beautiful women as much as I do, and many of
them are on the younger side," he said.[35] (Trump later claimed Epstein had
written the quote himself and had asked Trump if he could attribute it to
him. The future president said he had agreed.[36]) Epstein bolstered his own
reputation, too. In the early 2000s, when Mickey Drexler was still running
Gap Inc., he encountered Epstein at the Forstmann, Little & Company
conference in Aspen. It was an elite invitation—no media allowed—and
Drexler was there to schmooze and network. Drexler had met Epstein a
few years earlier at the White House. "What do you do exactly?" Drexler
asked. "I date young girls," Epstein answered.

Meister, the insurance executive who introduced Epstein to Wexner,
said he was disgusted to catch a glimpse into Epstein's world. In the 1990s,
Epstein showed up unannounced at Meister's apartment with five young
women in tow. "Epstein thought he was bringing me a gift," Meister told
Vanity Fair in 2021. "I told him, 'Get the fuck out and I never want to see
you again!'"[37]

Meister begged Wexner to stay away from Epstein, he said, but he was
too late. Epstein was a "loyal friend," as Wexner described him to *Vanity*

Fair in 2003. He said Epstein had "excellent judgment and unusually high standards," adding that "Jeffrey has the unusual quality of knowing when he is winning."[38] In the first decade of the 2000s, Epstein was certainly winning, flying Clinton to Africa on his private jet and hosting a science conference, attended by Stephen Hawking, on his private island.[39] His relationship with Wexner seemed unbreakable, especially to Epstein. Between 1991 and 2006, Epstein oversaw the sale of $1.3 billion of company stocks, held in trusts connected to Wexner.[40] "People have said it's like we have one brain between two of us," Epstein told *Vanity Fair*. "Each has a side."

/ / /

In December 2007, after more than sixteen years of close partnership, Wexner quietly revoked Epstein's power of attorney.[41]

Epstein's reckless behavior had finally caught up with him—or at least so it seemed. In 2005, a fourteen-year-old victim went to the police with her parents and said that after she had agreed to massage him for $200, Epstein had molested her at his home in Palm Beach.[42] The police began an investigation, and in 2006 charged Epstein and two assistants with multiple sexual acts with minors. When a grand jury indicted Epstein on only one count of prostitution, and not with a minor, the police urged the FBI to open its own investigation. Throughout 2007, as the US Attorney's Office prepared an indictment and issued subpoenas, Epstein's lawyers spent months negotiating the details of a plea deal.

It was also in 2007 when Wexner later said he first heard about the allegations against Epstein in Florida, according to a letter he wrote to his foundation in 2019. Wexner said Epstein denied any wrongdoing, but Wexner still decided Epstein "should step back from the management of our personal finances." In the fall of 2007, as he was breaking ties with Epstein, Wexner said he discovered that Epstein had stolen "vast sums of money" from him and his family. He never disclosed the total number. "This was, frankly, a tremendous shock, even though it clearly pales in comparison to the unthinkable allegations against him now," Wexner wrote, adding that Epstein returned part of the stolen money—$46 million—in 2008.[43]

Wexner neither reported Epstein nor went public with his discovery of the theft. Epstein's attorney at the time, Alan Dershowitz, recalled asking Epstein if he was concerned that Wexner might testify against him in court. "I have absolutely no fear of that," Epstein told Dershowitz. (Dershowitz told us in a 2022 interview that he assumed the reason was "something sexual.")

On June 30, 2008, Epstein pleaded guilty in Florida to a sweetheart deal. Though Palm Beach police had identified more than thirty underage victims, Epstein only admitted to one count of solicitation of prostitution and one count of solicitation of prostitution with a minor under the age of eighteen. The plea deal was filed under seal, hidden from the public record, and the agreement put a stop to the ongoing federal investigation. Epstein's victims weren't even informed of the deal until the following month. Epstein served thirteen months in the Palm Beach County stockade, though he was usually released during the day to work from his office in West Palm Beach. He served another year on probation, confined to his Palm Beach home and office, but he frequently violated the terms by traveling on his private jet. "Your body can be confined, but not your mind," Epstein told a reporter shortly before reporting for prison in 2008.[44] In the article, Epstein said the only client he could disclose publicly was Wexner.

Epstein finished his sentence in Florida in 2010 and returned to New York to mount a comeback as a "hedge funder with a zealous science background," as Forbes.com described him in an article that was later revealed to be written by a publicity firm.[45] Despite his new status as a sex offender, he found many of his friends eager to welcome him back and happy to take his word that his crimes were trivial. Even as some of his victims, including Virginia Giuffre, began a lengthy process of suing both Epstein and Maxwell, he hosted dinner parties at his Manhattan mansion attended by Katie Couric, Prince Andrew, and many others. His schedule was packed with meetings with politicians, academics, and other leaders, including Bill Gates, Woody Allen, and financier Leon Black.[46] Epstein attended events with the likes of Jeff Bezos or Elon Musk.[47] "I'm not a sexual predator, I'm an 'offender,'" Epstein told the New York Post in 2011. "It's the difference between a murderer and a person who steals a bagel."[48]

Epstein's grand rehabilitation plan appeared to be successful until the end of 2018, when the *Miami Herald* published Julie K. Brown's bomb-shell investigation into his criminal history. The paper quoted victims and investigators who had never spoken publicly before and questioned why the US Attorney had been so lenient. That prosecutor, R. Alexander Acosta, had recently been appointed US Secretary of Labor by Epstein's old friend Donald Trump. The FBI reopened its investigation.

On July 6, 2019, when Epstein landed at Teterboro Airport, in New Jersey, after a trip to France, federal agents and New York City police officers were waiting for him. He was arrested for sex trafficking dozens of underage girls between 2002 and 2005, and faced up to forty-five years in prison. Epstein's story became front-page news. How did he get away with such a light punishment in 2008? How much did his wealthy and powerful friends know?

The questions, the media attention—much of it led back to Wexner. Reporters pieced together Epstein's sketchy history. Victims like the model Alicia Arden came forward with their stories. The timing couldn't have been worse for Wexner. Victoria's Secret's profits were plummeting, and an activist investor was calling for him to step down as CEO of Limited Brands.

Wexner finally broke his silence on Epstein on August 8, 2019, in a public letter addressed to the Wexner Foundation, where Epstein once served as a trustee. Wexner's comments did little to quell the media storm. Two days later, Epstein was found dead in his jail cell in downtown Manhattan after previously attempting to end his life at least once while incarcerated. His death, ruled a suicide, only furthered the interest in his life—and spurred new conspiracy theories.

A few weeks after Epstein's death, Wexner tried to explain himself at the annual L Brands investor day meeting. He emphasized that his relationship with Epstein ended a "long time ago" and chose his words extremely carefully, never actually referring to Epstein by name. "In the present, everyone has to feel enormous regret for the advantage that was taken of so many young women and that's just unexplainable abhorrent behavior, and clearly is something we all would condemn." Wexner said he was embarrassed to be taken advantage of by someone so sick. "At some point in your life we are all betrayed by friends," he said. "And if we haven't, we're really fortunate to have lived a perfectly sheltered life."[49]

And with that, he got back to the business. The wider world, however, was not ready to move on.

/ / /

President Joe Biden was grinning from ear to ear one sunny morning just after Labor Day in 2022, addressing a crowd from a makeshift stage in a razed field in Licking County, northeast of Columbus. Trump won by a landslide there in both 2016 and 2020. "It's time to bury the label 'Rust Belt,'" Biden said. Behind him, an American flag hung down from the arm of a strategically placed idling excavator. "Made in Ohio and Made in America is not just a slogan," Biden said. "It's happening."[50]

The president had flown in that morning to celebrate the groundbreaking of Intel's largest-ever semiconductor manufacturing facility, a $20 billion investment touted as the largest economic development project in the history of Ohio. Semiconductors, the microchips that power everything from cars to smartphones, had become an urgent political issue. The pandemic had led to supply shortages and emphasized the precariousness of relying on Taiwan for chips when US-China relations were so strained. Ohio leaders competed aggressively to win Intel's business, offering $650 million in tax incentives over thirty years and lobbying for passage of Biden's CHIPS Act, which provided federal funding for the project. Intel announced its plans to build in Ohio in January 2022. At his press event, President Biden went through a laundry list of thank-you shout-outs, crediting Ohio's governor Mike DeWine, congresswoman Joyce Beatty, and many others. Columbus leaders trumpeted the city as the next American tech hub, "The Silicon Heartland." The slogan had become more than just marketing. Columbus was the fastest-growing city in the Midwest and one of the country's top cities for data centers and cloud computing.

Unmentioned onstage or in the press coverage that day was Les Wexner, the most powerful man in Columbus and the architect of New Albany. The suburb of eleven thousand people had beaten out forty other US cities for Intel's historic investment. It was Wexner's firm, the New Albany Company, that had packaged and sold Intel the thousand acres of land for its plant.

If things had gone differently, Biden might have taken the opportunity to visit Wexner's grand estate, not ten miles from the Intel construction site, as many other presidents had done before. When former president Barack Obama met with Wexner in Columbus in 2018, their meeting made national news: Wexner announced that he would no longer support the Republican Party. (Wexner considered President Trump to be abhorrent, especially after the 2017 white nationalist rally in Charlottesville.) But Wexner had become too much of a political liability to land a visit from Biden.

Today, he and Abigail no longer host large-scale public events at their mansion or its "party barn" on the property, where they once held an annual black-tie gala dramatically called "A Remarkable Evening." (Now the event is held elsewhere in New Albany.) Abigail's family-friendly horse show, the New Albany Classic, "hung up its helmet" in 2018 after running for more than two decades on Wexner's estate. The annual event once featured performances by Ariana Grande and the Jonas Brothers. In 2022, Wexner stepped down from his longtime role as the chair of the Columbus Partnership, the city's most powerful group of business leaders, which he had cofounded in 2002.

But Columbus has not rejected Wexner. His name remains visible on Ohio State's campus, where he endowed the arts center and the medical center. And every year, more than thirty million people visit Easton Town Center, the quaint outdoor shopping center village he developed northeast of Columbus more than twenty-five years ago.

Many locals still protect Wexner—not only former Limited Brands executives, but also leaders at the universities, hospitals, arts organizations, and Jewish groups to which he has contributed so much. Many of Wexner's former employees feel a range of sadness and frustration. Some are motivated to defend him out of fear that his misconduct might reflect poorly on them and on the work they did together. Ohio State University and the Wexner Foundation both launched investigations into their ties to Epstein and shared their results publicly. (OSU found Epstein had donated $336,000, and gifted the same amount to an anti–human trafficking group. The foundation determined Epstein played no role in its management or administration.)

As more information about Epstein has surfaced in the years since his death, the "why" of the relationship between Wexner and Epstein remains puzzling. Some people still believe the two men had a romantic relationship or that Epstein connected Wexner with young men, and that Wexner's money silenced their stories. Colleagues and acquaintances have questioned Wexner's sexuality since the 1980s, a speculation Wexner himself addressed (and denied) in the 1985 *New York* magazine profile. But those who knew Wexner were not aware of any romantic relationships with men. And no one has come forward with such an accusation. (Epstein denied having a sexual relationship with Wexner in a 2010 deposition.[51])

Brad Edwards, the longtime lawyer for several Epstein's victims, considers Wexner's claim of ignorance believable. "We have not seen where [Wexner] is in the company of Jeffrey Epstein at the time when he was engaging in these things," Edwards said in 2019. "In fact, it's very seldom that many of the victims actually even met him or saw [Wexner]. I do know that there's a lot of business ties to him, but other than receiving information about their business connection, I don't have any information to believe otherwise."[52]

Over the years, Wexner did maintain relationships with other employees that colleagues and associates viewed as unusual. Wexner handpicked a young man for Victoria's Secret marketing team in 1997 who was "dashing, flashy, well-spoken, phony—there was an attraction there between him and Les, clearly," according to one executive. The man was fired just months later after it was discovered that he had faked his experience. "The head of human resources had to take the fall," the executive said. "Who was going to challenge that one?"

Another employee with a prominent role in Wexner's life was Jamie McFate—the head of Wexner's strategic patterning division acting as in-house consulting firm. McFate was his ultimate yes-man, especially at the end of Wexner's retail career, someone Wexner and his wife Abigail treated like family. McFate often vacationed with the Wexners and even had a designated bedroom on the yacht *Limitless*. Wexner gave him extravagant gifts, colleagues said, including a Picasso and a Maserati. McFate's precise role in the business was unclear, even to those who believed they were in Wexner's inner circle.

Whatever its precise nature, Wexner's relationship with Epstein irrevocably tarnished his legacy. But Wexner did not slink away. While he stopped speaking publicly after the scandal, he remained actively involved in Columbus affairs behind the scenes. From the outside, Wexner remained all-powerful. "A divorce from Wexner is improbable, almost unimaginable," wrote David Ghose, the editor of *Columbus Monthly*. "How could the city cut ties with someone who is essentially the father of modern Columbus?"[53]

CHAPTER 15

No One Left to Say No

Les Wexner reasserts control—with disastrous results.

It was the last night of New York Fashion Week in September 2018, and the sweaty crowd milling inside a nearly pitch-dark warehouse in Brooklyn was growing antsy. Everyone knew that Rihanna was somewhere in the building.[1] The Barbadian pop star had summoned fashion editors and influencers to the borough's industrial Navy Yard "to enter the world of Savage x Fenty," the lingerie line she had launched four months earlier. Her brand offered a collection of sheer and lace bralettes, thong bodysuits, and garter belts—all sold only online. On the day of the launch, May 11, the e-commerce site crashed—just as Victoria's Secret's had nearly done twenty years earlier when the company first streamed its fashion show.

But Savage x Fenty was not Victoria's Secret. The line's designs veered unapologetically risqué, much like Rihanna herself. Unlike the other sexualized female pop stars of her generation, Rihanna carried a fuck-it attitude that made her seem in control of every element of her image and career. So when she explained her lingerie line was designed for women to please themselves, not men, the pitch felt authentic. "Savage is really about taking complete ownership of how you feel and the choices you make," she said. "Basically making sure everybody knows the ball is in your court."[2]

Inside the warehouse, an elevated circular set supported an earth science laboratory dotted with biomes full of leafy green plants, colorful flowers, and tide pools. When the "fashion show" finally began, dancers in the line's pastel and neon lingerie began floating through the space, posing and dancing like supernatural creatures in the stage's various dioramas. Several of the models who emerged to join them had appeared in Victoria's Secret shows, including the sisters Gigi and Bella Hadid.

But most of the women onstage would never have met the physical standards of Victoria's Secret, nor those of most designers showing at Fashion Week. Many of Rihanna's models had the athletic build of professional dancers typically seen in music videos. Several were plus-size. Two were very pregnant (a rarity on the runway). One, the model Slick Woods, was so far along that she went into labor backstage after the show.

Rihanna, notorious for abiding by no one's schedule except her own, often arriving hours after she is expected, appeared only at the finale of the show. She waved to the applauding crowd, wearing not her own lingerie but a clingy dress. On Instagram, however, she was her own best spokesperson, frequently posing proudly in lingerie and revealing a body that was curvier and softer than it had been at the height of her pop career. Like in 2012, when she performed during the Victoria's Secret Fashion Show cinched into a tight Vivienne Westwood corset gown. But she was no longer holding herself to a pop star's physical standards, and she seemed much happier for it. "I'm not built like a Victoria's Secret girl, and I still feel very beautiful and confident in my lingerie," she said in 2018 while promoting Savage, crediting her newly "thicc" body as the reason women clamored to buy anything she wanted to sell them.[3]

Women were responding to more than just the shape of Rihanna's body. Her version of sexy was more likely to be aggressive than coquettish. She and the models she chose were not just sex objects. They had a glint in their eyes that read: we are multidimensional, and we are not dressing up just for you.

Rihanna's message served the moment. A new wave of feminism had arrived, set off by the election of Donald Trump and increasing reductions to abortion access across the country. The #MeToo movement became a global campaign after several brave women and journalists unmasked Harvey Weinstein as a longtime serial predator in a series of investigative articles published in 2017. Across the country, spanning industries, women came forward with stories of sexual assault, cover-ups, and power games. For the first time, there was a sustained, unblinking national conversation about the ways men mistreated women, especially in the workplace. It seemed like every day, another powerful man resigned in response to accusations of abuse. Three of the most powerful photographers in fashion, Patrick Demarchelier, Mario Testino, and Bruce Weber, were largely excommunicated from the industry after several models told the *Boston Globe* and the *New York Times* the men had sexually assaulted them.[4] Terry Richardson, another prominent fashion photographer, also faced allegations of sexual assault and was dropped by most of his clients.[5] (In the years to follow, more photographers would face the same allegations and consequences.)

In a general, and perhaps subconscious, trend, many high-fashion designers shunned cleavage and miniskirts, and women's fashion turned conservative and oversize. High-rise pants replaced low-rise ones. (For example, see Gucci's maximalist layers from its blockbuster Alessandro Michele years, and all the mass-market brands that copied them, and the rise of the Valentino cape dress.) Advertising that catered to male expectations of traditional female beauty felt outdated at best and socially damaging at worst. More women looked at Victoria's Secret and wondered, *Why is this still okay? Why did I love this as a girl?* "For a lot of women, Victoria's Secret is an entry point for female sexuality," said Jill Filipovic, a writer covering politics and culture. She wrote about the brand's empty feminism for *Cosmopolitan* in 2016, describing the Victoria's Secret fantasy as "filtered through a really narrow, really unattainable male gaze–centric lens." She wasn't the only writer pointing out the same message. Even before Trump's election and the rise of the #MeToo movement, women were becoming more vocal about challenging everyday sexism. "Feminism" was no longer a dirty word.

Women who grew up never truly questioning the messages baked into *The Simple Life* or the slogans printed on Pink's hip-hugging underwear were changing, but Victoria's Secret wasn't evolving with them. The brand was still hawking the virtues of "training like an Angel" and the "inspirational" beauty of its slim and happy supermodels. Compared to Rihanna's Savage, Victoria's Secret seemed about as relevant as the dour department store lingerie floors it once replaced.

///

In 2015, three years before Rihanna launched Savage x Fenty, Victoria's Secret seemed unstoppable. That year in the United States, the brand brought in a whopping $7.7 billion in revenue and $1.4 billion in operating income, its best performance ever. In-store sales had grown every single quarter since the beginning of 2009. The brand's lingerie accounted for an estimated 60 percent of the total US intimate apparel market. American malls were attracting fewer visitors overall, but Victoria's Secret stores always tracked above-average traffic levels. Its parent company's stock price was sky-high for retail, peaking at almost $80 per share. More international expansion plans were underway. The first large-scale Victoria's Secret stores in China were due to open soon, in Shanghai and Chengdu. The fashion show was set for Paris in 2016 and Shanghai in 2017. Back home, a new four-story Manhattan flagship would soon open on Fifth Avenue, with a "museum" dedicated to the Angels and their fashion show costumes. And Victoria's Secret had expanded its television presence, packaging behind-the-scenes-style footage of its swimsuit catalog photoshoot in Puerto Rico into an hour-long *Swim Special* on CBS. Les Wexner's ambition to grow Victoria's Secret to a $10 billion business appeared inevitable.

Even as the brand's sales and profits continued to grow, some key dynamics of the business had shifted. Push-up bras were losing market share. Pink had become the brand's greatest growth driver. Between 2012 and 2015, sales of the teen line's bras and underwear increased by 50 percent, while sales of Victoria's Secret lingerie grew by 18 percent. The beauty division, which generated the fattest profits, had not grown in about five years.[6]

CEO Sharen Jester Turney found herself increasingly at odds with Les Wexner on how to move forward. She felt Victoria's Secret was long overdue for a technology upgrade. Digital channel sales had plateaued while, across US retail, online sales were outpacing brick-and-mortar. The brand had invested early in building social media audiences and upgrading its website for mobile-friendly shopping. But its e-commerce business was outdated and under-resourced by 2015. "The platform was archaic," said an executive in the division at the time, noting how all of Victoria's Secret's competitors had long since moved to popular e-commerce providers like Shopify and Salesforce.

Turney also believed the brand needed fresh marketing ideas. Calvin Klein's formula of using of-the-moment pop-culture personalities had allowed it to evolve with the times. American Eagle's intimate brand Aerie was growing quickly, fueled by its "no-airbrushing" marketing campaigns starring young women without visibly defined ab muscles. But over at Victoria's Secret, conversations about tweaking the brand identity went nowhere. In the pages of the catalog, almost every model was digitally altered to have deeper cleavage and thinner thighs. The fashion show somehow always looked the same, whether it was staged in New York or London or Paris. "We always reverted back to where we were," said Turney.

Turney was also frustrated with the corporate politics. Wexner's central group of executives—all men except for her—competed constantly for his approval. "He was always with four, five, six people following him," remembered a former merchant. In 2016, with only one year until Wexner's eightieth birthday, the succession question loomed large.

Above all, Turney disagreed with Wexner's emerging belief that Victoria's Secret sold too many types of products. For most of her tenure as the brand's CEO, she had pursued the opposite strategy. Introducing new categories, like swimsuits and beauty products and sports bras, gave shoppers more reasons to visit the stores and websites—and buy bras. Wexner had read a 2014 book called *The Good Jobs Strategy* by Zeynep Ton, a professor at MIT Sloan School of Management. Ton argues that companies offering customers fewer options are more successful than competitors that offer more options. Focused companies run more smoothly and efficiently and generate higher profits, she writes, pointing to grocery stores like Costco and Trader Joe's as examples.

Wexner wanted to apply the idea at Bath & Body Works and Victoria's Secret, where he urged Turney to consider cutting both swimwear and athletic apparel. He also considered reducing the number of sales associates employed in stores. Turney was opposed to these ideas. Victoria's Secret wasn't a grocery store, she thought. These strategies would not work in intimate apparel. But she held him off by canceling a few categories, like the brand's makeup line and the jeans and dresses still sold through the catalog.

As the divide between Turney and Wexner grew wider in 2015, she sensed he also resented her rising public profile. Wall Street and the media praised her for Victoria's Secret's record-breaking financial performance. "Meet the Woman Keeping Victoria's Secret at the Forefront of the Fashion World," declared *Vogue* in December 2015. Publicly, her relationship with Wexner seemed strong. When Turney was inducted into the Oklahoma Hall of Fame in November 2015, Wexner flew down to Oklahoma City and spoke warmly of Turney as he introduced her to the audience.

Finally, in February 2016, after sixteen years with the business and a decade as its CEO, Turney left Victoria's Secret. The official story was that she resigned to focus on her family. Instead of appointing someone to replace her, Wexner announced that he was taking over the day-to-day leadership of the brand.

Employees braced themselves for more changes. "We never understood why she was leaving," said one executive, while acknowledging her exit fit a pattern she had seen before. "Any woman that was intelligent, with a strong point of view . . . if you ever wanted to say what you really thought and it was going against the grain, you were gone."

Two months after Turney's departure, Pink's CEO, Denise Landman, went to New York on Wexner's behalf to address Victoria's Secret employees based in the city. Her news was grim: Victoria's Secret would wind down its swimwear business and stop publishing the catalog altogether, two moves impacting hundreds of employees. The staff was instructed to go back to their desks and await further updates. Most of the people on the swimwear and catalog teams were laid off.

The shutdown of the catalog was not a total shock. At the time, print advertising seemed like a waste of time and money. The best place to spend marketing dollars was online. Victoria's Secret had been cutting back on the number of catalogs it mailed out per year, and reducing the page count to cut costs. Without a catalog to consider, the brand could more easily merge the stores division and direct division, each of which still operated largely independently. But the catalog had served an essential function to the business. It sent out discounts and special offers that drew customers to the website and stores on a regular basis.

The decision to end swimwear was more puzzling. It was clear that Victoria's Secret swimwear business was unnecessarily complicated, indicative of the inefficiencies that can emerge in multibillion-dollar companies. The collection was "over-assorted," meaning there were too many options. Shoppers looking for black bikini bottoms, for example, had half a dozen styles to choose from in slightly different cuts and fabrics. The swimwear merchants in the stores and online divisions competed against each other for sales, further complicating the process.

But women loved the swimsuits. Online, the category was so popular, it often outsold bras during the spring season. In stores, swimsuits drew customers, especially young women, who wanted to try on swimsuits before buying them. Bikinis were often the first item teenagers bought from the main line, and Victoria's Secret had significant market share in US swimwear, around 25 percent. For most American women, the only other store offering well-made swimsuits for less than $100 was Target. While Victoria's Secret's swimsuits only brought in $500 million in sales each year, they had higher profit margins than many other categories—yielding about $200 million annually.

With swimwear winding down, Wexner wanted sports bras to more than make up the difference. Their sales growth had been slow in recent years, so he slashed the prices. A relaunched version of "Victoria Sport" arrived in the summer of 2016, with $15-to-$20 sports bras on offer instead of the $50-to-$60 versions sold before. The strategy reduced Victoria's Secret's profit margins on the category, but Wexner felt it was worth the hit to catch up on market share. "We probably sold as many sports bras in the last four weeks . . . now that they're at a lower cost and margin characteristics, as we did in the last calendar year," he told analysts in November 2016. "But it's going to cost a few bucks to eat somebody else's lunch."

In spring 2016, Victoria's Secret also finally started advertising its bralettes—the comfy wire-free bra tops that had been trending for more than a year, especially among younger women who wore them as crop tops on their own, or under open jackets and blouses. Bralettes were almost as easy to manufacture and sell as T-shirts. Victoria's Secret had quietly sold bralettes at the end of Turney's tenure, in the spring and summer seasons of 2015, and they sold well, priced between $10 and $20 each.

At Victoria's Secret, bralettes had historically been a touchy subject. Wexner and Razek disdained them. In meetings, Razek put their view plainly: "You're not getting fucked in that. Where's the glitz, where's the glam?" He didn't consider the soft, simple bra tops to be real lingerie.

In 2016, Wexner and Razek relented to the trend and gave bralettes the Angels treatment. Wexner hoped the style would draw young shoppers into stores, leading them to buy real bras, too. (Previous strategies to that effect, namely the free-panty coupon, were no longer working. Most women would claim their free underwear and leave without buying anything.) Razek did his best to fit the bralettes into his vision for Victoria's Secret. The campaign starred three of Victoria's Secret's youngest Angels—Elsa Hosk, Taylor Hill, and Martha Hunt—styled as if they were going to a music festival, in jean shorts and rain boots. (When a merchant explained to Wexner that bralettes became popular, in part, because young women wore them to the music festival Coachella, by then an established trendsetting event, he asked, "What's Coachella?") But the bralette ad's tagline—"No padding is sexy now!"—struck an odd note. Online, blogs and social media audiences asked the inevitable question. Was no padding ugly before?

Nevertheless, Victoria's Secret's bralettes sold well and Wexner doubled down on the style for fall, not appreciating that bra tops were more popular during the spring and summer than the fall and winter. By the end of 2016, bralettes were overstocked. Discounting ensued.

Wexner's barrage of changes—cutting swim and the catalog cold turkey when the rest of the business was showing signs of weakness—were painful. His executives wondered what had happened to Wexner's "test-and-learn" strategy. "[He was] asking us to do things that are not 'test and learn,'" one executive said. "No one would ever make decisions like that without a solution. What's plan B? His theory was 'You guys can figure that out,'" they said.

Victoria's Secret's profits, sales, and mall traffic numbers began to dip. In the third quarter of 2016, the total company's profit fell by 25 percent year over year. The L Brands stock price began to steadily decline. Competitors like Aerie, which Victoria's Secret executives had long dismissed as "ankle biters," were eating into its market share. By the summer of 2016, L Brands' stock price had slid 30 percent. And it would keep dropping for many more months to come.

Years later, some analysts would look back on this period, when Victoria's Secret lost two-thirds of its operating income in the course of just three years, and wonder if Victoria's Secret's peak in 2015 was not as magical as it seemed. They wondered if the brand relied on discounting to sell more products while sacrificing profits. L Brands only reported gross profit, the metric that best reveals the effects of discounting, across the entire corporation. Bath & Body Works was growing quickly and profitably, possibly camouflaging what was happening at Victoria's Secret. "It's rare in retail that your peak is a healthy peak, versus an overstretching peak," said Simeon Siegel, the retail analyst. (Turney refutes this view, saying discounts played a minimal role in the brand's 2015 performance.)

By the end of 2016, Wexner was back in a familiar position. Fifty years earlier, when his father had doubted his strategy, Wexner established himself as one of retail's great innovators. Now, he was again under pressure to prove his instincts were right, that he was following a sound strategy others could not understand. Wexner knew the profits would take an initial hit when he began to cull categories, like the catalog. That was to be expected. His conviction remained. "In hindsight the changes that we have made—I wish we had taken those actions two years ago, or three," he told analysts at the annual L Brands investor meeting in 2016.

Inside the headquarters in Columbus, Wexner's deputies grew frustrated and dismayed. One newly hired executive recalls joining a business review meeting hosted by Wexner at the end of 2016. "It's not about digital, it's about brick and mortar," he told the gathered staff, who represented different divisions of the business. No one questioned him. Stunned, the new executive vented into her notebook, *Oh my fucking god.*

/// ///

Tectonic plates in the fashion world shifted on August 20, 2013, when *Vogue*'s editor in chief, Anna Wintour, joined Instagram for the first time. The notoriously staid fashion editor posed for a cheeky sepia-toned picture on the magazine's official account, peeking out from behind the latest September issue wearing her signature dark sunglasses. "Anna Wintour reads #TheSeptemberIssue," the caption read. "Do you? We would love to see it! Show us your #voguestagram."[7]

Although magazines like *Vogue* and editors like Wintour remained powerful arbiters of taste and celebrity, the fashion bible was facing an existential crisis as shoppers spent more time online and less time flipping through glossy pages. The internet had propelled the rise of fashion influencers, whose loyal fans tracked every post on their blogs and social media accounts. Fashion brands took notice, impressed by bloggers' ability to sell out a handbag or a blouse, by simply posting a casual photo of themselves wearing the item with an e-commerce link.

So after years of telling *Vogue* readers what to wear and how to style their hair, its editors succumbed to the indignity of playing by social media's rules. Hence Wintour's cheesy Instagram appearance. In 2013, Instagram, just three years old, had almost two hundred million active users, a number that would triple over the next three years. A handful of bloggers—including the Italian Chiara Ferragni (known as "the Blonde Salad") and the Filipino Bryan Yambao ("Bryanboy")—emerged as major fashion arbiters (and earners). But no single influencer could supplant Wintour as the defining arbiter of American fashion tastes. Instead, Wintour was slowly losing ground to hundreds of digital mini-celebrities sharing their outfit ideas and makeup routines for free online. Many grew popular because they looked nothing like the models who had long dominated the pages of fashion magazines. They were Mormon moms in Utah or sorority girls in Atlanta or magazine assistants in New York City. Maybe they wore a size 6 or a size 12 or a size 16. Or they had acne or hyperpigmentation. Some were shopping on a budget, while others were wrapped head-to-toe in designer pieces. There seemed to be an influencer for every lifestyle, socioeconomic group, skin tone, hair texture, and taste profile.

These influencers initially confounded fashion's gatekeepers. Most online personalities were neither edgy nor avant-garde nor well-bred nor rail thin. They did not share many attributes the industry typically prized. Even the most-followed person on Instagram during the app's first five years, Kim Kardashian, struggled for acceptance and acknowledgment. Many in the industry had considered her tacky, unable to look beyond her highly publicized sex tape and her family's reality television show. But Kardashian's fortunes changed in 2012, when she started dating the rapper Kanye West. He opened doors Kardashian couldn't. Kanye upgraded her style, slowly remolding her reputation as a trendsetter, and introduced her to top designers and editors who soon realized the instant attention Kardashian could bring to their brands. The influential French editor Carine Roitfeld featured Kardashian on the cover of her magazine *CR Fashion Book*, in 2013, the same year Kardashian landed her first coveted invitation to Anna Wintour's Met Gala. Then came the ultimate industry milestone: an appearance, with Kanye, on the cover of American *Vogue* in 2014, photographed by Annie Leibovitz—he in a Saint Laurent by Hedi Slimane blazer; she in a Lanvin by Alber Elbaz strapless wedding gown. Some *Vogue* fans were upset to see Kardashian validated, but Wintour was unbothered. "I think if we just remain deeply tasteful and just put deeply tasteful people on the cover, it would be a rather boring magazine," she said at the time.[8] A fuller explanation might have acknowledged that, in a digital world where fashion trends could

emerge anywhere, subverting the classic rules of "good taste" was irreverent, democratic, fun. Also, necessary to survive.

Kardashian was more than just an internet celebrity. Her influence bled
into the culture at large. Her preference for heavy makeup and outrageous
curves, seemingly designed to pop on digital screens, shaped mainstream
beauty trends. More women began "contouring" their faces like Kardashian's, borrowing drag queen techniques to elevate their cheekbones
and eyebrows. In the United States, the number of silicone butt implants
doubled year over year in 2014, according to the American Society for
Aesthetic Plastic Surgery.[9] In 2015, lip implant procedures (a more inva-
sive method than injections) reached record numbers. American beauty
ideals drifted further and further away from the European runway model
standard.

Calvin Klein was one of the first major fashion brands to strategically
embrace social media influencers like Kardashian. In the mid-2010s,
the label was losing market share among young people and its denim
lines were struggling. Calvin Klein was also at the mercy of its distribu-
tors, which were primarily declining department stores like Macy's. The
founder left the business shortly after he sold it in 2003 to Phillips-Van
Heusen, a firm known for men's dress shirts sold in department stores.
In the years that followed, the brand kept up Klein's reputation for skin-
baring advertising campaigns fronted by runway models. Many of the
brand's campaign stars had been Angels or had walked in Victoria's Secret
Fashion Shows, although Calvin Klein's main female model after 2010,
Lara Stone, had never advanced beyond one runway show with Victoria's
Secret. (Razek hadn't liked her look. There was nothing cutesy or girl-
next-door about her; her scowl was part of her appeal.)

In 2014, Calvin Klein needed to grab the attention of an Instagram
generation inundated with a drip-feed of images and information. So the
company hired the teen heartthrob pop star of the moment Justin Bieber,
who, at twenty, yearned to prove he wasn't just a kid singer. In Bieber's
first Calvin Klein ad, in 2015, he shocked viewers by appearing shirtless,
cuddling with a smoldering Stone and giving the camera his best Blue
Steel. The print and television commercial generated endless headlines
and conversation, but it was just the beginning. The brand also tapped
a whopping sixty other celebrities, internet personalities with popular
Instagram accounts, ranging from beauty blogger (and future founder

of Glossier) Emily Weiss to former Angel Miranda Kerr to rising model (and Kardashian sister) Kendall Jenner. On Instagram, each influencer posted a lo-fi smartphone picture of themselves in Calvin Klein's distinctive white cotton underwear, with the hashtag #MyCalvins.

Regular people followed suit, posting their own intimate selfies in their Calvin Klein underwear to their own feeds. Suddenly, anyone could be an underwear model. Wearing lingerie was no longer just for private moments with a partner—it could be a public statement of freedom or confidence. More than six thousand people participated in the first months of Calvin Klein's campaign, all posting for free. All they needed was a pair of the brand's $20 bikini bottoms or $28 briefs and a smartphone. The success of Calvin Klein's campaign demonstrated the power of the social media celebrity. Young shoppers would respond to ads featuring models who looked like them, who *seemed* real and relatable.

One brand that immediately took a cue from Calvin Klein was Lane Bryant, the plus-size retailer that Limited Brands had sold to a retail group in 2001. In 2015, the brand hired high-fashion photographer Cass Bird and creative director Trey Laird, best known for his work at Donna Karan and Gap, to essentially re-create a photo story Bird had shot for *Vogue* a year earlier. Five plus-size models appeared together in stark black-and-white, each in lingerie. In the television commercial version, the models declared in unison, "I'm no Angel." Online, the brand encouraged women to post selfies with the hashtag #ImNoAngel. Though Lane Bryant's ads did not match the reach of Calvin Klein's campaign, the stunt generated widespread media coverage, too. And just about every article took a shot at Victoria's Secret's reputation for only casting "perfect" models.

One of the women in the Lane Bryant campaign, Ashley Graham, would soon become the first plus-size supermodel in fashion. A decade earlier, American *Vogue* had shot her for a story about plus-size shopping tips that was published in a "body shape"–themed issue fronted by Scarlett Johansson. ("Nobody's Perfect," the cover declared.) But in the years that followed, the magazine ignored Graham. Still, her career flourished in the plus-size market. Graham even designed her own line for the Canadian brand Addition Elle.

Graham, propelled by a natural charm, was a Heidi Klum for a new generation. On social media, she came across as goofy and honest. (At a dinner party hosted by Martha Stewart for influencers and editors, Graham once talked at length with one of the coauthors of this book about the joy of bowel movements.) Telegenic and well-spoken, Graham hosted a Miss Universe competition and *America's Next Top Model*.

Graham was an anomaly. Fashion's leading brands and magazines rarely hired plus-size models. In 2014, Graham's agency, Ford Models, decided to drop all its plus-size talent. Graham and her peers convinced IMG Models to represent them. The agent Mina White took them on, hell-bent on booking what the industry called "curve" models into high-fashion or mainstream jobs. Audiences had noticed the lack of real bodies in fashion advertising, too. "Body positivity" was a hot topic online, as social media users debated beauty ideals. When Calvin Klein, for example, cast a size-10 model for the first time in 2014, the images went viral on Twitter, a testament to the interest in inclusive fashion advertising.

In 2016, Graham became the *Sports Illustrated: Swimsuit Edition*'s first size-16 cover model, launching her past the two million follower milestone on Instagram. Graham was not just a model but a "body positivity activist," in the words of *InStyle*, where she wrote a monthly column called "Great Style Has No Size." She wrote and spoke often about the lack of fashionable options for plus-size women and of the rejection she had faced from the fashion industry over the course of her career. Graham emerged as the ideal supermodel for a changing America, where the average woman wore a size 16 to 18 and was tired of rarely seeing herself in fashion advertising or mainstream media.[10]

Of course, Graham's acceptance had its limits. When she appeared on the cover of British *Vogue* in January 2017, several high-fashion houses refused to provide clothing for her. (Typically, fashion houses clamor to get their clothing on *Vogue* covers, but few brands make samples of their collections for celebrities or models larger than a size 0 or 2.)

Graham made no secret of her ambition to model for Victoria's Secret. On the night the televised fashion show aired in December 2016, Graham posted an illustration a fan had sent her on Instagram. It was a portrait of her in one of the brand's lingerie costumes with the requisite fluffy wings. "Watching the Angels tonight like . . . ," Graham wrote. When Graham's IMG agents later pitched her to Razek and his team, there was no hesitation in their rejection. The reason given was Victoria's Secret's "fitness focus." Even though Graham trained regularly at Dogpound, the same trendy New York City gym popular among the Angels, Razek didn't feel she could sell the "Train like an Angel" lifestyle.

Razek wasn't alone in his thinking, of course. Even amid the body positivity movement and a growing awareness that metrics such as the body mass index were flawed measures of health, fat phobia remained prevalent, especially among older Americans. When Graham landed her *Sports Illustrated* cover in 2016, former *SI* model Cheryl Tiegs told a reporter, "I don't like it that we're talking about full-figured women because we're glamorizing them, and your waist should be smaller than 35 [inches]. That's what Dr. Oz said and I'm sticking to it."[11]

The fashion brands that hired Graham, like H&M and Revlon, did not mind the backlash. Her association let them market themselves as feminist and "inclusive," another favorite buzzword in an industry once built on exclusivity. Many "activist" models escalated their careers during Donald Trump's campaign and presidency, as the #MeToo and Black Lives Matter movements swelled. Models like Adwoa Aboah spoke frankly about their struggles with addiction and depression. Adut Akech, another model beloved by designers, recalled in interviews her childhood in a refugee camp in Kenya after her mother fled the civil war in South Sudan. Brands, seeking to appear socially aware, tapped these spokeswomen for their backstories as much as for their beauty.

Victoria's Secret ignored these tactics. None of its models had anywhere near a thirty-five-inch waist. When Razek appointed a whopping ten new Angels in 2015, five of the women were almost indiscernible from each other—a troupe of white honey-blondes with thin, toned bodies.

Two of the models, Jasmine Tookes and Lais Ribeiro, were Black, which represented a modest improvement. Previously, Victoria's Secret had only one Black model on its Angel roster at any given time. (First Tyra Banks, then Selita Ebanks, followed by Chanel Iman.) And a Black model never fronted any of the brand's advertising campaigns solo until 2020. It wasn't until 2015 that one of Victoria's Secret's show models, Maria Borges, was permitted to wear her Afro on the runway instead of extensions—a first the brand touted proudly.

Throughout the company's entire history, none of the Angels was Asian. In the early 2000s, casting director John Pfeiffer addressed the lack of Asian representation with Razek. Pfeiffer said Razek told him the brand didn't need Asian models because "we don't have a business in China." Liu Wen became the first East Asian model to walk in the fashion show in 2009. (After Victoria's Secret opened its first store in Shanghai in 2017, it hired Chinese models Sui He and Ming Xi not as Angels, but as the official faces of the brand in the country.)

While several Angels were Brazilian, none were Spanish-speaking Latinas, which would have represented one of the brand's largest and most loyal customer demographic groups in the United States.

Victoria's Secret also resisted hiring influencers. ("They're fat," Razek said once in a meeting about potential strategies, a colleague remembered.) Celebrity collaborations were still verboten in the 2010s, too. In 2015, employees remember a conversation about potentially linking up with Jennifer Lopez that went nowhere. Years later, as Lopez prepared to film *Hustlers*, about a group of strippers who con Wall Street bankers, someone in the film's production inquired about partnering with Victoria's Secret to sponsor the lingerie costumes in the film. The brand passed. *Hustlers* premiered to critical and commercial success (ultimately making more than $155 million at the box office) and earned Lopez a Golden Globe nomination. Other brands used these kinds of cross-promotional strategies all the time, but not Victoria's Secret. The Angels were Razek's only influencers.

Ultimately, the appeal of influencers lies in their off-the-cuff "authenticity." But the Angels never spoke frankly about their personal lives besides offering platitudes about motherhood or finding confidence on the brand's runway. They ticked through basic talking points: how they felt to be Angels, their workout routines, and their pets. Even the models with celebrity boyfriends and husbands—like Behati Prinsloo, who married Maroon 5 front man Adam Levine—did little more than blow them kisses from the runway. (Though, when Levine performed during the show in 2011, he and his then girlfriend, model Anne V, did walk down the runway together and kiss as he sang the band's mega-hit "Moves like Jagger.")

Razek saw the Angels as a modern version of the Marlboro Man, the rugged cowboy who advertised cigarettes for four decades. The Angels and the Marlboro Man were conceived as instantly recognizable, aspirational symbols of their respective brands (and shorthand for traditional masculine and feminine physical ideals). But as other consumer brands encouraged their spokespeople to get personal, the Angels stuck to their talking points. Victoria's Secret spoke for them, never the other way around.

CHAPTER 16

The Unraveling

The crisis in Columbus boils over, and the Wexner era
comes to an end.

Fashion loves a nepo baby. Gigi Hadid came to modeling with Hollywood savvy and pre-built fame from her mother's years, and her own appearances, on *The Real Housewives of Beverly Hills*.[1] Her bookers at IMG Models, one of the most powerful agencies at the time, aggressively pursued premier gigs for her. Many of Hadid's fellow aspiring models could only hope to catch someone's attention when parading down the runway, one of dozens of girls in each twelve-minute-long show. But at nineteen, Hadid was already followed closely by the *Daily Mail* and *Teen Vogue*. She had a teen idol boyfriend and lots of famous friends, many of whom were the children of celebrities, too.

It was no surprise when, in 2014, Tom Ford chose her to front his fragrance campaign. This was her first big luxury brand gig—a plum platform for introducing herself to the wider fashion world. In the ad, Hadid appeared completely naked, her limbs strategically covering what needed to be covered, and bathed in a luminous purple light. At the time, Hadid's body was her calling card. She later called it her "volleyball body," meaning she had muscles and breasts and curves, slight as they were. Her body shape and reality TV roots turned off some European designers at first, but they got over it quickly. In 2014, Karl Lagerfeld cast Hadid in her first major Paris show, for Chanel. Even among Lagerfeld's outrageously elaborate sets (the previous year, his models had walked through a fully stocked Chanel-branded supermarket), his spring 2015 ready-to-wear show was particularly memorable. In a bizarre response to the political awakening of women around the world, Lagerfeld staged a "feminist protest" on a cobblestone street built inside the Grand Palais in Paris. At the end of the show, the models marched together chanting slogans and holding signs that read, "Make Fashion Not War" and "Divorce Pour Tous." Hadid's sign read, "Boys Should Get Pregnant Too." Clearly, Victoria's Secret wasn't the only brand struggling to meet the moment. But even Chanel was trying *something*.

Hadid was the season's breakout star, with one million Instagram followers to boot. Still, Victoria's Secret would not have her. The brand thought her "volleyball body" was not lean enough. And her reality television roots also tainted her. Even when Hadid was good enough for Chanel and Tom Ford, the casting committee at Victoria's Secret (particularly Monica Mitro and the fashion show's longtime stylist Sophia Neophitou) would not stoop to what they viewed as a lowbrow association, according to several former colleagues.

It was the same for Kendall Jenner, Kim Kardashian's leggiest sister, who started modeling in 2014. "We were not allowed to speak her name," remembers a former employee. The brand's go-to photographer Russell James was a close friend of Kendall's mother, Kris Jenner, and had pitched Kendall to Ed Razek and the catalog team back in 2012. Like Hadid, Jenner was all over the runway shows in 2014, but Victoria's Secret turned her away. CEO Sharen Jester Turney agreed—she didn't want the brand to be seen as following the crowd.

The next year, Victoria's Secret relented and Hadid's audition tears became a viral moment. Jenner walked in the show that year for the first time, too. The brand featured both models in interview segments during the television program, a level of attention typically reserved only for Angels. Yet still, Gigi's younger sister, Bella, another rising model, was turned away in 2015. Razek and Mitro told colleagues they thought three reality television–connected models were simply too many. Bella had recently started dating one of the show's slated performers, Abel Tesfaye (aka the Weeknd), who threatened to pull out of the event unless his girlfriend was hired, too. Colleagues remembered Razek called Tesfaye personally and somehow appeased him—without casting Bella. (The model finally landed the show a year later.)

If all this sounds silly, it's because it was. Victoria's Secret was overlooking talent because of outdated ideas about aspiration and exclusivity. These young models were desperate to work with the brand. They were already massively famous among young American women, who tracked everything they wore. In 2015, Jenner was among the top-ten most-followed people on Instagram, with more than forty million followers, twenty million more than Victoria's Secret had at the time. (That year, according to Nielsen, ratings of the televised fashion show dropped to only seven million viewers.)

By the time Victoria's Secret realized it needed Jenner and Gigi Hadid as Angels, and put out offers, the brand was too late. The models were happy to walk in the television fashion show, but they had more exciting and lucrative opportunities that didn't require attending store openings and fragrance launches.

Throughout the second half of the 2010s, barriers to change were everywhere at Victoria's Secret. Instead of making major, needed e-commerce investments, Les Wexner prioritized remodeling the stores, which brought in 80 percent of the brand's sales. He believed updating and expanding the stores would bring in more business than the website ever could. But his remodeled stores were antiquated by modern standards. Shoppers couldn't buy online and pick up products in stores. The stores also lacked Wi-Fi, by then a common method for tracking the habits of customers in stores. (Even if you don't manually connect to a store's Wi-Fi network, the retailer can track your smartphone to see where you go inside the store and for how long. And they can hire data brokers to match your phone's unique identifying number to your age and spending habits.)

Few executives dared challenge Wexner. The perks of a job at Victoria's Secret helped reinforce a culture of complacency. Wexner still expected many of his executives and creative teams to "live like Angels." Dozens of employees—top merchants, heads of design, creatives on the "brand concept" teams in charge of setting seasonal trends—traveled around the world on expensive shopping trips four or five times per year. They stayed at five-star hotels and flew in the company's private jets. All in the name of research, all on the company dime. The regular stops were London, Paris, and Rome, but the globe-trotting could stretch to Mykonos or Saint-Tropez or Rio de Janeiro, depending on the season. In every major city, employees met with local "scouts," stringers recruited to arrange visits to the best local shops and restaurants and clubs. Primarily, the Victoria's Secret teams shopped, dropping tens of thousands of dollars at Selfridges in London and Agent Provocateur in Paris. "They always knew when Victoria's Secret was in town because the sales in one day were astronomical," remembers a former employee who traveled with the brand. On some days, as many as twenty-five Victoria's Secret creatives, designers, and merchants fanned across a city at once.

Back home, employees who the dropped Victoria's Secret's name often landed free hotel stays or impossible-to-get restaurant reservations, all because those businesses hoped to one day host the Angels. The company's salaries were higher than most of its competitors', even before stock options and the twice-annual bonuses, which could almost double salaries. To many employees, Victoria's Secret was a glamorous place to work and an impossible one to leave. What incentive was there to disrupt the status quo?

Another barrier to change was the company's hierarchical structure. Innovative ideas from younger merchants often failed to reach the real decision makers. "It was extremely bureaucratic," said a former merchant.

In the 2010s, however, various employees tried—and failed—to shake up Victoria's Secret's image. Razek told Turney's deputy Margaret McDonald to butt out of the show production when she suggested ways to modernize it, according to a former employee. His budgets were "locked away" from serious review. Suggestions of diverting money from basic cable advertising to digital went nowhere. Razek was known to shout down challengers.

The fashion show's longtime casting director John Pfeiffer proposed casting transgender models multiple times in his nearly two decades working with Victoria's Secret. In 2013, Pfeiffer invited the rising model Valentina Sampaio, who was openly transgender, to audition in person for Razek, Mitro, and the stylist Neophitou at the brand's New York City offices. After Sampaio left the room, Razek and Mitro admonished Pfeiffer, he remembered, for not warning them ahead of time that he was bringing in a trans model. Pfeiffer knew if he had asked them, they would have told him not to invite Sampaio to the casting. When it came time to choose the runway cast that year, she wasn't considered. "It was a very narrow definition of a VS girl at that point," said Pfeiffer. (A source close to Mitro said models were not rejected from castings solely because they were transgender.)

In 2016, Wexner hired Jan Singer, a former Nike executive and Spanx CEO to lead the lingerie division in the wake of Turney's departure. Singer proposed hiring the Kardashian family—including Caitlyn Jenner, who had come out as transgender a year earlier—to appear together in a campaign. Wexner and Razek were dead set against the idea. (Calvin Klein later pulled off essentially the same idea, in a 2018 underwear campaign—but only with the sisters.) The closest the Kardashians got to a Victoria's Secret ad came in 2018, when Kim's assistant contacted someone from Monica Mitro's team, asking to borrow some past runway costumes for a family Halloween costume. Mitro said yes. As the Victoria's Secret team packed up the tiny, bedazzled bodysuit that Candice Swanepoel had worn during the 2015 fashion show, a colleague remembers Mitro remarking, "Well, we're not going to get that back in one piece."

Razek cut down other ideas bubbling up in the divisions. In 2016, creatives in Victoria's Secret's beauty division pitched a new approach for an upcoming fragrance campaign. The concept was to hire former Angels, now middle-aged, as well as younger models with diverse body types and skin tones. They would appear together with the tagline "We are all Angels." The response was clear, according to a former employee. "They're not sexy," Razek said. When anyone proposed using older models, he was known to repeat, "We're not Jurassic Park." In these debates, Razek would often become angry or defensive. He believed that Victoria's Secret's marketing was not to blame for its troubles, according to former colleagues. "I don't opine on the design of the merchandise," he would say, "so you shouldn't get to weigh in on what I do."

Wexner's support of Razek was unquestioned—the "Right again, Eddie" mantra remained—even as the Angels' popularity faded. But Wexner's main concern, ironically, was how to keep the brand "young." Victoria's Secret's mainline customers had aged up, and Wexner had long neglected customers over thirty-five. They were more likely to be married and less likely to buy multiple bras a year. Wexner's obsession with youth could frustrate his merchants. In one of the Monday night merchants' meetings in 2017, the group was discussing a new style of underwear that was selling well. Wexner asked one of the younger female merchants present, "What panty size are you?" She laughed and was clearly embarrassed. Extra-small, she responded. "I want everyone who buys that panty to have your body," Wexner replied.

Wexner also shot down suggestions to sell maternity or mastectomy bras. He insisted that Victoria's Secret wasn't in the business of anything utilitarian—"hope, not help." The customer "would never get breast cancer, would never breastfeed a baby, and could never go past twenty-five," remembers a former creative executive.

Wexner didn't hide his views, not even from outsiders. In 2018, Victoria's Secret hired makeup artist Charlotte Tilbury to oversee all the makeup for that year's fashion show, using products from her popular namesake brand. Wexner was so impressed by her business that he met with her to discuss potentially carrying her brand in Victoria's Secret stores. When Tilbury explained that her makeup was designed for women of all ages, Wexner called customers over thirty-five "old and fat" and of no use to him. A former employee felt that the partnership ended right then and there. A few months later, Tilbury hired eighty-six-year-old actress Joan Collins as a spokesperson for her brand, which went on to become one of the fastest-growing labels in the American beauty market.

///

On the first Friday in November 2018, at the Victoria's Secret offices on Broadway in Midtown, the staff was finalizing the costumes for the annual fashion show. No one knew it would be the last of its kind. The lingerie lineup included tartan-print corsets and low-rise thongs, as well as a sheer bodysuit covered in strings of silver sparkles and a pair of "wings" that looked like the crown of the Statue of Liberty. The runway show would be staged and filmed the following Thursday at Pier 94, where a special goodbye segment was planned for Adriana Lima. After twenty years as an Angel, she was finally retiring from Victoria's Secret.

Nicole Phelps, an editor at American *Vogue*, arrived for a meeting with Ed Razek and Monica Mitro that day. Press coverage in the run-up to the fashion show was standard practice at Victoria's Secret, spawning articles that promised "inside access" to the women who graced the runway. But this interview was different.

Phelps had approached the brand's PR agency, KCD, a few months earlier with an interview request. She wanted to ask the architects of the fashion show if they felt the event needed modernizing. Her request was initially denied. But Razek became agitated by a narrative building in the media, one boosted by the rise of more inclusive competitors and reports of declining sales. Increasingly, the press was calling the Victoria's Secret fantasy into question. The show's ratings had sharply declined since 2013. So he and Mitro changed their minds about sitting down with Phelps. The interview would be a prime opportunity to defend the brand through a friendly outlet. Razek was the show's most passionate champion so why not let him defend it? He could be charming when he wanted to be. It was a "Hail Mary pass," said one employee. They assumed that *Vogue* would advocate on Victoria's Secret's behalf.

Inside the brand's offices in Midtown, Phelps was led through a maze of quiet cubicles to Razek's office, where he and Mitro waited. A colleague remembers that Razek was annoyed even before Phelps walked in. Earlier in the week, he had complained to other staff members about the fate of Les Moonves, the CEO and chairman of CBS, who had resigned two months earlier after a *New Yorker* article revealed that six women had accused him of sexual assault and harassment. "He's a decent guy, Les didn't touch anybody," a colleague remembers Razek saying. "Men are under attack. Let them come after me—I'm clean."

Razek wanted *Vogue* to understand that Victoria's Secret couldn't simply abandon its past because of a few naysayers. "The brand has a specific image, has a point of view. It has a history," Razek told Phelps.[2] "It's hard to build a brand. It's hard to build *Vogue*, Ralph Lauren, Apple, Starbucks." Phelps asked about the lack of model diversity, including pregnant models. "We've had three pregnant models walk the show," Razek said, failing to mention that those models had been so early in their pregnancies that it was impossible to know or that costumes had covered their bellies.

Razek complained about Instagram, where he felt bombarded by "people trying to tell me what an idiot I am this time of year." To demonstrate the inanity of the conversation on social media, he pointed out that one of the Angels, Sara Sampaio, was "constantly being criticized for being too fat." (Razek didn't mention that he himself had once criticized Sampaio's weight. During an interaction on set overheard by another employee, he told her "You look like shit," and to prove his point, he showed her an older picture of herself, from when she was thinner, on his phone.) "Nonsense gets written about us; God bless, we understand, we're a big target, a very big target," Razek continued. "We get it, we're enormously successful and have been for a very long time." He said the brand did not want to be all things to all customers. "I'm always asking myself . . . Why did we include that person? And did we include them to shut up a reporter? Did we include them because it was the right thing to do or because it was the politically correct thing to do? Do they take the place of somebody who worked for a year for the opportunity and cried when they found that they got it?"

Throughout the interview, Mitro, whose stepdaughter walked in the 2017 and 2018 fashion shows, focused on the positives. She reminded Phelps that Victoria's Secret had provided its models a national platform that otherwise did not exist in fashion. She pointed to the racial diversity of the models throughout the years. She noted that Lima was thirty-seven years old—virtually geriatric in fashion. She acknowledged that the brand had its haters, but said it also had a passionate fan base.

Halfway through the interview, Razek "hoisted himself on his own petard," as Phelps later put it. When she asked if the "Instagram generation" wanted something different from Victoria's Secret, Razek asked rhetorically, "Shouldn't you have transsexuals in the show?" using an outdated term. Answering his own question, he continued, "No, I don't think we should. Well, why not? Because the show is a fantasy. It's a 42-minute entertainment special. That's what it is. It is the only one of its kind in the world, and any other fashion brand in the world would take it in a minute, including the competitors that are carping at us." He said Victoria's Secret was no one's "third love," referring to ThirdLove, a smaller, online-only competitor that had recently launched a petition to boycott watching the Victoria's Secret Fashion Show, promising to send a free bra to every customer who posted about the protest.

Razek spoke with a surprising lack of awareness for an executive with more than thirty years' experience at the top of a Fortune 500 company. The *Vogue* interview went live online on the morning of November 8, the day the show was staged and taped, and panic set in among the brand's publicists. Razek came off as angry and imperious. Backlash was building on social media.

For ThirdLove, the callout was a boon. The brand's cofounder Heidi Zak published an open letter to Victoria's Secret in a full-page ad in the Sunday edition of the *New York Times*. "Your show may be a 'fantasy' but we live in reality," she wrote, quoting the cringiest parts of Razek's *Vogue* interview. "We may not have been a woman's first love but we will be her last."

In the month before the fashion show aired on ABC in early December, Mitro's team went into crisis mode. They canceled much of the press they had planned for the run-up to the premiere. (They'd intended to send models to hype the event on the *Today Show*, the *Wendy Williams*

Show, and *Jimmy Kimmel Live!* but canceled them all.) Mitro's team also scrapped a live pre-show she typically hosted before the television airing. "We went dead silent," said one of Mitro's colleagues. "We didn't promote at all."

In conversations with colleagues, Razek initially said that he was mis-quoted in the *Vogue* article, even though Phelps had recorded his com-ments and run them in full in the piece. But the day after the interview published, he apologized for his "insensitive" remarks in a written state-ment published on the company's Twitter account. "To be clear, we abso-lutely would cast a transgender model for the show," he wrote. "We've had transgender models come to castings. . . . And like many others, they didn't make it."[3]

When Razek's comments landed, the future of the fashion show was already in question. After the 2017 fashion show in Shanghai the previous year, a logistics nightmare that had cost a company record of more than $20 million to stage, CBS did not renew its TV contract with Victoria's Secret. Fewer than five million people in the United States watched the Shanghai edition, a 30 percent drop in viewership year over year. Razek pitched the fashion show to several other companies, including Netflix and HBO, with no success. Finally, ABC agreed to pick it up, with the option to air it for the next four years.

By then, even Razek understood that the fashion show should acknowl-edge and address its critics, albeit obliquely. The televised version of the 2018 show, staged again in New York City, opened with the words "What Is Victoria's Secret?" followed by direct-to-camera interviews with the con-tract models (recorded months before Razek's *Vogue* interview). "Empow-ering," answered Josephine Skriver, kicking off a chorus of responses that included "fierce" and, finally, "sexy." The models wore jeans and tank tops, sitting relaxed on tall stools against a plain backdrop. "It's difficult being a woman; other women understand that," said Elsa Hosk. They spoke about the Angels as a sisterhood. They said that some days they like to be in their pajamas and some days they like to be sexy, and there was nothing wrong with that. "And I don't care if you judge me," said Lais Ribeiro. "Be sexy for ourselves and who we want to be, not because a man says you have to be," said Taylor Hill. "It was never about that in the first place."

Later in the program, when the show turned to its requisite footage of the models exercising, each woman shared a fitness goal she had set that year that had nothing to do with weight or body measurements—like being able to push 135 pounds on a gym sled. Notably, Razek and Mitro did not make their usual appearances in the behind-the-scenes segments of the show. But there were no other notable changes. The models did what they had always done, strutting down a runway in kitschy lingerie costumes wearing cheerful smiles and winking for the camera.

Any programming changes could not offset Razek's comments, which featured prominently in the news coverage of the brand in late 2018. Victoria's Secret also announced Jan Singer's exit after just two years as the head of the main line's lingerie division. L Brands' stock price dropped more than 40 percent by the end of the year. "Victoria's Secret? In 2018, Fewer Women Want to Hear It," read a headline in the *New York Times*.

In many companies, a person in Razek's position would have been fired or pushed to retire. To many, he had deeply damaged the brand. But no one at Victoria's Secret was surprised when the holiday season passed, and Razek seemed to suffer no consequences for his actions. "If they hadn't fired him before, why now?" one employee put it. "It was just another thing on the list." In just a few months, a bigger scandal would eclipse Razek's offensive comments. By then, multiple people would have to take the fall for the good of the brand.

///

Les Wexner had a saying: bad inventory can make you sick, but bad real estate can kill you.

The idea was that stores required significant capital to build, maintain, staff, and renovate. Heavy fixed overhead costs become an unbearable weight as sales slide, especially for a brand like Victoria's Secret with well over a thousand stores. The impact on the bottom line can be fast and brutal. In 2018, even though Victoria's Secret's net US sales were the same as in the previous year—a whopping $7.4 billion—its operating income shrank by half, reaching its lowest level in more than a decade. After another painful, discount-heavy holiday season in 2018, L Brands announced that it would close fifty Victoria's Secret stores over the course of the following year. Even Pink, the reliable growth engine, began to decline in revenue after peaking at $3 billion in 2017.

Victoria's Secret's sister brand Bath & Body Works, however, was thriving. What started as a side project at Express in 1990 had become something like the McDonald's of cucumber-and-melon-scented toiletries. Cheap, ubiquitous, consistent. The brand's first CEO, Beth Pritchard, transformed it from a knockoff of the Body Shop, the beloved British body care chain, into a fast-growing, country market–inspired seller of lotions and face masks—nicer than drugstores and cheaper than department stores. After Pritchard retired in the early 2000s, the brand updated its rustic theme with a sleek, apothecary-style design. This shift helped Bath & Body Works continue to grow steadily and outlast upstart competitors from the cosmetics conglomerates. For a time, Bath & Body Works carried higher-end brands like Caudalie and Frédéric Fekkai. But customers preferred the cute and simple in-house lines, with comforting scents: "Strawberry Shortcake," "Sweet Pea," and seasonal specialties like "Leaves" and "Ginger Vanilla."

It was easy to overlook Bath & Body Works next to its glamorous sister company. The brand did not advertise. In 2010, it generated a little more than half of Victoria's Secret sales. Even its fictional origin story was modest: the counterpart to "Victoria" was "Kate," who grew up on a farm in the Midwest and made her own beauty products. The Bath & Body Works stores represented Kate's home. (The brand built a "replica" of her home in New Albany to inspire employees.) The store associates' gingham aprons nodded to the faux history.[4]

Once Victoria's Secret started to slide, Bath & Body Works took on new importance for Wexner. The brand's 1,700 stores were a magnet for people to sample the latest scents in person. Bath & Body Works had no serious competitors at the same price or distribution level. Between 2015 and 2018, its revenue increased from $1 billion to $4.6 billion, and its operating income rate held steady around 23 percent. During the same period, Victoria's Secret's revenue declined from $7.7 billion to $7.4 billion, while its operating income rate fell from 18 percent to 6.3 percent. Wall Street investors recognized an undervalued brand within L Brands' slumping stock.

In March 2019, an activist investor named James Mitarotonda hit L Brands with a damning public letter, describing Victoria's Secret as dated, tone-deaf, and imperiled. The letter lambasted Wexner's management choices since taking over day-to-day operations of the brand in 2016. Mitarotonda wanted to see the two L Brands chains split, either by spinning off Victoria's Secret or by taking Bath & Body Works public through an initial public offering, or IPO.

Mitarotonda's letter called out the L Brands board of directors for their age (an average of seventy) and lack of female representation (nine of the twelve directors were men). Mitarotonda also argued the board lacked the independence to challenge the company's leadership. Wexner's board was packed with friends, family, and business partners who had served for decades, including his wife, Abigail Koppel; Dennis Hersch, their family business adviser since Wexner stopped working with Epstein in 2008; and Wexner's very close friend Gordon Gee. (Gee was the former president of Ohio State and had led the university when Wexner made a historic $100 million donation in 2011.)

L Brands made sense as a target for Mitarotonda, even though Wexner maintained tight control of the company and its board. Wexner personally owned 17.3 percent of L Brands shares in 2019. And any proposals—a takeover bid, spin-off, or the removal of a director—required a 75 percent supermajority to pass. But Mitarotonda knew his recommendations would find support, if not among a board made up mostly of Wexner's allies, then among the larger investment community. (His firm, Barington Capital Group, had acquired less than 1 percent of the company stock.)

Wexner moved quickly to placate Mitarotonda, striking a deal with him before he could create any further trouble at the annual shareholder meeting that May. L Brands announced that it would appoint two new independent directors to replace Hersch and David Kollat, the former Limited Brands executive who had served on the board for forty-three years. Mitarotonda was appointed as a special adviser to the board. In turn, Barington agreed to not start a proxy fight, offer shareholder proposals, or nominate directors.

Meanwhile, problems continued to mount at Victoria's Secret, where stores sales declined 5 percent year over year in the first quarter of 2019. In a complete reversal from 2016, Wexner slowly reintroduced swimwear. He debated whether to host the fashion show again, keeping the production teams in a state of confusion. Shortly after the 2018 fashion show aired in December, Razek and Mitro informed the teams that the following year's show was canceled. Weeks later, they reversed course, informing everyone that the televised show was back on, sending producers scrambling to find a workable date and venue. Employees were unsure of what would happen next.

At times, Wexner and Razek appeared to double down on their Angels vision for Victoria's Secret. In the spring of 2019, they flew to New York City to personally review some of the lingerie for the upcoming holiday season. Such meetings at the Midtown headquarters weren't uncommon, but this one stood out to several former employees. Wexner and the brand's other top executives had rejected two previous iterations of the collection, deeming the lingerie "not sexy enough." At the last minute, the executives asked to see the lingerie on live models instead of the customary mannequins. The models took their turns walking around the conference room, some wearing sheer panties and open-cup bras, as the all-male executive team watched and remarked how beautiful the collection looked. "It was gross," said someone present at the meeting who felt the presentation, coming amid widespread criticism of the brand's attitudes toward women, was symbolic of the company's deep intransigence.

In the first months of 2019, Razek hired his final Angels. His choices were Alexina Graham, who colleagues saw as Razek's version of a diversity hire (the "first redhead" Angel), and Barbara Palvin, a slightly curvier model. Mitro's team struggled to promote the models in the press, eventually resorting to hiring YouTube influencers to appear with them to drum up interest for in-store events. Meanwhile, the fate of the 2019 fashion show remained unclear. Wexner's view was that Victoria's Secret needed to find a way back to its upscale, aspirational image. His big idea was to once again mine the brand's faux-British heritage. Mitro went to London to look at potential venues for a fashion show, including the exclusive members-only club Annabel's, where Victoria's Secret could stage something smaller and reminiscent of salon couture shows. But in May 2019, Wexner finally delivered the final word in a company-wide memo: this year, there would be no televised show.

Two months later, Jeffrey Epstein was arrested at Teterboro. Reporters bombarded employees, digging for any morsel of information about Epstein and Wexner. Inside the Columbus headquarters, speculation about the Epstein relationship ran rampant. Wexner sent out an internal memo denying any knowledge of his former financial adviser's crimes. "I would never have guessed that a person I employed more than a decade ago could have caused such pain to so many people," he wrote.[5] But Wexner's comments hardly calmed speculation. There were rumors that Epstein had an office at Victoria's Secret and even business cards. Still, most employees, even high-level, long-tenured executives, had never heard of Epstein. They had, however, heard the rumors that Wexner was gay, which fueled speculation and conspiracies about his relationship with Epstein. (Wexner's previous denial that he was gay in a 1985 article did not quell the rumors.)

Under unprecedented pressure to make drastic changes, Wexner did something once unthinkable. He turned on Razek. Wexner allowed his loyal deputy to resign from L Brands after nearly forty years with the company. In the final months of Razek's tenure, colleagues saw his exit coming. He retreated more and more to his office in Columbus with the door closed, on tense phone calls. "I never thought Ed would go," said one of Wexner's longtime executives. Razek's exit announcement came days after Victoria's Secret announced it had cast its first transgender model, Valentina Sampaio, one of the women Razek had turned away at a casting years earlier. "SO LONG PARTNERS," wrote Razek in an email to the company.[6] "With the exception of Les, I've been with L Brands longer than anyone. . . . But all good things must and do, inevitably, come to an end."

And then there was Monica Mitro, Razek's decades-long communications deputy. Her relationship with Razek had always been complicated. They were close friends, but employees who worked with both felt she had earned a level of respect that Razek rarely afforded her. (Once, when Mitro and Razek sat together for an interview, he motioned to her and told the reporter, "Don't look at her now, she used to be hot and beautiful twenty years ago.") Sometimes Mitro defended Razek, employees remembered, and sometimes she was the only one to stand up to him. People often asked her to broach a difficult subject with Razek on their behalf. Mitro's team was accustomed to her late-night calls venting about a rude email Razek had sent her or an apparent slight from upper management. She played hot and cold with her staff, asserting her control where she could. She could be cutting, making critical comments about her team's physical appearances. "All of us fought for her to love us," said one former employee, adding that Mitro had no awareness of the unhealthy work environment she created on her team of women. "Monica is the Regina George of Victoria's Secret," the employee added, referring to the bully in *Mean Girls*.

Once Wexner canceled the 2019 fashion show, Mitro sensed that her job was in danger. She was asked to cut costs to such a degree that it would have required laying off most of her small team. In August 2018, shortly after Razek exited, Mitro formally complained to an ally on the board. She was frustrated with the boys' club at the head of the brand.

The next day, at the office, the head of human resources told Mitro that she should only work from home going forward. Mitro seemed shocked. "She would not get out of her chair," remembered a former colleague. As it turned out, at least one of Mitro's colleagues had also made an official complaint against her, alleging that she had created a toxic work environment. (Mitro declined to be interviewed for this book.)

In the months that followed, it seemed as if Victoria's Secret handed out severance packages like candy, terminating a swath of employees, including Mitro and many of the people who worked with her and Razek. (In Ohio, emotional distress damages are capped, much to some employees' dismay, while staff based in New York could negotiate much higher exit agreements.) Such settlements were not unusual at Victoria's Secret. In reporting for this book, we rarely heard about any high-level executive who resigned without some form of a payoff in exchange for silence. Everyone seemed to have something on someone else. It was more pervasive in Columbus, which could still feel like a small town.

Mitro's colleagues speculated that she (or someone close to her) was a main source for a *New York Times* article, published the following spring, full of upsetting stories about Razek's inappropriate behavior with models. But by then, Razek was already gone. Soon, Wexner would exit, too, after arriving at a painful realization of his own: Victoria's Secret was better off without his leadership.

///

If anyone was going to buy Victoria's Secret, it was Stefan Kaluzny. In the 2010s, Sycamore, the $15 billion private equity firm he cofounded, was one of the only major players still interested in purchasing brick-and-mortar retail businesses. Many in the wider investment community felt retail was in an irreversible decline. But Sycamore had a track record for extracting profits from retail groups on the verge of bankruptcy, like Hot Topic and Talbots, by using a classic playbook: cut costs, close stores, outsource functions, and sell off the most valuable parts. Kaluzny was a traditional corporate raider with an aggressive reputation in an era when many private equity firms preferred to position themselves as brand stewards.

Kaluzny had already bought several businesses from Wexner. Before launching Sycamore in 2011, he was a managing director at Golden Gate

Capital, which had acquired a majority stake in Express from Limited Brands in 2007. Kaluzny joined the Express board and worked with Wexner and Express CEO Michael Weiss to take the chain public. Later, Sycamore bought a majority stake in the apparel sourcing division of Mast Industries, which Wexner off-loaded around the time he sold his apparel brands. (Wexner kept a sourcing division that focused on beauty products and intimate apparel.)

Kaluzny and his associates began evaluating Victoria's Secret at the end of the summer of 2019, analyzing its financials and interviewing current and past executives. Sycamore hired Boston Consulting Group, McKinsey, and other smaller firms to research the market and survey customers, as part of the monthslong due diligence process managed by Wexner's banker Stefan Selig. (Selig had advised Wexner on the sales of Express and the Limited at Bank of America. Between 2014 and 2016, he served as the Commerce Department's undersecretary for international trade, where he was investigated for extravagant spending related to travel and renovating his office.)[7]

Sycamore's view was that the Angels were not Victoria's Secret's biggest problem. After conducting customer surveys, the firm concluded the marketing needed to be more inclusive, but not completely overhauled, according to sources with knowledge of Sycamore's thinking. Simply put, they thought Wexner and his merchants had an inventory problem. Each season, they were overestimating how many bras and pajamas they could sell, furthering the need for discounting and thus decimating the company's margins. It was the kind of problem a private owner like Sycamore could address without the public markets' fixation on ever-increasing sales.

On February 20, 2020, Sycamore and L Brands announced a deal: Sycamore would acquire 55 percent of Victoria's Secret (including Pink) for $525 million, valuing the brand at $1.1 billion. The valuation was shockingly low, a quantification of Victoria's Secret's downfall. In 2019, same-store sales in North America were down 7 percent year over year, and the brand operated at a loss of $616 million in the same region. Internationally, Victoria's Secret was also bleeding, especially in Asia, where its wholly owned stores were unprofitable. (A fifty-thousand-square-foot flagship in Hong Kong was draining cash.)

Wexner coupled the announcement of the Sycamore deal with a personal statement. When the Sycamore deal closed, he would step down as CEO of L Brands and give up his role as chairman of the board.

By then, Wexner was the longest-serving American CEO of a Fortune 500 company. But he had lost the support of his board, especially Sarah Nash, who had just joined as a member in 2019, when activist investor Mitarotonda pushed for board changes. Nash was a former banker and the chief executive of a silicon manufacturing firm. Former colleagues with knowledge of the board's views said she and Stuart Burgdoerfer, L Brands' longtime CFO and one of Wexner's closest allies, had pushed Wexner to resign, arguing his continued presence was poisonous to the company. (A source close to Burgdoerfer denied this.) Speculation around Wexner's relationship with Epstein remained high. "Stuart, Sarah, and the board were judge and jury regarding the Epstein debacle—they just wanted it to disappear," said a former L Brands executive. "It didn't matter to them who ran Victoria's Secret as long as shareholders were delivered profits." The board announced that Nash would replace Wexner as chair of the board once the Sycamore deal came through. "I think about the endless possibilities ahead for this company," Wexner wrote in a memo to employees in February 2020. "And I've thought about where I fit in the picture. In keeping with this same thoughtful examination, I have decided that now is the right time to pass the reins to new leadership."

But Wexner had one more challenge to navigate as CEO. The Sycamore deal, announced in February 2020, would take months to close. On March 13, President Trump declared the Covid-19 pandemic a national emergency, and four days later, L Brands shut down all its stores. Two days later, Victoria's Secret also temporarily closed its online store. Wexner cut salaries for senior executives, canceled product orders, and held back on paying store rents. Victoria's Secret sales fell by 46 percent in the first quarter of the year. It was a bona fide crisis.

At Sycamore, the prospect of turning around Victoria's Secret suddenly seemed impossible. In April, the firm sued L Brands in a Delaware court, seeking to terminate the acquisition agreement. L Brands promptly countersued to force Sycamore to complete the transaction.

L Brands appeared to have the upper hand in the case. The acquisition agreement had specifically *excluded* pandemics from the list of calamities that could have allowed Sycamore to terminate the deal. Thus, Sycamore had to rely on a weaker legal argument: that L Brands had mismanaged Victoria's Secret in its response to the pandemic by closing stores and furloughing employees. (LVMH attempted a similar argument after its acquisition of American fine jeweler Tiffany & Co. right before the pandemic. In the end, LVMH chairman Bernard Arnault managed to shave $425 million off the purchase price.) Here, Sycamore was not just looking for a renegotiation; it wanted to walk away.

Though the terms of the deal were in their favor, L Brand's lawyers may have overlooked a crucial detail. In the countersuit against Sycamore, L Brands asked the court to force the completion of the deal—or, short of that, force Sycamore to pay L Brands "monetary damages." By seeking money from Sycamore, L Brands triggered a separate provision in the transaction agreements, effectively allowing Sycamore to blow up the funding for the deal. Kaluzny had won, and he didn't even need to pay to walk away. Wexner agreed to stand down, perhaps aware of the danger of spending millions on complicated litigation with all his stores still shut.

L Brands kept part of its original plan to separate its brands. Victoria's Secret would be spun out independently into a publicly listed company. And Wexner's tenure as CEO officially ended in May 2020. "I think everybody expects me to be sad," he said in his last call with executives as CEO. "Seeing the business grow not only to be large and successful but to be a really good company, I'm so proud even under the current circumstances. . . . We must control the things we can control, and the priority of protecting the company so that we weather the storm."[8]

Wexner remained on the L Brands board (as chairman emeritus) for another year. In March 2021, as Victoria's Secret prepared to formally spin off from L Brands, he announced that he and Abigail would not stand for board reelection. In the months that followed, as the L Brands stock surged in anticipation of the company split, Wexner sold off most of his shares. The stock price reached as high as $75 per share, just shy of its historical peak of $80 in 2015. His timing was right, minting him a hefty payday of more than $2.2 billion.[9] Even as a social outcast, Wexner remained a shrewd operator. The fattest cat. And the future of Victoria's Secret was no longer his problem.

CHAPTER 17

Apologies Aren't Sexy

Victoria's Secret pays penance, but its past remains
present.

In early February 2020,[1] as Wexner's lawyers finalized the deal with Sycamore, a bombshell report with a withering headline hit the internet:
"'Angels' in Hell: The Culture of Misogyny Inside Victoria's Secret," declared
the *New York Times*. The piece summarized the connections between Les
Wexner and Jeffrey Epstein and revealed Ed Razek as a toxic manager who
fat-shamed his colleagues, made lewd comments about models' bodies,
and invited the young women whose careers depended on him to private dinners. Wexner declined to comment in the article. Razek, who had
left Victoria's Secret six months earlier, denied all the accusations against
him. A representative for the Victoria's Secret board of directors expressed
regret and promised more accountability moving forward.

In the months after the article was published, groups of shareholders sued L Brands and Wexner in both Ohio and Delaware, alleging the
company's leaders damaged its brands by allowing harassment to go on
unchecked.[2] The Ohio suit accused Wexner, Razek, and the board of
enabling a "hostile abusive environment rife with sexual harassment . . .
making it impossible to either fix the Victoria's Secret business, or sell it
off for anywhere near its true value." L Brands agreed to designate a special committee to investigate the claims. (A year later, the company settled
the suits without admitting any wrongdoing, but agreeing to update its
sexual harassment policies and to stop enforcing nondisclosure agreements related to sexual harassment claims.)

For Victoria's Secret, moving forward seemed impossible. The
brand's reputation was undeniably tainted by months of declining sales

and negative press coverage. Former Angel Karlie Kloss distanced herself from the brand, telling a reporter in 2019 that she let her Angel contract expire four years earlier because she "didn't feel it was an image that was truly reflective of who I am and the kind of message I want to send to young women around the world about what it means to be beautiful."[3] (The reporter didn't ask Kloss why that view didn't stop her from returning to the Victoria's Secret Fashion Show in 2017.)

A month after the damaging *New York Times* report, as Wexner prepared to step down as CEO, the brand released its first ad campaign that one could reasonably describe as diverse. The model Helena Christensen— who had costarred in the very first Angels commercial more than twenty years earlier—photographed and appeared in the images. She was joined by a few recent Angels, as well as other professional models who were transgender, mid-size, and plus-size. The lighting was soft, the colors understated. The models looked straight on, with steely gazes. No vamping. They weren't being coy or cute. Another ad in the spring of 2020 featured another diverse mix of women photographed by another woman, Zoey Grossman. "When women come together, amazing things happen," read the tagline. The models looked relaxed but still serious.

These new campaigns were tasteful, but the abrupt change in tone from even just six months earlier was disorienting. This was a company best known for presenting its models as Photoshopped male fantasies. Internally, Victoria's Secret was roiling with turmoil in 2020. The first six months of the pandemic were terrifying for American retailers, who wondered if people would ever feel safe shopping in stores again. With stores closed, Victoria's Secret was losing money more quickly than anyone could have anticipated, and the mood was tense. In June, the brand's UK entity filed for creditor protection, after reporting an annual loss of £170 million ($214 million).[4]

Victoria's Secret lacked strong, consistent leadership, which added to the muddled strategy. (Remember that the Sycamore deal was off by May 2020, when Wexner officially stepped down as CEO. Victoria's Secret's remaining leaders had no choice but to charge forward with a turnaround strategy.) Leading the lingerie division, in charge of everything but Pink and beauty, was a relatively new CEO, John Mehas. Wexner had hired Mehas, a former Ralph Lauren and Tory Burch executive, at the start of 2019 to replace Jan Singer. Mehas had a mixed reputation:

good at his job, not so good at niceties. (Some called him a bully and elitist.) While he easily slipped into Wexner's corporate boys' club, he had a rough, *garmento*-style management approach that didn't sit well with the Columbus white-picket-fencers. Mehas was optimistic he could give Victoria's Secret the branding update it so desperately needed and reverse the sales slide.

Less than two years into his tenure, Mehas was abruptly fired. His exit came after a video conference call during which Mehas made what sources described as a derogatory comment about Victoria's Secret COO Dein Boyle. After the call, Stuart Burgdoerfer, L Brands' CFO filling in as interim CEO of Victoria's Secret, asked Mehas to apologize to Boyle. In an email, Mehas claimed that he had been misheard, and that he was referring to his "Aunt Jean," not Boyle. Shortly after this incident, Mehas was dismissed in November 2020.

According to people close to Mehas, the executive believed he was pushed out because he had broached the subject of Burgdoerfer's inappropriate behavior. Years earlier, Burgdoerfer had an affair with another executive at L Brands. The relationship became hot office gossip in Columbus when Burgdoerfer's daughter placed flyers on the windshields of hundreds of cars in the Columbus headquarters parking lot revealing her father's infidelities. "The stock is lower than ever, but he values his family even less," read the leaflets. "Hope you two can buy enough lingerie to make up for the damage you caused your families!!!" Burgdoerfer and the other executive both eventually left their spouses and married each other. "No one blinked," said an employee describing the internal reaction at the time.

Some executives thought Mehas's dismissal was unfair. Others saw it as just another symptom of a larger toxic, chaotic company culture. Either way, his exit added to the chaos at the company when it desperately needed stable leadership. (A representative for Victoria's Secret declined to comment on Mehas's departure.)

As the pandemic continued to disrupt business in 2020, Burgdoerfer responded with aggressive cost cutting. He laid off about 850 employees, or 15 percent of the workforce, and reduced inventory orders. The strategy would save Victoria's Secret $400 million annually, the company said. Those cutbacks, combined with 250 store closures in 2020, helped reverse the decline in operating income and gave investors hope for the brand's future. "It felt like they finally understood that they needed to shrink to grow," said Siegel, the retail analyst. Victoria's Secret remained the dominant lingerie seller in the United States, and its sales had weathered the onslaught of negative press in 2019 and 2020. In 2020, its lowest revenue year in a decade, Victoria's Secret's net sales were still $5.4 billion.

Meanwhile, a new leader ascended in Columbus: Martin Waters, the agreeable Englishman who had smoothly managed the international business for more than a decade. Although he wasn't part of Wexner's closest cadre of advisers, Waters understood the inner workings of the company. He was safe and clean. In November 2020, the L Brands board chair Sarah Nash named Waters as Mehas's successor. Leading Victoria's Secret's lingerie division, reporting to Burgdoerfer, would position Waters to assume the CEO role when Victoria's Secret completed its spin-off in August 2021.

Before his exit, Mehas raided one of the most important fashion brands in the world for a new creative director to replace Razek. Instead of going to a Parisian fashion house or an Italian leather goods giant, Mehas tapped Raúl Martinez, creative director of *Vogue*'s publisher, Condé Nast. Martinez was a bona fide fashion insider who had worked for Anna Wintour since 1988. In the mid-1990s, Martinez left Condé Nast to start a creative agency, AR New York, with his romantic partner Alex Gonzalez. Their clients included high-fashion brands such as Calvin Klein, Dolce & Gabbana, Valentino, and Versace, but also specialty retailers like Brooks Brothers and Banana Republic. In 2009, Martinez returned to *Vogue* to advise on creative direction and oversee the all-important covers. The *Vogue* staff loved him, as did Wintour, who kept increasing his responsibilities. By 2019, Martinez was head creative director for all of Condé Nast—overseeing twenty-one creative departments, every magazine, and the in-house advertising agency. The *New York Times* called him "the most powerful Latino in glossy publishing."[5] He had strong relationships with photographers and agents. He was also good-natured, never appearing to take himself or his job too seriously. At Victoria's Secret, Martinez's dual sensibilities—editor and advertiser—could come in handy.

Mehas also rehired Janie Schaffer as head designer. (Sharen Jester Turney first hired her in 2008, and she stayed until 2012.) Schaffer was up for the challenge again. "From a product standpoint, which is my role, I got it right for the times [in the 2010s] and I'm going to get it right for new times," she said in an interview.[6]

When Martinez and Schaffer reported to their new roles at the start of 2021, a major change was already afoot. The Angels, Victoria's Secret's iconic supermodel mascots, would be no more. In the first months of the year, the remaining modeling contracts expired. Meanwhile, for the first time in nearly two decades, the Angels' black-and-white portraits were quietly removed from the walls of many Victoria's Secret stores across the country. A museum-like exhibit of Angels costumes, installed in the top floor of the Manhattan flagship near Rockefeller Center, was dismantled.

In place of the Angels came the "Angels Collective," announced in the summer of 2021. Instead of assembling supermodels, the brand formed a new squad of celebrity ambassadors chosen for their accomplishments, not how they looked in skimpy thongs. The collective included women's soccer star Megan Rapinoe, the actress Priyanka Chopra Jonas, and the photographer and former 1990s It girl Amanda de Cadenet. The collective also included a few professional models too, such as European runway star Adut Akech and the plus-size trailblazer Paloma Elsesser, one of Victoria's Secret's most prominent faces since Razek's exit. The brand's new focus was women's empowerment. "We needed to stop being about what men want and to be about what women want," said Waters in an interview.[7] "In the old days, the Victoria brand had a single lens, which was called 'sexy.'" Rapinoe said the old Victoria's Secret was "patriarchal, sexist" and "really harmful."

The Angels Collective was just the beginning. Over the next two years, to Victoria's Secret's credit, Waters and his team tried a whole host of strategies to prove the brand's good intentions. (At the same time, Victoria's Secret continued to close stores, including the mega-flagships on Herald Square in Manhattan, Bond Street in London, and Causeway Bay in Hong Kong.) During 2021, the company seemed to announce a new campaign, initiative, or strategy every week: the first maternity bra, the first visibly pregnant model, the first model with Down syndrome. In 2022, the brand launched a new line, Love Cloud, billed as comfortable first and sexy second. The same year, Victoria's Secret made a small investment in the Los Angeles brand Frankies Bikinis, a cute line of skimpy swimwear and skintight knits popular with social media influencers and the young women who followed them. Then came the launch of Happy Nation, a short-lived genderless collection that sold online only.

By then, many shoppers had lost touch with Victoria's Secret's messaging. In early 2022, the brand conducted a survey that showed its customers weren't aware of its new marketing efforts.[8] When asked to identify images that portrayed the brand's identity, most respondents pointed to an image of Hailey Bieber, a thin model who would have fit into the Angels mold.

The report served as a reminder of the pervasive influence of Victoria's Secret's history. For decades, the brand had pumped out images of perfectly toned women frolicking on beautiful beaches in string bikinis or strutting through the streets of Paris in lacy lingerie sets and fluffy wings. This visual language was distinct and memorable. Now, its stripped-down, largely studio-bound campaigns looked nondescript.

And Victoria's Secret's try-hard attitude fell flat online, where commenters attacked what they saw as empty gestures of atonement. "All of a sudden, a lot of people didn't like them and *always* didn't like them," said Cora Harrington, a writer known for her blog *The Lingerie Addict*. "Now, when so much of the conversation happens online, a lot of folks have amnesia—they don't remember how big the company was, and how much a lot of people were invested in it emotionally."

In the summer of 2022, Victoria's Secret's haters found their anthem. An aspiring singer known as Jax went viral on TikTok when she wrote and performed a bubblegum pop–style song blaming the brand for her body image issues. "I know Victoria's secret / And, girl, you wouldn't believe / She's an old man who lives in Ohio / Making money off of girls like me," she sang. In the clip, Jax Photoshopped Wexner's face onto the body of a young woman in pink lingerie, bombshell-style curls framing his round face.[9] The song was catchy enough to land Jax a spot on Billboard's "Hot 100" singles list and a performance on the *Today Show*. The attention prompted an official pseudo-public apology from Victoria's Secret from the newly appointed CEO of Victoria's Secret and Pink, Amy Hauk, one of the brand's only top female executives. She penned a letter to the "VS Community" published on Instagram. "We make no excuses for the past," she wrote. "And we're committed to regaining your trust." (Hauk resigned six months later.)

Jax's Victoria's Secret earworm coincided with the release of a three-part Hulu documentary, *Victoria's Secret: Angels and Demons*. The director, former *Vanity Fair* writer Matt Tyrnauer, had previously made a popular documentary about the Italian designer Valentino. Tyrnauer and his lead producer, Corey Reeser, promised several of the executives they interviewed that the focus was the Victoria's Secret business. But in the end, the series fixated on Wexner's relationship with Epstein and discussed several conspiracy theories about Epstein, including the notion that he had been a secret agent for Mossad, the Israeli intelligence service. (After the series' release, some Jewish publications questioned if the documentary's portrayal of Wexner as a member of a shadowy, elite circle of influence was anti-Semitic. Wexner is known as a staunch supporter of Israel.[10] Tyrnauer did not respond to a request to comment.) The documentary may not have played fair, but it was effective television. Hulu reported that *Angels and Demons* was the most-watched documentary in the history of the streaming service.[11]

Between the catchy TikTok song and hit documentary, Victoria's Secret remained dogged by its past. But arguably the most damaging blow to the brand in 2022 came from an unlikely source: Kim Kardashian's shapewear brand, Skims. To advertise a collection of underwire bras, Kardashian used Victoria's Secret's playbook to her advantage. Skims hired two recent Angels, Alessandra Ambrosio and Candice Swanepoel, and two original Angels, Tyra Banks and Heidi Klum, to appear together in a photoshoot that winked at the past without trying to replicate it. Banks and Klum had aged, of course, but they didn't hide it. All four women looked fantastic, their bodies tanned and oiled, their hair in loose, tousled waves. Kardashian joined them, too, further twisting the concept. The handful of images generated a wave of headlines, and the photoshoot was documented on *The Kardashians*, the family's newest reality show, also airing on Hulu.

By simply borrowing a few former Angels, Skims found a way to reframe the market leader's legacy as light, guilt-free entertainment. Victoria's Secret, for its part, seemed incapable of doing the same.

/ / /

Every generation has its star merchants shaping the way Americans shop. In the first half of the twentieth century, department store magnates dominated. Men like Edgar Jonas Kaufmann in Pittsburgh, who turned temples of desire into pillars of their communities. The postwar period brought widespread change. When Sam Walton opened the first Walmart in 1962, he upended five-and-dimes with his vast inventory and deep discounts. Future superstores Target, Kmart, and Kohl's all launched that same year. Meanwhile, specialty retail chains began to chip away at department stores' dominance. The Limited's great innovation—trendy, imported fashion—helped democratize designer fashion and, in turn, became a powerhouse of the American mall. The internet led to the next great disruption. By the 2010s, online shopping was a death knell for the weakest malls in the country. Retailers responded by embracing data, prioritizing algorithms over instincts. The era of the merchant—visionaries like Wexner, the Gap's Mickey Drexler, and Abercrombie & Fitch's Mike Jeffries—seemed finished.

Jens Grede and Emma Findlay Grede, the duo behind Skims, entered retail just as the internet began to upend the fashion business. Jens was a soft-spoken Swede and Emma a fast-talking East Londoner. They met in 2006 while running separate divisions of a creative agency called the Saturday Group in London. Jens was the cofounder, creating advertising campaigns for luxury and fashion brands like Moncler and H&M; Emma connected brands with celebrity faces (like actress Natalie Portman and Dior). One day over a lunch meeting at Claridge's, Emma confessed her love to Jens, and the two have been professionally and personally intertwined ever since—living a plot straight out of a Richard Curtis romantic comedy.

The couple shared a sense of relentless ambition. Their skills—his as an operator, hers as a merchant—were as complementary as their personalities. And unlike many of their peers, the Gredes recognized that internet culture had become pop culture. When Jens and his agency suggested Calvin Klein hire Justin Bieber to promote its underwear in 2014, they recognized that images of the polarizing pop star might have meme-generating potential—and propel Calvin Klein into a national conversation.

But Jens and Emma wanted to do more than engineer hype for clients. They wanted to launch their own brands. In 2012 Jens started a denim line, Frame, with the agency's other cofounder, Erik Torstensson. (Erik's romantic partner, Natalie Massenet, the founder of Net-a-Porter, became a significant investor in several of the Gredes' subsequent ventures.) Frame played into the era's obsession with off-duty model fashion and launched exclusive styles and collections with models like Karlie Kloss and Sasha Pivovarova. Four years later, Emma launched Good American, a celebrity-backed denim line designed for curvy bodies. She enlisted Kim Kardashian's sister Khloé as a partner in the entire venture, developing a new model for celebrity-backed fashion. While Kardashian lured consumers in, the denim developed a sparkling reputation for its broad range of sizes, flattering fits, and trendy cuts. The goods—ultra-focused, in the Les Wexner vein—delivered.

The Gredes had found their formula: combine smart marketing and well-made products with an engaged celebrity partner, and watch the money roll in. The couple moved to Los Angeles and, in 2018, convinced Kardashian "momager" Kris Jenner to launch another line with them, this time with Kim Kardashian. The category was shapewear; the angle was Spanx but comfortable. Skims hit the internet in September 2019 with a line of stretchy bras, cinching bodysuits, and bike shorts in nine skin-tone colors and a wide range of sizes. At launch, the press coverage was price-less. The debut collection sold out the first day.

Skims was sexy in a modern way, in the Kim Kardashian way. In the years since she became one of the most famous women in America, she had, intentionally or not, reshaped the silhouette of the ideal American woman: ample, exaggerated rear end, tiny waist, and large breasts. Kardashian was a real-life version of Jessica Rabbit, the voluptuous red-headed cartoon from 1988's oddball animated feature *Who Framed Roger Rabbit*.

Through some combination of her tenacity, her vaguely exotic eth-nicity (half Armenian) and her husband, Kanye West, in the mid-2010s, Kardashian cracked the upper echelons of the fashion industry in an unprecedented way. In her appearances at the Met Gala in a gilded Versace dress, or on the cover of *Vogue*, or in ads for luxury brands like Fendi and Givenchy, Kardashian flaunted her silhouette as a status symbol. (Her crit-ics accused her of finding success by copying her look from Black women, presumably through plastic surgery, which Kardashian has denied.[12])

Her timing was perfect. In high fashion, the look of so-called luxury was shifting. Brands that ironically elevated "tacky" trends or branded merchandise into runway gear were minting money. European houses had been indirectly filching from hip-hop culture and streetwear for decades. But by the 2010s, they realized that embracing it directly—and even hiring designers from that world—would lure younger shoppers, particularly men. In 2015, few labels garnered more attention than Vete-ments, designed by a semi-anonymous collective led by Georgian Demna Gvasalia, which sold $1,000 graphic print hoodies and oversize trousers made of pieced-together vintage Levi's, the hem cut like a mullet.

Kardashian was polarizing but unflappable, moving through internet controversies unscathed, the Teflon influencer. She rarely second-guessed herself or showed any hint of shame. Her push-pull of openness and control was ideal for the time, when people feared raw sexuality but groaned at try-hard "woke" mantras. When Skims launched with an embarrassing gaffe—the line was initially named Kimono, a culturally insensitive play on the word for a traditional Japanese garment—Kardashian acknowledged the mistake, changed the name, and moved on. The internet's ire did, too.

Kardashian also had Kanye West in her corner. He was critical in upgrading her personal style and validating her with cultural snobs who considered him a musical and fashion genius. His line of Adidas sneakers, first released in 2015, was a smash hit. Kanye served as the "ghost creative designer" of Skims, Kardashian later explained, infusing the line with his influential aesthetic, borrowed from other designers, including Martin Margiela.[13] West introduced Kardashian to the Italian artist Vanessa Beecroft, who photographed Skims' early campaigns. He also linked Kardashian with Kim Schraub, a designer for his own influential apparel line Yeezy. Schraub was a founding designer at Victoria's Secret Pink, staying with the line from its introduction in 2003 through 2013, when she followed Pink's former chief financial officer from Columbus to Los Angeles to join Yeezy. In 2019, as Yeezy sputtered under West's chaotic leadership style, Schraub joined Skims as the brand's creative director. Schraub's personal taste was grittier than what her prior corporate design roles had allowed, but it fit well with Kardashian's new project. And she was a talented designer. The Skims stretchy bras and boy shorts were soft but flattering, versatile but not boring.

Skims had more than the hype of a celebrity founder. Whether they loved or hated Kim Kardashian, or fell somewhere in between, many people recognized she had created something comfortable and flattering. "Skims was selling self-pride," said writer and former *InStyle* editor Hal Rubenstein. "'When you look in the mirror you will like yourself.' That's a very different trajectory than 'buy this underwear so you can get laid.'" In a matter of months, Skims expanded to loungewear and intimates. The company wasn't just aiming to disrupt Spanx and disrupt the shapewear market. Skims had its sights on Victoria's Secret.

As it turned out, Skims CEO Jens Grede was a close follower of Victoria's Secret and an admirer of Wexner's retail genius. Wexner had used the mall to scale Victoria's Secret. Grede would use the internet to do the same for Skims. His priority was to build a high-margin online business driven by regular "drops" of product. In the late 2010s, the fashion industry was fascinated by the drops model, made famous by the streetwear brand Supreme. Instead of presenting customers with seasonal collections roughly four times a year, drops brands released batches of styles every few weeks. Companies that adopted the strategy—like Everlane, a digital reincarnation of Gap for a younger audience—learned that introducing a few new items every week kept interest high and helped avoid discounting and inventory pileups. Operationally, however, drops were tricky. They required strong supply chain relationships, careful planning, and must-have products.

At Skims, Grede had the capital and patience to build a strong drops model. But unlike Victoria's Secret, which scaled as it opened more and larger stores, Grede couldn't count on taking advantage of shoppers' store visits to sell them more products. They could find everything they needed online, from as many different retailers as they wished. Grede knew the brand could never compete against Amazon or Shein, the giant Chinese fast-fashion retailer. Skims would have to compete on fabric, fit, and reputation. The brand needed to very clearly sell hope *and* help. The media strategy, the Kardashian of it all, would ensure customers paid attention. Grede's strategy appeared to be working. By 2023, Skims was generating an estimated $750 million in revenue, valued at $4 billion.

Skims was in a class all its own. Few of Victoria's Secret's challengers had the capital or infrastructure to consider competing with the market leader. Even Savage x Fenty, Rihanna's lingerie line, slumped after its buzzy launch. That brand, launched by California's TechStyle Fashion Group, has raised more than $300 million through 2023 and has since opened a dozen stores across the country. But the product has a reputation for shoddy quality, perhaps a problem not even Rihanna's popularity can solve.

Emerging brands face deeper barriers. Take Parade, a direct-to-consumer lingerie line launched in New York City in 2018 that drew inspiration from the provocative technicolor images of United Colors of Benetton photographer Oliviero Toscani. Its founder, a twenty-one-year-old Columbia University dropout named Cami Téllez, designed a line of playful prints and kitschy details. She presented the lingerie on a cast of young, downtown cool kids of all ethnicities, genders, and sizes, photographing them in a raw, unselfconscious way. Téllez took cues from Glossier, raising venture capital funding and posting Parade stickers all over New York City and Los Angeles. The brand had a refreshing bite that played well on Instagram. But Téllez struggled to turn a snappy idea into a fully formed business. She quickly learned that a Victoria's Secret–style product and distribution pipeline was not easily replicable. Parade ran out of cash during its fourth year in business and couldn't raise more. Victoria's Secret executives considered buying the brand, but ultimately passed. In August 2023, Téllez sold the line to a little-known intimate apparel firm for an undisclosed sum—reportedly a fraction of its former $200 million valuation—and walked away with nothing.[14]

/ / /

New York Fashion Week, American fashion's most important biannual ritual, no longer occupies Bryant Park or Lincoln Center with giant outdoor tents and steady streams of guests at all hours of the day. But look around Manhattan each September, and you can still see signs of Fashion Week underway. Bumper-to-bumper black cars clogging muggy downtown streets. Sweaty guests, wearing too many layers for the sake of style, crowding red-carpeted doorways manned by publicists with iPads.

Wednesday, September 6, 2023, was no different. Earlier in the day, the beloved independent designer Rachel Comey introduced her latest collection on a little street in NoHo, just north of Houston Street. In the evening, fashion editor Nikki Ogunnaike celebrated her recent appointment as editor in chief of *Marie Claire* on the rooftop of a hotel on the Lower East Side. Nearby, the cohosts of *Throwing Fits*, a shock-jock-style fashion podcast, were throwing a cocktail party funded by an eager new e-commerce venture.

Meanwhile, farther uptown at the Manhattan Center, an entirely different kind of crowd gathered to witness a "reimagining" of the formerly iconic Victoria's Secret Fashion Show. Four full years had passed since the last show, and none of the guests knew exactly what to expect from the evening ahead of them. The low-lit, tiered ballroom was filled with what used to be called "bridge and tunnel" types, straight out of a liquor brand–sponsored party at a Meatpacking District nightclub, circa 2006. Some of the crowd seemed teleported from the old Victoria's Secret Fashion Shows: finance guys in striped banker shirts and charcoal slacks, women in tight dresses with blown-out hair. Young influencers and TikTok stars took turns posing on a hot pink carpet set up outside along Thirty-Fourth Street. Fashion models, including Victoria's Secret's current face,

Paloma Elsesser, dutifully showed up, too. A number of former Angels also appeared, including Candice Swanepoel and Adriana Lima. (In 2023, Victoria's Secret hired back a handful of its former models for different campaigns, mixing them in with new faces, as had been proposed years earlier.) They were joined by It girls like Julia Fox and Emily Ratajkowski, all dressed in skimpy, confusing looks. Martin Waters, Victoria's Secret's CEO, cruised the ballroom shaking hands, as did Raúl Martinez, the company's chief creative director. Mannequins in multistory cases lined the far side of the ballroom. Some displayed lingerie, others wore wings from previous shows—Angels history preserved in pink-lit vessels.

An hour into the party, the crowd quieted as the lights dimmed. Naomi Campbell and Gigi Hadid appeared on upper balconies, lit by bright spotlights. Campbell kicked things off by reciting a poem by the Nigerian writer Eloghosa Osunde. Then Hadid briefly introduced a video clip. There would be no models in lingerie that night; the main event was the screening of a trailer for an upcoming brand-produced film, *Victoria's Secret: The Tour '23*. The clips played on a jumbo screen draped across the ballroom's back wall. The guests, all standing, lifted their heads upward and watched silently.

The documentary-style film followed twenty young creative types, including four fashion designers, in four different non-American cities. They told their personal stories as they created fashion collections loosely inspired by Victoria's Secret—sometimes lingerie, sometimes not. Each segment culminated in a conceptual runway show filmed at the surrealist Espai Corberó building outside Barcelona.

After the extended trailer ended, two singers appeared without introduction: first the Colombian singer Goyo, and then Doechii, who performed back-to-back. The audience, too packed along the ballroom floor to dance, even if they recognized the songs, seemed confused. Was that all there would be? Indeed it was, save for a round of applause for the designers and filmmakers who emerged on an elevated side of the ballroom floor.

The full Victoria's Secret film was released two weeks later on Amazon. Hadid served as the narrator, addressing some of the inherent confusion of rebooting the show in such a different format from what once aired on CBS prime time. "I know what you're thinking, 'What the fuck? Where are the models and lingerie? Show me the girls in angel wings!'" she said, doing her best to bring a little levity to the project.[15] "It's been five long and lingerie-less years since my last Victoria's Show, folks." After a segment with Campbell and former Angels like Adriana Lima and Lily Aldridge strutting through the Corberó space, Hadid chimed in, "I mean, c'mon, we had to bring back a little bit of the old show." Otherwise, *The Tour* took great pains to distinguish itself from Victoria's Secret's past. There was no audience of gawking men on-screen. The featured designers and creatives received as much, if not more, attention than the models, who were more diverse in body shape and age than the brand had ever used before.

But those nuances were largely lost on social media. Online, clips of the former Angels back in lingerie racked up millions of views. A clip of Ratajkowski oohing and aahing over "archival" wings clocked more views than any other social media post the company had ever published.[16] Traditional media played along, too, with outlets as wide-ranging as the *Guardian* and the *New York Times* running pieces about the brand's new strategy. (KCD, the PR agency that ran the backstage and production for the Victoria's Secret Fashion Show for years until 2019, had picked up Victoria's Secret as a client again.) The press about the new show, from TikTok to newspapers, focused on the merits of a "woke" versus "sexy" strategy, wondering if the brand's turnaround efforts were clear or compelling enough to win over fickle contemporary audiences. "We are back in the conversation," said Waters a few weeks after the fashion show debuted, during a presentation for investors. He declared the project a success.[17] But Victoria's Secret revenue continued to decline, albeit slowly.

Internally, the show was seen as a failure and a waste of money. Before, Victoria's Secret faced criticism for chauvinism and crassness, but at least it had a clear point of view. Martinez was the obvious culprit for the misfire. He managed the production of *The Tour*, which cost close to $10 million to produce. He also had a track record of clashes with Schaffer, the chief designer, according to colleagues. In January 2024 only a few months after *The Tour*'s debut and three years after he left Condé Nast, *Vogue* announced Martinez was back at the magazine publisher, returning to his role as global creative director.

It seemed that Victoria's Secret was back to square one in its ongoing identity crisis, doomed to languish for years, if not decades, in its current state. With both sales and profits shrinking, the brand could be attractive for a private buyer, like an investment firm or a corporate raider masquerading as a strategic investor. Away from Wall Street's constant glare, the business might have better luck reinvigorating itself.

In early 2024, former Victoria's Secret executives caught wind of several fascinating rumors. Apparently, Skims had considered buying Victoria's Secret. Separately, John Mehas, the former divisional CEO, had approached Les Wexner with a proposal: Mehas wanted to raise money to buy Victoria's Secret and take it private, and he hoped Wexner would fund him. (A person close to Mehas denied the story, but sources close to Wexner said Mehas did pitch his former boss.) Regardless, Wexner, then eighty-six, was not interested. While he loves to reminisce, and he is still fascinated by the retail business, he had no interest in generating more headlines. And, more importantly, he knew better than to swoop in and try to fix Victoria's Secret himself.

❙❙❙

In 1999, Victoria's Secret "crashed" the internet with its first live-streamed fashion show. Back then, the brand's stunts were novel. Fashion shows were still insular industry rituals, alluring but hidden away behind closed doors in Paris or Milan.

That era is long over, as *The Tour*'s tepid public reception underscored. More than twenty years later, every fashion show is documented ad nauseam for each social media platform. Runway models now often include singers, actors, or former supermodels making surprise appearances. Brands seek ever more exotic venues, often in far-flung locations, like an arts museum in Rio de Janeiro or the streets of Havana. In the summer of 2023, Louis Vuitton marked the arrival of its new creative director, not a designer but the Grammy Award–winning musician Pharrell Williams. The Parisian house took over the historic Pont Neuf, the oldest bridge in Paris, for a runway show filmed from every angle by drones and camera cranes. Afterward, Pharrell and Jay-Z performed.

Whether or not they acknowledge it, the executives orchestrating these spectacles learned an essential lesson about the value of entertainment from Victoria's Secret—from the images of Claudia Schiffer in a bedazzled push-up bra, Heidi Klum strapped into a pair of twelve-foot-tall fluffy wings, and Rosie Huntington-Whiteley framed against an orange fireball in the California desert.

Judged against even Victoria's Secret's own history, *The Tour* could never measure up. The brand remains trapped under the weight of a past too thorny to unpack and too memorable to overcome.

Epilogue: Final Fantasy

When Roy and Gaye Raymond cofounded Victoria's Secret in 1977, they had a billion-dollar idea on their hands. But it was little more than an idea back then. The billion-dollar part—that became someone else's reality.

Gaye's life hasn't been easy. She and her two children endured the family's bankruptcy in 1986 and Roy's shocking, public suicide in 1993. In death, Roy became a cautionary tale, reduced to a parable about an entrepreneur selling out too early in David Fincher's modern classic *The Social Network*. The 2010 movie charts the origin of Facebook, the story of a young man who built an empire from someone else's stroke of genius. "This is a once-in-a-generation, *holy-shit* idea," says Justin Timberlake's Sean Parker, cautioning Jesse Eisenberg's young Mark Zuckerberg. "And the water under the Golden Gate is freezing cold."

When Les Wexner found Victoria's Secret, the Raymonds were desperate to sell. In the decades that followed, Wexner turned their little business into a mega-brand and, at some point, revised the origin story. He liked to say that he had set his sights on the lingerie business years before he first walked into the Raymonds' San Francisco store, in a way taking the credit for Victoria's Secret himself.[1]

Today, people who know the story of Victoria's Secret think of Les Wexner, the retail empire builder. Or Ed Razek, the Hugh Hefner wannabe behind the Angels. Or Jeffrey Epstein, the criminal predator who tarnished the brand's legacy.

Few people think about Gaye. She could be bitter about the past, but she's not. "Victoria's Secret was an amazing experience," she said in January

2022, in a quiet office in San Francisco. "I did it, I bought a house. I'm more or less debt free. I really enjoy my work." Gaye is in her midseventies now and still lives in the East Bay, working part-time as a physical therapist. She still looks much like her younger self, the woman who told Victoria's first story on television four decades ago.

Gaye now sees Victoria's Secret's billions as a poison. "All the money that Wexner has, all the money that he gave Jeffrey Epstein? How sad," she said. "I don't want to be anybody else, let's put it that way. I've grown to accept and appreciate who I am, and that's a pretty good place to be in life."

Gaye was the first in a long line of women behind Victoria's Secret who worked tirelessly to make the company a success, despite never being fully in charge. Wexner hired and promoted women to the highest ranks of his business in an era when men ruled retail. There was Verna Gibson, once his chief merchant at the Limited. There was Cindy Fedus-Fields and her catalog crew; Grace Nichols, the steadfast builder; Jill Beraud, the marketing maven; Marie Holman-Rao, the creative agitator; and Sharen Jester Turney, his star. While Wexner often hired, mentored, and promoted women, his closest advisers on the central corporate team were men.

And yet these generations of women, each impressive in her own right, were obsessed with their customers. These women routinely asked themselves the same question: "What is sexy now?" Some wanted shoppers to feel powerful in Victoria's Secret stores, to invite them to define "sexy" for themselves. Others wanted women to understand that "sexy" was more than a performance for their partners—it came from how they viewed themselves. Others didn't even want to use the word "sexy" at all. But those desires often got lost on the journey from the conference room to the television screen, from the concept board to the camera feed. Mass marketing is not always hospitable to nuance.

In the years since Wexner walked away from Victoria's Secret, the brand's sales have gotten better, then worse, then mostly settled into a state of slow and steady decline. The company is still massive, with more than $6 billion in annual revenue and about 18 percent of the intimates market share in the United States, more than double the share of its largest competitors.[2]

Victoria's Secret is far from dead, but it is no longer a bulletproof business or culturally relevant. It positioned itself so effectively as the standard- bearer of female beauty that the marketing ploy became reality. Its singular vision of sexy became America's vision of sexy. Until the wider culture began to recognize and expect multiple visions of beauty.

Many of the women who worked for Victoria's Secret in its heyday remain proud of what they accomplished there. But they are also saddened to see the brand reduced to its most lurid tendencies in the public consciousness. They are dismayed to see the brand associated with a notorious sexual predator. Those elements of the Victoria's Secret story obscure a far more interesting reality: the business was always more than just a clever marketing machine.

When Wexner opened his first store, the Limited, in 1963, not even his father believed anyone would come to shop just for casual women's sportswear. Now, Americans shop at one place for jeans, another for sneakers, another for bras. Specialty retail has dominated American shopping for forty years. Few were more successful or ubiquitous than Victoria's Secret, Wexner's greatest retail accomplishment. The multibillion-dollar business allowed more women than ever before to express themselves through the most basic parts of their wardrobes: bras and underwear.

At its height, Victoria's Secret had no serious competitors. The Angels personified a male fantasy, but many women loved them, too. You'd be hard-pressed to find anyone, especially in the United States, who didn't interact with the brand, its fashion shows, or its ubiquitous stores—even women who were put off by the Angels from the very beginning. People are full of contradictions. Victoria's Secret reflected an internal struggle many women feel, resentful of beauty ideals but also dogged by an obligation to fulfill them. Our personal values are not always aligned with our behaviors. Sometimes you just want a lace-trimmed push-up bra, with a tiny bow on the center bridge, wrapped up in a shiny pink-striped bag. Cheap, reliable, accessible thrills—brought to you by your local mall.

The story of one brand is also the story of a golden age in American retail, now come to a close. Fashion is a ruthlessly cyclical business. Les Wexner knew that better than anyone. No trend, no brand is forever. But he fooled himself into thinking Victoria's Secret could defy that rule. For a while, against all odds, it did. But that was just another fantasy.

Notes

Introduction: Dreams and Fantasies

1. Claire Zillman, "The Longest-Serving Fortune 500 CEO Is a Lingerie Bra Salesman," *Fortune*, June 5, 2015, https://fortune.com/2015/06/05/leslie-wexner-l-brands.
2. Emily Steel, Steve Eder, Sapna Maheshwari, and Matthew Goldstein, "How Jeffrey Epstein Used the Billionaire Behind Victoria's Secret for Wealth and Women," *New York Times*, July 25, 2019, https://www.nytimes.com/2019/07/25/business/jeffrey-epstein-wexner-victorias-secret.html.
3. Cited in Brian O'Reilly and Kim Bendheim, "Leslie Wexner Knows What Women Want," *Fortune*, August 19, 1985, https://money.cnn.com/magazines/fortune/fortune_archive/1985/08/19/66309/index.htm.

Chapter 1: Right Place, Right Time

1. This chapter relies heavily on extensive interviews with Victoria's Secret cofounder Gaye Raymond and early employees including photographer Peter Ogilvie; art director Ross Carron; Michele Rivers, who led retail; Barba Kandarian, the head buyer; and other sources who wished for our conversations to remain confidential.
2. The term "white space" was coined by management consultant Mark W. Johnson, author of *Seizing the White Space: Business Model Innovation for Growth and Renewal*. (Cambridge, MA: Harvard Business Press, 2010).
3. The Xandria Collection, "Sexual Aids," advertisement, *Cosmopolitan*, March 1978.
4. Elaine Benson and John Esten, *Unmentionables: A Brief History of Underwear* (New York: Simon & Schuster, 1996), 11.
5. Béatrice Fontanel, *Support and Seduction: The History of Corsets and Bras* (New York: Abradale Books, 2001), 11.
6. Colleen C. Hill, *Exposed: A History of Lingerie* (New Haven, CT, and New York: Yale University Press in association with the Fashion Institute of Technology, 2014), 22.
7. Elizabeth E. Ewing, *Fashion in Underwear* (London: Batsford Books, 1974), 28.
8. Fontanel, *Support and Seduction*, 31.
9. Quoted in C. Willett Cunnington and Phillis Cunnington, *The History of Underclothes* (Mineola, NY: Dover, 1992), 115.
10. Quoted in Cunnington and Cunnington, *History of Underclothes*, 115.
11. Cunnington and Cunnington, *History of Underclothes*, 197–98.
12. Quoted in Fontanel, *Support and Seduction*, 68.
13. Ewing, *Fashion in Underwear*, 78–79.
14. Fontanel, *Support and Seduction*, 66.
15. Ewing, *Fashion in Underwear*, 79.
16. Fontanel, *Support and Seduction*, 77.
17. Fontanel, *Support and Seduction*, 93.

18. Jane Farrell-Beck and Colleen Gau, *Uplift: The Bra in America* (Philadelphia: University of Pennsylvania Press, 2002), 17.
19. Fontanel, *Support and Seduction*, 77.
20. Mary M. Schweitzer, "World War II and Female Labor Force Participation Rates," *Journal of Economic History* 40, no. 1 (1980): 89–95.
21. Farrell-Beck and Gau, *Uplift*, 121.
22. Fontanel, *Support and Seduction*, 77.
23. Heather Vaughan Lee, *Artifacts from American Fashion* (Santa Barbara, CA: Greenwood, 2020), 269.
24. Robert Cross, "Hots Couture," *Chicago Tribune*, February 3, 1974.
25. Linda Witt, "King of Passion Fashions," *Courier-Post*, February 16, 1974.
26. Cross, "Hots Couture."
27. Frederick's of Hollywood catalog, 1971.
28. Witt, "King of Passion Fashions."
29. "Frederick's of Hollywood / Real People / George Schlatter," YouTube video, 3:39, posted by "Real People," October 5, 2017, https://www.youtube.com/watch?v=eNjQH2vXwmw, at 3:15.
30. Gregory Jaynes, "Grand Illusions: With Frederick's of Hollywood Fashion, What You See Is Not Always What You Get," *Atlanta Constitution*, February 28, 1975.
31. Frederick's of Hollywood catalog, 1971.
32. Tom Furlong, "Mr. Frederick, Inflation Fighter," *Washington Post*, January 11, 1981.
33. "Frederick's of Hollywood / Real People / George Schlatter," YouTube video.
34. "Fashion: Up, Up & Away," *Time*, December 1, 1967, https://content.time.com/time/subscriber/article/0,33009,712027,00.html.
35. Erik Hedegaard, "Catalog of Desire: Victoria's Secrets for Success," *San Francisco Chronicle*, September 22, 1991.
36. Steve Ginsberg, "Victoria's Secret Is the Subtle, Sexy Look." *Women's Wear Daily*, November 19, 1981.
37. Quoted in Subrata N. Chakravarty, "The Cleopatra Syndrome," *Forbes* 131, no. 10 (May 9, 1983): 74–79.
38. William Schack, "Neiman-Marcus of Texas," *Commentary* 24 (January 1, 1957): 212, https://www.commentary.org/articles/william-schack/neiman-marcus-of-texascouture-and-culture/.
39. Fred D. Reynolds, "An Analysis of Catalog Buying Behavior," *Journal of Marketing* 38, no. 3 (July 1974): 47–51.
40. Rachel Triesman, "These Are the Life Lessons Geena Davis Learned from 3 of Her Most Famous Movies," *Morning Edition*, NPR, October 6, 2022, https://www.npr.org/2022/10/06/1127158889/geena-davis-memoir-famous-roles.
41. Herb Caen, "Of All Things," *San Francisco Chronicle*, May 29, 1981.
42. Mitra Toossi, "A Century of Change: The U.S. Labor Force, 1950–2050," *Monthly Labor Review*, May 2002, https://www.bls.gov/opub/mlr/2002/05/art2full.pdf.

Chapter 2: The Rise of a Retail Savant

1. This chapter draws from interviews with early Les Wexner associates, including Pete Halliday and Robert Morosky; associates of Marty Trust, the founder of Mast Industries; and executives at the Limited, many of whom saw Wexner as a mentor and were involved in the early days of Victoria's Secret.
2. Leon A. Harris, *Merchant Princes: An Intimate History of the Jewish Families Who Built Great Department Stores* (1979; repr. New York: Kodansha USA, 1994), 204.
3. Stephen Miller, "Remembrances," *Wall Street Journal*, May 19, 2007, Eastern ed.
4. Harris, *Merchant Princes*, 339.
5. Jeff Suess, "Lazarus to Thank for Thanksgiving Date," *Cincinnati Enquirer*, November 27, 2014, https://www.cincinnati.com/story/news/history/2014/11/27/lazarus-to-thank-for-thanksgiving-date/19573889.
6. Isador Cabakoff, interview by Naomi Schottenstein, Columbus Jewish Historical Society, November 12, 1996, https://columbusjewishhistory.org/oral_histories/isador-cabakoff/.
7. Quoted in Pete Born, "Leslie H. Wexner: Uneasy Rider," *Women's Wear Daily*, February 27, 1985, 54–55.
8. "Les Wexner, Academy Class of 1990, Full Interview," YouTube video, 1:21:53, posted by "Academy of Achievement," July 12, 2017, https://www.youtube.com/watch?v=BF_jZdignxQ.
9. *Columbus Dispatch*, March 16, 1952.

10. Quoted in Nancy Nall, "High Profile: The Million-Dollar Style of Les Wexner," *Columbus Dispatch,* July 29, 1984.
11. Peter D. Franklin, "Thoughts on Being a Success," *Columbus Dispatch*, May 30, 1982.
12. Franklin, "Thoughts on Being a Success."
13. Samuel Feinberg, "From Where I Sit: Limited in Name Only, Not in Growth or Profit," *Women's Wear Daily*, February 22, 1977, 12.
14. Julie Baumgold, "The Bachelor Billionaire," *New York*, August 5, 1985, 33.
15. Feinberg, "From Where I Sit," 12.
16. Robert W. Reiss, "Limited's Growth Features Profits," *Columbus Dispatch*, February 3, 1974.
17. Pete Halliday, interview.
18. From one of our background sources.
19. Dana Thomas, "The High Price of Fast Fashion," *Wall Street Journal*, August 29, 2019, https://www .wsj.com/articles/the-high-price-of-fast-fashion-11567096637.
20. Feinberg, "From Where I Sit," 12.
21. Baumgold, "Bachelor Billionaire."
22. Quoted in Nick Paumgarten, "The Merchant," *New Yorker*, September 13, 2010, https://www .newyorker.com/magazine/2010/09/20/the-merchant.
23. Pete Born, "Limited: Mapping a Fashion Strategy: The Limited Strategy," *Women's Wear Daily*, December 22, 1986, 1–5.
24. Susan Dentzer, "Parlaying Rags into Vast Riches: A Brash Leslie Wexner Makes the Limited a Star," *Newsweek*, December 30, 1985, 30–32.
25. William H. Meyers, "Rag Trade Revolutionary," *New York Times*, June 8, 1986.
26. Quoted in Baumgold, "Bachelor Billionaire."
27. Isadore Barmash, "Lane Bryant and Ohio Chain in $100 Million Merger," *New York Times*, April 29, 1982, https://www.nytimes.com/1982/04/29/business/lane-bryant-and-ohio-chain-in-100 -million-merger.html.

Chapter 3: One Man's Failure Is Another's Opportunity

1. This chapter draws on interviews with Gaye Raymond, Barba Kandarian, Bob Morosky, several Limited executives, and relatives of deceased executives.
2. O'Reilly and Bendheim, "Leslie Wexner Knows What Women Want."
3. "Les Wexner, Academy Class of 1990, Full Interview," YouTube video.
4. Quoted in Johanna Schneller, "Death of a Dream Merchant," *GQ*, September 1994.
5. Schneller, "Death of a Dream Merchant."
6. Katherine Bishop, "An Elegant Kids' Store Fails," *New York Times*, December 27, 1986, https://www .nytimes.com/1986/12/27/business/an-elegant-kids-store-fails.html.
7. Steve Ginsberg, "Victoria's Secret Slated to Go National," *Women's Wear Daily*, January 5, 1983, 22.
8. Quoted in Michael Gross, "Lingerie Catalogues: Changing Images," *New York Times*, April 26, 1987.
9. Ginsberg, "Victoria's Secret Slated to Go National," 22.
10. Ginsberg, "Victoria's Secret Slated to Go National," 22.

Chapter 4: The Making of the American Mall

1. For this chapter, we spoke with people connected closely with A. Alfred Taubman; other long-term Wexner associates; and retail executives active during the period, many of whom knew Wexner or worked directly with him.
2. Malcolm Gladwell, "The Terrazzo Jungle," *New Yorker*, March 27, 2004, https://www.newyorker.com /magazine/2004/03/15/the-errazzo-jungle.
3. A. Alfred.Taubman, *Threshold Resistance: The Extraordinary Career of a Luxury Retailing Pioneer* (New York: HarperCollins, 2007), 36.
4. Taubman, *Threshold Resistance*, 34.
5. Quoted in Dan Alexander, "A Farewell Tribute to Alfred Taubman, by Les Wexner," *Forbes*, May 7, 2015, https://www.forbes.com/sites/danalexander/2015/05/07/a-farewell-tribute-to-alfred -taubman-by-les-wexner/?sh=302d4d1e70f5.
6. Quoted in Gladwell, "The Terrazzo Jungle."
7. Thomas W. Hanchett, "U.S. Tax Policy and the Shopping-Center Boom of the 1950s and 1960s," *American Historical Review* 101, no. 4 (1996): 1082–110.
8. Richard A. Feinberg and Jennifer Meoli, "A Brief History of the Mall," *Advances in Consumer Research* 18 (1991): 426–27.

9. Quoted in Meyers, "Rag Trade Revolutionary."

10. Eric Wilson, "Geraldine Stutz Dies at 80; Headed Bendel for 29 Years," *New York Times*, April 9, 2005, https://www.nytimes.com/2005/04/09/business/geraldine-stutz-dies-at-80-headed-bendel-for-29-years.html.

11. Meyers, "Rag Trade Revolutionary."

12. Born, "Limited: Mapping a Fashion Strategy."

13. Mya Frazier, "Once Proud, the Limited Now Weak Link in Wexner Chain," *Ad Age*, May 16, 2005, https://adage.com/article/brands-demandtrouble/proud-limited-weak-link-wexner-chain/103199.

14. Tracy Achor Hayes, "Specialty Chain Store Formula Now a Megahit in Fashion Field," *Dallas Morning News*, January 25, 1987.

Chapter 5: The Not-So-Ugly Stepsister

1. This chapter draws on interviews with Cindy Fedus-Fields, Laura Berkman, other Victoria's Secret executives from the period, several modeling agents, and models Carol Perkins and Frederique van der Wal.

2. Quoted in Gaby Wood, "How Do You Want Me? The Life of a Male Model," *Guardian,* January 11, 2009, https://www.theguardian.com/lifeandstyle/2009/jan/11/life-as-a-male-model.

3. Holly Brubach, "Mail-Order America," *New York Times Magazine*, November 21, 1993, https://www.nytimes.com/1993/11/21/magazine/mail-order-america.html.

4. Dodie Kazanjian, "Vogue's View: Victoria's Secret," *Vogue*, April 1, 1992.

5. Victoria's Secret catalog, summer 1993.

Chapter 6: Man About Town

1. This chapter draws on extensive historical research as well as interviews with Wexner's business associates and advisers, Gaye Raymond, and business associates of Roy Raymond.

2. Quoted in Born, "Leslie H. Wexner: Uneasy Rider."

3. Quoted in Born, "Leslie H. Wexner: Uneasy Rider."

4. Quoted in Born, "Leslie H. Wexner: Uneasy Rider."

5. Quoted in Born, "Leslie H. Wexner: Uneasy Rider."

6. Nall, "High Profile."

7. Ray Paprocki, "Inside the Wolfe Empire," *Columbus Monthly*, April 1986. https://www.columbusmonthly.com/story/news/2014/02/06/inside-wolfe-empire/4928316007/.

8. Quoted in Ray Paprocki, "Death of a Titan," *Columbus Monthly*, August 1994, https://www.columbusmonthly.com/story/business/names-faces/2018/06/12/death-titan/4928268007/.

9. Ray Paprocki, "Les Wexner's Impact," *Columbus Monthly*, March 1994, https://www.columbusmonthly.com/story/business/names-faces/2020/05/18/from-archives-les-wexner-s/1185489007/.

10. Jolie Solomon, "Limited's Founder Campaigns to Raise Hometown's Status," *Wall Street Journal,* December 9, 1986.

11. Herb Cook Jr., "Rinehart on Wexner: 'I Might as Well Be Talking to a Tree,'" *Columbus Monthly*, September 1985, https://digital-collections.columbuslibrary.org/digital/collection/cbusmonthly/id/25788.

12. Paprocki, "Les Wexner's Impact."

13. Quoted in Nall, "High Profile."

14. Lee Whelk, "Many People Like Columbus as It Is, Not 'Big,'" *Columbus Dispatch*, May 11, 1986.

15. Nall, "High Profile."

16. Betty Liu Ebron, "On the Upper East Side, Rich & Famous in Cleanup," *New York Daily News*, April 24, 1990.

17. Baumgold, "Bachelor Billionaire."

18. Baumgold, "Bachelor Billionaire."

19. Born, "Leslie H. Wexner: Uneasy Rider."

20. Bridget Foley, "The A Team," *Women's Wear Daily*, July 13, 1984.

21. "Eye Scoop," *Women's Wear Daily*, January 26, 1993, 4.

22. Harold Seneker and Delores Lataniotis, "The Forbes Four Hundred," *Forbes*, October 17, 1994, 272.

23. Ray Paprocki, "The Benevolent Billionaire," *Columbus Monthly*, March 1994, https://www.columbusmonthly.com/story/business/names-faces/2020/05/18/from-archives-les-wexner-s/1185489007/.

24. Ray Paprocki, "Power 2010," *Columbus Monthly*, June 2010, https://www.columbusmonthly.com /story/business/names-faces/2014/02/06/power-2010/2520377007.

25. Pete Born, "Wexner's Artistic Role," *Women's Wear Daily*, November 20, 1989.

26. Nancy Gilson, "Visual Arts: 'To Begin, Again' Explores the Origins and Evolution of the Wexner Center," *Columbus Dispatch*, February 19, 2022.

27. Quoted in Ray Paprocki, "Les Wexner Builds a House," *Columbus Monthly*, May 1990, https:// www.columbusmonthly.com/story/business/names-faces/2018/06/18/les-wexner-builds-house /986503007/.

28. Quoted in Dan Williamson with Ray Paprocki, "Les Wexner's Board Games," *Columbus Monthly*, April 2006, https://www.columbusmonthly.com/story/business/names-faces/2018/09 /24/les-wexner-s-board-games/9726099007/.

29. Schneller, "Death of a Dream Merchant."

30. Benjamin Pimentel, "Lingerie Firm Founder Dies," *San Francisco Chronicle*, September 1, 1993, A16.

31. Michelle Quinn, "Success, Bankruptcy . . . Suicide," *New York Times*, September 26, 1993, https: //www.nytimes.com/1993/09/26/business/success-bankruptcy-suicide.html.

Chapter 7: Victoria Grows Up

1. This chapter draws on interviews with several senior-level Victoria's Secret executives across marketing, finance, operations and merchandising including Jill Beraud, Cindy Fedus-Fields, Nancy Binger and Laura Berkman; former product developers Anne Enke and Cate Lyon; various modeling agents; and several colleagues of Dick Tarlow.

2. Kazanjian, "Vogue's View: Victoria's Secret."

3. Dyan Machan, "Sharing Victoria's Secrets," *Forbes*, June 5, 1995.

4. Sandra Palumbo, "Innerwear: Victoria's Secret Is No Longer Hush-Hush as Volume Has Boomed to $100 Million," *Women's Wear Daily*, March 12, 1987, 14.

5. Susan Faludi, *Backlash: The Undeclared War Against American Women* (Three Rivers Press: New York, 1991), 31.

6. Stephanie Strom, "When Victoria's Secret Faltered, She Was Quick to Fix It," *New York Times*, November 21, 1993, https://www.nytimes.com/1993/11/21/business/profile-grace-nichols-when -victoria-s-secret-faltered-she-was-quick-to-fix-it.html.

7. James Morgan, "Frisky Business," *Washington Post*, September 8, 1991.

8. Quoted in Christopher Palmieri, "Victoria's Little Secret," *Forbes*, August 24, 1998, 58.

9. Quoted in Ann Trebbe, "A Model's Secret: Jill Goodacre," *USA Today*, July 9, 1991.

10. Eileen Daspin, "Marketing/Media: Europe's New Supermodels," *Women's Wear Daily*, February 5, 1993, 12.

11. Christopher S. Wren, "Clinton Calls Fashion Ads' 'Heroin Chic' Deplorable," *New York Times*, May 22, 1997, https://www.nytimes.com/1997/05/22/us/clinton-calls-fashion-ads-heroin-chic -deplorable.html.

12. A copy of the brand book is in the authors' possession.

13. Quoted in Michael Musto, "La Dolce Musto," *Village Voice*, August 15, 1995.

14. Rene Chun, "The Man's Fashion Shows," *New York*, February 19, 1996.

15. A. J. Benza, "Sensuous Overload," *New York Daily News*, February 11, 1996. Quoted in "Victoria's Secret 1996," YouTube video, 1:51, posted by "90s Fashion," November 30, 2014, https://www .youtube.com/watch?v=Dq2kgs1i_8w.

16. Chun, "The Man's Fashion Shows."

17. Christopher Palmeri, "Victoria's Little Secret," *Forbes*, August 24, 1998, 58.

18. Billy Taylor, "Victoria's Secret Angels," *House of Style*, MTV Networks, May 9, 1997.

Chapter 8: Here Come the Consultants

1. This chapter draws on interviews with Marie Holman-Rao, various designers, senior-level Limited executives, associates of Marty Trust, and Michael Silverstein.

2. Jennifer Steinhauer and Edward Wyatt, "The Merlin of the Mall Tries Out New Magic," *New York Times*, December 8, 1996, https://www.nytimes.com/1996/12/08/business/the-merlin-of-the-mall -tries-out-new-magic.html.

3. Meyers, "Rag Trade Revolutionary."

4. Ronald A. Heifetz and Marty Linsky, "Leadership on the Line: Staying Alive Through the Dangers

of Leading," *HBS Working Knowledge*, May 28, 2002, https://hbswk.hbs.edu/archive/leadership-on-the-line-staying-alive-through-the-dangers-of-leading.

5. Steinhauer and Wyatt, "The Merlin of the Mall Tries Out New Magic."

6. Ylonda Gault, "The Limited Discovers Its Limits," *Crain's New York Business* 13, no. 51 (December 22, 1997): 199.

7. Reese Erlich, "Former Levi Strauss Workers Protest Texas Plant Closing," *Christian Science Monitor*, November 9, 1992, https://www.csmonitor.com/1992/1109/09072.html.

8. Karyn Monget, "Innerwear Report: Big 4 Bra Firms Take Lion's Share of Market," *Women's Wear Daily*, May 15, 1995.

9. Stephen MacDonald, "The World Bids Farewell to the Multifiber Arrangement," Economic Research Service, US Department of Agriculture, February 1, 2006, https://www.ers.usda.gov/amber-waves/2006/february/the-world-bids-farewell-to-the-multifiber-arrangement/.

10. Brandix Lanka Ltd., *Built on Trust: The Sri Lankan Apparel Industry Pays Tribute to Martin Trust*, 2015, http://www.brandix.com/built-on-trust.pdf.

Chapter 9: Making (Something Like) Movies

1. This chapter draws on interviews with Jill Beraud, Nancy Binger, Alex de Betak, models and modeling agents, and various associates of Ed Razek.

2. Quoted in Rebecca Quick, "Boss Talk: A Makeover that Began at the Top—the Road from Entrepreneur to Modern Manager Was Rough for Limited Founder," *Wall Street Journal*, May 25, 2000.

3. "Laetitia Casta révèle les secrets de tous les looks les plus iconiques de sa vie," YouTube video, 14:18, posted by "Vogue France," March 2, 2022, https://www.youtube.com/watch?v=mls6ZvF0Xkw&t=213s. (Note: YouTube includes a translation option).

4. Heidi Klum, *Heidi Klum's Body of Knowledge: 8 Rules of Model Behavior (to Help You Take Off on the Runway of Life)* (New York: Crown, 2004), 167.

5. Rene Chun, "Copy Catwalk," *New York*, December 16, 1996.

6. Quoted in Alex Kuczynski, "Trading on Hollywood Magic: Celebrities Push Models off Women's Magazine Covers," *New York Times*, January 30, 1999, https://www.nytimes.com/1999/01/30/business/trading-on-hollywood-magic-celebrities-push-models-off-women-s-magazine-covers.html.

7. Julie Baumgold, "A Perfect Merger," *Vogue*, September 1, 1998, 562–67, 670.

8. Mac Margolis, "Anatomy of a Fashion Star," in "Facing the Future Issues 2000," supplement, *Newsweek*, December 2000, 82.

9. Philip Weiss, "Health & Beauty: The Return of the Curve," *Vogue*, July 1, 1999, 192–95.

10. "Victoria's Secret Fashion Show 1999—Behind the Scenes," YouTube video, 32:33, posted by "gio-curve," June 25, 2014, https://www.youtube.com/watch?v=aR3hy5pRvMA.

11. "Victoria's Secret Fashion Show 1999—Behind the Scenes," YouTube video.

12. "Victoria's Secret Fashion Show 1999—Behind the Scenes," YouTube video.

13. "Hot Model: Gisele," *Rolling Stone*, August 19, 1999, 81.

14. Sally Singer, "Fashion Moment," *New York*, May 10, 1999, https://nymag.com/nymetro/shopping/fashion/features/864/.

15. Quoted in Suzanna Andrews, "Beautiful Dreamer," *Vanity Fair* (Spanish-language version), October 2004, 324–54.

16. Robert O'Harrow Jr. and Mark Leibovich, "Today's Hot Stock: Anything-Dot-Com; Some Fear Wall St. 'Mania' for Internet Firms Presages a Fall," *Washington Post*, April 23, 1998.

17. Lisa Napoli, "Was the Victoria's Secret Show a Web Failure?" *New York Times*, February 8, 1999, https://www.nytimes.com/1999/02/08/business/media-business-advertising-was-victoria-s-secret-show-web-failure-hardly-there-s.html.

18. Susan Kuchinskas, "Victoria's Secret," *Adweek*, June 28, 1999, 1.

19. Joshua Levine, "The Runway Leader: Alexandre de Betak a Slip of a Man with a Tintin Cowlick, Is the Frighteningly Fashionable Force Behind the World's Slickest Catwalk Shows," *Ottawa Citizen*, March 7, 1999.

20. Simon Mills, "Heavenly Creatures," *Sunday Times*, May 28, 2000.

21. Karyn Monget, "Victoria's Secret's Cannes: Cast," *Women's Wear Daily*, June 5, 2000.

22. Sandra Dolbow, "Marketers of the Year: Rattling the Chains," *Brandweek* 41, no. 40 (October 16, 2000): M86–M92.

Chapter 10: What Is Sexy?

1. This chapter draws on interviews with Jill Beraud, Marie Holman-Rao, various designers, and other senior-level executives who worked with Les Wexner and Ed Razek.

2. Quoted in David Moin, "IBI Giving Victoria's Secret Push into Global Prominence," *Women's Wear Daily*, September 29, 1999, 2–25.

3. Rebecca Quick, "Bra-wl! Push-Up Comes to Shove: The Effort to Build a Better Bra," *Wall Street Journal*, April 10, 2000, https://www.wsj.com/articles/SB955318658960353235.

4. Barbara Lippert, "Breasts R Us," *Adweek*, November 15, 1999, 30.

5. "SNL Transcripts: Ben Affleck: 02/19/00: Victoria's Secret," *Saturday Night Live*, https://snltranscripts.jt.org/99/99msecrets.phtml.

6. Penelope Green, "Quest to Soothe the Savage Breast," *New York Times*, July 2, 2000.

7. Amy Barrett, "Fashion Model: Gucci Revival Sets Standard in Managing Trend-Heavy Sector," *Wall Street Journal*, August 25, 1997.

8. Ariel Levy, *Female Chauvinist Pigs: Women and the Rise of Raunch Culture* (New York: Free Press, 2006).

9. Nancy Hass, "For Women Great and Small, Briefs Can't Get Much Briefer," *New York Times*, August 13, 2000.

10. Vanessa Grigoriadis and Ellen Tien, "Princess Paris," *Rolling Stone*, December 11, 2003, 63–66.

11. R. Ballie, "Study Shows a Significant Increase in Sexual Sontent on TV," *Monitor on Psychology* 32, no. 5 (May 2001), https://www.apa.org/monitor/may01/sexualtv#.

12. Jim Cooper, "Shocking Behavior," *Adweek*, June 14, 1999, S42–S46.

13. Jessica Kerwin, "Victoria Victorious," *Women's Wear Daily*, November 15, 2001, 4.

14. Kerwin, "Victoria Victorious."

15. Kerwin, "Victoria Victorious."

16. "ADVERTISING," *Time*, December 24, 2001, 88.

17. Alex Kuczynski, "Victoria's Secret's TV Tell-All; Fashion Show Raises Questions of Timing, Taste," *Chicago Tribune*, November 21, 2001.

18. Robert Sullivan, "Vogue View: Reality Chic: What It Takes to Sell a Bra," *Vogue*, November 1, 2001, 296, 298, 300.

19. David Moin, "No Secret: Victoria's Largest Store in Bodacious NYC Debut: Maximum Exposure," *Women's Wear Daily*, November 8, 2002, 1–29.

Chapter 11: On Wednesdays We Wear Pink

1. This chapter draws on interviews with Marie Holman-Rao; creative, marketing, and operational executives at Pink; and Casey Lewis.

2. "Lingerie Designers Launch New Pink Range," YouTube video, 4:02, posted by "AP Archive," July 21, 2015, https://www.youtube.com/watch?v=bz6m4IESv5w.

3. "Victoria's Secret Fashion Raids the Dorm, Targets College Crowd," *Standard-Freeholder*, July 30, 2004.

4. Azeen Ghorayshi, "Puberty Starts Earlier than It Used To. No One Knows Why," *New York Times*, May 19, 2022, https://www.nytimes.com/2022/05/19/science/early-puberty-medical-reason.html.

5. Margaret Talbot, "Girls Just Want to Be Mean," *New York Times Magazine*, February 24, 2002.

6. Talbot, "Girls Just Want to Be Mean."

7. "Event Brief of Q4 2005 American Eagle Outfitters Inc Earnings Conference Call-Final," Fair Disclosure Wire (Quarterly Earnings Reports), March 1, 2006.

8. "Aerie (2006)," YouTube video, 0:30, posted by "PastMeetsPresent," March 6, 2017, https://www.youtube.com/watch?v=6DjXhKs9tyY.

Chapter 12: Scaling Sexy

1. This chapter draws on interviews with Sharen Jester Turney, Jill Beraud, former senior-level L Brands executives, financial analysts, fashion editors, a former merchant, former marketing employees, and Nichole Naprstek.

2. Andria Cheng, "Victoria's Secret Puts Promotional Plans in Place," *Dow Jones Institutional News*, December 3, 2008.

3. Christopher J. Goodman and Steven M. Mance, "Employment Loss and the 2007–09 Recession: An Overview," *Monthly Labor Review*, April 2011, https://www.bls.gov/opub/mlr/2011/04/art1full.pdf.

4. Si Si Penaloza, "What's Victoria's Secret? Spend, Spend, Spend," *Globe and Mail*, November 29, 2008.

5. Vicki M. Young, "An Era Ends: Limited Sells Flagship to Focus on Global Growth," *Women's Wear Daily*, July 10, 2007, 1, 28.

6. Michael Clifford and Stephanie de la Merced, "Limited Brands to Cut Ties to the Limited," *New York Times*, June 17, 2010.

7. David Moin, "'No Regrets' for Wexner: Chief of Limited Brands Glad to be Out of Apparel," *Women's Wear Daily*, October 17, 2007, 1, 10.

8. Tim Feran, "Q&A Leslie H. Wexner: Forever Young," *Columbus Dispatch*, September 23, 2012.

9. "Limited Brands 2006 Investor Update Meeting—Final," Fair Disclosure Wire, November 6, 2006.

10. David Moin, "Wexner Wary of Overseas, Sees Limited Sales of $20B," *Women's Wear Daily*, October 20, 2011.

11. Moin, "Wexner Wary of Overseas."

12. "M&S Hires Knicker Queen Janie Schaffer," *City A.M.*, November 6, 2012.

13. Ylan Q Mui, "Victoria's Revelation; Brand Is 'Too Sexy,' Chief Says," *Washington Post*, February 29, 2008.

14. "Klum Knockers," YouTube video, 0:30, posted by "Gallery of the Absurd," February 18, 2011, https://www.youtube.com/watch?v=MsT6vphqx6A.

15. Alexandra Marshall, "Just Browsing," *T: The New York Times Style Magazine*, February 29, 2008, https://archive.nytimes.com/tmagazine.blogs.nytimes.com/2008/02/29/just-browsing-10/.

16. Ray Paprocki and Kathy Showalter, "Shaking Up Limited Brands," *Columbus Monthly*, December 2007, https://www.columbusmonthly.com/story/business/names-faces/2018/09/24/shaking-up -limited-brands/9726100007/.

17. Amanda Mull, "How Jeans Got Weird," *Atlantic*, October 23, 2019, https://www.theatlantic.com /health/archive/2019/10/so-many-jeans/600547/.

18. Kim Bhasin and Lindsey Rupp, "Inside the Fight to Design the Perfect Sports Bra," *Bloomberg*, July 24, 2017, https://www.bloomberg.com/news/articles/2017-07-24/inside-the-fight-to-design-the -perfect-sports-bra?embedded-checkout=true.

19. "Erin Heatherton Launches VSX Sexy Sport," YouTube video, 1:31, posted by "victoria list," September 1, 2013, https://www.youtube.com/watch?v=FOZuWUOMciI.

20. Emma Rosenblum, "Can the Internet Help Women Feel Better About Their Breasts?" *Bloomberg Businessweek*, October 2014.

21. Rosenblum, "Can the Internet Help Women Feel Better About Their Breasts?"

22. Kellie Ell, "Victoria's Secret Down, but Not Out," *Women's Wear Daily*, March 1, 2019, 6.

23. Rosenblum, "Can the Internet Help Women Feel Better About Their Breasts?"

Chapter 13: The Last Great Contract in Modeling

1. This chapter draws on interviews with models, modeling agents, and several Victoria's Secret executives and employees who interacted with models in different business capacities.

2. Gisele Bündchen, *Lessons: My Path to a Meaningful Life* (New York: Avery, 2018), 127.

3. Lynn Yaeger, "Va-Va-Boom," *Vogue*, September 2010.

4. Michael Gross, *Model: The Ugly Business of Beautiful Women* (New York: William Morrow and Company, 1995), 2, 4.

5. Anita Singh, "Linda Evangelista Claims Ex-Husband Abused Her," *Telegraph*, September 19, 2023, https://www.telegraph.co.uk/news/2023/09/19/linda-evangelista-claims-ex-husband-gerald -marie-abused-her/.

6. Agence France-Presse, "French Prosecutors Close Rape Investigation into Model Agency Boss," *Guardian*, February 15, 2023, https://www.theguardian.com/world/2023/feb/15/french-prosecutors -close-investigation-into-model-agency-boss-gerald-marie.

7. Jenn Abelson and Sacha Pfeiffer, "Modeling's Glamour Hides Web of Abuse," *Boston Globe*, February 16, 2018, https://www.bostonglobe.com/metro/2018/02/16/beauty-and-ugly-truth/c7r0WVs F5cib1pLWXJe9dP/story.html.

8. Yaeger, "Va-Va-Boom."

9. "The Victoria's Secret Fashion Show 2011," YouTube video, 7:00, posted by "Video Mix," December 16, 2012, https://www.youtube.com/watch?v=VSk8SMTpq4M&t=421s.

10. "Victoria's Secret Launch the 2010 Fantasy Bra," YouTube video, 1:41, posted by "adrianaFlima-com," October 21, 2010, https://youtube.com/watch?v=kFp7LN8zeiI.

11. Valeria Nekhim, "Q&A: Adriana Lima's Trainer Tells Us How She Got Back into Pre-Baby Shape," *Fashion*, August 16, 2010, https://fashionmagazine.com/beauty-grooming/qa-adriana-limas-trainer -tells-us-how-she-got-back-into-pre-baby-shape.

12. Ella Alexander, "Model Recovery," British *Vogue*, February 9, 2012, https://www.vogue.co.uk/article/karolina-kurkova-thyroid-battle.

13. "Backstage Victoria Secret Fashion Show 2003," YouTube video, 7:32, posted by "Gisele," November 6, 2022, https://www.youtube.com/watch?v=5b2RoJLFLoY&t=211s.

14. Melissa Whitworth, "Victoria's Secret Show: What Does It Take to Be a Victoria's Secret Angel?" *Telegraph*, November 7, 2011, http://fashion.telegraph.co.uk/news-features/TMG8872623/Victorias-Secret-show-What-does-it-take-to-be-a-Victorias-Secret-Angel.html.

15. Sara Hammel, "Adriana Lima Explains Extreme Pre-Victoria's Secret Show Diet," *People*, December 1, 2020, https://people.com/health/victorias-secret-fashion-show-adriana-lima-extreme-diet/.

16. Natalie Robehmed, "The Angel Life: How to Make It as a Victoria's Secret Model," *Forbes*, September 17, 2015, https://www.forbes.com/sites/natalierobehmed/2015/09/17/the-angel-life-how-to-make-it-as-a-victorias-secret-model/?sh=4ec791e81204.

17. Guy Trebay, "Model Struts Path to Stardom Not on Runway, but on YouTube," *New York Times*, February 14, 2012.

18. Romee Strijd (@romeestrijd), ". . . my body was under constant stress," Instagram, May 28, 2020, https://www.instagram.com/p/CAvVHSIsRmT/.

19. "Backstage@ 2014 VS Fashion Show, Karlie Kloss," YouTube video, 4:03, posted by "Klossy," July 24, 2015, https://www.youtube.com/watch?v=vPE6_cUpBxo.

20. Jonathan Van Meter, "Follow Me!" *Vogue*, April 2014.

21. Van Meter, "Follow Me!"

22. "Making of the Victoria's Secret Fashion Show 2015—Part 7 (It's Showtime!)," YouTube video, 4:09, posted by "TheScantilyClad," December 5, 2015, https://www.youtube.com/watch?v=pJbD3aObmEY.

23. Jessica Silver-Greenberg, Katherine Rosman, Sapna Mehashwari, and James B. Stewart, "'Angels' in Hell: The Culture of Misogyny Inside Victoria's Secret," *New York Times*, February 1, 2020, https://www.nytimes.com/2020/02/01/business/victorias-secret-razek-harassment.html.

24. "Victoria's Secret Angel Rings," J. Birnbach Jewelry, https://www.jbirnbach.com/victorias-secret-angel-rings/.

25. Silver-Greenberg, Rosman, Mehashwari, and Stewart, "'Angels' in Hell."

Chapter 14: The Epstein Factor

1. This chapter draws on interviews with Wexner associates and contemporaries, Victoria's Secret executives, and models.

2. Khadeeja Safdar, Rebecca Davis O'Brien, Gregory Zuckerman, and Jenny Strasburg, "Jeffrey Epstein Burrowed into the Lives of the Rich and Made a Fortune," *Wall Street Journal*, July 25, 2019, https://www.wsj.com/articles/jeffrey-epstein-burrowed-into-the-lives-of-the-rich-and-made-a-fortune-11564092553.

3. Safdar et al., "Jeffrey Epstein Burrowed into the Lives of the Rich."

4. Marc Fisher and Jonathan O'Connell, "Final Evasion: For 30 Years, Prosecutors and Victims Tried to Hold Jeffrey Epstein to Account. At Every Turn, He Slipped Away," *Washington Post*, August 10, 2019, https://www.washingtonpost.com/politics/final-evasion-for-30-years-prosecutors-and-victims-tried-to-hold-jeffrey-epstein-to-account-at-every-turn-he-slipped-away/2019/08/10/30bc947a-bb8a-11e9-a091-6a96e67d9cce_story.html.

5. Leland Nally, "I Called Everyone in Jeffrey Epstein's Little Black Book," *Mother Jones*, October 9, 2020, https://www.motherjones.com/politics/2020/10/i-called-everyone-in-jeffrey-epsteins-little-black-book/#1.

6. Nally, "I Called Everyone in Jeffrey Epstein's Little Black Book."

7. Gregory Zuckerman and Khadeeja Safdar, "Epstein Flourished as He Forged Bond with Retail Billionaire; Charismatic Financier, Now Charged in Sex-Trafficking Case, Built Ties with Executive Leslie Wexner that Extended into Shy Billionaire's Investments, Charities," *Wall Street Journal*, July 12, 2019.

8. Edward Jay Epstein, "My Many Run-Ins with Jeffrey Epstein," *Spectator*, May 9, 2023, https://thespectator.com/topic/curious-case-jeffrey-epstein-new-york/.

9. Leslie Wexner, Letter to Wexner Foundation, "Letter from Les," Wexner Foundation, Aug 8, 2019. https://www.wexnerfoundation.org/letter-from-les/.

10. Vicky Ward, "The Talented Mr. Epstein," *Vanity Fair*, March 2003, 300.

11. Ryan Smith, "These Celebrities Were Named in Jeffrey Epstein List," *Newsweek*, January 4, 2024, https://www.newsweek.com/jeffrey-epstein-list-celebrities-named-unsealed-ghislaine-maxwell-1857767.

12. *The Limited Inc 1996 Report* (Columbus, OH: The Limited Inc., 1997).

13. Laura Bird, "No Detail Escapes the Attention of Abercrombie & Fitch's Chief," *Wall Street Journal*, October 7, 1991, https://www.wsj.com/articles/SB876176611622798500.

14. Christopher Mason, "Home Sweet Elsewhere," *New York Times*, January 11, 1996.

15. Mason, "Home Sweet Elsewhere."

16. Andrew Keiper, "Bizarre Art, Porn, and Dolls: Inside Jeffrey Epstein's New York House of Horrors," Fox News, July 11, 2019, https://www.foxnews.com/us/inside-jeffrey-epsteins-new-york-house-of -horrors.

17. Caroline Davies, "The Murky Life and Death of Robert Maxwell—And How It Shaped His Daughter Ghislaine," *Guardian*, August 22, 2019, https://www.theguardian.com/us-news/2019/aug/22 /the-murky-life-and-death-of-robert-maxwell-and-how-it-shaped-his-daughter-ghislaine.

18. Gordon Thomas and Martin Dillon, *Robert Maxwell, Israel's Superspy: The Life and Murder of a Media Mogul* (Boston: Da Capo Press, 2003).

19. Safdar et al., "Jeffrey Epstein Burrowed into the Lives of the Rich."

20. Donald L. Barlett and James B. Steele, "The Lobbying Game: Influence-Brokers In D.C.: How Representatives of Foreign Interests Push Their Agendas Among Washington's Decision-Makers," *Philadelphia Inquirer*, September 17, 1996.

21. Barlett and Steele, "The Lobbying Game."

22. Jenni Fink, "Bill Clinton Responds to Jeffrey Epstein Document Release," *Newsweek*, January 3, 2024, https://www.newsweek.com/bill-clinton-responds-jeffrey-epstein-document-release-1857625.

23. Bradley J. Edwards with Brittany Henderson, *Relentless Pursuit: Our Battle with Jeffrey Epstein* (New York: Gallery Books, 2020).

24. Emily Steel, Steve Eder, Sapna Maheshwari, and Matthew Goldstein, "How Jeffrey Epstein Used the Billionaire Behind Victoria's Secret for Wealth and Women," *New York Times*, July 25, 2019, https://www.nytimes.com/2019/07/25/business/jeffrey-epstein-wexner-victorias-secret.html. For the police report, see Santa Monica Police Department Crime Report, *New York Times*, https: //int.nyt.com/data/documenthelper/1500-alicia-arden-police-report/04e6cef6bfb8b25c8684 /optimized/full.pdf#page=1.

25. Isabel Vincent, "Inside the Victoria's Secret Pipeline to Jeffrey Epstein," *New York Post*, July 14, 2019, https://nypost.com/2019/07/14/inside-the-victorias-secret-pipeline-to-jeffrey-epstein/.

26. Lucy Osborne, "I Woke Up and He Was on Top of Me," *Guardian*, May 28, 2022, https://www .theguardian.com/fashion/2022/may/28/jean-luc-brunel-abuse-six-women-epstein.

27. Emily Shugerman, Kate Briquelet, and Lachlan Cartwright, "Jeffrey Epstein's Modeling Ties Go Much Deeper than Victoria's Secret," *Daily Beast*, September 7, 2019, https://www.thedailybeast .com/jeffrey-epsteins-ties-to-the-modeling-industry-go-much-deeper-than-victorias-secret.

28. Shugerman et al., "Jeffrey Epstein's Modeling Ties."

29. Sarah Fitzpatrick, Nancy Ing, and Saphora Smith, "Jeffrey Epstein Accuser Virginia Roberts Giuffre Testifies Against Modeling Agent Jean-Luc Brunel," NBC News, June 16, 2021, https://www .nbcnews.com/news/world/jeffrey-epstein-accuser-virginia-roberts-giuffre-testifies-against -modeling-agent-n1270959.

30. Sarah Fitzpatrick and Tom Winter, "Epstein Victim Drops Her Lawsuit Against Lawyer Alan Dershowitz," NBC News, November 8, 2022, https://www.nbcnews.com/news/epstein-victim-drops -lawsuit-lawyer-alan-dershowitz-rcna56250.

31. Mark Williams, "Jeffrey Epstein Trafficking Victim Claimed She Had Sex with Billionaire Les Wexner," *Columbus Dispatch*, January 9, 2024, https://www.dispatch.com/story/business/2024/01 /09/jeff-epstein-les-wexner-linked-in-sex-trafficking-deposition-woman-says-she-had-sex-with -wexner/72166104007/.

32. Anna Kaplan, "Jeffrey Epstein Accuser Maria Farmer Holds L Brands CEO Leslie Wexner Responsible for Assault on His Property," *Daily Beast*, October 5, 2019, https://www.thedailybeast.com /jeffrey-epstein-accuser-maria-farmer-holds-l-brands-ceo-leslie-wexner-responsible-for-assault -on-his-property.

33. Mike Baker, "The Sisters Who Tried to Bring Down Jeffrey Epstein," *New York Times*, August 26, 2019, https://www.nytimes.com/2019/08/26/us/epstein-farmer-sisters-maxwell.html.

34. Baker, "The Sisters Who Tried to Bring Down Jeffrey Epstein."

35. Landon Thomas Jr., "Jeffrey Epstein: International Moneyman of Mystery," *New York*, October 28, 2002, https://nymag.com/nymetro/news/people/n_7912/.

36. Edwards and Henderson, *Relentless Pursuit*.

37. Gabriel Sherman, "The Mogul and the Monster," *Vanity Fair*, July 2021.

38. Ward, "Talented Mr. Epstein."

39. Shirsho Dasgupta, "Epstein Befriended a Slew of Scientists. New Records Contain 'Orgy' Allegation against One," *Miami Herald*, January 5, 2024, https://www.miamiherald.com/news/local/crime/article283847883.html.

40. Mark Remillard, "Billionaire Businessman Leslie Wexner Refuses to Reveal Full Scope of Jeffrey Epstein's Alleged Multimillion-Dollar Theft," ABC News, January 23, 2020, https://abcnews.go.com/US/billionaire-businessman-leslie-wexner-refuses-reveal-full-scope/story?id=68461262.

41. Release of Power of Attorney (Leslie H. Wexner, grantor; Jeffrey E. Epstein, grantee), County of Franklin, December 27, 2007, https://franklin.oh.publicsearch.us/doc/128235138.

42. Julie K. Brown, "For Years, Jeffrey Epstein Abused Teen Girls, Police Say. A Timeline of His Case," *Miami Herald*, November 28, 2018, https://www.miamiherald.com/news/local/article221404845.html.

43. Wexner, Letter to Wexner Foundation, "Letter from Les."

44. Landon Thomas Jr., "Financier Starts Sentence in Prostitution Case," *New York Times*, July 1, 2008.

45. Tiffany Hsu, "Jeffrey Epstein Pitched a New Narrative. These Sites Published It," *New York Times*, July 21, 2019, https://www.nytimes.com/2019/07/21/business/media/jeffrey-epstein-media.html.

46. Khadeeja Safdar, "Jeffrey Epstein Documents, Part 2: Dinners with Lawrence Summers and Movie Screenings with Woody Allen," *Wall Street Journal*, https://www.wsj.com/articles/jeffrey-epstein-documents-woody-allen-larry-summers-edb3e9b2?mod=article_inline.

47. Jodi Kantor, Mike McIntire, and Vanessa Friedman, "Jeffrey Epstein Was a Sex Offender. The Powerful Welcomed Him Anyway," *New York Times*, July 13, 2019, https://www.nytimes.com/2019/07/13/nyregion/jeffrey-epstein-new-york-elite.html.

48. Andrea Peyser, "Wait, He's Allowed to Have Kids?" *New York Post*, March 3, 2011, https://nypost.com/2011/03/03/wait-hes-allowed-to-have-kids/.

49. "L Brands Inc Investor Update Meeting—Final," Fair Disclosure Wire, September 10, 2019.

50. "President Joe Biden Visiting Ohio Friday for Intel Groundbreaking," YouTube video, 1:54, posted by "WLWT," September 9, 2022, https://www.youtube.com/watch?v=-uU0GfuS-_I&t=1s.

51. *Jeffrey Epstein: Filthy Rich*, episode 2, "Follow the Money," directed by Lisa Bryant, Netflix, 2020.

52. "Attorneys Will Speak on Behalf of Victims of Jeffrey Epstein," CBS12 News, July 16, 2019, Facebook Live video, 1:12:26, https://www.facebook.com/watch/live/?ref=watch_permalink&v=2403959823155915.

53. David Ghose, "What the Jeffrey Epstein Scandal Means to Columbus and Retail Magnate Les Wexner," *Columbus Monthly*, November 2019, https://www.columbusmonthly.com/story/lifestyle/features/2022/10/25/what-jeffrey-epstein-scandal-means-to-columbus-and-les-wexner/69589703007/.

Chapter 15: No One Left to Say No

1. This chapter draws on interviews with Sharen Jester-Turney, various senior-level executives at Victoria's Secret and L Brands, financial analysts, consultants, models, and modeling agents.

2. Chioma Nnadi, "Rihanna for Real," *Vogue*, June 2018, 77.

3. Nnadi, "Rihanna for Real."

4. Jacob Bernstein, Matthew Schneier, and Vanessa Friedman, "Male Models Say Mario Testino and Bruce Weber Sexually Exploited Them," *New York Times*, January 13, 2018, https://www.nytimes.com/2018/01/13/style/mario-testino-bruce-weber-harassment.html.

5. Sam Reed, "Terry Richardson Banned from Working with Conde Nast Publications," *Hollywood Reporter*, October 24, 2017, https://www.hollywoodreporter.com/news/general-news/terry-richardson-banned-working-conde-nast-publications-including-vogue-gq-report-1051343/.

6. Dan Eaton, "Why Wexner Launched a Shake-Up at Victoria's Secret Where Growth Was Stalling," *Columbus Business First*, May 27, 2016, https://www.bizjournals.com/columbus/print-edition/2016/05/27/why-wexner-launched-a-shake-up-at-victoria-s.html.

7. Vogue (@voguemagazine), "Anna Wintour reads #TheSeptemberIssue. Do you? We would love to see it! Show us your #voguestagram. Photo by @taylorjewell," Instagram, August 20, 2013, https://www.instagram.com/p/dPO2_iv62s/?hl=en.

8. Nolan Feeney, "Anna Wintour Implies Kim Kardashian and Kanye West Are Not 'Deeply Tasteful,'" *Time*, November 19, 2014, https://time.com/3595368/anna-wintour-kim-kardashian-kanye-west-vogue-cover/.

9. "Butt Augmentation, Labiaplasty on the Rise, Surgeons Say," NBC News, February 26, 2015, https://www.nbcnews.com/news/us-news/butt-augmentation-labiaplasty-rise-plastic-surgeons-say-n312996.

10. Lindsay Kimble, "The Average American Woman Is a Size 16 According to a New Study," *People*, September 26, 2016, https://people.com/health/average-womens-clothing-size-16/.

11. Melonyce McAfee, "Model Cheryl Tiegs Calls Plus-Size SI Swimsuit Cover 'Unhealthy.'" CNN Wire Service, February 26, 2016.

Chapter 16: The Unraveling

1. This chapter draws on interviews with with several senior executives at the company, specifically those who worked closely with Wexner, Razek, and Mitro; Nicole Phelps; modeling agents; and several people with knowledge of the Sycamore acquisition.

2. Nicole Phelps, "'We're Nobody's Third Love, We're Their First Love'—The Architects of the Victoria's Secret Fashion Show Are Still Banking on Bombshells," *Vogue*, November 8, 2018, https://www.vogue.com/article/victorias-secret-ed-razek-monica-mitro-interview.

3. Victoria's Secret (@Victoria's Secret), "Please read this important message from Ed Razek, Chief Marketing Officer, L Brands," Twitter, November 9, 2018, 11:01 p.m., https://twitter.com/VictoriasSecret/status/1061106626583822338.

4. "From the Heartland: Vintage Bath & Body Works," BBWHeartland, Tumblr, https://bbwheartland.tumblr.com/about.

5. Khadeeja Safdar, "L Brands CEO Les Wexner Says He Didn't Know About Jeffrey Epstein's Behavior," *Wall Street Journal*, July 15, 2019, https://www.wsj.com/articles/l-brands-ceo-les-wexner-says-he-didnt-know-about-jeffrey-epsteins-behavior-11563229415.

6. Kim Bhasin (@KimBhasin), "Victoria's Secret's top marketing executive is leaving the company. Ed Razek, the guy behind the annual lingerie fashion show, is out. Here's his letter to staff," Twitter, August 5, 2019, 6:57 p.m., https://twitter.com/KimBhasin/status/1158512289307344899/photo/1.

7. Lisa Rein, "Globetrotting Obama Official Traveled in Luxury. Taxpayers Footed the Bill," *Washington Post*, September 9, 2016, https://www.washingtonpost.com/news/powerpost/wp/2016/09/09/top-obama-administration-official-dinged-by-watchdog-for-the-cost-of-travelling-in-style/.

8. Tristan Navera, "Les Wexner on Retirement: 'When I Look in the Mirror, What I Feel Is Gratitude,'" *Columbus Business First*, May 14, 2020, https://www.bizjournals.com/columbus/news/2020/05/14/les-wexner-on-retiring-when-i-look-in-the-mirror.html.

9. Mark Williams, "L Brands Founder Les Wexner to Dump More than $2 Billion Worth of Company Shares," *Columbus Dispatch*, July 13, 2021, https://www.dispatch.com/story/business/2021/07/13/leslie-wexner-selling-2-billion-shares-he-control-l-brands/7957565002.

Chapter 17: Apologies Aren't Sexy

1. This chapter draws on interviews with members of the Skims team, current and former senior-level Victoria's Secret executives, and financial analysts.

2. Sierra Jackson, "L Brands Inks Deal with Shareholders to Exit Workplace Harassment Cases," Reuters, July 30, 2021, https://www.reuters.com/legal/litigation/l-brands-inks-deal-with-shareholders-exit-workplace-harassment-cases-2021-07-30/.

3. "Karlie Kloss: 'Only Now Do I Have the Confidence to Stand Tall & Know the Power of My Voice,'" *Vogue*, July 1, 2019, https://www.vogue.co.uk/article/karlie-kloss-on-modelling-faith-philanthropy-business.

4. Saabira Chaudhuri, "Victoria's Secret's U.K. Arm Files for Creditor Protection," *Wall Street Journal*, June 5, 2020, https://www.wsj.com/articles/victorias-secrets-u-k-arm-files-for-creditor-protection-11591349640.

5. Vanessa Friedman, "The Political Awakening of a Fashion Power Player," *New York Times*, November 3, 2016, https://www.nytimes.com/2016/11/03/fashion/raul-martinez-conde-nast-latino-presidential-election.html.

6. John Arlidge, "Can the Knicker Queen Save Victoria's Secret?" *Times*, July 18, 2021, https://www.thetimes.co.uk/article/can-the-knicker-queen-save-victorias-secret-clqhrlgsb.

7. Sapna Maheshwari and Vanessa Friedman, "Victoria's Secret Swaps Angels for 'What Women Want.' Will They Buy It?" *New York Times*, June 16, 2021, https://www.nytimes.com/2021/06/16/business/victorias-secret-collective-megan-rapinoe.html.

8. Khadeeja Safdar, "Victoria's Secret Is Trying a New Look. Can Customers Be Convinced?" *Wall Street Journal*, August 13, 2022, https://www.wsj.com/articles/victorias-secret-is-trying-a-new-look-can-customers-be-convinced-11660363214.

9. "I wrote a song called Victoria's Secret. It's out now," YouTube video, posted by @jaxwritessongs, July 10, 2022, https://www.youtube.com/shorts/nAZgebdEKT0.

10. Mira Fox, "Is Hulu's Victoria's Secret Documentary Trafficking in Antisemitic Conspiracy Theories?" *Forward*, July 25, 2022, https://forward.com/culture/511605/hulu-victorias-secret-more-jew ish-men-than-supermodels/.

11. BreAnna Bell, "Hulu Orders Sherri Papini Kidnapping Hoax Documentary from 'Britney vs. Spears' Director," *Variety*, July 25, 2023, https://variety.com/2023/tv/news/hulu-sherri-papini -kidnapping-hoax-documentary-britney-vs-spears-director-1235678694/.

12. Candace McDuffie, "Kim Kardashian Turns Her Back on Her Only True Talent: Stealing the Aesthetic of Black Women," The Root, September 7, 2022, https://www.theroot.com/kim-kardashian -turns-her-back-on-her-only-true-talent-1849508111.

13. "Kim Kardashian West and Kris Jenner (Plus Kanye West!) Talk About Their Empire, Jesus and Donald Trump," *New York Times*, November 6, 2019, https://www.nytimes.com/2019/11/06/style /kim-kardashian-west-kris-jenner-kanye-west-video.html.

14. Natasha Mascarenhas and Ann Gehan, "How Underwear Startup Parade Wiped Out Investors," *The Information*, October 6, 2023, https://www.theinformation.com/articles/how-underwear -startup-parade-wiped-out-investors.

15. *Victoria's Secret: The Tour '23*, directed by Lola Raban-Oliva, Korty Eo, Cristina Sanchez, and Margot Bowman, Pulse Films, Amazon, 2023, https://www.amazon.com/Victorias-Secret-Tour-Doja -Cat/dp/B0CG76GDRY.

16. 2023 Victoria's Secret & Co. Investor Day, webcast, October 12, 2023, https://onlinexperiences.com /scripts/Server.nxp?LASCmd=AI:4;F:QS!10100&ShowUUID=16260CD3–7185–42D0–84F8 –80B3F5418DAD.

17. 2023 Victoria's Secret & Co. Investor Day.

Epilogue: Final Fantasy

1. "Les Wexner, Academy Class of 1990, Full Interview," YouTube video.

2. Chantal Fernandez, "Victoria's Secret Returns to TV—but Its Challenges Are Bigger than Branding," *Financial Times*, September 26, 2023, https://www.ft.com/content/5d40d725-24ea-480f -8c9c-05d281006e79.

Acknowledgments

We'd like to thank our editor, Sarah Crichton, for believing in this project from the start. There was no person better suited for the job, and we're grateful for your guidance and care. We'll be forever indebted to you. Thank you to our agent, Eric Lupfer, a fine editor in his own right, who made our proposal better than it needed to be and understood why it was a story worth telling. Hilary McClellen and Alex Foster helped us cross the finish line with precision. Leigh Belz Ray, Marisa Meltzer, and Scott Sternberg offered essential feedback that upgraded the whole thing. Most of all, thank you to the countless people who spoke to us for the book, on the record and off, for hours upon hours. We hope you feel we got it right—at least most of it.

From Lauren

In some ways, this book started when I was in college, working at Victoria's Secret as a seasonal sales associate, where I discovered that every bra, apparently, "has a matching panty." I lasted two weeks.

Fast-forward twenty years, and that's when things really took shape. Thank you to Chantal Fernandez, my longtime reporting partner, for suggesting that the story of Victoria's Secret would be a good book, agreeing to write it with me, and being such a diligent coauthor.

I owe my editors at the *Business of Fashion*, Imran Amed and Vikram Kansara, quite a lot. Thank you for believing in me. To Tim Blanks, the best there ever was. And to Johanna Stout, Christian Layolle, and Anouk Vlahovic, my comrades in start-up life.

I'm grateful to *Puck* editor in chief Jon Kelly for granting me the time to write a first draft of *Selling Sexy*. Jon and the Content Boys™, Ben Landy and Danny Karel, have made my work better. Final *Puck* shout-outs go to Liz Gough, Alex Bigler, and the generous William Cohan, an early reader of this manuscript.

Pamela Lev, Emme Parsons, Leah Chernikoff, Britt Aboutaleb, Claire Mazur, Erica Cerulo, Hayley Phalen, Becky Malinksy, Leandra Medine, Danielle Nussbaum, Siddhartha Shukla, Scott Sternberg (again), Amanda Dobbins, Molly Creeden, Amy Power, Chris Black, Alix Rutsey, and the moms of Toddler Town made these years more fun. I always pick up the phone when Max Stein calls. Thanks to Mickey Drexler for teaching me so much about the business. Maureen Farrell did the kindest thing and offered to introduce us to her agent. I wish Long Nguyen, who died in 2022, was here to read this.

I owe my obsession with fashion to my parents, Michelle and Craig Sherman. Thanks to my mom for encouraging my ambition. And to Barb and Jeff Mikrut and Janet Kurka, who helped raise me. And thanks to my in-laws, Michael Frommer and Susan Shure, for their unconditional love.

Much of this book is about women who do the hard work while men get the credit. Dan Frommer, my husband and longest-running editor, has done everything in his power to ensure we both had the opportunity to succeed. He is also the greatest dad to Fritz, our funny, verbose son. Dan, I am so lucky, and everybody knows it. I love you.

From Chantal

This book wouldn't be possible without our sources. I'm grateful to everyone who picked up a call from an unknown Texas number and gave me a chance. Especially those who were initially skeptical about our intentions or still grappling with their own complicated feelings about the business. Victoria's Secret employed so many talented people throughout the decades. It was an honor to hear their stories, even the ones that didn't make it into this book.

My library cards proved to be some of my most powerful research tools in this process. Thank you to the New York Public Library, the Brooklyn Public Library, the Columbus Metropolitan Library, and the Bexley Public Library. I can't believe such valuable and extensive resources are free. I relied especially on the fantastic reporting in the *Columbus Dispatch* and

Columbus Monthly archives and on the guidance of the Thomas Yoseloff Business Center.

I'm indebted to the many people who have supported my writing by hiring and believing in me over the years, including Joshua Chuang, Chris Dixon, Graydon Carter, Leigh Belz Ray, Caryn Prime, Lauren Indvik, Brian Baskin, and Lindsay Peoples. Imran Amed and Vikram Kansara changed my career with their leadership, trust, and respect. And, of course, to my coauthor, Lauren Sherman, who believed in me before I did.

My parents never wavered in their love and cheers, even when they knew better than to ask me how the book was going. Thank you for always answering the phone. And finally to my best friend and husband, Daniel. My words here will never do justice to how you supported me and this book, so I'll just say thank you for your strength and brilliance. I would be lost without you.

Index

About the Authors

Lauren Sherman has been reporting from inside the fashion industry for more than fifteen years. Now a special correspondent at *Puck*, she was the *Business of Fashion*'s chief correspondent, and before that a staff reporter at *Forbes*. She has contributed to the *Wall Street Journal* and the *New York Times*, as well as *Fast Company*, *Women's Health*, and the *Gentlewoman*. She lives in Los Angeles with her husband and son.

Chantal Fernandez is a writer covering fashion, retail, luxury, and beauty with a focus on business and culture. She is currently a features writer for *The Cut* at *New York* magazine. A former senior reporter at the *Business of Fashion*, her work has appeared in the *Financial Times*, the *New York Times*, *Elle*, and *Harper's Bazaar*. She lives in Brooklyn with her husband.